MW00810760

MIDDLE OF DIAMOND INDIA

National Renaissance through Participation and Enterprise

SHASHANK MANI

PENGUIN
VIKING

An imprint of Penguin Random House

PENGUIN VIKING

USA | Canada | UK | Ireland | Australia
New Zealand | India | South Africa | China | Singapore

Penguin Viking is part of the Penguin Random House group of companies
whose addresses can be found at global.penguinrandomhouse.com

Published by Penguin Random House India Pvt. Ltd
4th Floor, Capital Tower 1, MG Road,
Gurugram 122 002, Haryana, India

First published in Penguin Viking by Penguin Random House India 2023

ISBN 9780670100194

Typeset in Sabon by Manipal Technologies Limited, Manipal
Printed at Thomson Press India Ltd, New Delhi

www.penguin.co.in

For
Dad and Mom,
Papa and Maa

and

Middle of Diamond Indians

Contents

Part IV: BUILDING: *A New India*

Introduction

A New Beginning at Seventy-Five

I have lived two lives as an Indian. In one, the long tail of colonial history, mores, linear culture and a metro city-led discourse in English guided me. The second, in the India of small towns and districts, which exposed me to a culture that is circular, complex and vernacular but exciting, emotive and full of possibilities. To discover that spirit, its culture and the hidden sources of its strength, I had to travel to that hinterland. My journey began in 2008 on a specially chartered train—an annual fifteen-day pilgrimage called Jagriti Yatra, to the four corners of India in the company of 500 young leaders—a journey that continues till date. But like the very circular throw of Indian traditions, these journeys took me back to my place of birth, a geography where Jagriti, a charity I incepted, was also born—Deoria, a Tier 3 district[1], with an ethereal banyan tree that has a canopy of forty metres. It seems as if that tree had been waiting 300 years for just this moment in our nation's history, to bless and inspire young Indians who pass under it every year during the Yatra, and it is where Jagriti is now building an enterprise centre. That banyan tree is fast becoming an organic symbol of inspiration for a movement to build India through enterprise—the focus of this book.

Many Indians are taking a turn at this second life— discovering our true centre and developing a new appreciation of the deeper resources of our nation. Every society has this urge for self-discovery, 'its own vision of reality, of the world in which it lived, and of itself and its relation to its past, to nature and to what it strove for'.[2] Now, when a generation born at the turn of Independence is taking a back seat at seventy-five, a new generation with new memories is exploring this self with new gusto. This moment is a turning point at which old ideas are being cast aside and new frameworks are being created. Central to that transition is a change in thinking about India as a *Pyramid*, to re-imagining it as a *Diamond*, with a majority in the Middle seeking a horizontal association that befits a republic. This change invites us to shed the top-down colonial and hierarchical thought process that guided us post-Independence and adopt a horizontal, collaborative approach in all walks of life. That is the Diamond-shaped India this book seeks to unearth, with an approach that can shine it.

The book traces voices, aspirations, needs and new methods of those in the Middle of the Diamond, who are no longer poor but are not particularly rich either. That Middle, through an aspirational economic process, is creating a new identity fuelled by its own culture and values. This identity supports a new confidence and collaboration egged on by technology in the hands of a young nation. A rise in the economic status of the country, led by this Middle, involves not just consumption but also production. It involves citizens not just in the act of voting but in the far more important act of building, balancing our democracy and giving it a creative bias. This process involves youth, women, enterprise, culture and technology, which will together spur development in a human-centred manner. It will shun the zero-sum economic thinking of colonial or mercantile systems, designed to divide resources and funnel wealth to metro destinations. It invites citizens to work together so that the total economic pie becomes larger and all of India prospers.

By the hundredth anniversary of our Independence, not only can India become the second-largest economy in purchasing power parity, it can also drive meaning and purpose for millions of citizens by making them active participants in shaping this growth through enterprise. By focusing on the Middle, the book points to a different path for this growth—decentralized, people and technology-driven, entrepreneurial and sustainable. The Middle represents 'and' thinking, balancing science and spirituality, economics and culture. Ideas and institutions born in the coming years based on this approach can guide other emerging democracies in Asia, Africa and South America—by putting focus on their Middle for their developmental efforts. This can counter the top-down approach, both of western industrial thinking and that of communist China, so that India emerges as a vibrant democratic voice in Asia with an economy that is dynamic. The success of this movement will depend on the act of shining Middle of Diamond India.

An experiential narrative

The book is a confluence of three stories. The first is the story of Jagriti, a movement scripted on a national canvas through the world's largest train journey and experiences in Deoria and Kushinagar, two Tier 3 districts to promote entrepreneurship. The second is the story of my experiences in the private sector, where I led the strategy arm of a consulting organization for over a decade, researching and proposing new ideas through which India could develop. Finally, and inevitably, the book takes an autobiographical turn through my personal experiences, growing up in small towns and districts, my travels and founding Jagriti as a movement with that inspiration.

In these varied interactions, on a moving train, in my corporate job and in the rice fields of eastern UP, a pattern emerged. Demographically, economically, socially and politically, that famous phrase of Prof. C.K. Prahalad—'Bottom of the Pyramid'[3] had lost its factual and emotional meaning. 'Middle of Diamond' is both factually more accurate and emotively stronger. Most of our population, a full 58 per cent, as detailed in Chapter 2,[4] reside in the Middle but are still being treated with methods of development that have ignored their innate strengths. While 'poverty traps' keep some in the country down, what we realized, and the book documents, is that the vast majority in the Middle have moved beyond that fate. This requires *enabling* citizens to rise using their own energy, context, culture and genius—the core thesis of this book. This insight came from the act of travelling, discovering, listening and building in that real India of small towns and districts.

Learning by wandering

My 'two lives' were made possible by wandering, exploring and learning from Middle India. While born and brought up in the Middle, by education and vocation, I had experienced the 'Top'. It was the act of living in small towns as the son of an army officer, and my years of travelling through the country on a train, that exposed me to an India residing in the Middle. Jagriti Yatra, a moving train of nineteen coaches that circles the country visiting role models who are working in that 'Middle', is a key learning ground, a social experiment of sorts that has been going on for fifteen years. We meet twelve inspiring individuals every year with committed co-travellers, and their aspirations, sacrifices and innovations are central to this book. We also learn from a district enterprise ecosystem where we are building a visionary centre to support enterprise in fifteen districts of eastern UP, referred to as Purvanchal. The act of circling the country in a train, with a special overnight halt in Deoria, has created the experiences that permeate this book.

At an event in the Rashtrapati Bhavan in 2017, the tenth anniversary of the Jagriti Yatra, President Ram Nath Kovind challenged all 500 present 'to convert the Yatra into a movement'.[5] That movement, I am pleased to say, is now being fuelled by a network of 7500 yatris, who have circled the country, and by entrepreneurs being nurtured in Purvanchal. Not only are these leaders doing inspiring work, they are the real hope of this book.

The book highlights an India proficient in vernacular but deficient in English. Issues surrounding youth and women's empowerment are analysed from a small-town perspective. The book leans on the culture and values of citizens in smaller towns and villages. The reader will discover an India where caste is a reality. If focus has been given to the period of colonial history pre-Independence and the economic drain that resulted, it is because the trauma still

hidden in smaller towns and districts was impacted most by
this period. The narrative brings out institutional dilemmas,
where old institutions with a focus on consumption
and distribution have to morph into those that focus on
production and creation. The use of technology explored
in the book focuses on impact in smaller towns with links
to local language. The narrative pushes against a Cartesian
world view and proposes a humanist approach centred on
India's culture and situation, suggesting a new modernity.
The book envisions a national transcendence where citizens
take part in nation-building using the tool of *udyamita*, an
expanded definition of enterprise that will energize local
economy and society, before the headwinds of demographic
ageing slow us down. The book describes how the Middle
and its original culture can help the process of intellectual
decolonization to chart a national rise over the coming
decades. It points to a fact that has become evident
recently—the ideological divide globally may no longer be
between the Left and the Right but between the dominant
forces of the Top and the rising energies of the Middle.

The tone of nation-building in the book, an unrequited
love for the country and the yearning for a positive future
may come across as too buoyant. That enthusiasm stems
from my experiences in smaller towns and districts and
my travels in the Yatra. It is a belief in a positive future
for India I share with many yatris and citizens, without
hesitation or apology.

The persona of Middle of Diamond India

On 15 August 2022, inspired by Prime Minister Narendra
Modi's call to action, I committed to the *Amrit Kaal* by

stepping away from my corporate life. I had gone to the Red Fort, accompanied by twenty other yatris, to see the Prime Minister unfurl the Tricolour as he announced the commencement of the Amrit Kaal. We heard the Prime Minister outlining his *Panch Pran*, the five vows, we have to take as a nation to become a developed country come the hundredth anniversary of our Independence. As I listened to the Prime Minister and heard the shifts he was proposing—the goal of being a developed nation, the need to decolonize our institutions, the pride in our roots, the need for national unity and creating a sense of duty in our citizens—it dawned on me that these were the very shifts I describe in this book. The rise of Prime Minister Modi has been explained by commentators through his personality and organization—his strengths as a leader, his connect with the masses and a strong party apparatus. But a wider narrative, at its core, points to the simple fact that he has emerged from the Middle. This book will help understand the deeper sources of history, society, economics and culture that have propelled a person like him to lead the country as India turned seventy-five and forms the core of his thinking. Curiously, 'MODI' is an acronym of 'Middle of Diamond India'. As I re-read chapters, edited them and mulled over the message of the Amrit Kaal, I realized the alignment was complete.

Our Prime Minister has not only risen from the Middle, he represents the aspirations of the emerging middle class. Today, inspired by his personality and achievements, they see themselves as having infinite potential. A belief has arisen that any citizen, even from the Middle, can become the Prime Minister. This gives our polity enormous *atma vishwas*, self-confidence, and our republic, new power.

An even bigger shift is the pride in our culture and a reimagined modernity that has been driven by the Prime Minister as the brand ambassador for the Middle. No longer are people seeking endorsement of dress, speech or behaviour from the elite or from the West. Progress is also wearing traditional Indian attire, the celebration of our festivals, the focus on yoga, a rediscovery of our heritage, and yet the acknowledgement and desire that over the Amrit Kaal, much more has to be done. The exponential increase in digital technology underlines this innovative endeavour to better the Indian reality while reaching the last person. The rise of Middle of Diamond India, as documented in these pages, offers a deeper analysis of the societal, political and historical forces that propel our Prime Minister. This rise can power the future in a profound way. That power will accelerate national growth as the Prime Minister's call for *sabka prayas*, everyone's effort, gets actioned, releasing republican energies.

Another leader in recent history who sought national renewal, looking to the future while rooted in our culture and heritage, was the other Narendra, the inimitable Swami Vivekananda, born Narendranath Datta. He graces this book at regular intervals, prophesizing the birth of an original India this book seeks to present.

Participation through enterprise

The book is divided into four sections—Framing, Learning, Changing and Building, with chapters within each as interconnected essays on 'Building India through Enterprise'. Attributes of Middle India emerge as a diamond-shaped demography in the first section, with details of two key segments—youth and women. The second section focuses on the historical trauma of the Middle, a comparison with the US at seventy-five and cultural features that distinguish India and its Middle. The third section focuses on how we can engage the Middle to participate through the tool of udyamita, shifting the location of development to the district and an approach to development that is citizen-led and digitally networked. The fourth and final section articulates a Banyan Revolution that is needed to energize all of India—the Top and Middle pulling up the Bottom, to spark a national renaissance over the coming twenty-five years. The appendices voice a commitment to the Amrit Kaal and a call to action for readers. The power of the Middle, the learning from different sources, the shifts that are needed to create a 'building bias' and a new modernity frame the narrative. My personal experiences and the process of founding and scaling the Jagriti movement serve as a scaffold for the book. The examples are real, though I have also quoted thinkers, experts and reports where required.

The book is aimed at the youth of the country and its *udyamis* (local entrepreneurs) starting with my co-travellers, the 7500 yatris who have experienced Jagriti Yatra and entrepreneurs being incubated at our centre in Purvanchal, each participant named in the appendix. The book seeks to energize those living in small towns and districts, and to signal this, 1000 villages of Deoria and Kushinagar district are also named in the appendix. The book will interest the lay reader, the active citizen of this country, who wants to contribute to nation-building. The private sector executive, the entrepreneur, the investor, I hope, take the thesis of this book, 'Building India through Enterprise', to heart.

The government leader and the policy expert may see in this book a way to reframe the progress of our democracy keeping the Middle in mind. The book would interest readers from other countries who see in Middle India issues and opportunities like their own Middle that can inform a new global debate between the North and the South. Ironically, this English book describes an India that does not read English. I see this more as an opportunity than a challenge. The English reader will discover an India often kept away from them by language.

A young and growing nation is building a new future. This movement relies on releasing the innovative and entrepreneurial potential in each citizen. In this, a new metaphor, 'Middle of Diamond India', can shape action, recognizing that the core is strong, but it needs polishing. Instead of focusing on the elite, this book draws attention to the awakening in the Middle. It analyses the past, only to shine a light on the future and to the act of polishing this diamond-shaped India. This shift will gain energy from the many challenges that India seeks to overcome in the coming twenty-five years. The US, that other large democracy, went through a civil war around the seventy-fifth anniversary of its independence to resolve the issue of slavery. Our provocation is more positive and perhaps more difficult—giving opportunity to the Middle, recognizing the size, strength and diversity of that demography. We must build the largest nation on this planet, through democratic action, involving the many. For this, we must build new healthcare systems, energy outlets, cities, roads and digital connects, strengthen agriculture, make more in India and look at finance from a different lens. But above all, we must develop and deploy the enormous entrepreneurial energy locked up in our citizens, especially those in the Middle. We must do all this knowing that our growth cannot be resource-intensive unless that resource is our people. We may have to take a different path relative to the West or to China, simply because Mother Earth may not have the capacity to allow the carbon-intensive path others have followed so far. The scale of the task in each sector or area of building is as daunting as it can be meaningful. That moment for action is now, before a twenty-year demographic window closes on us and future generations are left with headwinds of demographic ageing.

But the central proposition of this book is that, as a republic, that task is the task of citizen leaders. The government must be strong but focus on enabling this activity as a strong coach rather than a demanding captain. Young Indians, of the kind we see on the Yatra or in Deoria, are ready and willing to collaborate with each other to build a country of substance that future generations will applaud. We should let them get on with it. That unfettered building bias will redefine our republic and give meaning to millions of Indians in the process.

June 2023   Shashank Mani
From under the banyan
Barpar, Deoria, Purvanchal, Uttar Pradesh

Part I

FRAMING: *India beyond Seventy-Five*

The hidden soul of India lies in small towns and districts. To understand it, one must travel and explore this hinterland. Old paradigms that have defined India as a Pyramid, with the few at the Top running it, must change. Shifting centres of gravity to the Middle must be recognized and new metaphors created. Youth, a force for change in the youngest nation on this planet, must be motivated and mobilized through enterprise to create and build. A land defined by feminine energy must bring its women to the forefront, to take part in nation-building. Old world views, which the first generation after Independence held dear, must be discarded before we make a fresh start, a new framing.

1

Awakening: *A Journey into the Middle*

चरैवेति चरैवेति

—ऐतरेय ब्राह्मण

(Keep travelling, keep travelling)

—Etreye Brahman

I was woken up at midnight as the train passed Kasaragod, a train station in Kerala. Something was amiss. Swapnil, the executive director of Jagriti Yatra, quickly explained the situation. We had agreed to pick up Shree Padre, a national award-winning water expert, at Kasaragod. He was to travel with us till Kanyakumari to interact with the 500 yatris on our special train. At this point, though, the train, having passed Kasaragod, was hurtling towards Trivandrum with unbridled abandon. My task, I was told, was to convince the train's guard, with my bleary-eyed authority, to slow and stop the train at the next station. Thereafter, I was to convince Shree Padre to drive to this next station and come on board, having made him wait for three hours at the appointed station. And, by the way, I also had to explain to him as to why the train had not even slowed down as it whistled past him and his bewildered team.

Speaking on a walkie-talkie, I somehow managed to convince the guard to stop the train at the next station. Convincing Shree Padre on the phone was more difficult. I spoke to him, marshalling whatever arguments I could, to explain why his presence on this national expedition was important for our participants. How we had missed the appointed location of the pick-up, despite our plan to stop. After repeated appeals, he finally relented and got his white Ambassador to travel the additional 30 km to the station where our train was parked and where we were convincing the station master that we needed to keep it there till Shree Padre arrived. Irritated on arrival, when Shree Padre saw an entire nineteen-bogie train waiting for him, even at 2 a.m. he beamed gracefully. Appreciating the intent of this national journey and its learning possibilities, he got on the train and on to Kanyakumari with us.

The act of 500 participants circling the country over a fifteen-day journey in a special train wakes you up. It awakens the adventurer in you. It enables you to make a personal connection with the geography of the country as you travel from Maharashtra in the west to Odisha in the east, from Tamil Nadu in the south to Uttar Pradesh in the north. It awakens you to the physical beauty of our country as India's hills and valleys slip past your window. It awakens the optimist in you as you see how much has been done and highlights how much more is still needed. It makes you a pilgrim but reminds you that India itself has been defined by the footsteps of pilgrims.[1]

Leaders with heart

When we crafted the journey, it was with a simple insight—India needed young creative leaders, those who had the heart to give back to society, those who could build. Leaders who collaborated with others. Leaders who were inspired by the possibilities of the future and went into the real India to create it. Young Indians with the energy to change India within their lifetimes, recognizing that the next generation would not have the luxury of a positive demography.

It all started in 1997 when, with some friends and family, we decided to celebrate the golden jubilee of India by planning a national journey with young Indians who would live and build India's future. Even as the country looked back at 1947, the Azad Bharat Rail Yatra took 250 young students across the country on a twenty-two-day journey to discover the 'future of India'. India was still poor, answering to its description as a Third World country, but a subterranean energy was evident. We faced numerous challenges in organizing the journey, but the spirit of India's golden jubilee pushed us forward and we pulled it off. I remember paying for the last instalment of the chartered train's ticket using my credit card and those of four willing friends. This was one of at least a dozen hurdles where only providence seemed to be guiding us. That journey established that a train could be an invigorating vehicle to explore and envision India with those who would build it.

Exhausted physically by this effort and drained financially, I returned to my corporate job and to Gauri, my wife, who was to deliver our first child, a month after the journey concluded. Tarini, our first daughter, was born shortly thereafter but was delivered underweight, partially because Gauri had supported the organizing team well into her seventh month of pregnancy. I went about life watching my two daughters grow, with Isha, our second daughter, born three years later and Tarini, to our delight, growing to be the best sports girl at her school. Seven years later, in 2005, I decided to write a book to describe that journey. That book, *India: A Journey Through a Healing Civilization*,[2] was published in 2007 and was dedicated to my daughters.

Rebirth of a yatra

The words crafted as the story of that journey became the seed for Jagriti Yatra. But what got the Yatra germinated was the energy of those who had experienced the first journey and seen its impact first-hand. In 2007, I vividly remember a phone call from Gitanjali Banerjee, a participant in the first journey. By then, we had been trying to re-ignite the journey for a full year without landing a funder. In the call, she implored, 'We have to push one last time; this is too important a project to not try this once.' By that time, we were on the verge of giving up, exhausted by the refusal of funders who failed to understand why circling the country with young people on a train was a good idea. Gitanjali's willingness to relocate to Mumbai to lead the effort sealed the decision for us.

The second impetus came from those who understood the improbability of the venture and were attracted to it for that reason. Raj Krishnamurthy, an IIT Mumbai alumnus, got interested and signed up immediately when

I recounted the story of the first journey at an alumni get-together. Rewati Prabhu, a friend, snuck off to a vacation with the manuscript of my book and came back moved and convinced. Swapnil, an IIT Kharagpur graduate, tailed me at my book launch as his friend had gone on the first Yatra and this venture appealed to his sense of the unknown. I tested him: 'Are you truly convinced you can do this? It requires a different *"junoon"*.' This only served to increase his passion. Together with Gitanjali, he started the Jagriti Yatra office in Mumbai. Swapnil then proceeded to recruit Ashutosh, who had been a year junior to him at IIT Kharagpur and wasn't very happy with the cubicle life of his IT job in Chennai.

In a phone call, Swapnil asked Ashutosh in their campus lingo, '*Abbe, kuch dhang ka karna chahta hai* (Do you want to do something meaningful)?' and proceeded to outline the Yatra plan. Ashutosh quit his job, took a flight to Mumbai the same day, became part of the team and is the CEO of Jagriti today. These were true leaders. While the written word of my book created a proof point that the journey was possible, to believe in someone else's idea and to invest in it to grow it together was where leadership lay. This motley group came together every Saturday for team calls that continue till date.

The physical format of the train journey had been tested but the programme of learning had to be recreated. Growing up as the son of an army officer in towns such as Sangrur, Ahmednagar and Deoria, I had experienced a 'diamond-shaped' India. As we discussed the Yatra and its possibilities, as a team, we realized that in the smaller towns and districts lay the largest and most energetic segment of India's population. If exposed to enterprise, they would help themselves and pull up the poor who were at the bottom faster.

This was the Middle.

Slowly, as 2007 moved into 2008, four themes emerged to anchor our programme—Youth and Women, 'Middle India', Enterprise and Nation-Building. Today, having understood the importance of Digital, we have added that to form five attributes that frame our approach.

The first two themes, Youth and Women and Middle India, were with us right from the ideation stage. An enterprise approach came about as both Raj and I had run young companies as CEOs and had seen the power of entrepreneurship. Enterprise would also be applicable to this Middle. Employment had surfaced as a critical issue in small towns and districts, and young men and women were beginning to look at enterprise as a viable option.

But enterprise in a country like India, back in 2008, was still associated with large towns and metros. Infosys, Patni and other companies had demonstrated that enterprise creation was closely linked to a team. Capital and market would follow if teams could be built. We believed that nurturing leaders was the best approach to make enterprise broad-based in a country where capital was scarce and people were in abundance. Middle India was where national renewal would emerge and could galvanize action. That's where our leaders had to be identified.

Many counselled us to do something smaller. 'Why not a Maharashtra Yatra or an Uttar Pradesh Yatra?' they asked. We knew that a smaller journey would be easy to kick off but would likely perish as it would not catch the imagination of an aspirational democracy. We followed the dictum of 'no room for small dreams'[3] and attempted the largest train journey of its kind in the world.

We started the Yatra from a 10 feet by 20 feet office in Prabhadevi, Mumbai, generously lent to us by Rewati Prabhu and her family. Swapnil and Ashutosh would spend late nights preparing for the journey. Those were times when it was unclear if we would be successful in this mission but a sense of lightness and warmth enveloped these two pioneers. One night, as Swapnil and Ashutosh came out of the office at 1 a.m., Swapnil lowered the shutter and was about to lock the office. The moon was up and there was a buffalo tied to the lamp post outside the office, gently chewing the cud. In that surreal moment, Swapnil stopped in reflection and said, 'Not sure if the Yatra has given me anything yet, Ashutosh, but it has allowed me to fulfil one dream I've had since I was a child.' To this philosophical remark, made well past midnight, Ashutosh inquired, with some frustration, as to what that dream was.

Swapnil declared, 'When I was at the Sainik School in Nainital, I dreamt that I would have a small shop. That shop would have a shutter and I would lower the shutter every day and lock it after a satisfying day's work.'

These two young IITians, themselves from small towns, had given up corporate careers to lead this first Yatra. This exchange showed the carefree spirit that drove the effort.

We knew that participants would have to be top-notch for the Yatra to succeed. We advertised widely in the vernacular press to target smaller towns and districts and many people responded. We took a policy view to have at least 40 per cent women participation. Our programme emphasized collaboration. This was deliberately in contrast to the 'lone ranger' approach to passing examinations and 'lonely desk' approach to classroom teaching. We knew that in a country where human potential was unlimited, leaders needed to collaborate for national tasks.

Notwithstanding the complexity of travelling 8000 km in a train with 500 participants and 300 support staff, our solution was elegant. A participant would put his or her luggage in the train and take it out only when the train returned from its fifteen-day odyssey. The moving train would be where everyone would rest at night, with local visits on buses at each stop in the daytime. The railway network had served to extract the many resources of India and export it to Britain. It had brought manufactured products from British cities such as Manchester to the hinterland.[4] We would reverse the flow, bringing leaders from small towns and districts to explore the country and rebuild those areas through enterprise. We were subconsciously emulating Gandhi, who used a train journey to understand India on his return from South Africa in 1915 and shaped India's independence struggle based on those insights.

But as the date of the journey approached, we were struggling to find a partner and a sponsor. This is when a seminal meeting with R. Gopalakrishnan, 'Gopal' of Tata Sons, organized by Romit Chatterjee, their brand custodian, proved decisive. While the first journey gave prospective sponsors confidence, and my book documented it, for this journey, with a new orientation of 'Building India through Enterprise', a fresh narrative had been created. We needed a partner who would appreciate our long-term nation-building goals. The Tata Group understood this vision instantly. They knew the long-term aim of the Yatra was producing leaders and this matched the core values of the Tatas. They were also a brand that understood the power of enterprise, having seeded early enterprise towns such as Jamshedpur and Mithapur. What helped clinch the deal, I suspect, was the cheeky, under-the-breath comment by Swapnil as we exited our meeting, when he told Gopal that as a fellow IIT Kharagpur alumnus, 'You cannot say no to our proposal.' At the inaugural press conference in August 2008 to announce the partnership, Gopal described the start of the Yatra in poetic terms, '. . . the start of a small trickle at Gangotri or Talakaveri, which will soon become a roaring river as this movement picks up speed.'[5]

Our start was tumultuous. Roughly four weeks before the journey, I came back home one evening to see my TV screen showing smoke billowing from the Taj Mahal Hotel in Mumbai. This was followed by the gut-wrenching sight of a train station strafed by bullets from Kasab the terrorist's machine gun. His cocky figure walked past CCTV cameras, leaving a trail of mayhem behind. We froze as a team. This was a time when most participants, our sponsors and truth be told, even our team were uncertain if we could pull off this journey. Yes, it had been done once before but under very different circumstances and with half the number of participants we were proposing to take this time. The added worry was that participants would start dropping off given the starting point of our train journey was a stone's throw from the railway station where terrorists had struck on 26/11. Our partner, the Tatas, were also the owners of the Taj Mahal Hotel, the biggest target of the attack.

We held firm, as did the Tatas.

Finally, and most importantly, all participants arrived on the dot. There was a new charge and an energy in the air. The best answer to the negativity and chaos attempted by the terrorist attack was expressed by

Vibha, a team member: 'If the terrorists were maniacally committed to the negative cause of weakening India, we as a team are now even more committed to venturing out to build our country.'

A circle of inspiration

The Yatra has now been going for the past sixteen years.[6] We have circled the country thirteen times with such leaders since 2008, fourteen times if we consider the first Yatra organized in 1997 to celebrate the fiftieth anniversary of Indian Independence, sixteen times if we consider the digital format Yatras when, unbowed by COVID-19, we increased participation to 700 in December 2020 and 2021. In all, 7500 Yatris in batches of 500 have covered over 1,30,000 km in total or three times the circumference of the earth.

As the train circles the country, one can simply sit at a window for hours admiring the countryside, its hills and valleys. But often, this forms a backdrop for the millions of conversations that happen during the journey, creating new stories, friendships and a growing circle of trust that pilgrims also recognize.

Starting in Mumbai, the journey exposes participants to twelve role models—organizations helmed by individuals or teams that have accomplished something path-breaking. At Bengaluru, we host an IT session at an Infosys or a Mindtree and in recent years, an Udyam Mela that showcases enterprises relevant for a typical Middle India district. Madurai sees the spiritual inspiration of Aravind Eye Care. At Chennai and Sri City, we visit Elango Ramaswamy, who created a special village called Kuthambakkam, which brought Dalits and Brahmins together. Sri City is an example of an individual attracting scores of companies to set up their offices in what was an arid rural region of Andhra. In 2019, the Yatris were also taken to adjoining Sriharikota to study and understand the inspiration behind Mangalyaan. At Vizag, we visit Akshaya Patra, with its well-functioning mid-day meal programme, and have an equally inspiring visit to the naval dockyard, where, over the years, we saw the distant but growing silhouette of the Arihant, our strategic submarine, till it was launched.

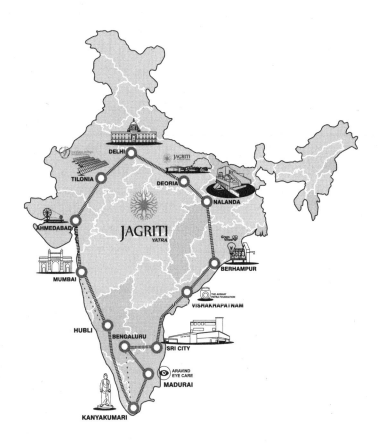

In the sixth Yatra, as I stood at the train station in Vizag, an inquisitive bystander asked me a question that is often on the minds of those who see our train: 'Where is the train coming from?' I said, 'Mumbai'. He then asked, 'Where is it going?' to which I replied with a smile, 'Mumbai.' Shaking his head, he moved away in disbelief!

At Berhampur, we meet Joe Madiath, the creator of Gram Vikas, who has shaped this region of Odisha into a centre of excellence for water and sanitation. Nalanda is the setting for an inspired debate on ancient India as its modern equivalent, the new Nalanda university, takes shape. Every year, we have a Yatri of Chinese origin and at Nalanda, we ask them to give the others a short account of their travels in India in remembrance of Hiuen Tsang, the famous eighth-century Chinese monk who lived there and took back scriptures that influenced Chinese civilization.

Around two-thirds of the way circling India, the Yatra shifts gears in a village called Barpar in the Deoria district of Uttar Pradesh—the only place all 500 participants stay off the train. This is where Jagriti was born, in the shade of a giant banyan tree. The tree inspired our logo and Raj coined a phrase for our stay and the business planning exercise that is conducted in this village, based on this inspiration—'Biz Gyan Tree', the 'tree of business knowledge'. By the time the train arrives in Barpar, we are ten days into the journey. The teams now understand each other as individuals and have been brought together by the exhilaration and fatigue of non-stop travel. The initial barriers of culture, ethnicity, language and often nationality have ceased to matter by now. The weather on 3 January, when we reach Deoria, is freezing and whatever residual barriers still exist thaw through the collective effort of coping with the cold. As participants alight from the train and board buses, dancing past a traditional welcome of *dhols* by local villagers, the winter fog evaporates with the rising sun. We divide the Yatris into groups of ten each, centred on a business idea that has been discussed in the train the day before. Each group is escorted to a nearby village by a local representative with a marker flag fluttering to provide direction. They test the hypothesis that forms the basis of their venture, with door-to-door discussions with villagers in their assigned area.

In the evening, each group gets a few minutes to present their plans and takes questions from a panel of judges. Usually, the insights are courageous and heartfelt. One judge, Sandeep Gambhir, who is the CEO of a company, took me aside after the competition and said, 'The openness with which one group presented a plan to manufacture sanitary napkins in the village was impressive. I seldom see these important issues being brought up even in urban settings with such clarity.'

Presentations over, a cultural evening commences. After ten days, the participants have come out of the narrow confines of a train and the resulting exuberance is memorable. At midnight, participants reluctantly retire to beds laid on the floor, with a mattress with straw underneath, to ward off the cold. That night on the floor, with temperatures dipping to zero, inducts many into the real India. The smell of the straw, the early morning walk in the fog to the giant banyan and meditation in and among its hanging tendrils, introduces them to the spirit of the Middle. This bonding cannot possibly happen by reading a book or watching a TED talk. It must be lived, experienced and felt.

The Delhi stop, with an inspiring talk by Anshu Gupta at Goonj, a social organization that has focused on the use of recycled cloth—and in 2017 with the President, Ram Nath Kovind—sets the stage for the concluding leg, when participants introspect on their journey beyond the Yatra. Tilonia, the stop after Delhi, has a setting as beautiful as any, with a village welcome topped off with a session with Bunker Roy, who brings all 'big city' thinking down to the ground. The final stop is in Sabarmati, where an introspective walk-through in Bapu Dhaam is followed by a boisterous valedictory and tearful farewells as the train leaves to complete its journey, returning to Mumbai.

Nuts and bolts

The smallest unit of interaction on the Yatra is a 'cohort', with six participants, either male or female, and one facilitator, a more senior Yatri, who sleeps in the same compartment. The facilitator spends his or her days and nights with participants, acting as an on-the-spot coach and mentor. In the daytime, two male cohorts and one female cohort come together in a group of twenty-one, appropriately called a 'Group'. The train therefore has approximately seventy cohorts and twenty-five groups.

Each cohort is assembled for diversity of geography and commonality of interest. Ten key areas of interest, including education, health, agriculture, handicraft, water and sanitation that are relevant for small towns and districts, are chosen as subjects for interaction with role models. For instance, a cohort could have yatris from Manipur, Kerala, Assam, UP, Madhya Pradesh or France with, say, a common interest in healthcare, and would be assigned Aravind Eye Systems, a prominent chain of eye hospitals in Tamil Nadu that has played a stellar role in eradicating blindness, to study their enterprise through a deeper dive into their activities and business model and see how it could be replicated elsewhere.

As part of the application process, we do not ask for any educational qualification. Instead, the selection process focuses on essays—in Hindi or in English—asking participants to outline what they have done for society, their role models and their plans upon their return from the journey. An interesting discovery is that many applicants from small towns and districts choose their parent as their first role model!

Motivating these leaders involves exposing them to other leaders who have trodden an entrepreneurial path. By taking them to the role model's *karmabhoomi* on our train, they experience the context and conditions in which their enterprise was germinated and is being nurtured. Critically analysing the work of these role models would further their understanding, which could be taken to their own districts on their return from the journey.

Learning from each other

The moving Yatra train consists of all sorts of people. Participants from small towns, metropolitan cities and international participants interact in its longitudinal belly. In the first few days, the English-speaking urban Yatris are vocal and their body language reflects this. They dominate group discussions and are seen leading the intellectual push. However, outlooks change after the 'time-lifeline' exercise is conducted on the second day of the journey.

In this exercise, each member of the Group is asked to share the ups and downs of their life in a candid presentation of five to ten minutes, using a chart paper to map their life on a graph. High points involve falling in love or clearing an important exam; low points reflect those moments when exams were flunked or friendships were broken. Participants talk of their achievements and failures with equal weightage. Often, this is the first time that those from metro cities hear the stories of people from smaller towns. As stories of each small-town person start to come out, it opens a window into the personal effort of the Middle. Soon, a positive combination of Bharat and India emerges.

I travel on the Yatra on an average for ten days, usually taking part in the first leg to 'settle' the train. In 2018, when we stopped in Kalkeri Sangeeth Vidyalaya near Hubli, our first stop on that Yatra, the first half of the day witnessed an inspiring presentation from Senthil Kumar, one of the directors of Selco Foundation, an enterprise that works in the sustainable energy space.

Solar power is now pervasive across the country, but Senthil outlined how, by financing it properly, its reach and adoption could be increased in districts and by smaller enterprises. We wrapped up the discussions and split into subgroups to wander the campus of the school to see the solar heaters and electric light fixtures Selco had installed. We then moved to the canteen. As I stood in the line to catch a meal, two participants, Geeta and Leena,[7] joined me and engaged in a conversation—which is the real forum for learning, both for the Yatris and for me.

The two girls were from well-to-do families from a metro city and were quiet to begin with. In a reflective mood, one said how 'humbled' she had felt that day. Her problems, which had seemed insurmountable till the day before, seemed insignificant compared to those of other co-travellers. Between bites of poori and sabzi, she talked of a woman leader she had met the day before, a fellow Yatri like her. This lady was in her thirties, a mother of three, and had started a women's cooperative society in western UP a decade ago, which now had 10,000 members. Her 'time-lifeline' had explained that at the inception of this enterprise, as a newly married woman, it was difficult for her to even leave the house. She often went out on the false pretext of going to a doctor. On one such visit, she opened a bank account for her organization and to 'cover up', brought back a prescription from the doctor in case her family members got suspicious. She revealed the creation of her 'social enterprise on the sly' to her husband and his family only when the organization was fully established and she could show them its success. Our two urban Yatris were inspired by this story and were crestfallen at the same time. Their lives till then had been spent complaining about what now seemed like the small and insignificant issues of prosperous India, when something as big as this had been created against existential odds without the support they took for granted.

People learn from other people. The horizontal association of citizens is the core of the Jagriti Yatra experience. When we named our smallest group a 'cohort' in 2008, we did not know that cohort-based learning would become a mainstream learning methodology.[8] The 'Middle' does not need gifts and advice from the Top; they require the ability to mingle unfettered *among* themselves, to find inspiration with each other.

As part of the Yatra, there are many inspirational role models we visit, each with a story that moves us. But on the journey, as in life, the real learning is from the extraordinary person around the corner. The person you meet going to the shower in the train, the inspirational facilitator whose house was firebombed by Naxals and who continued to work—these inspiring stories touch the heart as much as the head and exert a deeper influence.[9]

The single most explosive bonding between Yatris takes place during the Jagriti Geet. This song, written by Prasoon Joshi, rendered by Babul Supriyo with music by the late Aadesh Shrivastava, is a mere two minutes long. But Gauri, who is a choreographer, trains Yatris in a mass dance sequence during induction, when the Yatris arrive in Mumbai. This requires Yatris to move to a sequence that mimics the song's appeal, *'Kuch Badal Raha, Kuch Badlenge'*—some things are changing, some we will change. We repeat it every day during the Yatra on our visits to various organizations as a way of thanking them for hosting us. The results in mass bonding are astonishing as 500 bodies move to a common rhythm, expressing their gratitude to the hosting team at a role model location.

Role models form an axis of inter-generational learning. In Indian society, the concept of a guru passing on their insights to the next generation is well-known. But a 'classroom-only' approach to learning ignores the context that is critical for gaining knowledge. Traditionally, gurus did not just pass on knowledge but gave students the context of their lives by living with them. In the Yatra, we bring participants to the footsteps of the guru a.k.a. the role model in their location, where they have built an institution or an enterprise. That learning is facilitated by the workings of the twenty-one-member Group asking the role models questions that bring out their story in depth. This Group works between other sessions to create a presentation that details the work of the role model and is shared in the common room of the moving train a couple of days later after the role model visit.

If learning off the train is at the foot of the role model, the common room on the train becomes the epicentre of discussions and debate when the train is speeding along on the Yatra. Two air-conditioned chair cars, strung together, provide the arena for presentations and discussions once the Yatris are back on the train after the day's visit. Critical analysis and discussion are encouraged. For instance, an analysis of Gram Vikas, an Odisha-based rural empowerment organization, or an Aravind Eye Care may appreciate their work but also ask questions on what could be done to scale up this effort. Participants learn that enterprise-led developmental efforts are marathons, not sprints. Almost all enterprises and entrepreneurs speak of the 'dark nights' that preceded the bright mornings when they broke through.

Change and discipline

Change and discipline are two tracks of any enterprise and are an important component of our journey. Ideas, representing change and discussed with role models and in the common room, are important, but the act of getting a team to execute those ideas over a long term is essential to 'Building'. Early in the Yatra, we announce our intent to live disciplined lives. This is the only way we can bring back all 800 travellers, safe and sound, after an 8000-km journey. Doing headcounts before the train leaves, ensuring no doors are opened when the train is moving, fire and evacuation drills conducted for any eventuality, among other safety measures, are de rigueur. The single biggest discipline is the enforcement of no alcohol, no narcotics and no smoking rules. For this, Raj, Col Patil[10] and I climb the stage during the induction session for some straight talk. We make a light-hearted start by suggesting that smokers could use these fifteen days to kick the habit. But then a strict instruction silences the auditorium: 'Any whiff of alcohol or substance abuse will result in de-training at the next station. There is zero tolerance on this matter and we will enforce this discipline without any concessions.' Raj does this with utmost equanimity. On a few occasions, he has quietly but firmly got people to see the folly of their deeds on breaking these rules as they bid the train a tearful goodbye at some station deep in India.

The forty-odd international Yatris, who come from almost twenty different countries from all five continents, offer a unique perspective to the journey. They come because the act of circling the largest democracy has gained global appeal. They are usually experiencing India for the first time, and India, usually, is unmindful of personal space! In the initial days, they are hemmed in by the multicoloured, multifaceted, a question-a-minute Yatris and the sights, sounds and smells of the real India. But then, first a respect, and then a love for the journey, develops. Respect, because international Yatris have told me, 'This level of commitment and passion for building is seldom seen in my own country.' Love, as they see an India not on the tourist map. An India of small towns and districts that is brimming with hospitality and a respect for the outsider. Many have replicated the journey on their return to their countries. Five international journeys, modelled on the Jagriti Yatra, have been started, one each in the US, France, Peru, Portugal and the UK.[11] We are creating a forum for sharing knowledge across the world so that this learning format can be experienced by many others internationally.

A countrywide network

Sudhanshu Palsule, a teacher, an author and a friend, in a coffee conversation one Sunday afternoon in 2008, pointed to the power of 'travelling out to bring about transformation on return'. Having studied the lives of transformative leaders, such as Rosa Parks, who fought for black rights in Alabama, USA, went to live in Maine, far away from her home state, but then returned and started the black rights movement, Gandhi, who did a tour of duty in South Africa before returning to India, and others, he said, 'Incremental change can happen if you remain where you are from, but transformative change requires venturing out and then having the courage to return to your place of origin, howsoever difficult that may be.'[12] The Jagriti Yatra is just such a 'boomerang expedition': a fifteen-day train journey that exposes its Yatris to the possibilities across the country and examples of citizen builders working across India. But then to transform their own region, Yatris must come back to apply these learnings to their area. Many, we know, put the Yatra on their CVs and apply to an international university, a corporation, a bank or a consulting organization, but the majority return to develop their region through enterprise.

All put together, 6100 Yatris have been on the Yatra since 2008, with an additional 1400 travelling in a digital format. Over the years, we have documented the impact of these Yatris nationally. Approximately 28 per cent have created an enterprise, as per a recent impact report.[13] Many Yatris have gone on to work as volunteers in Teach for India[14] or as Gandhi and Ashoka Fellows.[15] Many others have gone about their lives in corporate or government jobs but with an inner awakening and a desire to impact society. Yatris talk of an intellectual rebirth that forced them to re-examine the basic assumptions of their lives in what they got and what they can give back to society. Many recognized that until the Yatra, they were skimming the surface of India and needed to dive deep into the real India to understand their country and contribute.

A network of 7500 Yatris is not enough to bring about change in a country as large as India. But then, one is reminded of what Margaret Mead said in this matter: 'Never doubt that a small group of thoughtful, committed citizens can change the world.'[16] Each of these citizens can, in turn, awaken their municipality, village, block or district. Before this journey, many felt alone in their mission of doing something for society. The Yatra, above all, gives participants a powerful gift—the knowledge that there are others like them. It provides evidence of what Pablo Neruda, the Chilean poet, once said, 'Our original guiding stars are struggle and hope. But there is no such thing as a lone struggle, no such thing as a lone hope.'[17]

Each Yatri, and I would say each person, holds this opportunity of returning to a meaningful life, a life awakened by 'struggle and hope', to contribute to their chosen area. Most Indians who live in metros and Tier 1 districts are one, at most two, generations removed from a place that is in Middle India. If they are in an urban area, they could choose their local municipality to give back. If young citizens of our country identify and adopt Tier 2 and Tier 3 districts and work to transform them, we can transform the country in one generation. The energies of the youngest large country in the world can shine the Diamond.

2

Diamond: *A New Metaphor*

समझो जग को न निरा सपना
पथ आप प्रशस्त करो अपना

—मैथिलीशरण गुप्त

(Don't see the world as a mere dream
Chart your path, your own destiny)

—Maithilisharan Gupta

The idea of a diamond-shaped India was first seeded in me by my fellow classmates in Kendriya Vidyalaya, Ahmednagar. As a cocky sixth grader who had come to plebeian Ahmednagar from tony Delhi, I was coming to grips with this sleepy town. My admission had taken place mid-term, as is the norm with displaced army children. My father went against the grain, admitting me to the recently opened Kendriya Vidyalaya and not the surer convent education others in his cantonment circle had opted for. As I entered the grimy campus, I quickly realized that this was a far cry from the spruced-up premises of the Junior Modern School, Humayun Road, Delhi, that I had left recently.

What the Kendriya Vidyalaya lacked in amenities, it made up in the character of its students. My initial haughty behaviour as a student from New Delhi quickly unfroze as I saw Ashok, the son of a subedar major, dressed neatly, always upright in his demeanour and usually first in the class too. Iqbal, the son of a schoolteacher, wrestled me, who was almost 6 inches taller than him, to the ground in one of those dusty sports field brawls which, on recollection, never had a real cause. Hailing from lower middle-class families in Ahmednagar, the students spoke broken English but their experience of life beyond the cantonment was more grounded than my own. The final cross-cultural experience, though, took place with my friend Ram outside school.

My father was a colonel in the cavalry. An important perk of Ahmednagar, the centre of training for the Armoured Corps, was horse riding. Early morning rides with my father were a highlight of our stay there. One summer morning, as we came around a bend at a fast trot, wearing the customary 'sola topee', I saw Ram, my friend, emerge from the bushes, having done his morning ablutions. Our eyes met for one small moment and then the gaze broke. The act of a colonel's son riding a beautiful bay, meeting his friend emerge from the bushes, was part of my realization that another world with similar hopes to mine, but different circumstances, lived beyond the cantonment hedge.

Kendriya Vidyalaya changed my sister and me, and I suspect many like us. It was where cantonment kids like us met real India. My father was then a mid-career officer and therefore my family was also middle-class. I observed my mother 'going slow' on essentials at the end of the month till my father's salary came in for the next month. But those in my class were 'emerging middle class', and this difference in economic and social status separated us from the people of Ahmednagar town. My three years in Ahmednagar made me understand that the aspirations of Ram, Iqbal and Ashok were like mine, even if they were marginally poorer and their English was broken. This has been the parallel narrative of our country. The act of these millions of 'emerging Middle' Indians rising from small towns and districts is the defining story of our times.

Morphing a Pyramid to a Diamond

As India crossed its seventy-fifth anniversary of Independence, this upsurge has picked up pace. Those from Tier 2 and 3 districts, such as Ahmednagar or my native Deoria, are now in the majority and asserting themselves. The aspirations of this segment are on the rise. The language barrier remains—Indian languages and hesitant English versus the annexe-honed English of the cantonment or a metro. But the centre of gravity has shifted firmly to this segment in the middle. This new centre will define the political, social, cultural and economic trajectory of the country over the coming twenty-five years.

In a paper published in 2002, C.K. Prahalad and Stuart Hart, two renowned management professors, came up with the phrase 'Fortune at the Bottom of the Pyramid'. Prahalad expanded this theory into a book,[1] which described the emerging market demography as a Pyramid. It invited corporates to search and seek a fortune at the

Bottom if they made goods and services to appeal to people with lower incomes and cash flows.

About a decade ago, analysts began to sense that this reality was shifting with the emergence of the Middle. A 2010 World Bank report divided the 7 billion of the world's population into four broad categories of countries. There were countries with a population of about a billion where per capita GDP was above $12,000. Another one billion lived in countries where the per capita GDP was between $4000 and $12,000. A third group of countries, to which India belonged, had a population of 4 billion and a per capita GDP range of between $1000 and $4000. Finally, one billion people lived in countries with a per capita GDP below $1000.[2] The vast majority—four billion—were in countries in the Middle. As the number of people in extreme poverty fell sharply, the vision of the world as a Pyramid, with a small number of elites gazing down at the poor from their perch at the top, was getting outdated.

Over the past decade, that 'emerging middle' has risen further, consisting of 800 million Indians and shaping countries like India into a Diamond.

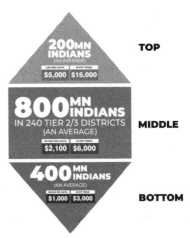

If we look at an economic classification of India in 2020, it had approximately 200 million Indians at the top with an average per capita GDP of Rs 4 lakh per year, or $5000, which in PPP terms is close to $15,000 per capita. The bottom segment consists of 400 million Indians, with a per capita income of Rs 80,000 per year or $1000, which translates to $3000 in PPP, poor even by sub-Saharan standards. The remaining 800 million people comprise the 'emerging middle' with a per capita income of Rs 1.5 lakh or $2100 per capita, which translates to $6000 in PPP terms, now a clear majority. The top of this Diamond-shaped India earns 2.6 times more than the middle and almost five times more than Bottom.[3] These numbers are averages, with each segment having higher and lower incomes. What the world calls Indian 'middle class' resides mostly at the bottom end of the Top. The vast majority of those in the Middle are 'emerging middle class', or simply 'Middle India'.

Middle India has around 800 million people, 11 per cent of the global population. On a PPP basis, the Middle has, on an average, a GDP that is the same as the whole of India, at $6000 per capita in PPP terms.

Middle India can also be broadly located in the 750 districts that make up our country. Each district will have some proportion of the Top, Middle and Bottom segment, but if we take an average classification, a diamond shape emerges here too. The top segment resides in thirty metro and Tier 1 districts, such as New Delhi, Mumbai, Kolkata, Chennai, Thane, Gurgaon and others, and on average coincides with the top income segment. When I studied at Modern School, Humayun Road, I was rubbing shoulders with the children of these Indians. These districts have approximately 160 million Indians, and in the main, they are prosperous. On the other extreme are 470 Tier 4 districts where 460 million Indians live, largely coinciding with the bottom income segment. These districts are smaller in size and on average are still poor, such as the district of Dhemaji in Assam or Gadchiroli in Maharashtra. Sandwiched between these two segments are 240 districts classified as Tier 2 and Tier 3 districts where 780 million Indians reside—57 per cent of India's population, in places such as Allahabad in UP, a Tier 2 district, or Ahmednagar in Maharashtra, a Tier 3 district.[4]

The US, that other large democracy, also witnessed a similar morphing after the Second World War as expressed by Edward Humes, 'After the war, economic distribution in the US began to resemble a diamond, relatively small number of poor and rich at either end, with a big fat middle at the centre.'[5] The post-Second World War growth of the US was also powered by a similar shift.

Damaging biases

The metaphor of a Diamond recognizes that most Indians are in the Middle, not only economically but also socially, culturally and emotionally (this is detailed later) and that their numbers are rising. This framing of a Diamond-shaped India liberates us from at least three biases that damage our democracy and slow us down.

The first bias is that the elite consider those in the Middle as poor, treating them as a liability rather than as an asset. The system ignores their self-worth and their ability to raise themselves with their own effort. This creates a self-fulfilling cycle of dependence, with government grants, doles and schemes being showered on them, when in fact what they need most is work. If this majority is seen as having innate capabilities, the government will focus on enabling these citizens, who can help themselves, and those around them. It will also save government money and effort, allowing it to focus on the truly poor at the bottom and create a safety net there. The Middle suffers from what some call 'the soft bigotry of low expectations'.[6]

By considering everyone below the Top as poor, a cottage industry of grants and subsidies had sprung up. The country remained obsessed with 'roti, kapda aur makaan', which is also the name of a film that is over four decades old but keeps getting run again and again. This was aided by a socialist mindset that insisted that tax and re-distribution was the answer, creating a structure of dependency. Political and administrative action must be differentiated in the approach to the Middle. Instead of 'rescuing' them from poverty through grants and doles, their strength must be recognized and utilized.

Arvind Rai, an entrepreneur from Kushinagar district in eastern UP, demonstrates this strength. Having gained initial success in retailing drinking water in the villages around Kushinagar, he noticed that many local businesses—milk vendors, dhobis and his own water distributors—needed a sturdy cycle that could carry a large load. Just as he was designing a cycle with a load-carrying capacity that would benefit local business—thicker tyres, better shock absorbers, a bigger back pillion—he noticed the proliferation of electric rickshaws. This is when he created the 'electric utility cycle', a cycle powered by an electric motor with a range of 45 km, which can be used by local vendors, entrepreneurs and artisans to ferry goods. This innovation did not result from a 'poor man' or a 'poor district' mindset, it resulted from living in a typical Middle India district, where a local need was discovered and addressed. There are hundreds of Arvind

Rais looking for encouragement and support, not doles or schemes.

The second bias is in thinking that Middle India is lacking in aspirations. On the contrary, Middle India is not satisfied with a cheap brand or positioning, even if value is important for them.[7] This was demonstrated by the dismal performance of Tata Nano. A low-cost car *was* required, but its branding as a 'cheap' car put people off. Had the Nano been positioned as a smart car, a yellow car, a women's car or some other attribute that went beyond low cost, it would arguably have made more progress.

This second bias was highlighted by Joe Madiath when we visited Gram Vikas in Ganjam district in Odisha in an early Yatra. 'The people of Ganjam may not be rich, but they do not deserve poor solutions,' he said. He had designed houses and toilets for tribals in that district with the same care as we would for citizens in prosperous India. As we visited the villages of Mohuda, where Gram Vikas has worked, we saw tribal families staying in neat two-bedroom houses, with a clean toilet and running water. Joe's actions are a rebellion against an 'unconscious apartheid' where the elite patronize the Middle with goods and services that are poor and designs that the Middle no longer aspires to.

We had to fight this bias when designing our enterprise centre in Deoria. The governing architectural equation for a small district remains 'Ordinary India equals exposed brick architecture'. Bucking this trend, we designed the centre with an aspirational façade, with all amenities, including digital connectivity, suited to the area. Had the same centre been planned in a metro city or Tier 1 town, people would not have questioned a design that was visionary.

The third bias is not understanding or appreciating the societal 'trauma' of historical repression that holds the Middle back. We see this first-hand in Purvanchal. Every development expert pronounces areas such as eastern UP backward, blaming attitude, lack of energy or people's inability to cooperate with each other. But we seldom discuss a history of oppression that drives a lack of trust and cooperation in society. The first war of independence in 1857 originated from Purvanchal and for ninety years, there was systematic oppression by the British to divide society for fear of another uprising. The dark irony of independent India is that those regions which fought most for independence suffered the most and are backward. In contrast, former presidency towns, which were part of the colonial system of extraction, have done well.

Countering this societal trauma takes time and effort. Examples of success must be demonstrated before we can re-establish trust and achieve the resulting social cohesion. Local leaders are essential to developing Middle India as they will empathize with this trauma and be patient as the ecosystem develops and societal trust is established. We see this in Yatris such as Gobinda Dalai in Odisha or Zubin Manav in Bihar, who come from these regions and are working to uplift them as a long-haul process. Zubin, in the Kishanganj district of Bihar, has created 'Project Potential' to grow rural youth into conscious leaders through his work for the community and environment since 2016. Gobinda has been working for livelihood creation in the smaller districts of Odisha. Outsiders, unless they had superhuman qualities, would have rushed back after a few months.

Aspirational energy

In *The Complacent Class*,[8] Tyler Cowen has documented the lack of dynamism that begins to afflict those who are well-off. As the Top of the Diamond achieves more prosperity, it gets complacent and has less incentive to drive change and growth. The Middle of the Diamond is hungry, aspirational and wants to rise, forming the potential centre of future growth for India.

Nationalism is best nurtured here, with development and economic prosperity as its focus. This Middle India, cutting across lines of caste, class and religion, wants a prosperous, secure and strong nation, anchored in and proud of its local identity and culture. The Middle wants future growth by sacrificing today and investing in tomorrow, much like an entrepreneur.

These voices from the Middle are gaining resonance through the power of social media. Their talents, even if expressed in Indian languages, can no longer be confined to those 'faraway' districts. They are as close as the nearest mobile phone, Facebook page or Twitter account. This is creating a churn and rupture as, for the first time, those in metro cities and Tier 1 districts are encountering a culture rooted in local traditions. With that comes discomfort. Kangana Ranaut, who comes from a small town and has an awkward English accent but is challenging those in the established circles of her industry, is an example of this phenomenon. The issue is the willingness of the Top to concede space to those from small towns and districts based on merit. But slowly, the Middle is gaining both confidence and acceptance, even from the Top, as Macaulay's pedagogy, colonial thinking and institutions are proving inadequate for an aspirational nation. The Middle was never co-opted into the British experiment as it was the 'other' and was oppressed by it. Middle India shows the same confidence that comes to countries such as Japan, which were never fully conquered. The confidence of a Dhoni is one example of that unfettered energy— somewhat quiet, often unassuming, but when put to the test, effective and explosive.

A startling example of small town and district confidence came to me from Chetna Gala Sinha, the founder of Mann Deshi Mahila Sahakari Bank, a bank for and by rural women headquartered in Mhaswad, located in the Mann taluka in the district of Satara, Maharashtra. With decades of experience serving women customers in smaller towns and villages, she says, 'Women who have been through a formal education are less open to risk taking and less confident than those who have not.' Her TED talk expands on this theme by describing an incident early in Mann Deshi's life. When Mann Deshi applied for a bank licence, the Reserve Bank of India (RBI) initially denied it because a majority of the promoting members were not literate. Most educated women would have accepted this decision as final, but the women of Mann, many of whom were uneducated, had the opposite reaction. They suggested Chetna organize literacy classes for them and set up another meeting with the RBI to explain the strengths of this banking segment. Sure enough, this time, their viewpoint hit home and they got the licence.

Against this rising tide from the Middle, in today's India '. . . civic life in the form of force, wealth, state action, ideas, social norms and the conduits through which it flows, institutions, organizations, networks, narratives and ideologies' favours the Top. Eric Liu calls this the 'power structure' of society.[9] This structure defines much of civic, economic, political and social life and its balance will either power or scupper India's nation-building project. We must give a new life to our republic by re-balancing that 'structure' so that the Middle can lay claim to its fair share and start contributing.

In today's India, the greatest determinant of whether a person will progress to health, wealth and prosperity is if he or she is lucky to be born at the Top of the Diamond. The definition of New India is that those from the Middle can do so with equal felicity and ease. That upward movement need not be led by the government. Our democratic systems and the arrangement of our polity, economy and society should allow millions to do this on their own, with the state enabling this process. That was the promise our founding fathers made—that *swaraj* would go beyond political freedom to encompass 'the freedom to be yourself' and that 'Swaraj was more than making India free; swaraj is the becoming Indian of the self of millions and millions of people.'[10]

The Middle as an anchor

The Middle can become a new fulcrum where Top, Middle and Bottom work in tandem for national renewal. An example of this mutuality and benefit is the story of Parvati[11], a young twenty-seven-year-old from a village near Deoria. Not highly educated, Parvati was roundly criticized by her brother and father when they observed her spending time on her rooftop peering into her smartphone. The signal for the smartphone was the best there, and Parvati was looking at designs of jewellery on the Internet.

Gaining confidence, she retailed some bracelets to shops in her village and then took her products to bazaars in nearby Deoria and Kushinagar. Her real break came when she came on board the Jagriti Yatra as a participant and sold some jewellery while the train circled India, proving that as a salesperson, there were very few who could beat her. Courageous and persistent, Parvati was not only making jewellery, she was also able to talk about her products with conviction and passion. She stayed back in Mumbai after the Yatra and decided that she would go back only after selling her stock.

Around this time, at a social gathering in Mumbai, she met Prerna, who instantly saw the beauty, both in the product and in the personal conviction that this girl from a Tier 3 district exuded. Over a couple of conversations, an unusual relationship formed between Prerna and Parvati. Prerna worked for a television company but had always wanted to do something on her own. In Parvati, she saw a mirror image of herself, but from a village of the type she had never visited. This bond was of common conviction and purpose as both wanted local women to benefit. Modern communication, logistics, the Internet and our network connected them in the unusual setting of a cocktail party in Mumbai. Prerna, a high-flying executive in Mumbai, and Parvati, the rebel daughter of a farmer from Deoria, came together to form a handicraft company.

Parvati and Prerna became equal partners in the venture. Parvati brought production knowledge and a team of locally trained women for jewellery and other artefacts to be produced in Deoria; Prerna brought business acumen and marketing flair. Prerna came up with an elegant design that positioned the brand such that the company could connect with the sophisticated upper end of the jewellery market. In a year, the duo had started creating jewellery that caught the attention of Fabindia and the first order was delivered. In subsequent years, their products were retailed overseas in Dubai and a graph of growth was charted. The small village from where Parvati hails has turned an unusual leaf. Those who were critical of Parvati's rooftop activities are now looking up to her. What a generation of women's emancipation could not achieve, this connection made possible within a few years.

The venture has gone through its ups and downs. Finance, marketing and hiring new people has not been easy. A key issue is that Parvati is often consumed by family and local issues that are part of rural life. When her mother is ill, she drops production and rushes to help her. When her fiancé had a bereavement in his family, she had to leave her business unattended. But as the infrastructure and ecosystem in Deoria improves, the journey has become smoother. It reminds us of the possibilities of what can happen when the Middle and the Top combine to influence the Bottom meaningfully.

Middle India must enable more Parvatis and there should be a network to connect them to more Prernas. Most economic acts in India—be it the ease of business, be it creating an SEZ or other infrastructure—still look at the Top of the Diamond as a safe bet. The belief still is that trickle-down will benefit those below the Top. A *direct focus on the Middle* as India turns seventy-five will impact the Top, Middle and Bottom together.

The Middle of the Diamond can be a better friend to the Bottom since, a few decades ago, they were themselves at the Bottom. Parvati recognizes the strengths and weaknesses of those at the Bottom and can pull poor women up based on mutual help and respect, caring and nurturing. Development, like any human endeavour, is seldom a financial or technical act. It requires helping in a human way, which Parvati understands as she is proximate to the Bottom. Tying a safety net for the Bottom to the aprons of those in the Middle will yield a far better outcome than a trapeze act from the Top. Over time, the poor at the Bottom one day may reduce to zero as the Middle bulges out and rises to the Top. I see a day where Prahalad's promise of a pyramid-shaped world may remain, but it will be an inverted pyramid.

Faith, family and community

Beyond per capita income, faith, family, community and meaningful work define the Middle.[12] As a Diamond-shaped demography emerges, the success of social and economic activities will depend on an understanding of what drives the average citizen within local social institutions. As we see when we circle India and in our district level work, three of these four factors are vibrant in the smaller towns and districts, while the fourth—work—is fast gaining attention.

Faith is the foundation of our civilization and is key to understanding small towns and districts. Not only have we thrived in having multiple faiths, spiritual traditions and religions, this has been our biggest export. The inner focus of Indian spirituality, the search for the sources of ignorance and the journey of ridding oneself of it have been an ancient tradition of India. Alexander the Great experienced this when he came as a conqueror to India and was reminded of the hidden empire within each human. Travellers such as Hiuen Tsang, Marco Polo and Ibn Battuta have testified to this. The philosophy of 'god within oneself' and an all-pervasive *brahma* are the basis of all Indic traditions, which leads to a faith that is innately bottom-up. It contrasts with Judeo-Christian traditions that begin with ten commandments issued from the top of Mount Sinai, indicative of a top-down approach.[13] In our travels across India and in our work in Deoria, I found faith to be an integral part of life in the Middle, guiding citizens in small and large decisions. The result is a process of self-regulation with a moral force for moderating behaviour, where society needs less monitoring by a formal church or a state.

Family is the second institution in the Middle that is a key to understanding and developing it. Family in small towns and districts is going through a transition and the structure of the family itself is circling back. The joint family structure remains common in smaller towns and districts, till people leave for big cities. Nuclear families are a natural by-product of urbanization and industrialization, and many Indians in the bigger cities live in one. Given that approximately 20 per cent of the Indian economy is industrial, and at the most, 15 per cent live in metro districts, the 'non-nuclear'[14] family predicted by Alvin Toffler should be re-examined as it already exists in Middle India.

Toffler described an industrial *second wave* relying on mass production, mass distribution, mass consumption and mass education, for which large-scale urbanization had been designed, which gave birth to the nuclear family. But gradually this would shift to a *third wave* economy, to services, technological customization and human centricity. In his mind, nuclear families were only a temporary product of the industrial era, and even in the West, he was questioning its efficacy.

However, joint families are troublesome if its members, particularly women and youth, do not find work. Patriarchal behaviour then smothers aspirations. This behaviour is aided by the predominance of land as an economic asset under the control of the patriarch and split, often acrimoniously, between family members. But in an enterprise framework, a family is the simplest unit of cooperation and accumulation of capital. In a family which is entrepreneurially active, youth and women can get 'economic space'. When a woman is economically active, she earns respect and space in the family not just because she brings home some bread but her work creates worth. This creates an atmosphere of abundance and growth, not limited to land as an asset. Parvati's company is a demonstration of family enterprise, where her father is now fine with her travelling and her dominating brother is now working for her!

Community is the heartbeat of Middle India. We have seen, relative to urban situations, how the community holds society together in a small town or district. They grieve together, celebrate together and are bonded in a fabric of local give and take. In one instance, I asked Safeena Husain, the founder of Educate Girls, a charity[15] that works towards girls' education in smaller, educationally backward districts, whether she could do something similar in a metro setting. She answered without hesitation, 'Thankfully, the villages of India are no longer the microcosms they once were. While urban

India has changed significantly, fortunately, the villages of India still have the sense of community intact. The village community plays a key role in ensuring that our system of girls' education is supported, and this is only possible in villages across small towns or districts. The community not only produces a cadre of committed volunteers, but it also provides a social feedback mechanism, which keeps our programme on track. I would never think of conducting this programme in a large metropolis or a city. The social cohesion required for its success is simply not there.'

This power, cohesion and the occasional interference that comes from any community-based effort is a critical asset of the Middle. This was recognized belatedly by the country when India instituted the 73rd amendment to the Constitution in 1992 relating to Panchayati Raj, explored more fully in Chapter 10. The difficulty of getting this amendment agreed to and the subsequent roadblocks in getting it implemented points to the bias in giving the Middle its share of power. Gram Pradhans are elected, but in the absence of spending power, schemes still require approval from district or state HQ. Schemes are limited to hand pumps, electrical poles, drains and similar basics, which are no longer topmost on the minds of the Middle.

The missing ingredient of work

The one area where Middle India is still deficient is in the department of work. Work is not just a means of earning a livelihood, it gives meaning to an individual, as '. . . work, not money is the fundamental source of our dignity. Work is where we build character. Work is where we create value with our lives . . . offering up our talents for the service of others'.[16] Work allows a person to start climbing the ladder of opportunity, giving him or her self-esteem, a connection with society and a shared economic stake.[17] Providing work is the single biggest challenge for the Middle, as agriculture, the mainstay of employment, is pushing out people as it gets mechanized and shrinks.[18] Industry, still controlled by the Top of the Diamond, is automating fast. Women are particularly compromised, as unlike men, they can't take a train out of the district to find work in cities. Those men who do migrate to cities stay in squalid conditions, often in jobs that pay just above minimum wage, as guards, drivers and construction workers. This creates tensions in the families who stay back, not to mention the squalor and crowding this creates in the urban areas they migrate to. It also creates what some call sagging in the Middle '. . . as higher paid jobs are created in high and low skilled occupations, not in middle skilled roles'.[19]

The Top of the Diamond has become economically strong through global connects, aided by the 1991 economic reforms. This segment dominates the economic language of the country, global trade and unicorn-directed entrepreneurship and is worth celebrating. However, the circle at the Top of the Diamond has become cosy and small, its members leaning on each other for economic transactions and relationships.

A signal of this small and economically successful club comes from the social settings I sometimes find myself in. In a country of 1.4 billion people, it shouldn't be difficult to find complete strangers. However, in most social settings in metro India, I find myself at a two- or three-degree separation from others. On greeting a total stranger at a get-together at a South Mumbai dinner, very soon I realize that a friend, a colleague or a distant relative knows us both from college, work or some other setting. While pleasing and often helpful, this points to the distance of the Top from the rest of the country. It points to a circle at the Top that is close to each other but largely cut off from the real India. The degrees of separation between Bharat and India is not six—it may well be sixteen.

The economic arch of our country is bending directly to the Middle. Most companies are aware that the small number of households in the middle class have many firms competing for the same market. As the Middle India of today becomes the middle class of tomorrow, most strategists are looking at ways of reaching this segment early. A whole industry has sprung up which talks of frugal innovation to design products and services for Middle India. As the reach into this Middle is difficult, new methods, including digital ones, have been put in play to reduce the cost of sale. The banking sector, for instance, has shifted most of its infrastructure to digital, reducing economies of delivery into the Middle dramatically. Customer surveys are discovering the complex value-conscious needs of this stratum. The Middle is not just consuming more toothpaste or sachets of shampoo, marketers are realizing that specific products such as high-quality air coolers, etc., need to be mapped to the latent demand there. Operational teams are seeking decentralized manufacturing to be close to their customers in case the supply chain gets disrupted.

There are numerous explanations for the surprising rise of Patanjali as a company, or the emergence of Sri Sri Ravi Shankar and the Art of Living. One tongue-in-cheek response from the despondent head of a fast-moving consumer goods (FMCG) company was, 'How do you compete with faith?' But the underlying reason is that many large companies ignored designing products and services for Middle India. A critical mass of such consumers, who are moved by yoga, by faith, by Ayurveda and by naturopathy, exists now, enabling a Patanjali to build a brand rapidly. Art of Living created a successful network in Tier 2 towns as it appealed to the search for spiritual meaning in the ordinary Indian. Heeding this calling, a friend from Lucknow gave up his lucrative dealership and became a full-time instructor at the Art of Living. People and households are attracted to a brand that emphasizes faith, family and community, rather than an aspiration relayed from the Top.

Over the coming twenty-five years, the Bottom of the Diamond will see citizens move into the Middle, even as many from the Middle will climb to the Top. This churn will be the defining political, social and economic movement as India reaches its hundredth anniversary. Much like the churning of the oceans in Indian mythology, both negatives and positives will emerge. But this will release new energies if the majority in the Middle is empowered.

A diamond gets its shine because it has many cuts and many facets. The more the cuts, the better the shine. India was known for its diamonds, the most famous being the Kohinoor. I saw this shining diamond locked up in a forlorn cage in the Tower of London some years ago. Kohinoor may not be the largest diamond in the world, but it is an emotive jewel for Indians, representing the multifaceted energies of a nation. It was in 1739, when Nader Shah raided India and took the Kohinoor to Persia, that our share of global GDP started to decline, as if our national heart had been snatched away. Maharaja Ranjit Singh retrieved it, but in 1849, by the terms of the Last Treaty of Lahore, the East India Company was 'gifted' the diamond by the ten-year-old Maharaja of Punjab, Duleep Singh.[20] The diamond-shaped demography of India today is akin to the Kohinoor—locked up but of immense value. Releasing and empowering it must become the central task of our republic.

3

Youth: *Our Growth Engine*

सेनानी करो प्रयाण अभय, भावी इतिहास तुम्हारा है,
ये नखत अमा के बुझते हैं, सारा आकाश तुम्हारा है।

—रामधारी सिंह दिनकर

(Warriors march fearlessly, the future is yours
As the stars in the night dim, the entire sky is yours)

—Ramdhari Singh Dinkar

India is an ancient land with a young population. The numbers are startling. As of 2021, 464 million people were between fifteen and thirty-four years of age—the highest in any country's history.[1] This is a hopeful situation, for youth are the harbingers of change. They are the generation that will carry the national baton forward now that Independence's first generation is retiring at the seventy-fifth anniversary mark.

In my years of being involved with Jagriti, I have found youth from smaller towns and villages hungry for change. They have high aspirations, but owing to limited opportunities, many migrate from their home districts

48

to larger cities. I have seen their possibilities, limitations and frustrations in the course of our work in Deoria and through the Jagriti Yatra. The youth are aspirational; they believe that tomorrow can be better than yesterday and yet, as Somini Sengupta puts it, '. . . aspiration is like water, unless given a path to flow, it can drown.'[2] That is, till you discover the ocean and have the courage to swim in it.

We did just this in the tenth Yatra, on 27 December 2017 in Kanyakumari. That same day in 1892, Swami Vivekananda had swum to the lonely isolation of a rock on the southern tip of India.

The year 2017 marked the seventieth anniversary of Indian independence and to mark this moment, the team had planned for a group of men and women to swim in the sea like Vivekananda had done. Trial runs had been done with twenty Yatri alumni off the Mumbai coast accompanied by a patrol boat, with Barkha Kedia, an Arjuna Award-winning Yatri and open sea swimmer, leading this cohort. At Kanyakumari, Tarini, my daughter, and I also joined in.

The sun was setting by the time the swim started. The glint of the sun on the town of Kanyakumari as we swam towards the shore will remain with me till the end of my life. As we came in on the last leg, exhausted and treading carefully on the sharp corals on the Kanyakumari fishing alcove, hundreds of Yatris standing on the adjoining jetty cheered us on. And true to our technological age, a drone from the Yatra camera crew captured this moment for posterity.

Positive freedoms

The youth of Middle India see the Top of the Diamond and its lifestyle through digital lenses—smartphones,

TV, Facebook and WhatsApp—resulting in heightened aspirations and expectations. At the same time, with agriculture unable to provide a livelihood for all and manufacturing fast automating, opportunities for gainful employment are shrinking. Should they stay back in their districts or should they head out to a big city? Can they get a government job? Should they start an enterprise? These are questions they grapple with daily. In north India, where the bureaucracy and politics are professions that accord respect, many drift in that direction. In other parts of the country, where private opportunities are greater, they struggle with the skills needed for those jobs. The net result is a loss of meaning, a crisis of employment and a culture of protest.

In an early Yatra, I uttered a phrase that ended up becoming a design principle for Jagriti: 'Protest is important, but building is far more important.' All the role models we visit on the Yatra are builders. Back in 2009 when the Yatra was still in its infancy, many well-wishers suggested that we invite Anna Hazare to the train. We discussed this seriously as Anna had built Ralegan Siddhi, a village we had visited on the 1997 Yatra. However, in his new avatar, he had drifted towards promoting his anti-corruption agenda. After careful discussions, we concluded that his current anti-corruption drive was 'anti', not 'for', something and while laudable on its own, did not align with the 'positive freedoms' we wanted to highlight. To resist the call to engage such a famous personality was not easy. Our team, well-wishers and participants, however, understood that a strong 'building bias' was the backbone of our movement.

Many youth are dissatisfied with the status quo and start with a posture of protest. This is guided by the language of our public life, which is tilted towards the negative. They grow up with a vocabulary of revolt, where it is 'cool' to protest, supposedly demonstrating courage when doing so. Words such as *'inquilab zindabad'* and *'azaadi'* slip easily off their lips. This is influenced by a culture post-Independence that believed that every problem required an oppositional response. This culture of 'doing something against' rather than 'doing something for' is not just an Indian problem but, in our case, it is much bigger if it influences 400 million youth.

When Yatris come with us on the journey, we attempt to shift the definition of freedom radically. At the very beginning, we describe 'positive freedoms' that come from a commitment. This is achieved not by throwing off shackles but taking on chains and using those to pull society forward. This commitment creates 'freedom to' rather than a 'freedom from'.[3] It is shaped by the commitment of a person, a group or a community to solve an issue and thereby move themselves and society forward. In the words of Tom Keller, 'Real freedom was not so much the absence of restrictions as finding the right ones.'[4] At the induction session, we gently suggest that if protest is in their nature, then the Yatra is not for them. In a lighter vein, we invoke the story of Morpheus from the movie *The Matrix* and the induction ceremony as a choice between the 'blue pill' and the 'red pill'. The blue pill will arguably give them immediate pleasure, which comes from protest, but the red pill will be an opening for the longer-term joys of building. Howsoever difficult the start, once the youth start building, it will give them lifelong meaning—a different kind of *azaadi*.

The induction auditorium packed full of 500 young men and women becomes a stage to enter a new world, a world of possibilities and exertions in the hinterland of India. We let them know that a fifteen-day journey will require constructive living with a building bias. 'If a tap leaks in the toilet in the train, instead of complaining, try to form a team and fix it' is one of our messages. We invite them to observe this bias in their co-travellers and role models. Each role model did not end up protesting on encountering an issue. They committed years of their lives to building a solution, usually through a social or economic enterprise.

As we create an enterprise ecosystem in Deoria, we have broadcast the same thought process. But mental models are difficult to change. As we were inducting an energetic young leader into our ecosystem, we asked his help to re-start a government-owned cold storage that had been lying unused for over two decades. The long defunct cold storage had been highlighted at a local meeting and we had discussed this with the relevant department in Lucknow, proposing a solution whereby an entrepreneur would repair it and take it on long lease. Our young inductee had been a student body president and as we talked through a revival plan, he blurted out, 'Where do we do the dharna?' His reaction in protesting against someone, someplace, rather than working towards a solution, is not atypical. But then I can't blame him; our social and political culture has been pushing protest for very long as an immediate Band-Aid that highlights the issue without focusing on the long-term commitment needed to solve it.

We cannot blame our youth for this situation if our media keeps highlighting the negative. Blaming the media for this situation is also not fair, for we are the buyers of those very newspapers with screaming headlines we later decry. If a culture of protest and cynicism overshadows the culture of building and positivity, we must seek out builders and *visibly* celebrate their lives. We need to make 'positive freedom' more desirous for youthful imaginations rather than the short-term freedom of protest. Youth then start seeing the many issues of the Middle as an opportunity to channel their energies.

Demographic dividend and youth bulge

There are two concepts that can help understand the dormant energies of Indian youth—the demographic dividend and the youth bulge. These are two related but slightly separate subjects. Demographic dividend speaks to the coming opportunity for growth, buoyed by the lower dependency ratio of India's population. Today, the number of people too old or too young to work and dependent on those in the working age—fifteen to sixty-five years—called the dependency ratio, is approximately forty-nine.[5] This has reduced from seventy-one in 1990 and some suggest that our growth spurt in the 2000s was aided by a sharp reduction in the dependency ratio in that decade. By 2036, this ratio will reduce to forty-six and then start to rise slowly. This means that for another fifteen years, more people in the working age population will support a smaller number of those who are dependent. After 2036, with an ageing India, that ratio will increase gradually, making more and more people dependent on fewer and fewer of those who work. By some estimates, our demographic opportunity will close in the next twenty years. In the northern and eastern states of India, the window is slightly longer, while in the southern and western states, that window is shorter. Roughly two decades of improving the demographic ratio will work in India's favour but only if the country is able to provide employment. If not, the dividend will convert into a liability even earlier.

The second concept, the youth bulge—what economists call 'youth in transition'—is the number of people entering the fifteen to twenty-nine-year age bracket. These young adults are looking for employment while coping with a transition as they come into adulthood. In these years, we need to find mechanisms where young people, awkwardly walking towards adulthood, continue to hold a positive view of society and the future. We also need to find employment for them as early as possible after their education has been completed. This employment is most needed in the Middle as much of the youth bulge will manifest itself here.

For India, the number of young people in the fifteen to twenty-nine-year age group in 2020 was an astonishing 380 million,[6] equivalent to the entire population of the US. Managing the transition of this many youths, giving them access to employment while keeping their attitude positive, is a critical challenge for India. This is a period where we need to keep youth confidence intact against personal and family anxiety to find employment. I have seen confidence tumble among youth in eastern UP as they attempt and fail examinations for qualifying for government jobs multiple times. Once their families and society start seeing them as failures, they start lounging on *charpais* in the mango orchards, away from the disapproving eyes of family and neighbours. Ultimately, they drift towards the city to find menial jobs. In this period of transition, many, frustrated with their situation, get drawn into activities on the fringes of society.

This frustration emerged dangerously on the Jagriti Yatra from a member of the catering staff. This incident occurred at a time when Yatris had returned to the train at a station in southern India. Headcounts had been completed and the train was preparing to leave. We had convened in the AC chair car common room to start a role model presentation by a group. As I settled down in my chair, I heard an urgent tap on the train window and saw that it was Ashutosh signalling to me to come out. On the platform, Ashutosh briefed me and asked me to follow him to the sick bay on the train. A young member of the catering staff, only nineteen years old, had taken a kitchen knife to a security guard on the train. Entering the sick bay, we found the security guard bleeding and getting medical attention. Thankfully, the gash was not deep and the doctors on the train had stabilized the injury. It turned out that the young man was from a small town and had been recruited in Mumbai. Feeling offended by a remark of the security guard, he reached for the knife in a moment of frustration.

But a bigger crisis was brewing on the train. The thirty-odd guards hired from a private agency were bristling with anger at one end of the train. The catering staff, around 130 in number, were gathered at the other end, preparing for a counterpunch. Col Patil and I walked down the platform to the security crew, telling them to stand down, else they would all be deboarded. We then walked the length of the train to the catering crew and suggested the same, telling them that strict action would be taken in case of any incident. Just as the signal was given for the train to move, we got the injured guard off the train to a local medical care centre. The youth had almost sparked off a minor civil war on the train, which could have escalated.

Across the country, incidents are on the rise where the underlying frustrations of our youth turn into larger conflagrations. The Jallikattu protest in Tamil Nadu and the Jat agitation in Haryana in 2017 are also grounded in the frustration of the youth. The Naxal unrest in the east and the anger of youth in Kashmir are ideologically charged manifestations emerging from anxiety. This stress can also be seen in the long queues of applicants for government jobs.

Challenges-as-inspiration

Our youth can be engaged in solving the many challenges facing Middle India. Challenge-as-inspiration provides purpose and meaning and can lead to large-scale employment if supported by a culture of building and enterprise. The challenges in India's small towns and districts are many, ranging from poor healthcare, average education, declining agriculture, lack of industries and need for energy to improving retail, financial inclusion, local urbanization and digital and physical connectivity, to name just a few. Instead of aiming for a job in a large city, the crisis of purpose, meaning and employment can be solved by matching the energies of this talent pool with the problem locally using an enterprise framework.

As the youngest large country in the world, India can present this matching process to its youth through a creative analogy. Kennedy created a national aspiration with a space programme, albeit one that was top down, challenging the US with the goal of landing a man on the moon and getting him back safely. He funded NASA and exhorted the country to get behind this act. As the story goes, when a janitor at NASA was asked his job description, pat came the reply, 'To put a man on the moon.' We can back a supra-national goal of greater economic prosperity, such as a $10 trillion economy in a timebound manner of twenty years. To do this, we must create our own district-level enterprise missions, mini-rural NASAs, that support youth at the grassroots. A young farmer in a Tier 3 district doing agro-processing, or a young mechanic in a Tier 2 town wanting to create a bigger garage, must believe, like that janitor, that his endeavour is part of our own national moon shot.

In the tenth anniversary Yatra in 2017, we threw a group challenge to the Yatris using Elon Musk as a provocation. This was done in Kanyakumari, after a discussion on Vivekananda and the sea swim described earlier. And there was an ironic link in that challenge. Nikola Tesla, after whom Musk had named his electric car company, was inspired by Vivekananda and sought to link his teachings of Vedanta with modern physics. Tesla had heard Vivekananda speak in New York and met him thereafter on 5 February 1896 for dinner, where Vivekananda explained *Sankhya* cosmology to Tesla.[7] Inspired by Tesla in turn, Musk had not only created one of the most valuable car companies by disrupting the electric vehicle-making industry, he had also disrupted two other industries—space flight and solar power.

We asked our participants to document three large disruptions India had achieved as a nation. We set this up as a question to be answered over the first half of the journey. Gradually, three answers emerged. The first was the Mangalyaan, our own Mars landing, which took enormous national effort and was accomplished at a fraction of the cost of other similar efforts. The second was Jio, the laying down of a telecom network across the country within a four-year period that disrupted the Indian telecom industry,[8] which had itself emerged from a technological leapfrog. Finally, Yatris also identified cooperatives such as Amul and Sewa as disruptions and a remarkable achievement that India could be proud of. But it was a struggle to name more game-changing disruptions in India.

In *The Geography of Genius*, Eric Wiesner identifies places such as Athens, Edinburgh and Calcutta which, at a certain point, due to certain circumstances, produced a flurry of genius.[9] The reigning location today is perhaps Silicon Valley. Wiesner traces the process that makes these spots gardens for genius to flower, with the role of culture being paramount. Instead of being marked by chic restaurants and comforting coffee houses, Wiesner's analysis reveals that these locations have both chaos and constraints for genius to take seed. He says, 'A little bit of chaos is good, as the mind goes into an "I don't know stage" which opens new windows and creates new breakthroughs.'[10] He believes locations that are invested in the status quo do not usually produce such individuals. The 'pot has to be stirred' for creativity to flourish. Debunking the belief that technology has a seminal role to play in the rise of Silicon Valley, he believes that the culture of that area, its 'creative ecology', is what drove technological success, not the other way around. Xerox Park in Palo Alto, California, provided another one of these places where a culture of curiosity took shape and spread to other parts of the valley.

The 7500 Yatris may not seek fundamental innovation or disruptions, for there is no 'formula' for genius. Middle India has a fair share of gentle chaos and a culture that is its own, where youth, as natural change seekers, can flower. As India climbs its own innovation curve, young genius can emerge from the Middle, which is our own undiscovered geography for genius.

The pursuit of meaning

Happiness became fashionable when the 1776 American Declaration of Independence employed it as a key phrase, announcing 'that all men are created equal, that they are endowed by their Creator . . . with certain unalienable Rights, that among these are Life, Liberty and the pursuit of Happiness'.[11] 'The pursuit of happiness' became an early goal for modern democracies. In the cities of India, this language and aspiration of happiness is in currency, with youth gathering at a Café Coffee Day, going for a movie, chatting on WhatsApp or other social media as they pass from school to college life, a job, friends and family. Youth in Middle India hang out together in village settings, are part of the Gram Mandali, take part in gully cricket, etc.— all these activities in the pursuit of happiness. But research has shown the straightforward pursuit of happiness is a sure route to unhappiness.[12]

Happiness on its own is a mirage; as you start drinking from it, it disappears. In contrast, 'meaning' targets a more permanent and longer-term goal, an 'inner world of reflective consciousness'.[13] To find meaning, a young person would have to use the 'positive freedoms' outlined earlier in this chapter. The act of making money, finding gainful employment is a *consequence* of the solution and leads to a meaningful life. As we travelled on the Yatra and took forward Jagriti's work in Deoria, I found meaning manifest itself through four pillars—Belonging, Purpose, Storytelling and Transcendence.[14]

Belonging, in the Yatra, starts with the act of sharing a 10-foot-by-7-foot compartment in a moving train for fifteen days with seven other participants. But it gets linked to the land by seeing the country as one, circling it together, offering a new sense of ownership. When Earth was photographed for the first time from space by the Apollo 8 crew in 1968, it provided humans with a new vantage point from which to contemplate their combined humanity. William Anders, the astronaut who took this photo, wrote, 'Earth's marbled beauty leaps from the darkness of space, amplified by the bleak monochromatic lunar horizon.'[15] The act of seeing Earth as one fragile planet, contrasted against the inhospitable lunar landscape, changed our sense of belonging and sparked the modern environmental movement. Recognizing that 'we belong together on planet Earth' creates a duty of care to protect, preserve and nurture that place. The Yatris have a similar epiphany when they circle India over a fifteen-day journey. Their thinking no longer remains limited to an association with a state or a district, a class or a creed; it fosters a belonging to the whole and engenders new meaning.

The second pillar of Purpose kicks in when Yatris meet role models who are motivated by a higher cause or fellow participants who have struggled under difficult circumstances. They are inspired by those who are 'givers' rather than 'takers'. Purpose may delay happiness but the creations that emerge or the relations that are strengthened in its pursuit make it worthwhile. The 'dark nights' each role model recounts, when they talk of the insurmountable obstacles they had to overcome, symbolize a purposeful struggle—perhaps not immediately happy ones but those that created meaning.

Each role model has a story of this struggle. Bunker Roy, who created Barefoot College at Tilonia, Rajasthan, which helps rural communities become self-sufficient, and has nurtured it for many decades, once talked of the day his organization was about to be shut down, recalling it like a scene from a Western movie. A local magistrate, having corralled the Barefoot College office in the village, was giving orders on a megaphone to 'give up', quite literally. Fortunately, a senior executive in the World Bank was visiting Tilonia and was staying with Bunker. Seeing this situation, the executive intervened, calling his head office, who pulled back the police posse.

That night was dark. Without the visiting executive, Barefoot College may well not have been around today.

The third pillar is in the magic of Storytelling. Stories are important for young people—personal stories of entrepreneurs and cultural and historical stories too.

We use this vividly in the time-lifelines of the first two days of the Yatra. I tell my own story to kick off the exercise: how I managed to win the three short sprints at school against a senior three years older than me. How I attempted the JEE after a year of listless studies at Delhi University, buying old Agarwal Classes papers. My somewhat lonely life in Aberdeen, Scotland and my training on an offshore rig, a short distance below the Arctic Circle in the North

Sea. Struggles of the 1997 Yatra, the joys of our children being born and the high of founding the Jagriti Yatra.

One time-lifeline that moved me was of Krati Gahlot. She described how she fought clinical depression and came out stronger, describing the struggles with herself and with society. She did not hesitate to show her vulnerability to 250 Yatris. The entire compartment, barring the clatter of a moving train, listened in pin-drop silence, the air heavy with meaning.

At Jagriti, we have also highlighted the story of Rani Laxmibai of Jhansi to good effect, creating a 'Har Ghar Laxmibai' programme for apparel and handicraft, detailed in Chapter 4. The women in this programme have their own stories to tell—the support given by a friend or a father or an act of personal courage—and these stories create ripples of meaning. These are moments when lives meld as their narration is an act of 'opening up', both for the teller and for the listener.

Transcendence and abundance

The final pillar of Transcendence is a heady mix of meaning and collaboration. Indian traditions are based on transcendence—'existence or experience beyond the normal or physical level'[16]. In the Yatra, the feeling of transcendence takes place in group settings, either when we slow the pace of the Yatra or when we amp it up—meditating in a group led by Tibetan monks on the hallowed grounds of the old Nalanda university or dancing to the Jagriti Geet with 500 others. These moments create meaning as they fuse many minds and bodies beyond the physical self. It creates a spiritual case for collaboration.

The visit to Aravind Eye Care not only brings out a spirituality inherent in that institution but also creates a comical tension between the temporal transcendence we experience in the Eye Care centre and the religious transcendence of the Madurai Meenakshi temple. After inspiring stories at Aravind Eye Care, visiting its different eye clinics and understanding its business models, we hear what Dr Venkataswamy, popularly called Dr V, the founder of Aravind Eye Care, articulated almost forty years ago. He said, 'Intelligence and capability are not enough. There must also be the joy of doing something beautiful.'[17] With this message ringing in our ears, we return to the train, parked a few hundred metres from the Meenakshi temple, when an 'otherworldly' transcendence complicates matters. Our exhortation to the Yatris to settle back on the train for a headcount before the train departs is difficult to enforce. There is an alluring offer, from no less than Devi Meenakshi, to break this rule and pay their respects at the temple. Every year, some Yatris sneak off to the temple, despite the whistle-blowing exhortation to stop and come back. One year, the organizing team gave in. We simply told all participants to proceed to the famed temple, with the organizing team joining in a prayer for a safe Yatra.

When belonging, purpose, storytelling and transcendence create meaning for youth, this leads to enhanced collaboration. Meaning creates abundance. Meaning can lead our youth to apply themselves to a cause, but abundance creates a pull to pursue that goal with others. Collaboration, the collective pursuit, comes more naturally to youth today, relative to my generation. The solo culture of my younger days is giving way to a culture that understands that any endeavour needs more than one.

This is partly a result of improved economic conditions of India and partly a realization that the old construct of 'my win is your loss' is the product of an extractive mindset. Collaborators are realizing that another's win can also lift them up, and this motivates our youth to conceive and achieve bigger goals. This new generation is revealing a republican India where working with each other is the primary means of progress. A more abundant mindset and environment, both economically and socially, is giving our youth a new playing field for collaboration.

Our education system lags in this shift. It is still geared to reward youth for individual effort, resembling a factory rather than a temple of learning. A temple must focus not just on the mind and the body but also on the heart, the human spirit. The education system is based on lines drawn many years back by an elite that created educational institutions for producing interlocuters in a colonial structure.

Our education system turned a corner when schools like Kendriya Vidyalaya or colleges like the IITs and IIMs came into being, allowing lower middle-class youth a shot at climbing to the Top. However, these new institutions continued testing for individual excellence. Other avenues to develop and test the heart, such as the National Cadet Corps and National Social Service, or sporting and outdoor activities that foster collaboration, remain limited. Institutions where character is built and young people can come together to pursue common goals need urgent attention. Psychologist and anthropologist Jonathan Haidt highlights the importance of socio-centric behaviour that benefits a group as much as the individual as a key axis of human success. He describes the joy of achieving something beyond the individual as the *bee-like* behaviour, which has been ignored for an *ape-like* behaviour that celebrates individualism and defines western life.[18]

National Enterprise Corps

A collaborative building process inspired by India's spiritual foundations requires a national framework for moral and economic growth. Udyamita, covered in Chapter 8, provides a template for organizing this. In this framework, societal capital combines with financial capital and state power. This requires a body for transference of knowledge so that local youth relate to others doing similar work nationally. This effort must focus on Tier 2 and Tier 3 districts where there is the most to do. An early form of such an association is being trialled through the Jagriti Ambassador for District Entrepreneurship (JADE) programme. Through this, each of the 240 districts in the Middle will have a Yatri evangelizing enterprise-led development in that district, but a national programme is needed to scale up this effort.

A National Enterprise Corps inspired by the journeys of Swami Vivekananda, who urged the youth of India to step forward keeping our own traditions in mind, might be an idea whose time has come. This could be conceived as a one-year compulsory stint for every young man and woman after graduation. This service would invite youth to a Middle India district to support local entrepreneurs and give real-life exposure and initial coaching with a learning-by-doing approach. It would not only expose these young facilitators to the real India, but through the act of supporting entrepreneurs, they would also get a rudimentary knowledge of starting an enterprise. Like the NSS, this service would give exposure to many young Indians to the joy of building in the real India.

I discovered Swami Vivekananda relatively late in my youth. As a second-year student at IIT Delhi, we organized a cycling expedition from Kanyakumari to Goa. Those were the days when a train journey to the south took three full days, with two nights of travel. Five classmates boarded the Tamil Nadu Express from Delhi for Trivandrum, with our cycles stored in the luggage compartment of the train. Time was whiled away charting the details of the journey, exchanging notes and enjoying the longest train journey in the country at that time. As we approached Trivandrum, I felt a fever creeping up on me. On reaching Trivandrum, I thought it best to check into the local army hospital, communicating with my family over a military phone as my father was posted in Jammu and normal phone communication was virtually non-existent. On examining me, the doctor declared this to be a case of mumps, which was not only infectious but required bed rest for a week. Reluctantly waving my friends off on the journey, I settled in for a few days of hospitality in a military hospital.

Having recovered from the illness, and with my friends already on their way to Goa, I decided to do the same length of travel on a bus. Arriving in Kanyakumari, I checked into the Vivekananda Mission on the shores of the Indian Ocean and the Arabian Sea. Like most do, I took a ferry to the Vivekananda Rock Memorial and meditated, returning to stay back in the simple premises of the Mission.

This is when I chanced upon an exhibition of the Swami, his journey and his wanderings for six years across the country, and his concluding stop at the rock I had visited earlier. There, he had a vision of a strong

nation built on the foundations of Indian values. This
led to his powerful declamation in Chicago at the World
Parliament of Religions in 1893, announcing that India was
spiritually rich but also hinting that it had to be materially
strong.[19] Vivekananda's guru and teacher, Ramakrishna
Paramahamsa, had already instructed him in the methods
of *bhakti*.[20] Here, at the foot of India, he came up with
the second method of salvation through the service to
others, leaning on the concept of *loksamagraha* outlined in
the Bhagavad Gita, which seeks social upliftment through
karma yoga. Vivekananda made the youth aware of their
infinite powers: 'Each youth who desires the good of the
nation as a whole, should try, whatever his walk of life,
to build up his character by developing courage, strength,
self-respect, love and sacrifice for others.'

That moment, in the premises of the Mission, was
a turning point for a young person like me. From that
location, one could technically look north and imagine
a land that was wise, with hidden energies waiting to be
unleashed. The romance of the place for me was sealed
when I learnt that Vivekananda had swum to that rock
for his three-day meditation. Taking inspiration from
Vivekananda, the National Enterprise Corps would create
a positive youth culture that celebrated building rather
than protest.

Organized in this manner, the youth can redefine nation-
building and find meaning in this act. Indian youth in the
Middle of the Diamond are not shy of expressing their
nationalism. But 'nationalism' that defines itself through
nation-building will require discipline, practice and time. It
does not rest on provocative speeches on street corners but
a long-term building bias that demands quiet leadership.

Youth can also educate elders that the time has come to shift gears.

The youth in the Middle of the Diamond are a resource pool waiting to take charge and accelerate our growth.

4

Women: *Creative Force Multipliers*

लक्ष्मीबाई नाम, पिता की वह संतान अकेली थी,
बरछी, ढाल, कृपाण, कटारी उसकी यही सहेली थी।

—सुभद्रा कुमारी चौहान

(Laxmibai was her name, the sole daughter of her father,
Sword, shield, dagger were her only companions)

—Subhadra Kumari Chauhan

Culturally, women define India. This has been mentioned
in our scriptures with women such as Gargi, Maitreyi and
Katyayani as leading thinkers. Women leaders played a
key role in our independence movement, with the vibrant
image of Bharat Mata uniting our nation. However, in real
life, we have consistently failed that description. This is
particularly true in our smaller towns and districts, where
the empowerment of women still lags behind the rest of
the country.

Women are endowed with natural creative powers,
something we notice in the Yatra and in our work in

69

Deoria. But this power is limited by the shackles Indian women have been put in. A lack of self-belief is instilled in them from an early age and remains a key hurdle in releasing the energies of women in India. Gandhi picked this up back in 1917 when urging greater involvement of women in our independence struggle: 'We have kept our women away from these activities . . . a kind of paralysis. *The nation walks with one leg only.*'[1] (italics mine).

As parents of two daughters, Gauri and I are personally invested in correcting this imbalance. We yearn for a day when our daughters' talents are recognized and they are accorded the same status as males. We believe they have even more to offer than men. But society makes women believe they are 'lesser beings' from an early age, in the very cultural traditions that hold up women as goddesses. The trenchant words of a Hindi woman writer, that 'Indian society has worshipped their women with brooms',[2] ring true.

Our family has a coming-of-age tradition as an *upanayan* ceremony, a rite of passage, where a young person is initiated to adulthood by seeking the guru's blessings. In my case, our family assembled in our ancestral home with my grandfather at its helm. Halfway through the ceremony, I had to enact running away to Banaras, to be placated by my maternal uncle, followed by my inevitable return. Shaven-headed, I got back to high school life in Lucknow, to a few friendly taunts, but with a quiet pride that society had noticed I was growing up. Later in life, I realized that my sister and the other women in our family never experienced that feeling. A woman growing up in India starts to feel 'micro exclusions' just when boys are celebrating brashly as they step into adult life. This confirms that 'the greatest source of suffering is not a handicap, it is the feelings of being useless, worthless, unappreciated'.[3]

Gauri, my family and I sought to change this in a personal way. We would do an *Upanayan* ceremony for our two daughters in our ancestral village. We researched and located a woman pandit from Varanasi who agreed to conduct the ceremony with four young women trainees so that the ceremony itself was 'powered by women'. This served to balance the wariness of our family pandit, who was watching these preparations inquisitively. Given the unusual nature of this event, Kiran Bedi agreed to give a talk to support the cause and flew into our hometown a day before the event. She shared her experiences growing up as a woman leader. How she started breaking down stereotypes as a national tennis champion and as the first Indian Police Services woman officer. The ceremony at Barpar was well attended and we were surprised by the positive response. Strangers have walked up to me many years later to applaud it, remarking on its symbolism. Society recognized that women's confidence cannot start when they are about to be elected as Gram Pradhans or are knocking on boardroom doors. The project of women's self-awareness, self-respect and ambition must start much earlier. If that bridge to confidence is not built early, we will continue, as a nation, to walk on one leg.

Balance sheet builders

Many years ago, speaking at a women's day programme at Bloomberg, I made a statement that belies my business training. I said, 'Women are balance sheet builders, while men are profit and loss people.' What this means is that given any resource, women are likely to use it for the long-term benefit of society. They invest in their child's health or in education, in an enterprise, etc. Men tend to spend much of the money on immediate needs—tobacco, alcohol, food, clothing. A World Bank report confirms this: 'In India, giving power to women at the local level increases provision of public goods such as water and sanitation and irrigation and schools and reduced corruption.'[4] Women also build balance sheets locally by holding the ground in the Middle, while menfolk often leave for a city to seek employment.

But this economic argument must be supplemented by a social one. In the Yatra, 40 per cent women's participation improves the quality of conversations. A confident woman contingent generates a creative and calming atmosphere. Not that men are not confident but the 'balance sheet' voice in discussions often comes from a woman.

We saw women power first-hand in Middle India when the 'Internet Saathi' programme was implemented in 2016 to train 17 lakh women in the districts adjoining Deoria. The programme was spread across seven districts, including some on the Indo-Nepal border that had 'jungle party', a euphemism for dacoits who used the jungles next to Nepal as a refuge. Unsurprisingly, this enormous project was led by a woman from a small town—Suvarna Tapkir.

I first noticed Suvarna in the Jagriti Yatra of 2014. Suvarna was a facilitator, and as I was leaving for home with my bags, she walked up to me at the station and handed me a pouch filled with crumpled notes. 'I collected it during the Yatra by giving facials and massages to other women on the train,' she said in a matter-of-fact way. 'I want to donate it to Jagriti as a sign of my gratitude.'

In a fifteen-day journey, she had found the time to open a beauty parlour for women Yatris! Married early, Suvarna was then in her mid-thirties but entirely a self-made woman. Post-marriage, she put herself through graduate studies and then did an HR management course. Her husband had suffered an accident and she juggled her time caring for him while bringing up her two sons.

When Google and Tata Trusts approached Jagriti to roll out the Internet Saathi programme in 2016, we were unsure. We advertised the project within the Yatri group to elicit interest. Suvarna was the first to step forward and that gave us the confidence to move ahead. But relocating from Pune to eastern UP for a period of a year was not an easy decision. One Sunday afternoon, Gauri and I found Suvarna outside our door, wanting to get counselling on the idea, with a request that we telephone her husband, who was reluctant about this move. We discussed the pros and cons and together discussed the move with her husband, giving him a sense of the impact the project would create. Her husband finally convinced, Suvarna led one of the largest implementations of Internet education in the country with 1.7 million women—more women than in the country of Mongolia.

Suvarna started by hiring and training 2400 women, each of whom were given tablets and phones. Each woman would cover four villages adjoining their own, training women—and some men—with house-to-house visits. Going door-to-door, they would convince reluctant parents and husbands to let women experience the world through the Internet. They discovered unusual personalities in the process, such as Akanksha, a twenty-one-year-old Internet Saathi. When Vanita, our board member, met her while researching the role of family in Middle India enterprises, she asked her in Hindi, 'Why don't you start a business with your brother?' Akanksha was quick to retort, 'It would not work out; *he does not have the right attitude.*' This intrigued Vanita and she probed, 'What do you mean by attitude?' Akanksha deadpanned, 'I know that the right attitude is important for business success from reading Shiv Khera's Hindi books.' In the middle of rural eastern UP was a twenty-one-year-old woman who wasn't going to be confined by her surroundings and was intent on transforming herself through self-help.

Women power lifts everyone

Executing the programme, providing tablets, training, distributing and then monitoring progress had its challenges. Some grumbled about how the programme could 'spoil' these women through 'too much exposure'. Some felt that their sisters, daughters or wives would be 'unsafe' on the Internet. But a more insidious theme hung in the air—if women got ahead, men would fall behind. This is the old 'one or the other' argument. Research though tells us that when women get ahead, the whole of society, including men, get ahead too.[5]

We saw a shift in attitudes, both in women and in men, due to the Internet Saathi programme in the Deoria region. There was a new confidence and a curiosity to go beyond Internet training. A critical mass of women came together and that gave them peer confidence. The formation of an apparel cluster and SHG groups involving women started in earnest and more women sought work. While some naysaying parents, brothers and husbands remained, several women became entrepreneurs, inspired by the doors the Internet opened for them. The circle of confidence that has been created is expanding every day.

The euphoria and positive energy generated by this programme turned out to be short-lived when women's Labour Force Participation Rate (LFPR) in India was examined. The LFPR of women in India has dropped from an average of 31 per cent at the turn of this century to 24 per cent by 2018.[6] In comparison, the global average in 2018 was exactly double that of India at 48 per cent. Bangladesh's large apparel industry and cooperative movement has seen its women LFPR rise from 26 per cent at the turn of the century to 36 per cent by 2018. A 24 per cent labour force participation means that three-quarters of Indian women do not even attempt to seek employment.

Indian women are getting educated in large numbers. Results for board examinations from across the country, particularly from smaller districts such as Deoria, often see women come out as toppers. They are diligent and hardworking. And yet, by the time they can start participating in the economy, they have been sent into oblivion within their married homes. Rural women and those from backward classes have a higher labour force participation owing to agricultural employment. Women in urban areas have a lower labour force participation relative to their rural sisters. Their balance sheet building qualities remain confined to family chores.

By creating a successful enterprise near or in their homes, women from small towns and districts can break out. The first 'balance sheet building' activity entrepreneurs like Parvati undertake is investing in other women.

Every woman thus employed will in turn invest in her children—food, nutrition and the resulting good health, creating a cascade of societal goodwill. A second major shift that takes place is that by becoming local, believable role models, they provide inspiration to other women to become entrepreneurs. Parvati has become a role model for other women, with many others looking to join her in the enterprise creation game. A pickle-making venture has sprung up, supplying pickles for orders received on the Internet, with Delhivery, the logistics provider, stretching its logistics chain to pick up bottles from a village on the outskirts of Deoria town. Another woman has started a business making sanitary napkins. An apparel cluster is being designed alongside other activities that promote women SHGs and micro-enterprises. Finally, inspired by such enterprises, other women step forward to create infrastructure for women. In 2017, another Yatri, Manisha Mohan, who hails from a small town but has worked in MIT, USA, who has devised technology for women's safety, began working with local entrepreneurs to create a women's safety device.

Women in urban areas and Tier 1 districts can play an important role empowering their sisters in the Middle. Like Prerna, who became a market partner for Parvati by bringing sales, marketing and design elements to their enterprise, Indian women at the Top of the Diamond too can be force multipliers. Women require coaches, mentors, market connectors and financiers who bring these elements to the Middle. A rural-urban 'sisterhood' creates a forum for better sales and more funding but also creates an emotional connect beyond just business. Prerna coached Parvati in a manner that may have been difficult for a male partner. Women at the Top can be a key support for women-led development in the Middle.

Beyond the 'weak woman' stereotype

Our positive narrative often came up against a 'weak woman' story everywhere we went in Deoria. Almost every school function I attended had a play on a women's theme. But inevitably, it had girls enacting tearful scenes of helplessness with the 'rescue' of women as its conclusion. But the women we saw in the Internet Saathi programme, and women like Parvati and Suvarna, were far from helpless. This is what Robert Caldini and others call a 'big mistake', wherein an overuse of a negative message, instead of solving the problem, inadvertently normalizes the situation.[7] The 'women as weak' stereotype in Middle India is also a case of the 'soft bigotry of low expectations'.[8]

Our emphasis was on a super-narrative which moved beyond the 'weak women' story, and this too was led by Suvarna. We were convinced that society does not have to emancipate women; actually, women would emancipate smaller towns and districts. This required a fresh language of women's empowerment, one that believed that women were inherently strong. Once such a narrative was built, the 'second leg' whose lack Gandhi bemoaned would become active.

We leaned on a local heroine from history to create our narrative. Rani Laxmibai is remembered for protecting Jhansi against the British, but as a girl, she was Manikarnika, born in Varanasi in eastern UP. Rani Laxmibai's birth in Purvanchal could be used to make our point, we felt. She exemplified everything we knew the young girl in Purvanchal was—smart, energetic and as effervescent as Laxmibai's childhood nickname, Chhabili, suggested. The many young girls we find roaming fearlessly in the villages of Deoria till they get to the age of ten or eleven are like the young Manikarnika. Then they get burdened by the norms of society and the lack of women-supportive infrastructure.

This is when we created the Har Ghar Laxmibai programme in support of women-led development using the icon of a woman warrior from that region. Through our outreach programme, we attempted to communicate that every house had potential Laxmibais. Building on our work in the Internet Saathi, we sought to combine an iconic historical personality with economic activity through an apparel cluster. We created the largest cloth mural of Rani Laxmibai ever made using embroidery and stitching—a 30-by-20-foot picture of the rani on horseback, showing her fighting the British carrying her son on her back. This was a picture every woman in the Middle recognizes only too well, as this metaphor plays out in her daily life. Helpfully, the word *Laxmi* also denotes the goddess of prosperity.

We organized tents in each of the sixteen blocks of Deoria where smaller cloth sections of a larger mural would be embroidered and stitched together. Hundreds of women embroidered her image, neatly broken down by Suvarna and her team into twenty-five separate pieces. Together, this was stitched into a giant cloth fresco on which her image appeared as a whole. This image was unveiled on a public ground in the virtual presence of Kiran Bedi. The impact was electrifying for both women and men. Almost

2000 women came forward as part of the unveiling; with them came 1500 men. The act of a large cluster of women creating a large mural of their favourite heroine together motivated many to start apparel enterprises, often helped by their husbands. This shows that once women-led development commences, the other half also joins in. An apparel cluster was given life that day, catalysed by the collective effort of women in that region.

The inclusion of women as combat soldiers in the army and air force can be perceived as powerful demonstrations of women's strength. The selection of a woman helicopter pilot, Shivangi Singh, by the navy from Deoria in 2021 made news across the region. The act of a woman police person carrying a carbine on a train station or airport sends a signal that they can also protect. Individual women athletes have consistently won more Olympic medals for India than men. There are many such examples which, once highlighted, will remove mental blocks, revealing that women are strong, even if their strength is different from men and even more in need now.

Another ancient civilization, the Greeks, also recognized the powers in the feminine. *Athena Doctrine*, a book by John Gerzema and Michael D'Antonio, outlines this theory with deep research.[9] Athena, the Greek goddess of industry, arts and crafts, gave the Greeks the olive tree, their equivalent of the banyan. Athena sustained Greek economy and culture. She was venerated for her skills, civilizing influence and fairness. The authors of this book undertook research that polled over half a million people in twelve different countries, asking questions on 'masculine' and 'feminine' traits in the modern networked world. They found feminine traits most attributed to words such as interconnectedness, openness, adaptable, committed, creative, planning, imaginative, humble, empathetic, expressive, affectionate, caring, nurturing, etc. 'Masculine traits' were closely associated with words such as dominant, analytical, proud, self-reliant, resilient, competitive, direct, confident, competent, career-oriented, etc. These attributes actually exist in both genders and each are required in society. But an overwhelming number of those surveyed identified the first with the 'feminine' and the second with 'masculine'. Once definitions were established, they polled respondents to link these attributes to three desired positive outcomes—leadership, success and morality. Which attributes were necessary to be a good leader, to be a successful person and to live a moral life? With minor variations, the survey showed that feminine traits in a *networked world* were more relevant in *all three* outcomes.

The twelve countries were then assessed in having a 'predominant feminine' or 'predominant masculine' orientation. There was evidence that those countries that cherished 'masculine' traits were less developed than those that cherished 'feminine' traits. One can question what comes first—whether economic progress results in more respect for 'feminine' attributes or more 'feminine' attributes lead to a better economic situation. But the values of the feminine in a post-industrial economy were evident from this study. In the Indian cultural context, relevant for the Middle, one does not have to go very far back to discover that the idea of the *Ardhanarishvara* expresses that feminine and masculine balance. It exalts, rather than diminishes, the importance of women balancing a 'man only' world at the apex of the Indian pantheon.

The unpleasant side of gender imbalance

While a positive message is important, the darker side of the gender situation must be confronted. Large-scale trafficking of women, violence within marriage as well as acid attacks and rapes continue in India. These gigantic issues and their impact have been glossed over. Society, including the police, is not sensitive to these serious manifestations of gender bias and mostly ignores or covers these incidents up without the needed nuance and sensitivity. The nearest analogy that Kristof and WuDunn[10] draw with the issue of women trafficking—still a roaring business in Asia—is the slave trade. Today's India largely sweeps this ugly issue under the carpet.

At the Top, gender discrimination is usually a matter of unequal pay, lower sports participation or unwanted sexual advances, highlighted by the #MeToo movement. In smaller towns and districts, gender discrimination is sometimes lethal, literally so. As a World Bank report asserts, 'Parents are less likely to take their daughters to be vaccinated than their sons—those alone accounts for one-fifth of India's missing females.'[11] Girls in India from one to five years of age are *50 per cent* more likely to die than boys of the same age.[12] This does not account for 'silent murders'—those killed before they are born. Those girls who survive are often undernourished, evidenced by widespread stunting of women in India. This is also reflected in India's ranking in the Global Gender Gap index—105 out of 135 countries. Even if we account for some bias in this reporting, the Laxmibai image takes a beating with these numbers. The saving grace is the relatively high ranking in political participation of women in the global index. This remains in evidence with strong women chief ministers and Cabinet ministers, which are partially the fruits of the 73rd Amendment. Despite examples of strong women in mythology and historical heroines such as Laxmibai or the Rani of Kittur, the tradition of treating women as second-class citizens continues.

These concerns bring up the two-pronged character of the debate on women's empowerment in the Middle. There is the 'lean in'[13] theory that seeks 'women powered by women'. A second theory says that for women's advancement, we must create 'women's infrastructure' for women to live lives of safety, security and dignity while being able to work in a small town or district. The Laxmibai idea draws from the 'lean in' theory, where a woman, feisty at birth, brought up with male companions, groomed in the art of war, stands up and defends her kingdom. The second theory seems to suggest that not everyone can be born a Laxmibai, a Rosa Parks or a Sheryl Sandberg. It calls upon society to make changes at the field level through women's infrastructure. It seeks systemic change so that over time, it is easier for an ordinary woman to find purpose and happiness of the kind her male brethren enjoy. Middle Indian women need both. We must inspire the Laxmibai in each woman and also create an environment and infrastructure so that when women step forward, they feel supported.

Women's infrastructure should recognize that women need special support, not just as workers but also as managers. There is enough and more to do close to the village. In our experience, apparel making, food processing and handicrafts are starting points. If we want women as managers, then the burdens of the family that are lumped on them must be resolved. Common child creches, a facility for the care of elders by a common pool of nurses and the reorientation of men to understand that women have an important economic role are only some of the items on that list. After the COVID-19 crisis and large-scale working from home, the discomfort in working out of home is less, for both men and women, and this can be another impetus for better home infrastructure for women.

Blind spots and risk taking

With 40 per cent women's participation, the Yatra is a testing ground for gender behaviour. The first time, a pattern was pointed out by an outsider—Jude Kelly, the founder of Women of the World and the former artistic director of the South Bank Centre in London. Ignoring my warnings that the Yatra was a tough journey, she has travelled thrice on it for short durations of three to five days each.

On her second journey, she pointed out something that had gone unnoticed by us—men were dominating conversations when women had more to say. In the sessions on the train, at the end of every role model presentation during the question-and-answer session, Jude noticed the men take up positions in the front line, with women in the second or third row. The women would push forward, parting the wall of men, to make their points and would then withdraw. Women's interventions were equal, but they had to fight through this wall of men to be heard. When Jude mentioned this, we realized it as well. At a role model stop, when we had the attention of the entire group, we asked Jude to address this issue with the participants. When Jude pointed out this behaviour to participants, the message went through with surprising ease. These were blind spots that men had not noticed.

In real life, this happens far too often. Women are expected to be in the second row of life, while men are driving from the visible front. We need to bring women to the driver's seat, alongside men.

HEC, a business school in France, elected to do research on the Yatra by sending a team on the journey that polled participants, giving us further insights on women's empowerment. They analysed the impact on participants with 'before and after' questions, interviews and surveys. They interviewed Yatris as they began their journey and repeated this on the last day, when they finished. There were many observations that were of interest to us, with 99 per cent of all participants saying the journey had a deep impact on them. But the most heartening finding was women participants gained the most from the journey.

At the time of starting the Yatra, their propensity to take risks was low, but when they disembarked, they recorded the highest *increase* in risk-taking attitudes. The study ascribed this to the company of other women, a fast-paced fifteen-day journey, but it also pointed to the men as catalysts. Men were supportive and, discounting the blind spot pointed out by Jude, wanted women to do well, helping where possible. Women will help women, but men will have to do this as well.

The 'lean in' vs the 'women's infrastructure' debate was brought out in Odisha. In one visit to Gram Vikas, we posed a question on women's empowerment to Joe Madiath, its founder. We were flush with theories behind the success of different enterprises. We had seen how women were the silent force behind the many enterprises we had visited.

The women nurses in Aravind Eye Care did the jobs of paramedics, keeping the cost of surgery low. We had also seen the role played by women at Kalkeri and Selco. With this in mind, we asked Joe how he saw women play a larger role as entrepreneurs. To this, Joe had a counter-intuitive answer, 'Women are already burdened. They keep the kitchen fires alight, they fetch water for the family, gather firewood, rear children and ensure their houses are clean. Now you want to add another chore to this list—find work through enterprise.'

While this was not the answer we were looking for, it points to the 'hidden jobs' and 'hidden economic value' that measures such as the GDP do not account for. Does an additional role of entrepreneur saddle them with an additional burden? We discussed Joe's reply back in the train. The conclusion we reached was that while this was an additional role, unless women took on this role, they would always be the 'homemaker' accorded little economic value and marginal standing in their family. For further economic standing, we need to create women's infrastructure to support women leaders.

Breaking barriers: a Middle Indian woman's perspective

One idea for the provision of finance to support women came from a woman from Deoria but in picturesque Kanyakumari. At key points in the Yatra, a panel discussion is organized with eminent social and economic personalities. On that day, we had organized a discussion on women's empowerment with Shaheen Mistry, Madhura Chatrapati and others,[14] with Venkat from the CNBC TV18 channel moderating the session. 500 Yatris from across the country sat listening as the panel debated the predicament of women. At the question-and-answer session, Richa from Deoria asked a question that reflected the grittier dilemma of the Middle. 'Madam,' she said in Hindi, 'My father has kept aside Rs 10 lakh for my dowry. How do I convince him to put this as an investment into starting my own enterprise?' So far, the panellists had been fielding glacial questions on breaking the glass ceiling in boardrooms from metro Yatris—this was Day 2 of the Yatra. This question landed with the full force of the choices faced by the Middle. I cannot remember if Richa got a satisfactory answer but an idea was born that day in Kanyakumari.

Dowry, illegal in India, continues in small-town settings. Our idea at Jagriti is to convert this into enterprise finance. What was previously earmarked for a dowry or an expensive wedding could be invested in a venture jointly owned by the newly married couple. Instead of a glitzy celebration and the customary scooter or fridge that is presented, in this case, they would have the opportunity to make lifelong earnings through an enterprise. The woman would enter the house as a worthy enterprise owner, an idea that is slowly germinating in the region.

In my experience, power is seldom given—it must be taken. In a democracy, the best way to do so is through the ballot box. The biggest hope for women's empowerment in small towns and districts is coming from voting trends. Women in Middle India are voting in large numbers and they are voting for those who help them. The 2009 Lok Sabha elections saw that the female votes polled were 4.5 per cent below the male vote. In 2014, that number reduced to 1.8 per cent, and in the 2019 parliamentary elections, the women's vote equalled that of men at 66 per cent.[15] More importantly, women are voting with a mind of their own. Research shows that women are voting for issues that are important for society.[16] This is a democratic balance sheet vote of 50 per cent of India's population—400 million votes—and has transformative powers for India. As there are 50 per cent women in every family, if women start voting with a mind of their own, the politics of development we all seek will come with a rush. More women politicians are entering Parliament—already, the 2019 Lok Sabha has the highest number, even if it is a paltry seventy-eight.[17] We hope the balance created by women in the Yatra with 40 per cent participation for sixteen years will soon be seen across the country.

Can India achieve a 'women's dividend' through women-led development as it tries to achieve growth and a better Human Development Index?

Ultimately, the answer to this question will come from women. Our experience shows that once women are given power, they take other women along with them, as was done by Suvarna in the Internet Saathi and Har Ghar Laxmibai programmes. Once women come forward, so do men. This is when the two legs of society start walking in tandem for national renewal and growth. The women's voice ensures a longer-term view with a building bias. With the vote an important instrument of power, women can accelerate their development through their franchise—a voter no longer guided only by others—but by voting for those who promote her interest. This will multiply every resource of the nation given the balance sheet building qualities of women. Women's empowerment through enterprise in the smaller towns and districts of our country can start a virtuous cycle. This will not only be a victory for women, but it will also be a victory for our democracy.

Part II

LEARNING: *From History and Culture*

As a nation, we can learn from our history, from other democracies and from our culture. The Middle has witnessed many traumas in gaining freedom that remain hidden and need to be understood for a full appreciation of its circumstances. The behaviour of that other large democracy, the US, at the time it turned seventy-five can provide insights for our national journey. Our culture remains distinct and original in these locations, ignored by the post-colonial elite and therefore less tampered with and more authentic. This culture, if rediscovered, can give our nation a new field of growth, one driven by the human spirit. Discovering our revolutionary history, forces of democracy and new sources of culture can give our nation poise and stability, moving us further and faster to create a prosperous nation.

5

Revolutions: *Lessons from the Middle*

खड़ी शत्रु की फौज द्वार पर, आज तुम्हे ललकार रही
सोए सिंह जागो भारत के, माता तुम्हे पुकार रही

—श्याम सुंदर रावत

(The enemy is standing at your doorsteps, challenging you today
Awaken o lions of the nation, Mother India needs you now)

—Shyam Sundar Rawat

As revolutionaries, Mangal Pandey and Mahatma Gandhi were opposite in temperament, but their efforts at different times vectored the British out of India over ninety years of struggle. Both of them carried the spirit of the Middle, and while their methods were different, their origins and early life in small towns and districts powered their actions. Leading up to Independence, the Middle played a frontal role in the freedom struggle and it was punished the most by the British. During the course of my work in Deoria, a district adjoining Ballia, the birthplace of Mangal Pandey, I see the scars in society through the punishment meted out to this area by the British after 1857. Gandhi too derived his political strength by mobilizing those in small towns and districts. Post-Independence, this role and sacrifice was not acknowledged and the Middle was relegated to the national back seat.

I discovered Gandhi through his autobiography, but a family memory also gives me a spiritual connection to him. Gandhi visited Gorakhpur in February 1921, shortly after the non-cooperation movement had been launched. As the train carrying Gandhi steamed into Gorakhpur, my grandfather was one of fifty students from his college assigned to receive him. As a sea of humanity swept on to the platform, this fragile student cordon broke. The Mahatma was saved only by the intervention of the Ali brothers and Dr Bridges, the principal of St Andrews College, where my grandfather was a student. At the guest house, my grandfather was stationed as a guard outside Gandhi's room. After a few minutes, Gandhi proceeded for his public meeting. Two lakh people showed up for his rally at Baleka Maidan, where, according to my grandfather, Gandhi '. . . spoke in his feeble voice and broken Hindi.'[1] The person who impressed my grandfather the most was Maulana Mohammad Ali, who spoke with verve and clarity of thought. The event made a lasting impression on many and while my grandfather did not give up his studies as part of the non-cooperation movement, he understood that a revolution was in the making.

But India's modern revolutionary history commenced sixty-four years before that time with the sound of a bullet on 29 March 1857, when a man from Ballia took aim at the British empire. Mangal Pandey hailed from Nagwa village in eastern UP. He had enlisted in the British army but was known for his self-esteem, even under the overpowering discipline of the army. The revolution he called forth was a private one and it sparked a war that started with a defence of culture. On the Barrackpore parade ground, when he took aim, Mangal Pandey probably knew that the consequence of his revolt would be death. Once he saw he was going to be overpowered, he tried to kill himself. Shortly after his capture, he was hung at the gallows on 8 April, eleven days after he had raised his gun. With his death came alive an India that had been tormented for 100 years—tormented by the British but also by its own weakness and contradictions, which had allowed British rule. The spark of 1857 awoke the country and over the next ninety years, the Middle served both as catalyst and key actor in the struggle for independence.

India's First War of Independence was 'led by the lower-middle-class men whose status and livelihood were most severely corroded by the tactics the British used to protect their rule.'[2] That lower-middle-class man, Mangal Pandey, challenged the dominance of the British in a frontal way on a military parade ground. Till that time, 'Company Bahadur' was a name respected and feared by Indians. From the Battle of Plassey, 100 years prior, the East India Company had established their rule in India, converting a company listed on the London Stock Exchange into a 'joint venture' with the British government through the Charter Act of 1833. In the time leading up to 1857, the East India Company was a '. . . regime suspended from above the lives of its subjects . . . having only the thinnest connection with the people it was supposed to rule.'[3] This system was based on a method of control instituted by Cornwallis around 1800, elaborated later.

The draconian aftermath

The reprisals that took place after 1857 left India, particularly the north, reeling. A private company that had encroached on a civilization as old as human history sought to bring it to its knees. The East India Company lashed out at India as if it had belonged to them from antiquity. Atrocities were committed on both sides, as in any civilian theatre of war, but the British acted to stamp out the very spirit of society through visible violence. Mass executions, many at the mouth of a cannon, and public hangings were common. Forces from outside of UP, Bihar and Bengal were brought in to quell the rebellion. A significant cantonment was created in Lucknow to keep military firepower close by. British administration was given teeth and anti-citizen laws to protect the administration from its own people were formulated. Local zamindars and rajas who helped the British quell the revolt were co-opted, while others were persecuted. English settlers were already present as indigo farmers in towns such as Campier Ganj in eastern UP and they became the local eyes and ears, with friendly zamindars acting as trojan horses across the districts of Purvanchal and Awadh.

The police force was strengthened and early battalions of what later became the Pradeshik Armed Constabulary (PAC) were instituted. The objective was not to protect citizens from the disorderly but to protect the British and their collaborators from citizens. As historian Jon Wilson put it, 'The government's anxiety was based on their perception that Indian society was always in a state of emergency.'[4] British leaders such as John Malcolm who designed this approach thought 'the law needed to be an instrument of command not a mechanism to contest state power'.[5] This rule *by* law continued even after the East India Company was dissolved and the British Crown took control of the 'joint venture' in 1858, continuing to build an apparatus of shock and awe. The administrative system focused on preventing another revolt that could send the British tumbling into the sea. While before 1857, *Purabia* soldiers such as Mangal Pandey were the backbone of the Bengal army, recruitment from these areas was stopped and the idea of 'martial races' was formulated to encourage military recruitment from other regions that supported the British.[6] UP, Bihar and Bengal came under a particularly strong police and military radar. If an ordinary individual like Mangal could light a spark that could ignite the country, who knew how many such Mangals existed?

This history of revolution and repression sheds light on the social trauma of the Middle in general and of Purvanchal in particular. The empire's future was dependent on ensuring that another revolt did not emerge from this area and draconian methods were employed to subdue and divide society. There were similar, less well-advertised mini-revolutions against the British, which are important to understand the Middle in other regions. An early rebellion depicted in *Anand Math*, a novel by Bankim Chandra Chatterjee, took place in Bengal between 1770 and 1820, when a troop of sanyasis took up arms. The Polygar wars, waged by Veerapandiya Kattabomman of Tamil Nadu from 1799 onwards, were a brave resistance to the British East India Company. In Kittur, within present-day Karnataka, a lady ruler, Rani Chennamma, defied the British between 1824 and 1829. The Indigo Rebellion gripped Bengal from 1859 to 1862 when British indigo farmers used extractive and unfair rules to cultivate their lands. The Santhal Rebellion took place from 1855 to 1857, just before the First War of Independence. The story of Birsa Munda in what is now Jharkhand around 1900 is another case of a tribal leader challenging the British.

While some early revolts by local rulers were to protect their own mini kingdoms, the ones that had a lasting impact were those that involved ordinary people. Remarking on the 1857 rebellion, Jon Wilson comments, 'The insurrection was led by north India's dislocated lower middle class. The rebel leaders particularly called upon soldiers, clerics, artisans, petty officers, minor landlords and merchants to join the revolt.'[7]

These mini revolutions were soon forgotten, for the kings of the princely states, local lords and the upper crust—which later came to constitute the Top—were co-opted by the British into the colonial network. 'The heart of colonial society remained in the presidency towns where many Indians continued to absorb and adapt alien influence and ideas'[8]. Today's metropolises—Mumbai, Chennai, Calcutta and Delhi—progressed as entrepots to this exploitive network that stretched deep into the hinterland. Understanding these mini revolutions is important to understanding the backwardness of the Middle, as the very regions that sparked independence were singled out for oppression. The societal distrust and social trauma in these regions, their economic backwardness and their relationship with the administration are part of this historical and social trauma of the Middle. The Top, which sided with the British after the 1857 rebellion, seldom experienced this, and if they did, they ignored these slights

for they benefited from the Raj. In my view, novels such
as *Anand Math* and history books such as Veer Savarkar's
The First War of Independence were kept off the reading
list by the Top for they challenged the civilizing world
view that the Top accepted. That colonial patina remained
unchallenged even after Independence.

The British exploited India, simultaneously constructing
a myth that the empire was benevolent. The colonial
administration collapsed our economy and society as
'. . . the first half of the nineteenth century saw the retreat of
artisans and traders, warriors, and nomads to the villages,
and to a lifestyle that relied on the direct cultivation of
the soil'.[9] The Raj quelled uprisings and distanced itself
from the real India. Its officials took refuge in gated
enclaves or hurried off to hill stations by creating idyllic
conditions resembling Britain. If the conscience of some
in the British ruling class was pricked, they took refuge
in the act of proselytization. The empire was not just a
conquest of land and economics—the soul of the 'primitive
heathen' had to be rescued too. The war of 1857 failed
to liberate India, but it made Indians fully aware of the
true intentions of the British. It also put the British on
notice that missionary activities would not be tolerated.
The proclamation of Queen Victoria declaring India as her
dominion on 1 November 1858, as a result, had statements
of benevolence and circumspection on faith, including a
promise to respect the rights and beliefs of all her Indian
subjects.'[10] The first real revolution had been put down by
a public show of violence, but it had created the first moral
and spiritual counterattack on the empire. However, the
procedures of governance instituted in 1793 by Cornwallis
were made even more obscure by what Charles Dickens

satirized as the 'circumlocution office' of the Victorian bureaucracy, serving to create a state with an impersonal, inward-looking culture based on complexity.

Co-opting the elite

But to rule a country the size of India with a few thousand officers required more than villainy, brute force, economic sleight of hand, missionary zeal and bureaucratic obfuscation. By 1931, when India's population was about 300 million, the number of people of British origin was only 1,64,000. Of these, 4000 were civil servants while 60,000 were in the army.[11] These numbers required large scale 'psyops'—psychological operations—to co-opt our elite and make them believe in the empire. Colonialism, capable of large-scale violence, merchant companies with an extractive agenda, a missionary church bent on conversion and a bureaucracy trained to control required legitimacy. This needed institutions to brainwash those in power to create a brand for the Raj the country would respect. The rest would follow as these leaders, once indoctrinated, would in turn explain the virtues of the empire to those below them. In any case, the ruling class had been ambivalent about war in 1857; 'it was the governed not the governing classes who rebelled'.[12] Brainwashing the elite to justify imperial culture as a civilizing force was a key element of a colonial ecology.

I studied in an institution that had once specialized in this effort. Colvin Taluqdars' College is a well-known school in Lucknow where I enrolled after my stint in Kendriya Vidyalaya in Ahmednagar as my father moved to a field posting in Aizawl, Mizoram, without the family. Living with my mother, sister and younger brother, Lucknow served as a 'separated family' location for my last five years of school.

As its name suggests, Colvin had colonial origins. Designed for the sons of local *taluqdars*,[13] it opened its portals in 1889, three decades after the First War of Independence. With its school and hostel buildings built in the style of the medieval *kothis* of the Nawabs, its large playing fields tucked away on the edge of the Gomti river and its motto, 'Noblesse Oblige', which translates to 'privilege entails responsibility', the slant of privilege Colvin stood for was evident. An annual sports function called the 'Durbar Day' had featured caparisoned elephants in the days gone by. This was where the young wards of the ruling families of UP were sent for a rite of subservience that was part of a bargain made with the British after 1857. As Jon Wilson puts it, 'The British state . . . had to stand forth as a protector of the sub-continent's ruling class guaranteeing their security for their submission.'[14] At the time I was a student in this school, the British had long since left; it was their memories we had to bow down to.

With the UP Board as the examining body, the education was mostly in Hindi but with a keen focus on physics, chemistry and maths which later helped me clear the JEE. In retrospect, the school was designed to train us to be the guardians of the Top. As gentlemen scholars, we were expected to go to Delhi University, or if luckier, to Oxford or to Cambridge. We were framed as generalists who, by superior access and networks, could walk on water, crossing the sea of Indian life with ease. Even more famous public schools such as Doon, Mayo, Scindia, Sanawar and the Hyderabad Public School carried a similar leitmotif.

Colvin gave me a balanced education and thanks to the UP Board, I was exposed to the joys of Hindi literature. In Jaipur, where my father was posted after Mizoram, my English consistently failed the standards of the cavalry mess. I fumbled for words as the sons and daughters of other officers conversed in fluent English. But, in the end, I could not shake off Colvin's colonial ethos. The comings and goings of Governors and Viceroys were thrust on us when the lifting prose of *Anand Math* or the speeches of Vivekananda were waiting.

Colvin Taluqdars represented the hyphenation created by Macaulay's famous Minutes. Colvin was one of the regional governors and taluqdars, the landowners through whom he governed. The school became a setting to create '. . . a class of persons Indian in colour and blood, but English in taste and opinion, in morals and intellect'.[15] The indigenous education system, which was well-developed across rural and semi-rural areas, as documented in *The Beautiful Tree* by Dharampal,[16] was sundered and the focus shifted to educating the privileged in English. Missionary schools that came to India from the middle of the nineteenth century also continued portraying colonialism positively while carrying on missionary activity across the country. Macaulay's aim was singularly imperial and technical—to 'subjugate the actions of British officers under a single set of rules and so make the empire whole and united'.[17] These rules enabled 2,00,000 Britons to rule 30 crore subjects.

The administration was architected with the 'state as a commander and builder, not a nurturer of human capacity and talent'.[18] As an example, in 1859, the state spent Rs 1 lakh for education in the whole of Bengal, the same amount spent rebuilding the barracks in that year.[19] The infrastructure built was directed towards the economic gains of the imperial economy. Large infrastructure projects in waterways, railways, ports and roads allowed British products to come to the hinterland and commodities to be taken out. Last mile connectivity was neglected, with an indigenous 'bullock cart revolution' serving to close this gap. The infrastructure built was designed as a conduit to the Top, leaving vast swathes of the Middle unconnected. Besides suffering a lack of infrastructure, smaller towns and districts were administered through a bureaucratic process bereft of dialogue. A distrust, therefore, developed between ruler and ruled and also between different segments of society. Divide and rule was in effect 'oblige and rule' and took place not just between different segments and regions of the country but crucially between the elite and the masses.

A gradualist movement and a revolutionary

The Indian National Congress was founded in 1885. Among its founders was Allan Octavian Hume, an enlightened Scotsman. The association was given sanction by the Viceroy as a relief valve for those in the higher echelons of society. Hume created the Congress to 'make a resolute struggle to secure greater freedom for yourselves and your country, a more impartial administration, a larger share in the management of your own affairs'.[20] This appeal to the elite also sprang from the rationale of privilege. The revolutionary ardour sparked by 1857 was to be *regulated* rather than supported. It was an appeal to create another set of political interlocutors between the British parliament, the Viceroy and the common man.

In its early years, the Congress played the role played by trade associations in economic circles today, relaying the voices of the elite in an orderly manner. Many early appeals for self-rule were rejected and as a result, more revolutionary voices such as Bal Gangadhar Tilak arose asking for full freedom, which split the Congress. During the First World War, the two extremes of Congress leadership had to come together and in the 1916 session of the Congress in Lucknow, they asked for 'self-rule', a hesitant call to arms.

But by 1916, an individual with revolutionary ideas had come back to his native land a year earlier. Born and educated in the small town of Porbandar in Kathiawar in modern-day Gujarat, trained in London as a lawyer, he already had a lifetime of work behind him at the age of forty-five. Having experimented with different forms of civil disobedience, he had already propounded and tested the idea of *satyagraha*—appeal to the truth. This man, who went by the name Mohandas Gandhi, understood that India resided in its villages when he toured the country on a train. More than two decades earlier, it was a train journey that had set his life's course when he was thrown off a train in Pietermaritzburg in South Africa in 1893. His Indian train travels were prompted by Gopal Krishna Gokhale, who exhorted him to explore the 'real India'.

During his Yatra, Gandhi understood that India's salvation lay beyond the negotiations of the Congress with the Viceroy in Delhi. He linked the rejuvenation of India with its small towns and villages and to its culture. He recognized that this segment of India had not been co-opted by the British in its colonial infrastructure.

Only the strength and spirit of these people would enable independence from an empire on which the sun was refusing to set. Mass action for true independence would also come from here. Gandhi's ideas of *lok samagraha* or integration and of satyagraha found a channel here, and its execution caught the British off guard for it targeted 'two previously strongest areas: military might and moral assuredness . . . Ahimsa denied the relevance of British armed strength while the spiritual dimension challenged the whole basis of imperial self-assuredness'[21]. Gandhi talked of the coming together of society to overcome the ills of the nation by reviving its spirit, which was not to be limited to political independence. The healing of a civilization like India had to start in the heart, not in the head, and hence his focus on spirituality and culture. By taking on the garb of an ordinary Indian, he signalled his oneness with that India. The mind of the country's elite had been captured by a colonial dispensation, but its heart in smaller towns and districts could be rescued.

When Gandhi returned from his Rail Yatra, there was a spring in his step. He had seen the issues India faced from a third-class train compartment. His conversations with fellow passengers ratified the approaches he had experimented with in South Africa. With the force of his personality, he proceeded to give this as a plan for freedom to the Congress. The lawyer of the Inner Temple used the spirit of Porbandar and a philosophy of non-violence experienced in Kathiawar, and led a fearless campaign for freedom. 'By meeting British violence with Indian non-violence, Indians were essentially civilizing their oppressors'[22]. Starting from Champaran and Kheda, Gandhi won battle after battle against British iniquities, bringing to the fore the other India. The debating society of the Congress was now galvanized into action.

The defining journey that forced the hands of the British in 1930 brought this message to all of India. By now anointed 'Mahatma', the great soul, Gandhi came up with the idea of 'salt as a symbol', communicating the inequity of *namak* to the common man. The Dandi March was positioned as a pilgrimage creating a 'new crossing' or a *tirth* for the country.[23]

The media followed every step of this novel act of defiance. The British, unable to gauge the movement, kept quiet and let the march roll on. The march changed our independence struggle; it brought our masses into the movement, charged by the cultural wellsprings of India.

In this duration, the spiritual inheritors of Mangal Pandey and Laxmibai continued to torment the British. More Mangal Pandey-type insurrections continued, parallel to Gandhi's efforts through ahimsa. The valour of Veer Savarkar escaping as a prisoner while being transported in France and fashioning an alternate story of revolution has been celebrated recently. Aurobindo Ghose had retreated to his ashram in Pondicherry but continued his spiritual quest in seeking India's rebirth.[24] The stories of Bhagat Singh, Chandra Shekhar Azad and their martyrdoms always inspired us as children. Azad breathed his last in a park in Allahabad, keeping his promise that he would never be caught by the British, when he used the last bullet on himself. Subhash Chandra Bose, who was also born in the small town of Cuttack, took to joining the enemy's enemy and died fighting for India. Soldiers of the Indian National Army, the INA raised by Bose, included a women's regiment named after Laxmibai, which fought valiantly in Burma. After the end of the war, three key leaders from the INA—Gurbaksh Singh Dhillon, Prem Kumar Sehgal and Shah Nawaz—were put on trial, which only served to unite the whole country. The spirit of 1857 returned; 'the mood now in 1945 was not different to that in 1857'.[25] The mistreatment of naval ratings who had returned after spending years defending the empire in the Second World War, and their uprisings in Mumbai and Karachi, was the final straw that gave us independence. Each revolutionary chose their own path, each wanted a change in the status quo—Pandey through the defence of culture, Gandhi through satyagraha, Aurobindo through spiritual upliftment and Subhash Chandra Bose through armed insurrection. Directly or indirectly, each derived their energy from a small town or district.

Freedom at long last

After ninety years of struggle, in the end, India got freedom but without fundamental rupture. It is true that the revolution Pandey sparked and which Gandhi and the others completed, aided by the naval ratings mutiny, left no doubt in British minds that they had to leave. But the republican revolution of involving masses from that other India in the project of shaping a new nation, post-Independence, was consumed by the fires of Partition. Pandey's attack was a push against the perceived encroachment on culture, while Gandhi wanted more than just political freedom—he was looking at a cultural, social and economic revolution. Involving the ordinary Indian in the task of nation-building was as critical as the fight for independence. But after Independence, the *ancien regime* continued, with the revolution imagined by our founders brushed under the carpet.

My encounter with *My Experiments with Truth*, the uber-honest autobiography of Gandhi, took place in my last year of school. The book—Gandhi's candid self-appraisal and the sources of his thinking—shook me. But in the open-air canteen near Karakoram, my hostel in IIT Delhi, attempts at explaining this book to my friends was drowned out by an India pursuing the US dream. Very soon, I too was getting inducted into the world of the Beatles and Pink Floyd. My first-year Rendezvous festival at IIT Delhi had rock bands, complete with an old-fashioned fight, in the open-air theatre in our campus. As a Kishore Kumar fan with *Chalti Ka Naam Gaadi* as my favourite movie and Agyeya's *Shekhar: Ek Jiwani* as a defining book, I was in unfamiliar territory, but the need to fit in was overpowering. *Zen and the Art of Motorcycle Maintenance* was a book recommended to me by my friends who came from the metros. As I read the account of this bike journey across the US, Munshi Premchand and *Namak ka Daroga* faded into the background. But a full induction to this culture took place at Machan, a restaurant at the Taj Mansingh, Delhi, redolent with images of a tiger shoot in the British Raj and its brand of aristocracy.

We came to Machan for its 'as many refills as you want' Rs 100 Cona Coffee, but we stayed back for its ambience—air-conditioned environments, front desk receptionists described in IIT dorms as Greek goddesses and unaffordable club sandwiches, which was a welcome contrast to the burnt tandoori roti of our hostel mess. The atmosphere of leisure and abundance contrasted with the messy bustle in restaurants we could just about afford in Malviya Nagar, Delhi. Machan was quintessentially Raj, and even decades after Independence, that location was alive and aspirational in Delhi. The mountain of imperial extraction, the penury of our citizens through colonialism and the degradation of culture was forgotten between sips of Cona Coffee. 'Experiments with truth' became utopian and redundant here. As we left late at night, for some reason, we never forgot to tip the turbaned *durwan* at the gate.

This imperial brand flourished even after Independence as the energies of the Middle, harvested by our founders to achieve our freedom, were forgotten by the Top post-Independence. There was no rupture in the colonial ecology at the Top. Post-colonial India forgave the empire for the loot, plunder and mismanagement India had endured. Instead of assessing and revealing the extraction India had endured during the colonial period, the elite took control and sustained many of those very traditions. As Priya Satia comments, 'The moral case against empire encounters stubborn ambivalence despite the history of anti-colonial struggle.'[26] This is because those who struggled and gave us independence were left out of the power structure and the very elite who had collaborated most with the British continued to script our national narrative. While independence gave India geographic unity, the long-nurtured divisions of the Top with the rest were sustained. The elite, to my mind, were victims of a massive Stockholm syndrome as an unconscious survival mechanism, when 'people get attuned to the people with power above them and learn to adjust themselves to their expectations to please them'.[27]

Political consolidation but at a price

India had a very difficult birth as a nation and this external chaos aided lack of internal rupture. The British left against a backdrop of widespread mayhem, chaos, loot and pillage as two countries were born out of undivided India. This was done by a handsome viceroy and his elegant wife, but it was an unmitigated disaster. This kind of beginning to Independent India could not have been worse. The Partition was planned poorly, rushed through and executed in a slipshod manner by a retreating empire that had enriched itself over two centuries. The Partition was planned as most things had been by the British—in the hallowed halls of London and Delhi, removed from reality. It was the work of Sir Cyril Radcliffe, who had never been to India prior to 1947, let alone having knowledge of those who would bear its consequences. It led to a rushed exit scarring generations on both sides of the border.

Sardar Patel, who recognized the talents of smaller towns and districts, had another problem to tackle at Independence. As the home minister and the Deputy Prime Minister, Patel understood that the administration he and others had fought for decades had to be used to consolidate India. This was not his strategic vision but a tactical necessity to achieve the goal of keeping India intact. Once this decision was taken, he delivered India politically, bending the wills of kings and princes to that of our democracy. This brought in crores of citizens to democratic India from princely states, and with a few exceptions, he achieved this bloodlessly. Patel, who most understood the vision of a people-centric republic, had to turn inwards. He had to use the administrative and police services to consolidate the country. His generation and the other founders understood that at that point, the sanctity of the nation was paramount. Political consolidation came at a price; administrative rule, much the same as when the British ran India, returned. People power, the promise of our republic, had to be sacrificed at the altar of consolidating the country. India was born a democracy that could boast that elections were taking place every five years but without a clear agenda for republican action where the common citizen could be considered an active participant.

This behaviour is not unnatural at the birth of democracies. We will see later a similar postponement of slave emancipation at the founding moment of the US. In India, the Fabian socialism of Nehru, which relied on state power, failed to shift the approach from the days of the Raj and a dynastic trend cemented this false start.

On the one hand was the 'steel frame' of an administrative system focused on control in the district, and at the other extreme, the nation got busy climbing the 'commanding heights' of the economy, allured by the success of the Soviet Union. That split the nation open in two opposite directions. The administrative set-up at the district level lacked incentive for economic development. Its core spirit had been honed for almost two centuries to destroy and inhibit local industry to make space for British goods. Post-Independence, its revenue collecting role was reduced, so it did what it knew second-best—control. Cottage industries, the unfinished project of Gandhi, petered out without a strong helmsman. At the other end, Nehru started building 'Temples of Modern India', which were intended to benefit the masses but were guided by the vision and energies of a technocratic elite and created a dynamic of 'trickle down' that continued thereafter.

The founders of the United States gave its democracy the gift of graceful transitions, a topic covered later in the book. George Washington retired at the end of his two terms with John Adams taking over, followed by Thomas Jefferson for two terms after he beat Adams. The rise of Mrs Indira Gandhi shortly after Shastri's death took away this opportunity for India. Shastri, a simple man born in the small town of Mughalsarai, died early and in mysterious circumstances. This diminutive leader was deeply influenced both by Vivekananda and by Gandhi. In his brief stint of two years as the Prime Minister, he ushered in the Green Revolution in 1965 and won a war with Pakistan, coining the slogan of 'Jai Jawan, Jai Kisan'. After the sixteen-year tenure of Nehru, and a mere two years of Shastri, another family member took control of India. Without a base or a track record, Mrs Gandhi started polishing her only asset—the family name. This resulted in the exercise of power through palliatives such as the nationalization of banks and a centralized and increasingly corrupt administration. If Mrs Gandhi was already removed from the real India, she distanced herself further by governing through her advisers, a 'kitchen cabinet' of sorts. Then in 1971 with the 'Garibi Hatao' slogan, she attempted to retain power through a grant and subsidy model, creating layers of dependency. The proclamation of the Emergency in 1975 was the last throw of this dice and the death of her younger son, Sanjay, in 1980 paved the way for another dynastic transition.

The slogan of 'Garibi Hatao' was very much in the air when I was a child. In Modern School, I even faintly remember being photographed with the architect of this slogan at the wedding of my maternal uncle. Wearing the sherwani of a *sahbala*, the young 'best man', I am seen dwarfed in this photo between Y.B. Chavan, my maternal grandfather, and the diminutive Mrs Gandhi. My thrill at being photographed with the Prime Minister soon turned into childhood panic when one morning, my mother informed my sister and me that our father was leaving for Bangladesh to fight a war, where his regiment, the 63rd Cavalry, was being deployed. On the triumphant liberation of Bangladesh and his return, Mrs Gandhi was redeemed in my nervous imagination. Inspired by this victory, I even wrote a letter to the editor of the *Pioneer* newspaper in Lucknow while in school, praising her ways, little realizing that the structures of dependency were getting stronger every day.

Her son, Rajiv Gandhi, another scion of the dynasty, understood the weakness of 'Garibi Hatao' and the grant-and-subsidy model—he admitted that only 15 per cent of it really reached the poor. But by then, the country had become comfortable with a state barely loosened from the days of the British Steel Frame. The many millions who were poor were its focus. Our private sector at the Top was comfortable with this articulation, selling smaller and smaller sachets of shampoo to the poor at the Bottom of the Pyramid.

A modern revolution thwarted

Rajiv Gandhi attempted a mini revolution to balance the power structure for the Middle, but this was largely thwarted by his own administration. A Yatra role model, Ramaswamy Elango, the village head of Kuthambakkam near Chennai, recounts the day it was given final shape

by Rajiv Gandhi. Elango was in Kanyakumari when Rajiv
visited the location. This was a time when Rajiv was
struggling with the question of introducing the Panchayati
Raj Bill as a constitutional amendment. The thought that
India required a representative government at the village
level had been around since the time of the framing of the
Constitution—Gandhi's influence had seen it inserted as a
Directive Principle of State Policy. This new structure could
balance the district bureaucracy and aim for development
that had local involvement. But committee after committee
had come and gone with no one having the appetite to
make this move.

In Kanyakumari, at the Sunrise Beach, Rajiv mulled over
the policy and its consequences if presented in Parliament.
Elango says, 'Rajiv was to visit the Sunrise Beach for only
a few minutes but stayed back, pacing barefoot for hours
after the sun had risen.' He finally made up his mind and
went back to Delhi to introduce the bill in Parliament in
1989, although he could not muster enough majority in
the Rajya Sabha to get it passed. The legislation finally got
approval only in 1992, his death at the hands of a suicide
bomber creating the political space for its passage. The
Panchayati Raj came up with the bold suggestion of 33 per
cent reservation for women. Gram Pradhans were given the
power to decide what must be done in their villages, but
financial powers largely remain with the administration[28]
with implementation not given adequate focus, particularly
in the north. Those states in the south that have devolved
power faithfully as per the Panchayati Raj Bill have a better
economic and social record.

The 1991 economic reforms cannot be called a
revolution, but it created enormous space for enterprise

at the Top. Narasimha Rao created a turning point like Deng Xiaoping had done in China in the late 1970s. It was confined to giving private enterprise space at the Top but deserves to be celebrated regardless. In the end, though, it did not impact the Middle, where the majority lives, barring a tepid economic trickle down.

In fact, the forces of reform, whenever they came near the Middle, were pushed back as the existing structures felt threatened by the possibility of real power with the people. In India, that Middle has grown over the past decade to become the largest segment, no longer in extreme poverty and now having a distinct voice. The rise of Prime Minister Modi symbolizes that rising energy. The clear mandate to the BJP in 2014, led by Prime Minister Modi who comes from the Middle, is a first indication of this shift. The call to mobilize the energies of ordinary citizens is encapsulated both in the Panch Pran, where the responsibilities of citizens have been listed, and his call for *sabka prayas*.

The approach to bringing up this Middle through its own energy can become the centre of our next revolution. The war of independence in 1857, the Dandi March in 1930, our political independence in 1947 and post-Independence revolutions of economic reforms in 1991 and Panchayati Raj in 1992 were moments when the country shifted a gear. Since 2020, after the COVID-19 shock, India has also reset equations, with a realization that the Middle needs direct support and participation for enterprise and employment essential for growth. The first three events taught us different methods to revolt against a repressive regime, and they were all led by the Middle. The ones post-Independence moved our political and economic thinking forward. The rise of the Middle must recognize that this time, there are no British to chase into the sea. Instead, over the coming twenty-five years, we must create a new independence through a participative model that can inspire our rise. India, post-independence, thought 'divide and rule' of the British was based on region, caste or creed. The real forces that kept colonial thinking alive was the 'divide and rule' between the elite who were coopted by colonial forces and the rest.

Tagore spoke of decolonization in visceral terms: 'We have for over a century been dragged by the prosperous West behind its chariot, choked by the dust, deafened by the noise, humbled by our own helplessness and overwhelmed by speed.'[29] Much like Mangal did growing up in Ballia and Mohandas did in his train travels, I see the spirit of the Middle rising. This spirit is breaking the mental chains that have held us prisoners to colonial institutions or the rationale propagated by the industrial West. Only by invoking that spirit will we honour those revolutionaries from the Middle who truly gave us our independence.

6

Democracy: *Two Nations at Seventy-Five*

पन्द्रह अगस्त का दिन कहता- आज़ादी अभी अधूरी है
सपने सच होने बाक़ी हैं, राखी की शपथ न पूरी है

—अटल बिहारी बाजपेयी

(The day of 15 August says, Independence is still incomplete
Dreams are yet to be realized; the vow of Raakhi is still to
be fulfilled.)

—Atal Bihari Vajpayee

At birth, every nation is a vulnerable child. It goes through adolescence with its petulant phases, ultimately morphing into a mature individual with its own identity and self-image. New voices emerge when the generation that gives it birth retires or passes away. This happened in that other large democracy, the US, too. By the early 1860s, the founding generation that had given it birth had passed away. Off balance, it went through a crisis when an attempt was made to abolish slavery, culminating in a civil war and paving the way for the US we know now.

Events leading to the US's independence and the first seventy-five years after its independence can provide insights for India. In this comparison, there are some obvious differences as well as some commonalities. However, they have *two* themes in common: the *postponement* of a key issue at the time of independence and the *rise of a new generation seventy-five years* after independence to address that issue. This was made possible in the US where Lincoln arose around its seventy-fifth anniversary, shifting the power structure in the process.

The rebirth of the US at that time was instigated when slavery was rejected by a new generation. In 1781, when the US wrested freedom from the British after a protracted revolutionary war and its constitution was written, slavery remained, with some founders themselves as slave owners.[1] The US tolerated slavery as long as Washington, Jefferson and others, who were slaveholders, ran the country, until a generation later, when the likes of Jackson and Lincoln came of age.

When India became a democracy, its circumstances were different from those of the US—it was an ancient civilization, heavily populated and culturally strong. But it had sustained wounds from 200 years of imperialism, which had drained it economically and intellectually. Independence came, but the nation that was birthed on 15 August 1947 remained under an elite DNA, resembling the British. A true rupture that could have created a different governance model was smothered in an effort to keep the country stable politically. Come seventy-five years of independence, and as that first generation retires, a new churn is taking place, led by voices from the Middle. India at seventy-five is re-birthing as the Middle gets its voice, discovering its own genius, giving space to citizens as actors beyond voting, finding its voice and a place in the world as it gains confidence as a free republic.

Many democracies can give comparative lessons from history, but most are just too small or too young. The US, which has a democratic history of 230 years, is likely the best comparison for India, although its population currently is the same as when India gained independence. The first seventy-five years of US history, between the Battle of Yorktown in 1781 when the US gained independence and the rise of Lincoln about seventy-five years later, holds numerous lessons and points of departure for new democracies. History may shrink with time as technology accelerates change, but democracies are measured in human lives, for citizens ultimately decide its course. The core beliefs of humans, formed at an early age, are held over a lifetime and are difficult to change. With the ballot box deciding the ruler, when the number of citizens is large, the 'wisdom of crowds'[2] kicks in and creates a rise and fall of nations that is similar. A time-delayed comparison, even if the points of birth are 175 years apart, will give us key insights. The age of seventy-five, considered a good measure of human life, is a good timespan for a comparative study of the US and India as two large democracies.

My discovery of the US

When I joined Schlumberger, an oilfield services company, after college, I was motivated by my early vows of *ghumakkadi*—wanderlust. In these wanderings, I saw and experienced the influence of the US and its culture, led by Hollywood and global corporations. I initially experienced this culture in Singapore where I was sent for training. In my batch of trainees were three Americans, a Mexican, a Japanese, an Indonesian and myself, the sole Indian. Aspirations were shaped by happenings 'Stateside', a euphemism for trends in the US that our American co-trainees used frequently. Weekend outings were to McDonald's, Burger King and other US fast food franchises, which had all opened branches recently.

My first posting was to North Yemen, with Tomohisa Nawate, the Japanese trainee, as my partner. Sanaa, the country's volatile capital, was our base location. Life was spent on a land rig in the Rub Al Khali or 'the empty quarter', shuttling to Sanaa in Toyota Land Cruisers, often negotiating with Kalashnikov-toting teenagers with the traditional dagger or *jambia* on their belts and a mouth stuffed full of *quat*. Our client was the Hunt Oil Company and its culture was brashly American.

After spending a year in the searing deserts of Yemen, I was posted to the freezing climes of Scotland in Aberdeen on the SEDCO 704 drilling rig situated in the North Sea. My life revolved around two-week shifts on the offshore drilling rig in different departments, with two weeks onshore as a rig engineer in the office in Aberdeen. Every moment of offshore living was full of adventure, living as we were on the edge of the world on an offshore rig also built in the US.

It was during this time, aged twenty-four, that I decided to explore the US on a Greyhound 'bus tour'. Starting from New York, I travelled to Boston, where I spent time with a friend who was working with me in Aberdeen as a rig engineer. I had a picnic dinner with his family on the banks of the Charles river and watched the Boston Pops serenade a 4 July fireworks display, celebrating US independence in the state that had initiated the independence movement. Back in New York City, I met Ram Challa, my friend from IIT–Delhi, who took me around Greenwich Village.

As I browsed through US history books in a bookstore, eager to understand how this nation had been shaped, a small but telling altercation took place with the shopkeeper. He asked me if I was looking for a true history of the country. He then proceeded to tell me to 'stop looking at those books', pointing to a second set of shelves which, he said, 'talk of the settling of the continent, and the original inhabitants as well'.

Steeped in the lore of this successful democracy and having just returned from a 4 July celebration, I was irritated and asked the shopkeeper to mind his own business. But the shopkeeper, to his credit, kept insisting that I explore this alternate narrative. On the verge of a confrontation, Ram pulled me out of the bookshop. I was puzzled by this behaviour but later understood that the shopkeeper was hinting at the history of his land before Europeans had colonized it. It was a time when its indigenous people roamed freely, buffaloes grazed the land and there was plenty of deer and elk in the forests.

From New York City, I hopped on a Greyhound bus that took me to Philadelphia, the birthplace of US democracy. On the journey, I encountered the thrill of travelling across a vast new land but was also made aware that such a journey was for the predominantly black, underdeveloped segment of the United States—their 'Middle America'. I was charmed by the black bus driver's drawl but on getting off in Philadelphia, I saw a divide that was reminiscent of my own experience in Ahmednagar: black communities, with young adults roaming the streets, separated from white neighbourhoods 'safely' tucked away in hedge-lined suburbs. As I tried to find my way to a youth hostel in Fairmount Park that evening, I heard catcalls, which prompted me to abandon that idea and I retreated to a safe hotel room across town. The next day, my visit to the Liberty Bell, the location where the US Constitution was written, turned out to be a mild disappointment. Coming from a country where monuments go back millennia, a history stretching back 200 years seemed unsatisfying.

Visible freedoms

A few days later, in Washington DC, my encounters were more illuminating. Given my army upbringing, a visit to the Pentagon was a must. A bunch of us, predominantly international visitors, were part of a group tour that had a young black US army lieutenant with a rakish cap as our tour guide. I was expecting to be frisked as I entered the building, having seen the many checks on a similar visit to the army HQ in Delhi. So I was pleasantly surprised when the lieutenant announced, 'Ladies and gentlemen, you can take photographs anywhere except inside the offices of the generals and the admirals, as they get disturbed.'

A few hours later, walking into the Senate, a similar lesson awaited me. When I inquired which senator to contact to arrange a pass, the receptionist calmly said, 'Please deposit your bag in that closet and walk through the door to the gallery of the house.' These were deliberate acts of 'democratic experience' through which the US was voicing that they were an open democracy where the common man or woman was given access to the corridors of power. From Washington DC, I made my way to New Orleans. I then took a flight to Oregon, where I did a week-long rafting course on the Deschutes river. This expedition brought me back to the hidden forks of US history the bookshop owner in Greenwich Village wanted me to discover. The expedition, consisting of two rafts with sixteen young Americans, worked its way down the river, navigating rapids, with nights spent under the stars. One fellow rafter was Jennifer Oppenheimer, a descendant of Robert Oppenheimer, the father of the atomic bomb and a Sanskrit scholar. During the expedition, we had permission to bank only on the right of the river as the left bank was a Native American reservation (they were previously referred to as American Indians). When we sighted these 'Indians', it was not wild tribesmen wearing feathered headbands and riding ponies but young adults in denim driving pick up-trucks. These Native Americans had been re-settled in this reservation, having been uprooted from their original location further south as the US expanded westwards. As the 'real Indian', I could not help but feel a tinge of empathy for their displacement.

Historical and philosophical resonance

Starting with the search for India or 'the Indies', there is a curious 'life length' resonance in the histories of the two nations. Columbus, leading the Spanish effort, established landfall in what is now the Bahamas in 1492, claiming discovery of the Americas while searching for India. Vasco Da Gama, a Portuguese, took the correct turn and landed on Indian soil in 1498. The *Mayflower*, a ship with 108 of the first settlers in North America, landed in America in 1620, while the British East India Company established its first factory in Surat in 1613, close to the birthplace of Mahatma Gandhi in Porbandar. The Battle of Plassey, under an ambitious British clerk, Robert Clive, established the rule of the East India Company in 1757 and at about the same time in 1754, the Seven Years' War took place in North America, establishing British influence over Florida. When India's first war of Independence took shape in 1857 with the uprising in Barrackpore, the US was readying for a civil war. Finally, in 1947, when India gained Independence, the US, after the Second World War, was creating institutions at the Bretton Woods Conference, which shaped the post-war world.

Important personalities who shaped the thinking of the two democracies were attracted philosophically to common themes and ideas, creating a relay race of thought exchange. In 1850, Thoreau, the American philosopher, was deeply influenced by the Gita and the Upanishads. As one work on him states, 'The origins of Thoreau's cosmology were to the East where the boundaries between people and gods, and God and nature, were more porous.'[3] Thoreau went on to coin the word 'civil disobedience'. Vivekananda made the US his wandering ground after his speech in Chicago at the World Congress of Religions in 1893. He talked of a material West needing the balance, wisdom and spirituality of the East. Gandhi was influenced by Thoreau when he was mulling the use of civil disobedience in fashioning satyagraha. Ambedkar completed his thesis in Columbia University in 1915, a few blocks away from the black heartland of Harlem. Martin Luther King in turn was influenced by Gandhi when he decided to adopt non-violence in his struggle against an obstinate administration. Finally, the Dalit movement in India borrows from the Black Rights movement.

In part inspired by this exchange, Patrick Dowd, a Fulbright scholar from the US, attended the Jagriti Yatra in 2009. On his return, he started a similar train journey in the US called the Millennial Train Project (MTP), the first of which travelled from San Francisco to Washington DC. He understood that the concentration of capital and the business ecosystem on the east and west coasts in recent years has created doubt whether the US has a 'wide and deep' enterprise-led society, since almost 80 per cent of the start-ups are concentrated in California, New York and Boston.[4] The MTP attempted to convey the message that enterprise must be a widespread engine for inclusive growth. This American version of the Yatra is a continuation of the intellectual and people-to-people collaboration between these two large democracies.

In recent months, that connection acquired a deeper dimension. As destiny would have it, Patrick married Camilla Rockefeller, a wedding I recently attended at the Rockefeller estate in upstate New York. Camilla is a descendant of John D. Rockefeller, the billionaire oil magnate at the turn of the twentieth century, who met Swami Vivekananda and was influenced by him to focus on philanthropy, which, in part, led to the creation of the Rockefeller Foundation a decade after that meeting.

The first seventy-five years

The starting pistol for a historical comparison of the US and India is 1781 when, at the Battle of Yorktown, the

British were defeated by George Washington's Continental army and his French friends. If you add seventy-five years to that date, you arrive at around 1856, when Abraham Lincoln was bending the arch of American history, starting his political efforts to unite the country with slavery as a key issue. Seventy-five years after our independence in 1947, the year 2022 could mark a similar turning point for the Indian nation. A deep dive into the early history of the US, even after accounting for the differences in culture, economic strength and relative population size, can provide insights that could be valuable for how India could negotiate its way forward—some lessons to learn and some mistakes to avoid.

Society in the US in its early years was based on the idea of a fresh start. Immigrants shed their intellectual baggage when they left Europe. As they entered the isle of New York, the main entrepôt to the US, they were intoxicated by the possibilities of this vast tract of real estate and its fierce work ethic. They settled and tried to create living conditions that were like the Europe they had left recently. Each of the thirteen colonies at the time of the Declaration of Independence in 1776 had some form of legislature, even if only landowners could vote. The zeitgeist of the new arrivals was an aversion to the 'class-based' mores of their motherland and a more horizontal, practical approach to opening up the continent. This required agility and enterprise from the beginning. The north, the areas near Boston and New York, became the urban, business-oriented edge of the country, while the south had large estates in the countryside which copied the English manor lifestyle of rural England. The state of Virginia, named after Queen Elizabeth I, the 'Virgin Queen', became the epicentre of this rural lifestyle.

There was a surprisingly strong network of communication with many pamphlets and almanacs in circulation. Many of these pamphlets gave advice on living a simple life. Tom Paine's 'Common Sense' was an example of this pamphlet revolution and was read in small towns across the colonies. Much like Tilak's call for *Purna Swaraj*, it announced for the first time that both the British king and the British parliament were corrupt and anti-American. Before this, like Indian independence movement leaders, those fighting for American independence were still playing both sides. They were judging whether a compromise formula with limited autonomy, representation and taxation could be brokered with the Crown. 'Common Sense' and other pamphlets sharpened that debate and involved the citizens as active participants in independence.

George Washington and Thomas Jefferson, two prominent founding fathers, were still living semi-colonial lives in Virginia. Washington had won fame as a warrior fighting Native Americans alongside the British and lived on a giant farm at Mount Vernon. His prodigious energy, calm, regal demeanour and ability to fashion victory in any situation of war were legendary.[5] Jefferson, an enigmatic, supremely talented writer, had 11,000 acres of land and then married a lady who brought an additional 15,000 acres.[6] Both Washington and Jefferson lived much like their English forefathers, insisting on clothes being stitched in London and eating from cutlery and crockery imported from Europe.

The US was enjoying the bounties of unlimited land, 'settled' by displacing its indigenous people. The number of Native Americans came down from around 7 million in 1492 to 4 million by 1776 in North America[7], culled as much by guns as by disease brought in by settlers.[8] This fanned the flames of slavery, particularly in the tropical south, for in the absence of local labour, slaves were imported to settle the continent. Economic opportunity came naturally as a democratic polity combined with the energy of a pioneering people and exploited the bounties of nature. An abundance of timber, cattle, ore and other resources—for instance, whaling in Nantucket and oil at Spindletop—made this a material society, intellectually unconstrained by natural resources.

The US's Jallianwala Bagh

The fires of independence were stoked in Boston, whose revolutionary fervour came to the fore in 1773 in an incident known as the 'Boston Tea Party'. A ship sent by the East India Company had its tea upended into the Boston harbour. A message was sent to the British that taxation and unilateral trade would not be tolerated. What turned the revolution violent was an incident in Lexington in 1775, when a group of Bostonians challenged British troops militarily. While many on the revolutionary side were killed, more casualties were registered on the British side. This emboldened the revolutionaries and when the Second Continental Congress, a gathering of representatives of the thirteen states, took place in Philadelphia in 1776, the Declaration of Independence was written and signed.

Many of the grudges listed resembled those in the Indian struggle for freedom—taxation without representation, arbitrary rulings against the colonies, tariffs that benefited Britain, an obstinate king who thought of these five-odd million people of the US as his direct subjects, even when local legislatures existed, and so on. These demands brought the colonies together under the Continental Congress, a cohesive national body, which prevented the British from enforcing their divide-and-rule policy they used so effectively in India, not to mention the advantage of a society without ancient rifts and almost all of its people hailing from the same stock.

The US benefited from the experience of incipient democracy in each of the thirteen states, each having recognized the benefit of working together. The US struggle for independence, like the Indian struggle, had different actors. The actors of Indian independence ranged from a militant Mangal Pandey and a peaceful Mahatma Gandhi to a revolutionary Sri Aurobindo and even to an out-and-out military man in Subhash Bose, who, between them, forced the British out. The US struggle, one can argue, was also a similar effort, obtained jointly by the pen of Jefferson, the convening abilities of Adams and the sword of Washington.

The first salvo was fired by the elegant pen of Jefferson, aided editorially by Benjamin Franklin, the polymath pamphleteer. The Declaration of Independence does not have an exact Indian equivalent, but the Purna Swaraj document of 1930 comes closest. The declaration, which has just 1337 words, started with words borrowed from Thomas Locke: 'We hold these truths to be self-evident, that all men are created equal, that they are endowed by their Creator with certain unalienable Rights, that among these are Life, Liberty and the pursuit of Happiness.' It goes on to say, 'To secure these rights, Governments are instituted among Men, deriving their just powers from the consent of the governed.'[9]

When the Declaration of Independence was written in 1776, the signatories understood that an army had to be raised, and Washington was made in-charge. At that point, the Continental Congress had little by way of collective strength except the desire to get rid of the British, who had not kept their word. This was like India in the 1920s, when promises of self-determination were broken by the British after the First World War and Gandhi initiated the Non-Cooperation Movement as a mass movement. Republican steam was built in the US through the power of pamphlets. The soaring words in the Declaration of Independence were soon read across the continent. This served as the intellectual equivalent of the Non-Cooperation Movement in India, bringing the masses into the struggle for independence. The republic got behind this band of brothers with the Continental Congress as a convening body, each state sending militia to be part of Washington's army. Eight and a half years of revolutionary war led by George Washington culminated in the Battle of Yorktown as a decisive victory that gave the US its independence. In this duration, Washington fought eleven battles and won only three. Ultimately, what sapped British will was, like in India, the cost of keeping the empire going was just too high.

Two fathers

Freedom won, Washington retired to Mount Vernon, acknowledged as the person who single-handedly delivered the US a military victory and its freedom. He was promptly summoned back to chair the constitution-making body, which produced a simple yet effective document balancing the executive, legislative and judicial powers of the government. The executive got a stronger role, given that most thought Washington would be the first President, which is ultimately what happened. The first government was sworn in with great care to ensure that no semblance of imperial pomp crept into the ceremony. Washington, the father of the nation, chaired the constitution-making body and when elected its President, ran the country for two terms thereafter.

The situation running up to the independence of India was like that in the US, but the path to gaining independence was very different. Washington adopted war as his strategy, while Gandhi chose the path of satyagraha. Washington's military victory was fashioned by mobilizing the republican energies of the American nation to sanctify and participate in revolutionary war. The war was a battle of wills and staying power between ideologies and a way of life that were similar, including weapons, systems and a common underlying Anglo-Saxon culture. Indian independence was driven by a more fundamental clash—one of two different cultures and methods. Gandhi and other freedom fighters, such as Bose and Savarkar, used iconography and culture to inspire our nascent republic, which brought people from ordinary backgrounds into the struggle for independence. Our founders, all avid students of history, understood that a 'Washington approach' may not be as effective. They also believed that a mere copycat republic was not the ideal of independence.

Both fathers—Gandhi and Washington—had great clarity of purpose, yet suffered moments of doubt. Both were hard-working, fastidious writers. Both were struggling with the ills of society—Washington willing that his slaves be liberated after his demise and Gandhi devoting considerable time to the emancipation of Dalits. They were opposite in demeanour—the 6-foot-2-inch Washington with a heavy martial gait as opposed to Gandhi in a loincloth and a toothy smile. The inner aura and strength, though, were similar, but they took different energies from their respective nations—material for the US and humanist for India.

Deferred responsibility

But both republics had one thing in common – postponing a key issue that was difficult to address at the time of independence. In the case of the US, it was the 'dark hole' in the heart of the republic, the blot of slavery. In the case of India, it was the lack of a meaningful role for the citizen as power was handed back to the structures of colonialism. Post-Independence, a meaningful role for citizens was forgotten or, in any case, postponed. For the US, their moment of redemption came seventy-five years later, when Abraham Lincoln, emerging from the mid-west, a 'Middle America' of sorts, held the union together while abolishing slavery and created a second independence.

The seventy-fifth year of India's independence is heralding a similar era for India.

It is difficult to predict how this moment will unfold for India. Seventy-five years after independence, the US underwent a bloody civil war to resolve slavery. Some suggest a north versus south divide that could spark similar civil strife in India. That is too linear a projection of history. The rationale for independence and the colonizer—imperial Britain—may have been the same, but the methods of independence and the cultural wellsprings that drove them are diametrically different. India's method of redemption will also be different, based on India's civilizational strengths. Tracing the post-independence sequence of events in the US should give us some clues on how India may want to progress.

Post-independence, Alexander Hamilton was its chief 'centralizer'. James Madison gave the constitutional document its substance. The constitution of the US had started to be developed as a living document during the revolutionary war, starting with the declaration of independence. In matters of arms, creating a continental postal system, raising taxes, coercing citizens to join the army, eight and a half years of revolutionary war were a dress rehearsal. The constitution was therefore partially tested and created by the very people who were now looking at making it whole. But on the topic of slavery, it remained flawed. The constitution avoided the word slave or slavery and introduced an administrative compromise proposed by Madison. Blacks were counted as 'three-fifth' of freemen in the states they were present, without voting rights. This was pointed out as a contravention of their own founding principle—'all men are created equal'. Similarly, white women were denied voting rights till 1920, another glaring compromise. The constitution was also silent on Native Americans, only mentioning them in the context of regulating commerce 'with foreign nations, and among the several states, and with the Indian tribes'.[10]

Despite these shortcomings, the adoption of the US constitution by all the thirteen states, with a blueprint for other states to join as they were created, was a major achievement. George Washington's convening presence in this setting was crucial. But the American constitution preserved slavery and allowed many founding fathers to continue as slave owners in their thousand-acre plantations. Lip service was paid to greater ideals when Washington willed that after his and his wife's death, slaves on his plantation be freed. Jefferson expressed his opinion intimately, allegedly by having an affair and children from a slave woman. Others in the north kept quiet, knowing a time would come to press the case.

The missing citizen

At an equivalent time in India's life, the Constitution was being framed by our Constituent Assembly, but the father of our nation was absent. The republican ideas of the Dandi March, satyagraha, *sarvodaya* and other elements of our freedom movement were understated. Instead of following our own genius, relying on the spiritual and humanist origins of our nation, our framers scoured the world for ideas. A Westminster form of parliamentary democracy was barely tweaked as it got adopted. The India Act of 1860 and several laws that originated during British colonial rule were kept intact, and ideas that relied on the Westphalian system of the nation state also became our national framing.

To be fair, the assembly was working in the backdrop of extreme anxiety. The fires of Partition had consumed half a million lives and displaced upwards of 15 million people.[11] Nehru, for instance, talked of 'not injuring the structure' on 3 April 1948 in the Constituent Assembly, stating, 'One has to be careful as not to injure the existing structure too much . . . there has been destruction and injury enough . . . I am not brave or gallant enough to go about destroying it more.'[12] The resulting constitutional document, with its ideas from the Australian, US, German and French constitutions and of course, British Common Laws, had the underlying tenor of a colonial state still intact. The document was 1,11,000 words long, the lengthiest constitution in the world and one rarely read by Indians beyond the first few pages.

With Gandhi absent from the Constituent Assembly, Nehru enamoured by Fabian socialism, and Sardar Patel as home minister anxious to get the princely states integrated, we committed our own 'original compromise'. The citizen went missing from the document and heavy official language took over, making it a document of rules and regulations rather than a principle of governance. The republic was reconstituted without rupture from its colonial past. The sacrifice, mobilization and induction of the common man in giving us freedom was ignored, and their role was confined to voting. The 'Directive Principles of State Policy' as strictures, instead of making the Constitution timeless, used socialist language that would soon become obsolete. The old order led by the state took charge and started running this vast country much the same as before 15 August 1947. Like the US founders, one could argue, it was 'just too difficult' to loosen up when a new country was enduring the trauma of Partition and had to be consolidated. But then we must also recognize that instead of a proud republic, we started as a democratic copy of a colonial regime.

Many key issues were dealt with successfully by our Constitution—the creation of universal franchise for millions, including voting for women, the upliftment of backward communities by including reservation for Scheduled Castes and Scheduled Tribes, creating a developmental framework with the Planning Commission, howsoever flawed, and so on. The consolidation of princely states and the creation of an election machinery that provided smooth oversight to the largest franchise in human history were singular achievements. But the core was without rupture; it did not incorporate values of people's involvement, societal values, the local energies that had been released by the struggle for independence and existed in small towns and districts and had been used by Gandhi, Patel and earlier by Vivekananda, Aurobindo and others to gain independence.

Owing to the anxiety of Partition, the leeway that the Continental Congress gave to Washington, Jefferson, Adams, Hamilton and Madison to devise levers of power in a deliberate manner was not available to our founders. Nehru, Ambedkar, Patel, Azad, Naidu and others were focused on the more immediate task of organizing the state to stay afloat. As a result, barely any institution was touched. The I in Imperial was changed to Indian. For example, the ICS (Imperial Civil Service) became the Indian Administrative Services (IAS). At the provincial level, United Province was glibly changed to Uttar Pradesh. The colonial script used since the First War of Independence, which was used to co-opt the elite, continued. India meekly agreed to be part of the Commonwealth, a symbolic bow to the very queen who had made India destitute over two centuries of her rule.

Nehru could have driven a more original inception of the state as Gandhi's chosen protégé, but instead, in a bizarre move a mere sixteen months after the Constitution was adopted, he forced a change to key clauses that weakened the right to free expression.[13] He chose the benefits of a smooth handover and consolidation of state power rather than a longer-term, more comprehensive rupture involving citizens. Patel as the new home minister consolidated the nation, in which the colonial institutions of control came in handy, but his passing away in December 1950 gave Nehru all but unlimited power. To be fair to the founders, the Constitution was a herculean achievement, but it was framed at a difficult time by the elite and remains incomplete. Much like the US, our founding fathers may have realized that another generation would rise, giving visibility, power and creative responsibility to the citizen.

Hindsight is 20:20. Today, instead of critiquing the past, we must take on that unfinished task. The generations following those who gave independence to the US tackled the unfinished task of the abolition of slavery. We must similarly rise to bring the citizen centre-stage. Ideas born in one lifetime require another generation to rise to create that rupture. This happened to the US, starting with Andrew Jackson and concluding with Abraham Lincoln.

The US was remarkably lucky that three architects of the American revolution ran their country post-independence and their perspectives complemented each other. They consolidated the nation, brought together different states and created political and economic unity. George Washington retired gracefully to Mount Vernon after his second term. John Adams gave his best in the one term he served after Washington. He was ousted by Jefferson, who brought in several reforms. The Lewis and Clark expedition and the Louisiana Purchase enlarged and consolidated the nation's boundaries. Alexander Hamilton's role in outlining the federal nature of the United States was remarkable and James Madison laid the financial foundations of the US economy. But all of them were mini aristocrats, part of an increasingly closed elite. Later, in 1825, the presidency of John Quincy Adams, the son of John Adams, signalled that attitude of the elite who wanted to keep power within their lineage.

A change of guard

The presidency of Andrew Jackson (1829–37) began the transition in the US. Jackson came to the national stage in opposition to attempts by the elite to keep power to themselves. A visceral politician, he had proved himself through military campaigns in Mexico as a consummate frontier man. Jackson won the elections in 1824 but through an act of collusion between Quincy Adams and Henry Clay, the speaker of the House of Congress, was denied the presidency.[14] Four years later, he won a clear mandate, bringing to Washington DC the spirit of the frontier and the aspirations of the underprivileged millions. His core election strategy was 'throwing out the privileged'. He was a natural leader, a charming, cussing president that the country swooned over. Jackson set the stage for democratizing the US where, after the initial euphoria of independence, political life had become corrupt and dominated by the elite. He positioned himself as someone claiming the republic back for its people. The Jacksonian presidency ensured that the voice of the people came back with raucous efficiency, with the common men and women invited to the White House for the first time. The old order felt uncomfortable with this display of plebeian political might.[15] This reflects our own post-Independence leaders, raised in western style, bristling about the rise of a Mulayam, a Mayawati, a Mamata or in recent times, Prime Minister Modi.

The question of abolishing slavery hung in the air but was given fodder around the 1820s when a religious ardour rose in the US, absent at independence.[16] In Europe, slavery had been abolished and moral pressure was rising from across the Atlantic. However, there was commercial pressure within the country from the south to continue slavery. With the mechanization of cotton ginning, cotton exports had increased exponentially and this was the bedrock of the southern economy, with slaves forming the spine of cotton farming. While bringing slaves into the US had been banned by 1808, the existing slaves and their offspring continued to remain in bondage within the republic, their trade even picking up pace, with many in the south equating slaveholding with social prestige.[17] But there were voices wanting a comprehensive solution to this 'dark hole' in the heart of the US.

The clearest of those voices was from Abraham Lincoln. He entered political life with a passionate interest in solving the issue of slavery. Lincoln came from what was 'Middle America', having educated himself on his own. Lincoln framed the issue of slavery not so much as a north versus south divide but as an issue that was at the heart of a united country. For the 'union' to survive, slavery had to be seen by those in the south as inimical to the progress of the entire nation. A second birth of the 'United States' happened with this insight.

The details of how he won the civil war, and ultimately lost his own life, are beyond the purview of this book.

But his story is a lesson in the historical predicament and parallels of democracy, and one from which India can learn as it crosses its seventy-fifth anniversary. In the US, the north was economically stronger while the south had more political heft, an inverse of the situation that India finds itself in. The sheer determination of Lincoln to hold the line on slavery not only emancipated 4 million blacks, it also paved the way for an equal society in other spheres of life. It took seventy-five years for the power structure in the US to shift as new ideas emerged in society with the rise of a new generation that had been born and raised in an independent USA. In between, Andrew Jackson had swung the pendulum to the other side and wrested power forcefully from the elite who had started passing the presidency among themselves, eventually paving the way for Lincoln.

India's opportunity at seventy-five and beyond

In India, the privileged few who took charge post-Independence were hailed as revolutionaries. But behind the elegant prose of *Discovery of India* lay the thought process of the departed British. This is not just a Nehruvian issue; most in the ruling elite suffered from it. A clean rupture, possibly due to the bloodshed around Partition, partially because of Gandhi's absence and Patel's early demise, did not take place. Colonial institutions were rejuvenated in the body politic. The nation continued to highlight the elite while paying lip service to the other India. In recent years, the Middle has become prominent, yet we continue to patronize and give palliatives to citizens, which does not recognize their innate strength beyond voting. The colonial institutions of the Raj continue to dominate life in the Middle, for the district apparatus remains unchanged. This is truer in the poor north and east that had rebelled in and after 1857 and where the colonial apparatus created stringent systems of control for ninety years thereafter.

Democracies have a habit of first consolidating and then expanding, and this process accelerates at around seventy-five. The writer and thinker George Friedman, who has investigated these institutional cycles, says that at around seventy-eight years, 'The broad framework of the Constitution stays in place, but the federal and state institutions change their relationships with each other and change the way they work.'[18] In the case of the US, this institutional shift was catalysed by a war on slavery.

India won its freedom not by the bayonet but by satyagraha. If satyagraha was a tool, then a more positive tool, one that will empower citizen leaders in the Middle, is needed now. Lincoln made the case for abolishing slavery through his 'house divided' metaphor, asserting that a house divided on the question of slavery would ultimately fall. We too are suffering from a 'house divided' syndrome, where the Top of the Diamond still has access to the lion's share of privileges in our democracy. A revolution that seeks to engage the citizen from the Middle does not require us to get rid of the elite in some revolutionary putsch. Instead, the Top and the Middle can collaborate using their respective strengths to take the country forward as an integrated whole.

I see this happening on the Jagriti Yatra, where young people from larger cities, once they understand the importance of the Middle, collaborate wholeheartedly. The north and the south must work together against a future I see described in articles foretelling an imminent clash. We must push our developmental philosophy internationally by outlining the 'Middle-up' approach to other developing nations who have gone through colonial trauma like India and are being wooed by an authoritarian China. Our rich culture will make this case across Asia stronger as made by a democratic, multifaceted country, and a culture powered by its people. That is only possible if the full talents of our republic come into play, not just those of the creamy layer.

Recognizing this approach, this unity over surface differences is the starting point of creating institutions for the Middle and a nation-building process Middle-up, rather than Top-down. These institutions and this movement will take shape in a decentralized manner, close to those leaders who will give it mass and momentum. Instead of designing institutions from up top, we must inspire leaders to understand this responsibility locally. I believe 7500 Yatris, expanding each year by 500 young leaders, can play a key role in this process. This India, and this group, can potentially throw up our own mini-Jacksons and mini-Lincolns who will develop their own area in the Middle, utilizing its strengths and getting support from a network of similarly motivated citizens. We are at the cusp of creating our second republic, which will pay true homage to our founding fathers and complete the task they began.

7

Culture: *Inner Resource of National Strength*

कस्तूरी कुंडल बसे, मृग ढूँढत बन माहि।
ज्यो घट घट राम है, दुनिया देखे नाही।

—कबीर

(The musk deer roams the forest in search of an aroma that
resides in its navel
In the same manner as Lord Ram is everywhere, without the
world seeing him)

—Kabir

The world can be broadly divided into six civilizations—
Christian, Islamic, Chinese, Latin American, African
and our own, Indic—making up much of the global
population. Each civilization boasts its own culture, an
abstract yet important aspect for national growth and
renewal. Culture is 'a reservoir of behaviours, thoughts,
feelings, values and mindsets that people share . . . like

tacit knowledge, a culture can't be managed by controlling; but its impact is concrete.'[1] National culture changes gradually, but it is critical for the nation-building project. Clarifying cultural contours is best done by contrasting it with another culture, recognizing that each is unique to its own heritage, geography and context. Such a comparison can generate clarity, pride and even humility, as one learns from another culture.

The Chinese culture offers a worthy comparison for a cross-cultural examination of Indian culture. The Chinese civilization is of equal vintage to India's and has developed on the same continent, with the Tibetan plateau and the Himalayas a formidable yet porous border between the two[2]. In recent times, the rising and expanding Chinese nation is both an example of and a contrast in how culture impacts the growth and development of nations. Recent accounts call it a 'Hare and Tortoise race',[3] with widespread acknowledgement that China has outpaced India on all measures of material growth. But in that story also rests hope that, with a cultural boost from the Middle, India can still compete and finish ahead in the long-term.

I got an up-close exposure to Chinese culture when my family and I stayed close to the Forbidden City in China for the Beijing Olympics in 2008. We have encouraged our girls to follow their passion for sports and, when possible, try to take them to watch the Olympics. For the Beijing Olympics, my parents also came along, and the event did not disappoint us. The Bird's Nest stadium was enormous, with our lucky draw getting tickets to the stadium on both days when Usain Bolt broke the 100 and 200-metre Olympic records. But in the ceremonies and our stay, we also observed the many differences in Chinese culture relative to India. The mass parade and drills in the opening ceremony, with civil society drummers acting as if they were trained by the military, was one indicator. A communist regime seemed to have depleted Chinese architecture from ancient Beijing, the imperial seat of Chinese dynasties, apart from the circle around the Forbidden City, where we were staying.

But it was in the common person's behaviour that we got a true glimpse of Chinese culture. One night, returning from the Bird's Nest stadium, the public bus broke down. A bus full of passengers sat in complete silence for over half an hour. It was only when my father and I got down to investigate and help the lonely driver who was trying to fix the bus that others stepped forward. It was as if people were waiting for someone from the government to appear and fix things for them. I knew that Chinese society was state-led, but this experience gave me a personal glimpse of what that meant in cultural terms. In India, an incident like this would have resulted in half the passengers pushing the bus and the other half trying to help the driver repair the fault, even if he did not need that help! Self-organizing citizen participation is guaranteed in India in any such situation.

Other experiences of Chinese culture in recent years point to this state-led, top-down approach. Recently, a Chinese business executive in Europe proudly recounted how the Chinese police had found her wallet within an hour of it being lost, when dense police surveillance cameras filmed citizens and helped identify the wallet in a taxi, where she had dropped it. The lady saw no threat to citizens' privacy in this Orwellian incident. The treatment of Tibetans and Uighurs in China recently indicates a similar effort at control and uniformity by the Chinese state. The hidden code of not mentioning the 3Ts—Tiananmen, Tibet and Taiwan—informs public life in China.[4] Of late, one can observe the projection of a top-down approach from China overseas, with the Belt and Road Initiative (BRI) in which large infrastructure contracts have been signed with states that have dictatorial governments. A signal of this was the day Xi Jinping, the Chinese President, amended the Communist Party constitution in 2018; in 2022, his appointment was confirmed as President for a third term with the worrying title of 'the Helmsman', last used for Mao.[5]

Direct government action with a top-down culture has many advantages. It can make decisive shifts in the economic status of its citizens. It can push through large infrastructure projects without opposition; for instance, even the Bird's Nest stadium, where Bolt won his medals, was a result of displacing over 74,000 people.[6] Not to be outdone by nature, Beijing attempted to seed clouds to avoid rain at the opening ceremony of the Olympics. China has created electronic walls that give its companies advantages by keeping data under state control and creating the 'Great Firewall of China'. A strong state makes sure citizens and nature behave, marching along a path laid out by the Politburo, the local party chief or sometimes by the People's Liberation Army (PLA). Many in India look over the Himalayas wistfully, believing they too should engineer a state-led march like China.

A culture in contrast

Before India thinks of copying the Chinese state-led model, let us examine the history of both countries to clarify their contrasting cultures—one state-led, and the other citizen-oriented.

To pick up the story of this difference, one must go back to the Warring States period of Chinese history, coinciding with the Qin dynasty circa 200 BCE. This period created the backbone of political organization in China. The Qin dynasty combined the hard structures and the formulaic lines of the legalist system which had preceded it with the moral principles of the Confucian system, which was reinstated as a guiding philosophy in government. Chinese emperors held a 'mandate from heaven' that gave them power, and the state created state systems to enforce that power. A common script and a strong bureaucracy led by Mandarins, the root of which name is the Indian word *mantri*, formed key components of state power and allowed China to rule from Beijing. The Chinese state delivered large state-funded projects, bending nature to its will. The Great Wall of China stands out as one of the largest inter-generational infrastructure endeavours; less well known are China's feats in hydraulic engineering and joining rivers, shaping nature for its own purpose. This reflects the Confucian mindset of nature as a resource to be exploited, ignoring its own Taoist traditions that 'emphasized the fundamental oneness of all phenomena'.[7]

This culture celebrates the primacy of the state, giving it an unusual degree of power to control both citizens and nature. Other cultures vest a higher authority in religion within a self-regulating moral order, before temporal law comes calling. China has a diffuse equivalent in the Confucian canon but nothing that explicitly restricts the power of the state. As Francis Fukuyama puts it, 'In the west, in India and in the Muslim world, there was a body of pre-existing law, sanctified by religion and safeguarded by priests and clerics, that was prior to, and independent of the State . . . This law was binding on the ruler . . . Rule of law in this sense never existed in China.'[8] The 'mandate from heaven', if broken by an unjust or ineffective monarch, allowed scope for rebellion and overthrow of the regime. This is not to be confused with a popular mandate from the people. It was a 'safety valve' that aggressive generals and family satraps used to take charge, cleanse and re-model imperial power using force and war.

In later years, as other warring factions managed to assert control, a rise and fall of dynasties continued, ending with the Qing dynasty at the beginning of the twentieth century. This is when the Kuomintang took over, initially supported by the communists, later followed by the breakaway communists achieving victory in 1949 inspired by Lenin and Stalin under the urgings of a global Comintern. The Long March undertaken by the communists, in which both Mao and Deng participated, drew its energies from rural China. But the net result was class war in the manner Marx had ordained and a state focused on material success. Over the centuries, indigenous rulers and foreign invaders, and in recent times communists, adopted a state-led political structure. War was a constant feature in Chinese historical and societal memory, much before the Long March, and before Mao's famous statement, 'Political power grows out of the barrel of a gun.' Culturally, the Chinese are comfortable with this top-down mandate.

Indian society took a different turn around 600 BCE. Till then, society was organized in pastoral tribes, from the time the Gangetic and Indus plains were settled with small kingdoms. The organization of society into *varnas* and *jatis* gave local organizations, built on caste lines, moral and economic clout that kept the power of the raja in check.[9] Religion and spirituality became an important bulwark against state power. The creation of metaphysical systems that 'explained all aspects of the phenomenal world in terms of an invisible transcendent one . . . shifted emphasis from one's own genetic ancestors and descendants to a cosmological system encompassing the whole of nature.'[10] This retained authority and power in society, serving to limit the power of the raja, while making it local. This development remained an oral tradition for a very long time till it was codified by the *Manav-Dharma shastra*. Power did not spring from political authority as it did in China but from 'a source independent of and superior to the political ruler . . . where the king exists to protect the system of *varnas*, and not the other way around.'[11] While the state in China wielded both political and moral power backed by a strong bureaucracy from early times, in India, local society had the upper hand moderated by *dharma* and the *shastras*.

Remarking on this local, horizontal association, the Buddha is purported to have said to his man Friday around the fifth century BCE, 'Have you heard, Ananda, that the Vajjians foregather often, and frequent public meetings of their clans . . . So long, Ananda, as the Vajjians foregather thus often, and frequent the public meetings of their clans, so long may they be expected not to decline, but to prosper.'[12]

The twenty-first century is being talked of as an Asian century.[13] The south-east Asian countries have borrowed from both Indian and Chinese cultures. India, China and south-east Asia together account for just under half the world's population, and therefore this culture will likely become the dominant planetary culture over time. Chinese culture is top-down and promotes long-term state-led authority, while Indian culture has republican characteristics, where society ultimately will have the final say. The question that must be asked is which culture— Chinese or Indian—will influence Asia most. This has become an urgent concern with the creation of China-led institutions a whole-of-society issue[14] as China projects its way of life and governance in Asia, Africa and Latin America, subverting state systems to promote the Belt and Road initiative. India has an opportunity to offer a cultural counterpoint that has a stamp of her own civilization, making it different both from China and the West. Crucially, its culture will help with its growth trajectory, not just in numbers and in GDP involving its citizens but also in the quality and direction of that growth. Powered by its cultural wellsprings, India can chart a more people-centric, inclusive and environmentally sound approach.

The idea that India has unifying cultural traits had many detractors. British leaders such as Sir Ian Strachey in the 1880s rubbished the concept of India and gave the British credit for creating the country, a well-known colonial ploy. But 2000 years before Strachey and others tried to diminish India as a conglomeration of warring states, Alexander the Great was given a very different perspective on his arrival at the north-west edge of India. After the battle with Porus in what is now Punjab, local informants, as reported by Greek historians such as Strabo, Arrian and Eratosthenes, described the land of India as a rhomboid: 'An unequal quadrilateral in shape, with the Indus on the west, the mountains on the north, the sea on its east and south.'

They also reported the dimensions of this rhomboid, giving for instance 19,000 stadia (2183 miles) along the western coast from the point of the cape to the mouth of the Indus.[15] Alexander Cunningham, who rose to be the director of the Archaeological Survey of India, confirmed that 'the close agreement of these dimensions, given by Alexander's informers with the actual size of the country is remarkable.' This rhomboid was united by culture, which was often carried across great distances by its pilgrims, including those who took Buddha's message to China.

Spirit and consciousness in the modern world

At the heart of Indian culture lies spirituality, a moral force, that elevates, unifies and instructs the human condition through *sanskriti*. If India has shown a unique richness of different religions, ethnicities, languages, food, lifestyles and ways of life within a single civilization, this cultural unity has been a key force.

In truth, as young Indians, we felt guilty that our culture has overdone the 'spirit' part. Indian culture had engendered multiple religions, philosophy, traditions, dance styles and singing *gharanas* but had left 'matter' to others. We felt this resulted in the West equipping itself with better arms and equipment that were used to colonize us. This governed how the world has been run, with industrial might and a mindset of conquest over nature, something readily copied by communist China. In recent years, the West and China have expressed a hesitation and regret at this mindless rush towards material growth, ignoring nature and the human spirit, causing irreparable damage to the planet and to society.

New thinking in psychology, philosophy and biology aided by modern physics is offering an alternate narrative to back this human-centric world view. This was articulated by Fritjof Capra, a modern scientist with a mind open to the philosophy of the East. His study of links between particle physics and eastern spiritual traditions started with a conversation with the Indian seer Jiddu Krishnamurthy in California.[16] When I read his first book, *The Tao of Physics*, in college, its call to challenge a Cartesian world view resonated with me. Through modern physics, he revealed another world that reconciled with Indian Vedanta and Buddhist thought. Quantum physics and the principle of uncertainty allowed a perspective beyond Newtonian give and take, action and reaction. It opened a window where the observed and the observer were not apart, as surface 'reality' indicated. Experiences which were 'directly felt' without breaking down issues into sub-components created a holistic alternative. This provides an argument for synthesis and intuition to counter Western industrial society, which atomized mind and matter. We can begin to understand that taming nature and the use of machines to change the world may be only one of many cultural narratives.

In recent years, Capra has highlighted the Santiago theory of cognition, which creates space for spirituality and consciousness in the modern world. This theory, based on human connections, can be seen every day in the culture of small towns and districts of India. The Santiago theory starts by critiquing the Cartesian world view, developed about 400 years ago, and links consciousness to 'self-generating and self-perpetuating living networks'.[17] It sees cognition not as an observation of matter and its control by the mind but as 'the process of life'. Reality manifests itself when an organism is self-renewing and creates new connections with other living beings. The theory suggests that humans are only one version of a living being and creates a link to the wider network of nature within which humans operate and are a part of. This belief in a wider connect with nature is something one observes constantly in the lives of those in the Middle, with animals and birds, crops and trees as part of daily life, making connections and networks that reflect the Santiago theory.

The theory also clarifies the concept of the spirit or 'soul', which finds mention across Indian philosophy as *atman*, and goes on to suggest that this atman connects the entire realm of living beings—plants, animals and humans—as a 'Supreme Universal Spirit'. Capra concludes in a paragraph reminiscent of the Bhagavad Gita, stating, 'When we look at the world around us, we find that we are not thrown into chaos and randomness but are part of a great symphony of life. Every molecule in our body was once a part of previous bodies . . . and will be a part of future bodies. In this sense, our body will not die but live on, again and again, because life lives on.'[18] Similar words reflecting African vitalist traditions are said by Mufasa to his son Simba when explaining the 'circle of life' in the movie *The Lion King*.

India's culture is taking on a new importance as this alternate view gains weight, no longer imbued by the thought process of the elite, who borrowed their cultural moorings from the industrial West. The frameworks used by those at the Top to examine our culture suffer intrinsically from the limitations of English language, which twist the outcome.[19] To understand our culture, we must explore the small towns and districts of India. Will Durant, the philosopher-historian, summarized this pithily: 'Culture suggests agriculture, but civilization suggests the city.'[20] The 'neglected culture' of communities in smaller towns and districts, if revived through an explicit cultural rediscovery, can recharge our nation. Within the nation, each region will have its own sub-culture. A Diamond view of India understands that each crystal of the diamond has its own unique glint.

A pride in our culture, the passing down of our civilization through culture, change driven by culture and the resulting 'cultural dividend' can be one of the most fulfilling chapters in the growth of India. The core of this uniqueness is a focus on the human spirit.

To examine the culture of smaller towns and districts, we must investigate four aspects of Indian life—art, the family system, the social system and value systems. In each, there is a rich tapestry to draw from in Middle India. In each district, each town or village, there are cultural traditions that can be celebrated and tied to a modern republican ethos, a compass to guide our actions. For the coming twenty-five years, understanding and synthesizing our culture from the Middle up will refresh it, giving the nation new meaning, confidence and unity.

The little traditions of the Middle

Some time ago, I took part in a Ram Lila event in Pandeypur village near Deoria. This village has a tradition of the villagers coming together to act in the Ram Lila. For more than a hundred years, they have preferred local, home-grown talent to professional actors. The performance, spread over several nights, began with a puja of Ram, Laxman and Sita dressed for their part, complete with bows and arrows, representing the 'real-time' presence of good within society. This was followed by a real-life drama triggered by the anchor, a well-to-do resident of the village, who was excluded when the puja was being performed. Taking the mic, he proceeded to publicly berate the organizing committee amid giggles and laughter from the crowd gathered for the evening. Once he calmed down, the Ram Lila proceeded and was enacted for a full fourteen days till on the last day, Ravan's navel was finally pierced by Ram's arrow, sealing the victory of good over evil. This was a part of the yearly fabric of life in that village, with similar renderings in different parts of the district.

This presence of Indian art in the daily life of many Indians points to a creative gene that surprises most visitors. Today, it seems to many that Indian art is confined to cities in theatre settings, exhibitions, dance recitals and music concerts—the 'great traditions'. But that is only half the story. Middle India, on the other hand, is a giant repository of 'little traditions', where art is a part of life. I see this contrast having experienced one form of the 'great tradition' at close quarters for over twenty-five years, being married to Gauri, who is a professional Kathak artist. The solo performance of Kathak sparks emotions that startle me even today. Such performances are meditative and the effort is to connect with a mystical and almost yogic concentration of audience and performers, with an aesthetic purity.

On the other hand, the 'little traditions' produce art with an emphasis on total sensory awareness and a high level of audience participation, often involving singing, dancing and drama all together. Cultural performances, such as the Ram Lila and Muharram processions as well as art forms such as *rangoli*, are part of such traditions. Audiences participate in them with gusto. During a visit to Ganjam, Joe Madiath, our role model, reminded us of this cultural unity. He says, in a tribal setting, 'If one person dances, everyone dances.'

Our nation-building project and developmental solutions must recognize the importance of these little traditions that connect with the masses. Only by incorporating the idea of 'art as a living process' in smaller towns and districts into our overall imagination will we make our culture whole. Jude Kelly, the artistic director of the South Bank Centre and a global arts leader, reminded me of this during the 2012 Yatra. In a village setting in Ganjam district, I provoked her by saying that Indians would get to art once they had satisfied their need for food, clothing and shelter. Jude protested instantly. She said, 'Art is a need that is synonymous with our humanity; you cannot ask the citizen to reach a certain economic threshold before asking her to be artistic.'

The family as a cultural unit

The family is another unit of investigation that has unique cultural attributes and its true manifestation is in Middle India, as outlined earlier. The joint family in a small-town or village setting brings together different cultural spheres, ranging from the societal and economic to the spiritual, and gives them a safe space within the family to flourish. Old-world rules for women within a joint family still need loosening, as does its tendency to suppress the individualism of many of its members, demanding that they toe the line. But it does give its members a sense of community and belonging. Our literature worships the mother but also characterizes the women as a distractor—'as a wife she seduces her husband away from his work and spiritual duties'.[21] The image of a confident, knowledgeable woman must return with force as a balance sheet builder and as the anchor and cultural glue of the family that she usually runs.

It is in our nature to pass on civilizational and cultural mores. The family is the most important entity for passing down cultural norms, often through myths and stories. My own childhood was replete with stories about my grandfather's elder brother, who was known as Babua. The stories of his courage were retold at family gatherings by my father and uncles to the extent that in tough sports matches at college, I invoked his spirit and strength. When living with my maternal grandparents, my grandmother was the chief source of cultural stories. She would tell us stories of the Ramayana and the Mahabharata. To me, these stories defined heroism and personal sacrifice. As a high school student in Lucknow, I saw my grandmother's cultural habits as outdated. I was growing up as a rational young citizen revelling in the possibilities of science, and her insistence on ritual seemed out of place. But now that I look back on her life, she was living our culture in these very rituals and perhaps I should have given her more credit for it.

In a Middle India village setting, the family is usually a joint family. Those who migrate to a smaller town close by, like Deoria, live together till the pull of a metro city makes their family a nuclear affair. The Indian joint family has been attacked as retrograde and inimical to industrial growth, but recent thinking by futurists considers 'non-nuclear' families viable[22] as the world decentralizes post-COVID-19 and the headlong rush to large cities is no longer a given. With improvements in connectivity, both physical and digital, a more spread out urban growth theory is emerging and justifies larger families living within local societal networks, as outlined earlier. With approximately 12 per cent of India living in the top 100 cities with a population greater than 5 lakh,[23] much of India must recognize and use the family for enterprise creation and economic growth process.

The caste system, its challenges and opportunities

International visitors or friends gingerly pick up the subject of caste in Indian society only after the initial banter. Indians answer equally gingerly, often opining that caste may still be practised in rural India, but in most urban settings it has been erased. Caste is a form of social stratification that is unique to the Indian Subcontinent and has proved highly resilient. Beginning initially as an occupational division of society, it ossified in India over time to the point that it became counterproductive, and in the case of Dalits, inhuman.

The Indian Constitution outlawed caste discrimination and mandated affirmative action for those from disadvantaged castes. But this form of social organization continues in a social sense. Some of its features—apprenticeship, a guild-like structure, farming and artisanal bonds—can be used in a modern context, for enterprise. At the same time, injustices to Dalits and other backward classes still need to be fully eliminated. I have seen this structural shift take place in

Purvanchal, with Gram Pradhans no longer coming from the upper castes. While inter-caste marriages are still rare in rural settings, increasingly, societal forces are rearranging caste equations and creating new ties and configurations. Some commentators ascribe the faster growth of enterprise in southern India over the past thirty years to the lowering of caste barriers.[24] This will accelerate social and economic development and foster further breaking down of caste rules and structures.

Values, our fourth and last component in a study of culture, are changing rapidly in small towns and districts. Television and, in recent years, smartphones have 'levelled' the value exchange with urban and international settings. However, our culture has an in-built resilience, leavened by stories and mythologies that guide ethical behaviour. This resilience is grounded in the basic postulate of *sila*, character, which stems 'from the experience of singleness in the depth of the mind, rather than in the heat of action'.[25] It is also guided by three *gunas* or traits of *sattva*, *rajas* and *tamas*, and three moral principles of *dana*—to give others their due, *daya*—sympathy with fellow creatures and *dama*—a restraint on passions. The four *purusharthas* of *brahmacharya*, *grihastha*, *vanaprastha* and *sanyas* also give an individual a lifelong compass to live with. These concepts have created values that get refreshed through India's oral traditions and has kept our value systems in the Middle original. The power of these values and our faith is what also explains the resilience of our culture, which was 'sustained by the unrelenting application of mind, in every field—metaphysics, philosophy, art, creativity, polity, society, science and economics . . . a holistic interconnectedness that informs it'.[26]

Enterprise within culture and tradition

In this cultural context, the inception of enterprise in small towns and districts will require a 'circle of trust', a concept Vanita Viswanath, Jagriti's board member and a person who has worked extensively in rural areas, has written about. She says, 'Development . . . requires the crucial lens of culture and traditions (C&T). Culture, as a composite of relationships, norms, long established in "circles of trust" that include immediate and extended family members, gurus, social and religious group members, and the relationships and responsibilities that have evolved to sustain them.'[27] Vanita, who worked extensively with the World Bank, goes on to argue that ignoring culture and tradition has caused many philanthropy programmes to fail.

In our quest for enterprise-led development in smaller towns and districts, we cannot ignore the context, the opportunities and the challenges posed by culture— art, family systems, social systems and value systems. These cultural aspects can act both to channel energies and sometimes as an impediment to innovation. Culture seldom changes quickly; it evolves. Our task is to use it for the nation-building project and change it through that process. For instance, caste may break society into smaller and less cohesive segments, but in rural areas, each caste still has a natural propensity and a family apprenticeship in a vocation. Caste need not be used in the limiting sense that would hinder enterprise but in a manner where existing strengths and skills are utilized. This will reverse the ossification that has taken place, with modern economy playing the role of a lubricant in loosening old-world strictures based on caste.

Indian culture can also contribute to the recent debate on Environmental, Social and Governance (ESG) measures, where the business world is trying to reconcile industrial and consumer enterprise with a wider debate on capitalism harming both our planet and our society. At the core of Indian culture is the belief that nature—plants and animals—have salience of their own, which indicates cultural parity with humans. This is reflected in our mythology and the region-specific nature of our history, with stories of Hanuman, the Kalpavriksha—a wish-fulfilling divine tree—and the temples one sees under trees in small town and districts. The 'sacred geography' of India grants agency not just to humans but to all living creatures. This requires a relationship of respect and interdependence between humanity and the environment it lives in. I see this in the 'lived lives' of those in small town and districts, where wild animals such as monkeys, snakes and others are tolerated, and in some cases, even welcomed. Much before recycling had become standard or zero-based farming was talked about, Indian culture applauded circularity, borrowing from its belief in the cycle of life. Indian culture, with its focus on vegetarianism, cultural sects like the Bishnoi who protect wildlife, and women from the likes of the Chipko movement who protect trees, has been celebrated, but these ideas have not been utilized. Such traits are not unique to India; other civilizations exhibit them, like the Native Americans and Chinese Taoist traditions. Owing to its long years of colonial rule, India has ignored this culture in a mindless rush to westernize.

No wonder the Greendex, a ranking of consumer behaviour in countries as it relates to sustainable practices, ranked India at the top.[28] This would not surprise the person in the smaller towns and districts who mostly lives symbiotically with nature. However, rampant use of plastics is now degrading small towns and districts with the presence of plastic increasing in our rivers, something we observe crossing railway bridges during the Yatra. The answer is to consider the cultural wellsprings in our own society and promote growth that is sustainable from inception, a topic covered more fully in Chapter 12.

One cultural factor which has a bearing on the economic prosperity of the Middle is vocational orientation. The concept of vocation, at the heart of Indian rural society, was systematically attacked by the structures of the British Raj and the education system Macaulay gave us. The focus of the British educational system was not on training young people to be dextrous with their hands, as that would produce competing goods that would work against the British monopoly. The educational system they championed for India valorized clerks and civil servants rather than vocation and enterprise. Certain pockets of mercantile activity continued, though, for instance the mercantile communities around the Gulf of Cambay, in Kutch, Kathiawar, Saurashtra, Marwar in Rajasthan, and similar pockets of enterprise and commerce in the Konkan, Tamil Nadu, Hyderabad and other locations. In contrast, till very recently, the Indian middle class in a small town continues with non-commercial, non-creative pursuits, as government servants, lawyers, college teachers and doctors as vocations that are most aspirational, with enterprise only a recent addition.

Our cultural inheritance

To shift this culture and make entrepreneurship mainstream, we will have to present enterprise in a more holistic manner to the Middle. The search for meaning and purpose must inform our definition of enterprise, creating a wider definition of udyamita, elaborated in Chapter 8. In India, spiritual and moral growth matters as much as a material one. This was a sentiment used fully by Gandhi in gaining independence. His crossover position as a political figure, a social reformer and a man of religion were all key factors in mobilizing the masses. By fusing concepts such as sarvodaya and satyagraha with a mass experience, such as the Dandi March, he was able to forge the independence movement. The next spurt of economic and social growth must use this cultural quotient and strength.

Our 'cultural dividend' is not a given. We must shape and nurture it so that the country can benefit from it. Its real dividend is in a society that is driven sustainably, meaningfully and one that works together towards a larger national goal. This is not the first time we have tried to use it. The concept of Ram Rajya, Ashoka's edicts, Akbar's attempt at a syncretic religion, Shivaji's attempt at cultural unification, Gandhi's invocation of the Gita, our Constitution shapers' use of symbols and cultural motifs and the 'integral humanism' of Pandit Deendayal Upadhyaya, illustrate that our leaders have used culture successfully, and over the next twenty-five years, we must keep this precedent in mind. The recent construct of the Amrit Kaal is as much a cultural call to action as an economic one.

The paradigm adopted by the Top of the Diamond relies on the imagination of a nation as a Westphalian construct, or in some quarters even admiring the Chinese leviathan. In the late 1940s, China committed to Karl Marx and imitated a philosophy born in industrial Europe, which lured the Middle Kingdom away from its civilizational foundations. As Richard Evans has noted, 'Mao wiped clean the old slate of tradition, and Deng finished that job by filling the resultant vacuum with the aspiration of "catching up with the west".'[29] In this imagination, a nation's political borders, its constitution, its legal system and a singular rush towards material growth defined modern China, as it did the industrial West.

On the other hand, India has been sketched not just through the legal constructs of state and physical boundaries but by a strong culture that has held it together. This culture offers a systematic vision of how the different parts of the human experience can be integrated.[30] It was shaped over a long duration, morphing and regenerating itself over centuries as the process of 'transforming life into a site of learning'.[31] In its instincts it is experiential and evolutionary in nature, rather than seeking a revolutionary break from the past. Much like our modern-day Yatra, it is defined by the journey of pilgrims that have travelled the four corners of the nation centuries before our present-day political boundaries were drawn by Radcliffe. A favourite cultural argument of mine, made by Harvard Indologist Diane Eck, who credits travellers with defining our country when she says, 'India is a land linked not by the power of kings and governments, but by the footsteps of its pilgrims.'[32]

Part III

CHANGING: *Our Developmental Approach*

Based on a deeper understanding of the Middle, a new approach to development can be adopted. This will use the methods of udyamita, an expanded definition of enterprise that will energize local economy and society. Not solely defined by material gains, it will encourage participation across all segments of society, pulling in citizen builders, recasting them from voters and consumers into builders and creators. For this, action should shift to the Middle district, which is emerging as a new theatre of focus, neglected since Independence and saddled with a colonial administrative system. To accelerate impact, we must use human-centred digital networks and platforms that best support udyamita and help create an ecosystem. These changes will mobilize our republican energies, creating associations between citizens to accelerate our nation-building project.

8

Udyamita: *New Thinking, New Building*

कर्म यज्ञ से जीवन के स्वप्नों का स्वर्ग मिलेगा
किन्तु बनेगा कौन पुरोहित, अब यह प्रश्न नया है

—जयशंकर प्रसाद

*(Through sacrificial fires of action, will we realize
the heaven of our dreams
But who will propitiate those fires, is the question
that still remains)*

—Jaishankar Prasad

My village in eastern Uttar Pradesh, Barpar, is named after a banyan tree that grows on its outskirts. Thanks to this tree, *'bar ke par'*—the other side of the banyan—is the lyrical name given to our village. The tree's canopy spans 40 metres end to end, almost half the size of a football field. From the time I was a child, I remember the distant silhouette of the banyan standing guard near our village. Women from our village would line up to pray in the cavelike temple nesting in its trunk. We played in its shade, using its dangling shoots as swings. In the summer months, with a charpai as our bed and a good book under our arm, we would lounge under the tree and could hear the twitter of birds and see the fields around the tree being tilled and tended. But we never climbed the tree; it was holy. No one cuts its branches for the same reason. It has stood like this for over 300 years, exuding a unique spirit.

In Indian mythology, the bargad or banyan symbolizes the life-giving tree, Kalpavriksha. From ancient times, Indian village communities have used its massive canopy to hold gram panchayats and gatherings. Shiva first narrated the story of the Ramayana to his wife Parvati sitting under a banyan on Mount Kailash. The Buddha meditated under a bodhi tree, a relative of the banyan, for enlightenment and gave his first sermon from under a similar canopy. It was named the 'banyan' when early European traders saw Baniyas trade under its copious shade. In 1855, it was under a banyan tree in Mumbai that the first stock exchange opened, with twenty-two traders gathering and conducting their business at a tree close to what is today Horniman Circle. They shifted a decade later to a place under another banyan tree on what is now Mahatma Gandhi Road. In 1874, the stock exchange secured permanent accommodation on what is now Dalal Street. The banyan also features on the court of arms of Indonesia, where it symbolizes strength. If further proof of its strength is needed, a visit to Angkor Wat in Cambodia would rest the case, where the banyan has taken over the city from which the Angkor kingdom withdrew.

When our founding fathers chose the banyan as our national tree, they understood its ancient strength, its role as an ecological marvel—a mini forest of sorts—the symbolism of village gatherings under its canopy, its spiritual resonance and its connection to the story of enterprise in India.

This tree also witnessed the contrasting fortunes of India's economy. The stock market in Mumbai flourished under its shadow as the economy in our metros grew in colonial times. In contrast, the tree in my village witnessed the steady decline of the hinterland as enterprise was chased out of the Middle. Extraction of commodities, extortionate *lagaan*, an ecosystem of revenue 'collection', the smothering of handicrafts and the dismemberment of guilds and artisanal societies were a direct by-product of colonial extraction and subsequent neglect. It was the same system that relegated our 300-year-old banyan, with a story of its own, to the position of *Ficus benghalensis*, a mere name in the Linnean system of botanical classification. The mighty banyan was reduced to a catalogued plant in a western explorer's imagination, which was focused only on colonial extraction and exploitation.[1]

A systemic economic exploitation

The economic exploitation of our hinterland had killed small industries and handicrafts by the time we gained independence. Gandhi drew attention to the economic bankruptcy in villages and smaller towns in the run-up to Independence through the symbolic act of spinning the *charkha*. His encounter with extreme poverty was purported to have taken place while on his way to Champaran in Bihar. An apocryphal story tells of the moment when Gandhi, walking in the heat, stopped at a village hut and asked for some water. The only inhabitant, a lady, answered plaintively from behind her door, 'How can I give you water when the only cloth I have is washed and is drying on the clothesline?' This brought home the penury of our country to the Father of the Nation in a personal and visceral way.

Numerous famines, most notably in Bengal just before the Second World War, underscored this situation. Between the two World Wars, India serviced its debts and 'home charges', which were to the tune of 50 million pounds—3.1 billion pounds in today's money[2]—every year to the UK, not to mention sending millions of her sons to fight wars that were not of its making. In the First World War, India gave a one-off 'war gift' of 100 million pounds to the British and took on an additional 100 million pounds of war loans from American banks.[3] The infrastructure the British built was for 'maximum return, most importantly in increased revenue payment'[4] rather than for the benefit of the local economy. As a result, the average economic growth nationally was zero in the 200 years prior to Independence and as the population doubled, per capita income halved.[5] Over the same period, the per capita income of Britain grew ten times.[6] A violent Raj mandated that money flowed out from India and ensured the ingress of British goods to its markets. The inventions of industrial Europe were not enough to raise Britain; it was the subjugation of India that cemented this process. As Philip Mason comments, 'Plassey appears to be the midwife of the Industrial Revolution.'[7]

Our GDP just after Independence was $30.6 billion, of which approximately 50 per cent was in agriculture, with every three out of four persons reliant on agriculture for employment. Services constituted 30 per cent of GDP and manufacturing was at 16 per cent.[8] Manufacturing was not only small, what existed around Independence was in urban enclaves controlled by the British or the Indian elite. At the time of Independence, the balance sheet of the country was both weak and lopsided, with wealth and enterprise being concentrated in the three presidency cities of Mumbai, Calcutta and Madras, with New Delhi gaining importance as India's administrative capital. Just before Independence, Britain ruled over 380 million Indians—including what is now Pakistan—and owned a significant portion of the subcontinent's wealth. Pre-Independence total foreign assets in 1939 accounted for $2.8 billion, almost 10 per cent of GDP, of which $1.4 billion was in private investments in tea, plantations and the jute industry.[9] At the time of Independence, wealth was transferred to Indian industrialists and as a result, capital remained concentrated in the same large towns where it had accumulated pre-Independence. While land reforms played a role in soothing the nerves of the hinterland, significant acreage remained with large litigant landowners.

Post-Independence, India started its economic journey intellectually split into, at least, three camps. The Nehru camp proposed large-scale industrialization with the state playing a key role. A second camp, the authors of the Bombay Plan, proposed economic prominence for large private sector initiatives but agreed that capital-intensive industrialization would be driven by the government. A third camp, the Gandhians, were keen to promote a 'molecular' economy,[10] which sought to expand cottage industries in the 5,00,000 villages that made up rural India then. They understood that the rural economy had been destroyed by colonialism and needed urgent repair.

Nehru won, with planning linked to national integration as a top-down process: 'Behind the Plan lies the conception of India's unity and of a mighty cooperative effort.'[11] He imitated the planning methods of the Soviet Union in his bid to operationalize the concepts of socialism. Instead of addressing the extensive damage done to our economy in the smaller towns and districts, our gaze shifted to the 'commanding heights' of large industrial and public sector enterprises. Patel saw the lack of focus in this planning process when he compared the plan to the Mahabharata— without a clear strategy. The nascent Jan Sangh, formed under the leadership of Shyama Prasad Mukherjee, took up the case for a mixed economy and sought to become a vehicle of middle-class aspirations, but the untimely death of Mukherjee in 1953 stalled this project. Enterprise creation was soon ensnarled in the rigmarole of bureaucracy; whatever made headway was limited to the larger towns and cities.

Institutions for the Top

The onset of the Licence Raj combined with crony capitalism in the seventies and eighties ensured that enterprise and economy in the smaller towns and districts deteriorated. By the end of the twentieth century, the share of agriculture in our GDP had plummeted to 15 per cent, even though 42 per cent of Indians in rural areas were still dependent on it.[12] The services sector took off and is now 60 per cent of our GDP, while the manufacturing sector still hovers at the 21 per cent mark, much the same as at

Independence.[13] As the Indian economy grew, the growth in services and manufacturing continued to happen in urban enclaves. A variety of scientific and educational institutions were created to support the economics of large companies at the Top, starting as early as 1952, with the IITs, AIIMS and thereafter the IIMs. The mindset in these institutions, however, borrowed techniques from developed economies to foster growth in large industries, rather than understand the needs and markets of the real India, where a majority lived.

I happened to study at one of these institutions— the IIT. A high degree of peer pressure was the core of the learning experience at the IITs. Those who made it through the entrance exams were academically strong, and as grades were relative, fellow classmates kept us on our toes. Many came from underprivileged backgrounds, their entrance a final push to the Top which would ensure a new life for them. However, barring a few exceptions highlighted below, practical teaching was missing, and an understanding of the issues India faced was largely absent. Our labs in mechanical engineering were no doubt well-equipped as IIT Delhi had been assisted by the United Kingdom when it was built, but the approach emphasized theory over practice and international experience over Indian.

The only experience I had of real-life learning was when Professor Dhar, one of the finest professors at IIT-Delhi and my final dissertation counsellor, bussed my class to a hotel construction site in Delhi where heating, ventilation and cooling equipment were being set up. This was the most insightful day for me in the entire four-year course. By limiting exposure to the world outside their well-tended campuses, the IITs were preparing us to become useful to another country—usually the US. The kind of challenges that India needed to overcome would have energized us. Instead, we spent nights theorizing on the hyperbolic paraboloid rooftop of the Convocation Hall at IIT Delhi. Given its lofty height, those conversations were literally cut off from the real India.

Professor Dhar, himself a Gandhian, insisted on exploring local solutions. At the time, he was investigating how thermal springs could create a heating, ventilation and cooling device that would preserve medicine in a remote district of Uttarakhand. Professor Dhar also took a humanities course, 'Science and Humanism', and in this he drove home a point our well-appointed campus was unable to make. Unless we used our expertise in technology for the good of society, it was not worth much. The course pointed out that India, its values and its spirituality, mattered. Through this course and his life's ideals, Professor Dhar did more than ask us to look outside the campus. He gave voice to the creative Indian and asked us to understand our own humanity—a humanity driven by a moral purpose, perhaps a national purpose. He made us see that our institution was not just a place to learn, it also had to train us to contribute. Many of us kept that lesson under our belt, hoping to contribute in some way in the future, but many also bid goodbye to it as they kissed the tarmac before boarding a flight to a US university, never to return. The recent success of Indian-born CEOs of major global tech companies is worthy of applause, but it is also a measure of lost talent, much of which could have been retained if we had exposed engineers to the real challenges India faced and created a positive environment for enterprise.

When leaders stayed back and stood their ground in smaller districts, enterprise flourished. The success of Amul is an excellent example of this contribution. Amul was created by the entrepreneurial actions of a committed leader, Varghese Kurien, supported by the enterprise DNA of the Gujarati community. During the Jagriti Yatra, we have seen the stainless-steel towers of milk in Anand—an inspiration for any entrepreneur. Amul is a rare business that created infrastructure that helped farmers and women in situ. In urban areas, there was an attempt to promote khadi, which became a fashion of sorts when a starched kurta became a political uniform in Lutyens Delhi, but it hid a hypocrisy towards small-town enterprise. Small businesses in a typical district, the biggest source of local employment, fell victim to a licensing regime stunting growth, making them unviable.

I have observed first-hand the decline of the carpet industry in the district of Mirzapur much before Kaleen Bhaiya—from the OTT series *Mirzapur*—became famous on Amazon Prime. My maternal grandfather's family owned a carpet business in Gopiganj in Mirzapur. This business prospered in my childhood, with maternal uncles visiting international locales, bringing back export orders and presents for me! I would roll and trim carpets with their employees on my vacations, coming home smelling of singed wool, much to my mother's annoyance. Our large house in Gopiganj, where the joint family of my maternal grandfather and his four brothers lived, hummed with hope and activity. But the family knew that the expansion of their enterprise above a certain revenue would attract the attention of a state that was keen on nationalization and they would also forfeit the benefits of small-scale industry.

Ultimately, the family kept the business small, and it was slowly divided among the brothers instead of being scaled up as a whole.

Around the same time in 1984, Deng Xiaoping in China tasked the equivalent of our District Magistrate (DM) with setting up Township and Village Enterprises (TVEs), which created large-scale employment outside big cities. In our case, the creation of District Industrial Centres (DICs) was promoted, but the performance metrics of the district administration were not changed. The DM continued to be involved with every decision in the district and lacked the bandwidth for promotion of enterprise, which should have become a focus of the district administration long ago.

India stands a good chance of becoming a $10 trillion economy over the coming fifteen years,[14] with the potential of 9 per cent GDP growth. This can only happen if the smaller towns and districts in the Middle undergo an enterprise revolution. Without large-scale participation of small towns and districts in economic production, neither will we grow fast, nor will that growth be inclusive. The Gini coefficient, a measure of inequality, shows that India, the largest democracy in the world, is becoming worryingly unequal. As per an IMF report, our Gini coefficient has gone up from 0.45 in 1990 to 0.51 in 2013.[15] Growing inequality created a veritable political storm in Trump's USA, May's Brexit and Erdogan's Turkey and could hit our shores too.

Giving more than taking

Efforts to grow the economy focus on macro-economic interventions. Economists talk of reforms in land, labour, fiscal policy, industrial policy and liquidity measures. But at its core, this language of enterprise still favours trickle-down economics. The mindset and tools remain much the same as when the Linnean system catalogued a 300-year-old banyan, with a unique story in its own context, as an inanimate plant ready for extraction. The word 'enterprise' got associated solely with material growth and money making and was distanced from the human spirit and societal associations that are important in India, where the ethic of community and the ethic of divinity also matter. To create a widespread enterprise movement directly in the Middle, where culture, context and collaboration matter, we need to offer a wider explanation of enterprise that focuses on human connections and spirit. This is particularly important in a country where services continue to be the largest segment of the economy.

An oft-quoted phrase from Adam Smith, on first reading, presents enterprise as selfish. In his book *The Wealth of Nations*, Smith wrote, 'It is not from the benevolence of the Butcher, the Brewer or the Baker that we expect our dinner, but from their regard for their own self-interest.'[16] This seemingly selfish phrase, in fact, makes a case for 'giving' rather than 'taking'. The butcher, brewer or baker makes money by understanding and satisfying an unmet need *of another person*. Enterprise at its core is dependent on solving problems for society, by creating an extraordinary experience *for someone else*. Money as the starting point of this process is misplaced; it is the value that you create as an entrepreneur by 'giving', 'serving', 'sacrificing' and 'building', if done better than others, that drives commercial success. Aravind Eye Care, which has a relentless focus on 'curing unneeded blindness', generates money, but that is only because the entire operation is designed to serve millions who are suffering from an eye ailment. A more prosaic enterprise—say a *dhaba*—also succeeds in making money only if it serves customers better than others.

The 1991 reforms created an ecosystem for enterprise in Metro and Tier 1 districts and, as a result, the economy at the Top grew rapidly. Our next revolution has to create a similar ecosystem for enterprise in the Middle so that we deepen and widen the economy. An ecosystem approach that resembles a garden or a forest which is interdependent and connected. Kevin Kelley, the innovation expert, says: 'Just as in a forest, the success of one species depends on the success of others . . . ecosystems are governed by coevolution, which is a type of biological co-dependence, a mixture of competition and cooperation.'[17] We will then start moving away from a linear, Cartesian and mechanical system of looking at the Middle as a source of extraction of commodities that sees citizens merely as consumers. We can then locate a movement of creation and building in the Middle for national growth and renewal.

Redefining entrepreneurship

Traditional entrepreneurship is defined as the 'discovery, creation and profitable exploitation of markets for goods and services'.[18] Jagriti's experience with enterprise promotion in smaller towns and districts has given us a more expansive and collaborative language based on udyamita. This definition starts with the energy and purpose of a local leader who solves problems our growing democracy faces based on local strengths and local resources. In doing so, the enterprise creates markets and connects with resources, locally, nationally and internationally, rather than focus on extraction. The entrepreneur 'assumes accountability for the inherent risks'[19] and gains economically and socially as a result. An ecosystem is essential for udyamita to take root, for it is not only supported with market connects, mentorship and money, but it is also supported by stories. This approach must go beyond the 'subsistence entrepreneurship' of SHGs, microfinance and others to 'transformational entrepreneurship' that involves new ways of collaboration, production and service as a 'real engine for growth for the economy, since these entrepreneurs start firms that grow rapidly and create jobs and innovation in the economy'.[20] Some enterprises will graduate to becoming large companies, in the manner of a Nirma in India or a Walmart in the US, both with small-town beginnings. Other enterprises will create hospitals, schools, sports clubs, horticulture businesses and local companies that clean streets or clear garbage, often in partnership with local government. Some will shoot up to become unicorns. Cumulatively, they will solve the many needs and challenges of Indian society, and thereby provide large-scale local employment in the Middle. In this manner, national economy will grow 'Middle-up' as we involve more people in the production process. Then economic activities will not remain confined to what some call 'fripperies'[21]—elite goods and services that are for the pleasure of the few—and instead focus on solutions that impact the many.

Ludwig Erhard, Chancellor of Germany after the Second World War, drove its economic recovery from 1948 to the 1960s with an economic philosophy that was similar, as it focused on the Middle.[22] Some call this 'supply-side economics' but in the case of India, this is simply the enabling of the vast Middle to be productive.

The idea of satyagraha as articulated by Mahatma Gandhi outlined an India-specific framework that got us political freedom. Deendayal Upadhyaya's 'integral humanism' offered a method to bring society together. Udyamita offers an India-specific framework that can give the majority in the Middle economic freedom. Satyagraha worked as the participation of those from smaller towns and villages widened and deepened the freedom struggle from the 1930s onwards. Integral humanism has succeeded as it has created a language based on cultural unity that brings diverse people together. The next spurt of growth and prosperity will only take place if we widen and deepen economic participation through an ecosystem approach based on udyamita in a context in which the majority live and work. This movement must pay more attention to the regions of the north and the east, such as Purvanchal, which were singled out for punishment by a colonial system and as a result remain 'enterprise dark' today.

Udyamita starts with a truth that is as old as humanity—to build today to benefit tomorrow for the benefit of many. A sense of sacrifice and purpose is key—something that creates a moral force for strengthening society, linked to the wider challenges that India must overcome, and not just remain confined to making money. With this positioning, udyamita can offer solutions to the real issues faced by India—better health, clean water, effective education, renewable energy, local transport, last mile logistics, etc. This will use local resources—manpower, agricultural product, handicrafts and apparel, etc.—

creating local employment in collaboration with national and international expertise and resources. Unlike the aim of many start-ups, where getting a pizza delivered one minute early sometimes becomes the goal of entrepreneurship, the problems and solutions here build the nation. Making money will remain an important component but as a means of keeping count of success and reinvestment. This sequence—societal problems, contextual solutions and economic benefits—is at the core of udyamita. A narrow money-making position will limit this movement to those few who are already entrepreneurially minded. Techno solutions that were proposed by the 'maker movement' in the West[23] attempted to democratize building but remained confined to technologically driven solutions. Udyamita focuses on the human motivations of entrepreneurs and solutions that solve real issues of society locally, which may well include technical solutions but are not defined by them.

At Jagriti, we have seen enterprise-led development grow visibly over the past decade as we circled the country and udyamita took root. In 2008, we saw disbelief when we took udyamita to smaller towns and districts through our train journey. Many at that time thought that skilling was sufficient. But the last few years has seen the country and the Middle turn an enterprise corner. We observed how the hidden springs within Indian civilization are filling the well of udyamita from society. In our travels, we saw a pursuit of meaning and purpose through this process. No wonder the word *arth* in Indian philosophy translates not just to material growth and accumulation of wealth but also to meaning. The definition of enterprise imported from Silicon Valley may be important for a venture capital and private equity-led process at the Top. The unicorn dream defined by a billion-dollar valuation focuses on singular scale and creation of a monopoly in the way Peter Thiel describes in his book *Zero to One*[24], and will remain in currency. Our definition of udyamita takes it out of urban enclaves, singular scale and exploitation through monopolies, and makes it dependent on many udyamis with a free exchange of value and widespread economic growth. By understanding our own national spirit, connecting it with the social and cultural underpinnings of small towns and districts and a language based on a pursuit of meaning, a large-scale economic movement is possible.

While government can enable this movement, 'it is much more difficult to find examples of successful government enterprise programmes . . . the failure of government-subsidized venture capital funds or direct investments in start-up firms'[25] is an indication of this problem. The government is naturally risk-averse as its money is accountable to the Parliament. An enterprise revolution must be seeded from society and the private sector as a people's movement, where 'inherent risk, accountability and benefits' are aligned. The government can support this movement by creating 'enterprise infrastructure'. Enterprise infrastructure includes physical space and digital platforms and an approach to governance that encourages the 'association of people' led by citizen leaders. Enterprise-led development cannot be *pushed* on people by the government; it will be *pulled* by citizens connected to the market and this ecosystem. The creation and early success of the Swavalambi Bharat Abhiyan[26] is an example of a society-led effort for enterprise and employment in India. Even the TVEs of China, which made profits for

Communist Party officials, discovered that government involvement became untenable in the long run.[27]

The starting resource for this movement is abundant in Middle India—local leaders. Leaders such as Parvati Singh and Rahul Mani, both local entrepreneurs in districts such as Deoria, or Gobinda Dalai in Odisha and Savita Munde in Maharashtra—each a Yatri who has started an enterprise after the Yatra. Hernando de Soto, a Peruvian economist, has outlined the hidden capital that remains locked in physical property which can promote economic growth in emerging markets.[28] He focuses on assets in real estate in the poorer parts of the world, placing this global hidden asset base at $9 trillion. Our experience points to another source of hidden capital, *entrepreneurial human capital*, locked up in countries such as India, primarily in the Middle, which udyamita can help unleash. This capital lies dormant in citizen leaders and better education is only one way of releasing it. The entrepreneurial capital in the Middle has to be unlocked through market connects, mentorship and money in a do-learn-do process that goes beyond classroom learning. By enabling these millions of citizen leaders from the Middle, growth can be both explosive and inclusive.

Real leaders address problems

As we circled the country and worked in Purvanchal, broadly two types of leaders or udyamis and two types of problems or 'markets' emerged. These leaders, markets and enterprise archetypes are being enabled by digital techniques—Jan Dhan, Aadhaar and Mobile (JAM)—irrespective of their sector. Udyamita requires 'earned income', which differentiates it from charities.

The first type of udyami is a leader who is motivated by social success and operates in the local market or location. A local school or hospital run by a private person, at a profit, would qualify. Udyamita solves a local issue—health, education or sanitation—often using some grant funding to supplement earned income from local usage. Social enterprises, such as Aravind Eye Care, that have scaled up this local effort qualify, and they have also created what Clayton Christensen, the celebrated innovation expert at Harvard, describes as 'market making' innovations.[29] Such innovations create an entire new market—in the case of Aravind Eye Care, small-town eye surgery and blindness prevention at a scale that makes it one of the largest eye care systems in the world.

A second udyami is motivated by a local need for a profitable cause, such as the contracting businesses run in a district like Deoria. They drive construction of a road auctioned by the Public Works Department (PWD) or through the Member of Parliament Local Area Development Scheme (MPLADS) fund and build schools, hospitals and colleges. As local infrastructure is created, local urbanization grows, local institutes are built and municipalities created, these businesses will likely flourish. Rama Bijapurkar, a leading market research expert, believes that 'matching the quality of basic living, i.e., infrastructure, with the quality of consumer goods people have is one of the biggest needs and opportunities'.[30] We need faster urbanization in mofussil towns, creation of healthcare systems, creation of schools and colleges, availability of 24x7 power and energy, transportation links to benefit agriculture, digital connectivity and others.[31]

The third type of udyami is a leader who is addressing a national or international market or need, with a product or service that is produced locally. Vyanjanam in Deoria sells pickles under its brand name to urban markets across India. In this case, the product is being marketed to the larger cities and metro towns, although some quantity is also sold in the adjoining district. This has led to employment for over 100 women, with Delhivery, a supply chain company, picking up packages from Baitalpur on the outskirts of Deoria. The leaders in such enterprises are usually local, getting help from market connectors sitting in a large city who become market partners.

Finally, with the Internet, many local enterprises can become what are called 'micro-multinationals'. They can address viable markets nationally and outside the country, much like a handicrafts company has done from Deoria. High-speed connectivity does not distinguish between a large or a small town, or its proximity to a port or a road, and so starting a business that is global from day one is incredibly cheap.[32] A recent report outlined how 50 million small businesses on Facebook are selling globally—Alibaba alone has almost 10 million such businesses.[33] This requires understanding the needs of customers, their tastes and their attitudes overseas, but even that is being facilitated through global connects.

Market, mentorship, money and *mahaul*

Market connect is the crucial ingredient for udyamita to succeed, much more important than money, for it gives access to a large and sustained source of money—the customer. Market connects will require enterprises to become a part of the value chains of private sector companies and the rapidly growing e-commerce world. Corporations looking at new sources of innovation and value are collaborating with the incubation islands of Hyderabad, Bengaluru or Delhi. However, insights required to solve the real issues, the next frontier of needs in Tier 2 and Tier 3 districts for servicing the 800 million in the Middle, can only happen if these corporates partner with enterprises from these districts. Businesses built on solving these real problems can scale up globally as 4 billion people live in the 'global Middle'—in countries such as Nigeria, Indonesia, South Africa, Brazil, Mexico, Vietnam and others—with issues similar to our own Middle. Corporates must move beyond CSR to include supply chain integration and ask managers to contribute through mentorship. By considering such enterprise as part of their value chains, they can penetrate deep into the hinterland, which is preferable to enterprise-led development led solely by charitable effort. With this comprehensive approach, the benefits and the relationship with the Middle become strategic and our economy expands naturally.

Mentorship, sometimes through peers and through more experienced udyamis, is a critical element for the success of udyamita. In a rural and small-town setting, it is the modern approximation of the cultural approach of a guru-*shishya* relationship. I have personally experienced the power of such an approach through the blessings of three gurus who have shaped my life—Professor Dhar being one of them. Similarly, the facilitators' mentorship is a critical element of the success of the cohort-based group process in the Yatra, where the facilitators act as mini gurus. By definition, the guru is less interested in personal or immediate gain; they want their protégés to succeed, creating a virtuous circle of inter-generational learning. With the help of digital meetings and messaging platforms, a remote mentoring relationship can now be fostered with experts.

A recent conversation with the founders of Barmer Bazaar, a venture initiated by four Yatris—Dr Mukesh Panwar, Dr Surendra Singh, Nehpal Rathore and Dilip Gehlot—who came in sequential years to the Yatra from Barmer, Rajasthan, gave me an insight on how udyamis learn through mentorship. The founders of this local aggregator that sells items ranging from dates to handicrafts and other locally produced items told me, 'The Yatra and the Biz Gyan Tree exercise in particular was transformative. It taught us to look at a venture holistically and plan with a three to five-year ambition. Before this experience, our approach was focused on money and we believed that itself would drive success. The mentorship of those in our group taught us to take a longer-term, holistic view.'

After markets and mentors, money is another plank of enterprise creation. Angel finance, venture finance, private equity, bank finance and infrastructure finance must be re-examined keeping the approach of udyamita in mind. Finance must understand that a significant proportion of the economy is service-led. It is not just assets that need to be assessed in lending, it is also the quality of the entrepreneurial team. Examining their integrity, quality, drive, hunger and staying power will become even more important in the funding process. The banking system is still wary of lending to entrepreneurs, with local bankers caught between entrepreneurs who come to them with half-baked funding plans and a banking system that is egged on by the government to meet lending targets set nationally.

At a grassroots level, mahaul or environment for udyamita is critical for success. This mahaul is often marred by corruption. Corruption, as Yuen Ang, an author who has written a book on corruption has documented, is of broadly four kinds—'petty theft', where officials take a cut in local transfers, 'speed money' to facilitate movement of documents, 'access money' that allows them access to the influential and 'grand theft', where large-scale siphoning of money takes place at a national or state level. While in the global corruption index both India and China, countries with large and complex governance structures, are ranked almost the same, the nature of corruption is different.[34] In India, speed money and petty theft dominate while in China, access money and grand theft are key drivers of this index. This points to a burden on the ordinary entrepreneur in India and to the behaviour of local administration, which is often unsupportive of an enterprise. On the other hand, access money, which is the dominant form of corruption in China, sometimes supports business growth. Of course, any kind of corruption ultimately catches up, illustrated by the spectacular fall of Bo Xilai, the mayor of Chongqing, who was convicted on bribery and embezzlement charges. In contrast, in India the volume of corruption is high while the value is low and this must be addressed if last-mile mahaul for udyamita has to be improved.

A Banyan Revolution for the Middle

The seventy-fifth anniversary of India can trigger a movement where the Middle participates more fully in economic activities. We need a Banyan Revolution named after our national tree focused on udyamita which starts with the 'pursuit of meaning'. Solve a problem well, service a client with humility or create a product that surprises a customer, and the entrepreneur and employee will find meaning and economic success. Meaning creates a wider movement of enterprise, not the 'hedonistic treadmill' that has seduced Europe and North America, pumped unnaturally by an extractive economy that was primed originally by colonialism. The language of enterprise must be shaped by motivations that drove the success of satyagraha, sarvodaya and swadeshi in giving us Independence, and the philosophy of integral humanism. This new spirit of udyamita is more difficult as it requires participants to observe the long-term discipline of building. It is less glamorous, takes more time, shows results slowly, but once results start to flow and the flywheel of enterprise starts to move, it can give lifelong meaning to citizens, create employment for our masses and transcendence for our nation. This micro focus on udyamita can be aided by the macro narrative of development in a time-bound fashion. To be productive and in the service of another person is the first step towards engaging not just with enterprise and nation-building, but with life.

We see this in action with the catering staff on the Yatra train. Every year, almost 130 catering staff feed the train with a zeal for service that is extraordinary. They are young Indians from ordinary backgrounds, usually from small towns, as recounted earlier in the book. They get up at 5 a.m., often in the freezing north Indian cold, and serve tea and breakfast in time before Yatris deboard to visit role models. They then board a truck to serve lunch at the role model site, hurrying back to arrange tea, followed by dinner and thereafter some haldi milk as the train cuts into the cold north in the second half of the journey. But these young caterers find enormous meaning in this work and there is palpable joy in their service. Invariably, on New Year's Eve, woollens and sweater distribution is organized by the Yatris for these caterers without our prompting. The caterer has devised a system where he is able to cater across 8000 km of our journey, purchasing vegetables and condiments across the length and breadth of India. But he has also created meaning in the lives of these young men in the difficult confines of a moving train with a smile and good humour.

The biggest cultural hurdle to our meta narrative of udyamita is the 'stigma of failure'. A secure government job is still the primary aspiration of young India and their parents, particularly in the north and the east. One reason—a strong alternative is simply not available. The second—government servants are seen to have inordinate and unidirectional power with marginal accountability. This motivates hundreds to apply, even if it is for the job of a peon. And finally, the Middle lacks an ecosystem, 'enterprise infrastructure' and stories of success. Institutes, thought processes, management systems, technology and media have pivoted towards the Top of the Diamond, leaving those in the Middle, 'enterprise orphans'.

As we look at creating a movement based on udyamita, the cultural effort of removing the stigma of failure in any enterprise will be the most difficult to overcome. However, recently, we have seen youth in smaller towns and districts finally understanding that there are no alternatives. Every district has an army of young people who have lived in coaching centres trying to pass an administrative service examination, or preparing for the police or military through sports, and failed. In recent times, they are seeing the success of role models both locally and nationally, who are showing a new path of economic growth and livelihood through udyamita.

The Banyan Revolution should focus on what some would term as 'mezzanine enterprise'—neither very small nor very big. Over time, entrepreneurs can scale these middle-sized enterprises to large ones, moving the economic needle much faster and at a wider and deeper level. Micro enterprises have done well as they could flourish simply on the societal trust that exists in such a setting, with Grameen Bank and other microfinance institutions leading that charge. Mezzanine enterprises require more support and enablement—enterprise ecosystems, network and infrastructure. They require connections to local, national and global markets and a mentorship infrastructure essential to guide and support leaders. Once such an ecosystem is in place, it will power development on its own steam.

This movement will require an inventory of those who are capable of starting and nurturing enterprises. By identifying leaders who can be motivated, trained and mentored to take on enterprises, local issues can be addressed and export of products from these districts to national and international locations can be fostered. Our 7500 Yatris are a key part of this enterprise human capital pool nationally.

The Banyan Revolution will have to re-educate the country that the socialist and collectivist theory of state-directed 'common good' is outdated, and has failed in countries that have tried it over the past fifty years. For a country as large as India, with such diversity of language, climate, occupation, cultures, faiths and local solutions, udyamita creates common good, locally and more naturally. Our stable democracy over the past seventeen general elections has given citizens confidence in the right to vote. At the seventy-fifth anniversary of Independence, it is time we created a meta story for the 'right to build'.

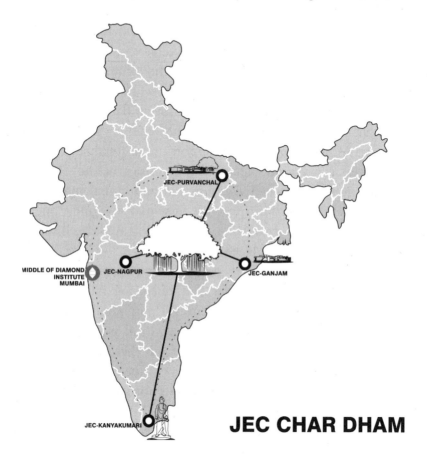

JEC CHAR DHAM

Creating national transcendence

Our founders created a meta story for national liberation to secure Independence. We must create a similar story for the coming twenty-five years that powers our society and economy. The Jewish state of Israel managed to achieve this on two occasions. In the initial years of independence, they created national transcendence when faced with an existential threat where 'fear of loss often proves more powerful than the hope of gain'.[35] They rallied together to achieve the seemingly impossible, be it the Yom Kippur War in 1973, when they fought Egypt and Jordan simultaneously, or the rescue of hostages at Entebbe in 1976, when an El Al plane was hijacked, and later in creating a culture of enterprise that is both deep and wide. At the core of this transcendence was a sense of 'national meaning'. After thousands of years of wandering, the Jews returned to their own station in Palestine and founded a state in 1948, a year after India's independence. National transcendence informed not just Zionist leaders such as David Ben-Gurion, Golda Meir, Shimon Peres and Yitzhak Rabin, but citizen leaders in daily life. It motivated the fighter pilot who flew over hostile territory to destroy an enemy nuclear reactor, or the Sayeret Matkal commando who risked his life as he went out to rescue hostages. In this first instance, post-independence, it was directed by the state to create infrastructure and national strength guided by a national purpose.

But after going through a traumatic phase of economic slowdown in the 1970s and 1980s, Israel decided to convert the same national mission into igniting widespread enterprise. National purpose informed the gutsy entrepreneur Shai Agassi, who left a promising career as a top executive at SAP to try his hand at creating an electric vehicle revolution. It is seen in the rigour of the training in its army institutions, which thereafter lead to entrepreneurial careers for many soldiers and a booming defence industry. It is also underpinned by a national structure of enterprise created in universities.[36] Understanding that the nation comes first, young and old have gotten behind this national mission of high-tech enterprise.

I doubt we can copy the high-tech enterprise model that Israel has engineered. Our innovation quotient is still low, our service percentage is high, our capital base per capita is small and our nation is much larger and more diverse. If Israel spends 4.9 per cent of national GDP on R&D, India hovers around 0.7 per cent.[37] However, we can foster an enterprise movement in Middle India that is innovation- and productivity-driven, service-centric and supported by enterprise ecosystems. With an economy more than two-thirds service-based, service enterprises will play a key role in our growth. It may not be as productive as the Israeli microchip manufacturer, but it requires less of money and more of human capital—something India has aplenty.

The udyamita tide is finally turning. The Banyan Revolution is within our grasp. It can create a moment of 'national transcendence' directed at the Middle laced with meaning and potentially be a source of employment to millions of people. This will take time, as the task of taking on a positive endeavour, enlisting people, showing success and creating an ecosystem are not instant. The good news is that without too much prompting and supported from the bottom by 'molecular' enterprises that Gandhi seeded pre-Independence, we have become a leading hub for small and growing business. If we can accelerate this, the Banyan Revolution over the next twenty-five years will help shine the Diamond.

9

Citizen: *Our Protagonist for the Middle*

कहइ रीछपति सुनु हनुमाना। का चुप साधि रहेहु बलवाना।।
पवन तनय बल पवन समाना। बुधि बिबेक बिग्यान निधाना।।

—तुलसीदास

*(Jamavant, the king of bears, says, why are you so silent,
o powerful Hanuman?
O son of the wind, you have strength, intelligence,
wisdom and science)*

—Tulsidas

Citizenship forms the basis of democracy as 'only by the consent of the governed does the ruler get his legitimacy'. India has experienced democracy, shaped by local kinship, caste and spiritual obligations, from the times of the great *sanghams*. Its success as a 'constitutional democracy' is largely a result of this historical memory. Our founders yoked the common man from smaller towns and villages to the struggle for independence. At Independence, their imagination for the citizen was not to stop at the finishing line; after breasting the tape of freedom, the citizen was to keep running, continuing to pull the nation forward. While the citizen expected to benefit from a free India, our founders also wanted them to be engaged in its development. This involved political, social, cultural and economic freedoms and effort. Instead of 'freedom from' British rule, post-independence, our citizens would create 'freedom to' a prosperous and more cohesive nation. However, the rights enshrined in our Constitution and a state-led approach post-independence created a one-way narrative for the citizen to be served by the state.

Citizens' responsibilities were conspicuous by their absence in our Constitution. Citizens were given many rights, covered in fifteen pages and twenty-three articles in the Constitution of India. For good measure, the state was directed to help the citizen in the 'Directive Principles of State Policy', which covered four pages and fourteen clauses. But expectations from citizens were weak, covered in one page and one article, 51A of the Constitution. Citizens could vote, had to be law-abiding and could do no harm to others and their environment. But beyond that, the largest democracy said nothing to its 330 million citizens, now 1.4 billion, to act and participate. Citizens were the inspiration for the Constitution, but it was a one-sided formula; they were asked to 'vote' and 'behave' but there was no exhortation to 'create' and 'build'. Our constitution framers were understandably anxious to signal that citizens, who had experienced oppression by a colonial system, were now free and would be fully supported by the state. However, to assure our citizens that we were finally free, rights were declared without remembering that a young republic is also built on responsibilities. The reciprocal relationship and responsibilities, starting with local civic involvement and a call to bring their energies to the national arena, were muted. Public servants and 'public service' became the coda after Independence, where citizens would benefit through state action. A socialist start to our polity cemented that approach of 'first government then citizen'.

I grew up in this environment. My grandfather retired as a senior public servant in Uttar Pradesh. My uncle was a senior police officer, retiring as a director general. My father got admission to the Indian Military Academy in 1955, and retired from the army as its deputy chief after forty years of distinguished service. As we grew up, in dinner table conversations we were expected to contribute but through government as the medium. The state was the custodian of wisdom and it would serve citizens through institutions largely untouched after the British left. I cheekily questioned my father on the traditions of the cavalry, where old regiments showcased 'silver' in the cavalry mess, reflecting a colonial heritage. My youngest cousin answered the calling to serve our country directly, becoming an air force fighter pilot. My grandfather hesitatingly approved of my private sector career in Schlumberger only when he recognized that my salary was a few multiples higher than what others were getting. These traditions created a sentiment of 'society and country first', but in those days, the conduit for action was the singular channel of government service.

Statism and populism

Citizens have experienced two phases of this state-centric approach over the past seven decades. The first, a strong socialist phase, involved a process started by Nehru which was continued by his daughter, Indira Gandhi. This was a time when the energies of our citizens were not just wasted, they were largely absent. Heavy state-run machinery in large public sector organizations focused on industrialization while the citizen was seen largely as a voter and a consumer. Just over four decades into Independence, the reforms of 1991 created a counter-force at the Top, releasing the energies of the private sector, and a growth surge resulted. These enterprises at the Top created trickle-down development that also impacted the Middle, albeit indirectly.

A second phase started with populism when citizens were wooed and served by a clientelist government. The state was coerced by different segments and castes to give them their pound of flesh. Reservation, with Mandal as a primary example, became the rallying cry for citizens in this phase, with the state trying to provide government jobs based on caste reservations. This resulted in a fragmented polity as divisions in society, created by caste politics, also created unstable governments. Over time, caste segments started discovering that this bargain was not yielding social or economic benefits for them. For instance, in Bihar, there was a pushback against clientelist politics when citizens recognized that by capturing votes as a block, those who got elected took their caste base for granted, relieving them of the pressure to perform. This was aided by the women's vote, which is less motivated by caste equations, when they recognized how a ban on alcohol had increased safety and reduced domestic violence. This phase has still not come to its end but seems to be receding.

A third, republican phase is emerging based on the vast majority of citizens in the Middle, and is likely to dominate citizen mindset and political trends over the coming twenty-five years. We observed the emergence of this republican energy over a decade of Jagriti Yatra and our work in Deoria. With the vast majority in the Middle no longer in extreme poverty, today's citizen sees through the socialist or clientelist approach. Indian citizens and civic and political leaders are realizing that a republic is not just the transfer of power from the citizen to the ruler for a period of five years at the time of voting. A true republic is where citizens help create better circumstances for each other and the nation, with the government serving as an enabler. Tocqueville pointed to this relationship as 'the art of associating together must grow and improve in the same ratio in which the equality of conditions is increased'.[1] Colonial institutions tried to weaken and break this association. A socialist approach spoon-fed its citizens through an inefficient government and clientelist politics split citizens into smaller segments asking for more from the government. Now that the Middle has gained strength and gravity, with a mature democracy beneath us, we must build new institutions that put citizens at the centre of our national and political experience, not just as voters but as builders. The recent focus on Janbhagidari and the Prime Minister's call for *sabka prayas* signals the beginning of this phase.

Size and complexity

In mobilizing our citizens, relative to a Western democracy such as the UK, there is another complication—one of size. The UK, a society of 50 million at the time of our Independence,[2] could be governed by a Westminster form of government with welfarism as its driving motive. It was possible to access citizens, communicate with them, nudge them, listen to them, create representation and forge governance links in a typical constituency. In our case, when a typical constituency is twenty times larger in number of votes, the approach must change. Today, a Member of Parliament in the UK, on an average, has 1 lakh citizens in their constituency. Contrast that with the 26 lakh citizens on an average per Member of Parliament in India. District population has increased, on average, from just under 14 lakh citizens per district in 307 districts at the time of Independence to 19 lakh citizens on average per district in the 740 districts today.[3] Increasing administrative layers at each level—national, state, region, district, block, village—causes snags in any service well before it reaches the citizen, with the lowest layer at the Panchayat level still searching for financial powers. Such disproportionate representation makes it difficult for elected representatives or administrators to listen to and serve citizens.

If numbers and layers make matters difficult, complexity multiplies this manifold. As India has modernized, societal complexity has increased 'the multiplication and diversification of the social forces in society. Kinship, racial and religious groupings are supplemented by occupational, class and skill groupings'.[4] The modernization of society is happening at a rapid rate, multiplying groupings and connections. As India modernizes, 'major clusters of old social, economic and psychological commitments are getting eroded or broken and people are available for new patterns of socialization and behaviour'.[5] This is aided by rapid infusion of digital connections through smartphones, which are penetrating the Middle rapidly. This complex citizen landscape is difficult to manage through a typical welfare state as imagined by western democracies around the Second World War. A new alchemy is needed where the citizens themselves becomes the creator and the association between citizens becomes a key goal of governance.

Ordinary citizens, extraordinary characters

As I wandered in Deoria, I met citizens from across its social segment, each of whom had a unique story of contributing to society. Each person has a different achievement, age, economic profile and spirit. These three characters show how ordinary citizens are contributing to a Tier 3 district. These are not entrepreneurs supported by Jagriti, described elsewhere in the book, but ordinary citizens with a unique story and potential that defines our republic.

I first met Barrister Yadav on the banks of the mighty Narayani river. He has a handlebar moustache that sits on a face weathered by toil and thirty years of hard work. He talks deliberately, pausing with a self-respecting tone, never letting it be known how humble his background is. Barrister was born in a small village called Pipra Ghat in 1956 and he still lives there today. When he was in Class V, his mother passed away, and this was the biggest shock of his life. Having finished his intermediate education at the local school, he took a train to Delhi and found work as a labourer in Patel Nagar in a *kabadi* shop at the age of seventeen. He worked for Rs 8 per day to begin with, but over three decades, managed to gradually climb up the economic ladder till he had two shops of his own in Patel Nagar and had bought a small flat for himself. His two daughters and two sons were born there, but once they were settled, he returned to Pipra Ghat. In 2013, the river flooded his village, but he stayed back and continues to go back and forth between his village and Delhi, where his children live. He says that having successfully married off all his four children, he is now 'free to work on solving the issues in his areas, helping locals at the *thana* or with work in his village and adjoining areas'. Having worked his way up from poverty, he could easily have stayed back in Delhi. But Barrister, having seen the full circle of life, returned to where he belonged.

Ganga Singh Kushwaha was a Member of the Legislative Assembly from Fazilnagar in Uttar Pradesh and was born to a family of farmers in a village called Narayanpur Kothi. Since he was the brightest among his siblings, his mother encouraged him to pursue studies, supporting him through the many ups and downs in his life. In 1953, he travelled to Deoria which is 25 kilometres from his village, and studied in an intermediate college there. Coming in contact with the Rashtriya Swayamsevak Sangh (RSS), he became a lifelong member. Having got admission to St Andrews College in Gorakhpur, he graduated with a BA, but his brothers encouraged him to study further for his Bachelor's in Education and then his Master's in Education, which he completed in Kushinagar, the adjoining district. This is when he was offered a job at a handsome salary, above the market rate, at a school in Deoria. But Ganga Singh had another passion—to build an educational institution. He sought the help of the Raja of Tamkuhi to support this institution, which was first established in an old, abandoned building that the raja vacated and gave to Ganga Singh for this purpose. His brothers were annoyed, asking him to take up the well-paying job as a schoolteacher, but Ganga Singh persisted, supported in this endeavour only by his mother. After a hard day at the school, he would return to his home to have his meals and then sleep at the school itself to ensure that the next day began on time. In time, he was elected a Block Pramukh and then an MLA, winning a second term from this constituency in 2017. The sincerity of his work is evident. Even though he is more than eighty years old, the desire to do something for his area remains. When I see him today, I see the same young man getting up early and sleeping late to build his school, which has educated thousands in the region.

Priti Pandey, who is in her late twenties, comes from an ordinary family in Deoria. She lost her father at an early age and her mother and brother brought her up together with her younger sister. Neither her mother nor her brother ever allowed the sisters to accept a job in a private company, fearing that this would be looked down upon by society. As a result, Priti turned down a job offer as an airhostess when her family prohibited this. She joined Nehru Yuva Kendra activities locally, where she gained prominence as a good speaker. A chance to go to Hyderabad to be part of the Global Entrepreneurship Summit gave her confidence and insights when she met other women from different parts of the world pursuing their entrepreneurial dream. That was a turning point for Priti and she decided to focus on the cause of women's enterprises, helping to motivate and challenge girls to take economic risks. She has helped other women start enterprises by becoming a mentor to them. These enterprises include one for sanitary napkins, which are being distributed across the district through her efforts. She is practical in the realization that her life will take her where marriage takes her, but we know that wherever she goes, she will keep the women's empowerment agenda close to her life's work.

These citizens bring out the ordinary lives, aspirations and striving that are an unheralded part of Middle India. They are ordinary people who saw the struggles of life as inevitable and yet contributed. They continue to contribute to the district and society where they belong, standing their ground in the district square.

The village square balances the tower

Niall Ferguson explains a perennial societal dynamic in his book *The Square and the Tower*[6] as the contrast between the village square, where citizens such as Barrister, Ganga Singh and Priti reside, and the tower, from which the ruler keeps control. In a networked world, the traditional power of the tower is being eroded as the square is energized by citizens and their association. For many decades after our independence, we were dominated by the tower. Through the vote, the citizen could change governments and caste politics created social upliftment for the marginalized. Now that the Middle has critical mass, a new phase is possible where the aspirational common citizen in the smaller towns and districts, able, motivated and networked, can accelerate development to add to the political benefits of democracy. The Square in the Middle will add to our republican energies and bring the nation to life. The tower will continue to play an important role as a regulator and arbitrator in society. But with 800 million citizens gathering in the 'Middle Square', the country needs a new dynamic and building role involving the citizen, with increased opportunities to associate.

The size, complexity, use of technology and modernization of the Middle Square is asking for a new horizontal relationship among citizens. This will supplement existing vertical relationships with government. The Tower must remain and in some cases should be strengthened, but it should not overshadow the Square. In this imagination, the government would cater to the Bottom of the Diamond directly, not a trivial number at 250 million citizens, who remain poor and require direct support. Citizens in the Middle, on the other hand, must be given enabling platforms to associate and build. Instead of using the state to serve the vast majority in the Middle, we need to reimagine development by *enabling* citizens, a goal our founders believed in. This does not require copying the West in welfarism or changing the Constitution; it can be achieved by recognizing the importance of the Square in our republic and recasting government as an enabling watchtower.

Our current approach for serving the citizen imitates the method adopted by the UK, France and Germany, who designed the state to work in welfare mode after the Second World War. The UK, France and Germany increased their spending on welfare services by increasing government spend from 10 per cent of national income to 40–50 per cent of national income between the 1950s and the 1980s.[7] At 10 per cent of national income, the government was primarily focused on the 'regalian' functions of police, courts, army, foreign affairs, general administration, etc. The state expanded considerably after the Second World War. Anxious about post-war recovery, it increased its spend, which added 30–40 per cent of GDP as government spend over three decades. This increase was split into two broad buckets—providing health, education and other services and replacement and transfer payments to the needy. The spend of the state stabilized at the 40–50 per cent of GDP range in the 1980s even though in the UK, the Thatcher regime and in the US, the Reagan administration sought to lower it.[8]

Today, in India, the government spends on average 15–20 per cent of GDP, combining Central and state spending.[9] This takes care of both the 'regalian' functions as well as welfare activities. India must plan an increase in this spend as it increases its tax base. However, instead of creating a bloated welfare state, it can use its republican energies to keep government spend limited to the 25 per cent range. It must invest in improving the core functions, with higher spending in state institutions, and allocate higher amounts for a safety net for the 250 million citizens at the Bottom. In the Middle, it should rely on citizens to provide services while regulating these activities better to unleash greater civic action. This service, regulated better by a stronger state, will not be from a centralized top-down entity but will be local, contextual and therefore more effective and efficient, also generating local employment. Instead of implementing policies and spending money mechanically, it will seek citizens' participation by easing their path and providing behavioural nudges.[10] India still has an opportunity to avoid the path Europe took, creating a bureaucratized state that smothers societal action. It should also not go down the laissez-faire route of the US, where big business at the Top, the 1 per cent, dominates the economy. This will further exacerbate economic disparities in the largest democracy in the world, which is unsustainable. The state must take a middle path by

Welcoming 500 leaders at the induction ceremony of a fifteen-day odyssey (Photo by Priya Goswami)

Induction speech, explaining the hardships and joys of the fifteen-day journey (Photo by Priya Goswami)

Flagging-off ceremony of the Jagriti Yatra with guests and yatris (Photo by Priya Goswami)

Ceremonial breaking of a *narial* (coconut) at the start of the journey (Photo by Priya Goswami)

Common room in the train—the location for discussions on the move (Photo by Sarah Hickson)

Participants deep in conversation on the platform before boarding the train

At Aravind Eye Care, Madurai, learning at the feet of the role model

Kanyakumari—at the edge of our country, taking an oath for the Amrit Kaal (Photo by Priya Goswami)

Nalanda—meditating on the hallowed grounds of an ancient university (Photo by Priya Goswami)

Tilonia, Rajasthan—where women from across the world are learning about solar technology (Photo by Fahad Yunus Mohammed)

Walking back from the banyan in the fog in Barpar, Deoria (Photo by Ayaz)

Biz Gyan Tree exercise in Barpar (Photo by Sarah Hickson)

Valedictory photograph in Bapu Dham at the Sabarmati Ashram (Photo by Maneesh Agnihotri)

Planning the Banyan Revolution with the mighty banyan in the background (Photo by Maneesh Agnihotri)

The Internet Saathi programme is being implemented in Deoria and six adjoining districts (Photo by Maneesh Agnihotri)

The Jagriti Enterprise Centre—Purvanchal (JECP) Phase I multipurpose hall that started functioning recently (Photo by **Rajeev Rai**)

improving its core functions and building capabilities to enable enterprise and economy in the Middle, where the majority lives, so that societal action is used locally and with greater efficiency. The police, army, administration, judiciary and foreign affairs are functions ready for an inter-generational overhaul at the seventy-fifth anniversary mark. These capabilities will strengthen what some call the *'Power On'* approach to ensure that social strife, national calamities, regulatory functions and national defence can be managed well. This will take up bandwidth, energies and investments from the government. The second capability that the state should build will enable citizens to experience a different type of state power described as *'Power To'*,[11] which will give flow to the republic and support 'positive freedoms', especially in the Middle. A smaller but stronger state with an enabling function for powering 800 million citizens in the Middle, including provision of local service through enterprise, will keep our fiscal burden low and the services localized and effective.

This can happen only if the government actively brings people together. Over seventy-five years, our democracy has classified citizens through the process of voting every five years. We can use this knowledge to bring together citizens on a continuous basis in the act of building. A first step has been taken through JAM, but this still serves as a conduit of digital service from government to people, albeit an efficient and safer one. The requirement is for a stronger association that enables collaboration 'between citizens', aided by technology and platforms, a topic covered later in Chapter 11. This must start by changing our mental framework towards citizens, labelling them as creators who come together to build, rather than mere voters who vote a government into power. Advances in technology, connectivity, attitudes and a can-do spirit in our Middle will allow this model to succeed. This change in narrative would require courage from citizens, civil society, the private sector and government leaders and a departure from unilateral welfarism, which has created a complex and inefficient state in Europe but is still seen as a key goal of governance. In the Middle, the government should 'shift from offering solutions driven by the national bureaucracy to incentivizing, enabling, and inspiring experimentation and innovation from the local and individual upward'.[12]

The Swachh Bharat Mission is an example of such a partnership and an example of Power To, where the government played the role of a convener and enabler and the citizen participated actively. Open defecation is an issue that could only be solved through large-scale citizen participation. Various civil society organizations, including Yatri alumni, were mustered to build capacity, and large-scale communication was used to create awareness, which has been elaborated in Chapter 13. While this programme was a national initiative, it was largely powered by local citizens at the district, mandal and village level.

Harnessing collective intelligence

For similar citizen collaboration, insights from Thomas W. Malone a.k.a. Tom's study on collective intelligence could come in handy. Tom is a professor at Massachusetts Institute of Technology (MIT), where he founded the Centre for Collective Intelligence. I met Tom in Tokyo during a conference where I was presenting the story of emerging markets and the transformation of India as a rapidly growing economy, while Tom was taking a session on the role of information technology. Tom hides his razor-sharp intellect behind an easy-going manner. Over the course of a dinner conversation, Tom discussed the findings of a research his team had done recently to understand the collective intelligence of a group. Individual intelligence, which is quantified through tests such as the JEE or the SAT, helps understand individual performance. Group intelligence, on the other hand, measures the intelligence, and therefore the relative performance, of groups of people working together to solve an issue. Three attributes marked successful groups which were therefore classified as intelligent—'social perceptiveness', 'equal contribution by members' and the 'role of women' in that group. Most importantly, performance was not related to the sum of the individual intelligence of members in the group. It proves what we sense in life—very intelligent people seldom make for a successful collective. It is a socially strong group, where participation is strong and where the women's voices are included, that gives societal results.

In a subsequent book, *Superminds*,[13] Tom expanded this theory, outlining how collective intelligence works by joining groups of people to create impact. Categorizing *Superminds* into five broad segments—Hierarchies, Democracies, Markets, Communities and Ecosystems— he outlines how a collective has more potency than just improved computing power. People *plus* computers, connected through a network, results in successful societal collaboration. The narrow technological use of robots, automation and machine learning does create human progress, but if people relate to computing power, society progresses faster through the use of collective intelligence.

Tom says, 'Groups of people and computers, together, are far more collectively intelligent than was ever possible.'[14]

To understand the underlying ethics that inform collective action and citizen mindsets, we can refer to research by psychologist Jonathan Haidt. Haidt talks of how the WEIRD (Western, Educated, Industrialized, Rich and Democratic) category of citizens has dominated citizen narratives as protagonists, stating, 'The WEIRDer you are, the more you see a world full of separate objects, rather than relationships.'[15] In contrast, Haidt asserts that eastern societies look at situations and form associations keeping in mind the context, the relationships and the morality, which goes beyond individual fairness or harm. In discovering this contrast, three concepts of morality were uncovered—the ethics of autonomy, the ethics of community and the ethics of divinity. Haidt, himself from a rational WEIRD background where autonomy dominates, came to the state of Odisha in India and himself struggled to come to terms with the two ethics beyond autonomy. He discovered that Indian society lived by an ethic in which community played a key role—'people are first and foremost members of larger entities such as families, teams, armies, companies, tribes and nations'.[16] The third ethic of divinity was even more difficult for Haidt, an atheist, to grasp, but it was evident that divinity played a key role for Indians. The ethics of divinity commands that 'people are . . . temporary vessels within which a divine soul has been implanted . . . not just animals with an extra serving of consciousness'.[17] The ethics of community and the ethics of divinity can occasionally lead to oppression and strife. But not recognizing these ethics is tantamount to not understanding the core of a citizen's world view in a typical non-WEIRD society. With this understanding, we can communicate, motivate and develop citizens not simply based on an economic, rational, utilitarian view but consider the deep influence of community and faith.

Both Malone and Haidt's work are relevant for Middle India. While the Middle does not have high-end computing power, with smartphones, citizens can enhance group intelligence, connecting with each other in larger numbers. Similarly, following Haidt's insights, while we can encourage citizens to chase the economic, utilitarian dream in large cities, most in smaller towns and districts have community and divinity as part of their reality. These two, combined with increasing autonomy, will create a higher form of societal group intelligence relevant for India.

Challenging the Pavlovian Pyramid

Traditionally, citizens and workers are still seen as Pavlovian opportunists, incapable of aspiring to anything but a hierarchy of needs. Another Pyramid that defines this imagination is being challenged both by the behaviour of the Middle, and by thinkers such as Balagangadhara. Abraham Maslow's Pyramid of Needs, an idea first documented in 1943, starts at the bottom with 'physiological needs' of food, clothing, shelter, leading upwards to 'security needs' for safety, leading next to 'belongingness and love', to 'esteem', before culminating in 'self-actualization needs' at the top. Mimicking the Bottom of the Pyramid metaphor, we equate the motivations of millions with *roti, kapda aur makaan* as linked to physiological needs. Some time back, this picture was comprehensively punctured when microfinance demonstrated that belonging needs, alongside food, clothing and shelter, are equally important for the poor. Tata Nano's dismal sales, outlined earlier, hinted that positioning a car as 'cheap' turned off those it was targeting—clearly esteem mattered to those in the Middle. The explosion of mobile telephony carries with it the belonging need of communication, as evidenced by the surprising growth of smartphones in the Middle despite its cost relative to the average income. Art and culture, once seen on the self-actualization frontier, are part of daily life in the Middle.

Balagangadhara asserts that Maslow's 'need hierarchy' reflects a specific western cultural and religious tradition. The pyramid borrows heavily from a mechanical conception of humans and the image of God commanding humans from up top. It classifies different hierarchies that consider happiness a consequence of satisfying *desires*. Indian traditions, he suggests, focus not on satisfying desires but on removing ignorance caused by desires. By addressing ignorance, which is not a result of material needs but is based on an inner compass, the hierarchy may not dissolve fully, but it is softened. Balagangadhara and others believe a 'need-based approach' is culturally specific to a certain tradition. Indian culture takes initiative away from external needs and gives power to the inner motivations of citizens, which include material growth but are not limited or defined by it. If this is at the core of citizens' motivation and guides our theory of growth and development, it may also offer a more sustainable path of development for India.

Looking at the citizens in the Middle in this manner— as aspirational but in control of their desires, creating happiness through meaning—could lead to a new approach to citizen association. We can begin to measure human progress through a focus on associations and service, which remains the dominant sector of our GDP and is poised to grow as India becomes the largest country on the planet. We should encourage manufacturing but without the anxiety that it has to form the bulk of the Indian economic experience. Instead of capital being the dominant resource for fostering growth, human capital and enterprise would lead the factors of production, redefining well-being and national growth, with material growth being only one component of this approach.

This citizen-centric approach, led by those from the Middle, would also shape a new national identity and a new modernity. The nation-building sprint over the coming twenty-five years would be defined by our citizens and our own culture. It is best led by citizens from the Middle, the largest segment, who collaborate both with the Top and the Bottom, creating a new modernization that considers the needs both of community and society[18] elaborated later in the book. They will modernize as old patterns of kinship to family, religion and caste give way to wider patterns of association based on interests, vocations and geographies, and to the act of nation-building. Some of this will be driven by urbanization, which forges new associations, but this can also happen in smaller towns and districts, with widespread connectivity creating a dispersed and decentralized urbanization close to community and often imbued by divinity that is anchored locally. This is more likely after COVID-19 seems to have discredited metro cities in the eyes of those living in the Middle.

Beyond political and civic leaders, this national identity will be shaped, as Fukuyama says, '. . . from the bottom up by poets, philosophers, religious leaders, novelists, musicians, and other individuals with no access to political power'.[19] This is based on cultural and value-based associations that have been the hallmark of citizen groups in India. It is also based on the theme that 'social mobilization . . . is a by-product of the emergence of new identities as people become aware of shared experiences and values'.[20] The social mobilization of millions of Indians in the Middle, a shared experience as we build and new aspiration will be the core of this national identity.

'A nation built by building'

Citizens coming together to build should be the very definition of citizenship. As David Brooks puts it, 'A people is made by making. A nation is built by building.'[21] To promote this definition, one must power community building, which has been weakened in small towns and districts. If previously, the bonds of village life kept communities together, gathering in moments of bereavement, birth and marriage, then today, we need to create communities where citizens come together to build. In these conversations, the starting points are the possibilities of the future, our heritage and the issues of the present. Strength-based community building takes off from local pride but creates a superstructure of joint ambition, achieving what was not possible by individuals. In this, udyamita can be the micro-process that disciplines nation-building, giving it structure, strength and spirit.

We took this thought back to Deoria, where Jagriti is building an enterprise centre and encouraging udyamis by creating a group of citizens who can change that area through a regional mission.

'Naya Deoria' was one such local effort aimed at re-envisioning the town of Deoria Sadar. This small town became a district HQ when Deoria district was carved out of the Gorakhpur district just after Independence; at the time, Deoria had a population of 1.5 lakh. Today, it has a population of 4 lakh and in addition, during working hours, at least another 1.5 lakh people come for chores such as buying vegetables, going to the court or government offices and other errands, creating a daytime population almost four times the original. This results in a traffic jam at Subhash Chowk, the main town crossing, at 11 a.m. that puts the 10 a.m. traffic snarl in Gurgaon to shame. It also creates local mess and confusion. The realization that something had to be done was evident. Led by Jagriti's Urbanization Centre of Excellence, we rallied the mayor of Deoria, Alka Singh, the local MLA, Janmejaya Singh, and others into a forum where two other issues beyond traffic jams were also highlighted for joint action—a more efficient cleaning system, including a modern sewerage system, and a digital network that provides safe access to the Internet for the whole of Deoria.

We shared this vision with the community and the District Magistrate. With the mayor in attendance, we organized a meeting in the local town hall with sixty to seventy local citizens. As we discussed each of the three issues, suggestions came thick and fast. Citizens accurately pointed out which roads could be made one-way, where the sabzi mandi could be shifted, how a sewerage system could be created ahead of time in those areas where the town was expanding and so on. Those attending the meeting realized that garbage collection required active participation of the citizens to tackle this issue by using dustbins provided by the mayor. This also relaxed the tension with the mayor as those in the hall recognized their role as partners in this process. This dialogue created a shift from Power On efforts by the government to Power To efforts by the community, where both administration and citizens saw their roles more clearly. Lumping all problems on the administration was as wrong, as blaming citizens for the garbage that lay outside their homes. This initiative created a group of eleven leaders who, in turn, are working with other citizens on this project, which we hope to fructify shortly.

India can make rapid strides if it incentivizes the Tower to foster greater associations between its citizens in the Middle Square. But if 'revolutions are rare, reforms, perhaps are even rarer'.[22] Those wanting to reform the local administration while simultaneously involving citizens must fight both extremes of the spectrum, keeping the revolutionary in check and the conservative egged on. Citizens are not looking for a sudden transformation of society which can be done through a dramatic, emotional appeal. Hence, the reformer must present the project with care and in detail using a cultural appeal as much as a developmental one. The reformer requires far more skill, courage and endurance than the revolutionary and needs the support of institutions.

A nation is the combined soul of citizens in action. Leaders such as Pandit Deendayal Upadhyaya called this 'chitti'[23], a spiritual manifestation of nation that is not limited to its political border. National meaning for a young republic is manifested through citizens' efforts, articulated in recent years as *sabka prayas* by Prime Minister Modi. As we look beyond the seventy-fifth anniversary, jettisoning old memories and creating new stories shaped by citizens, a new identity is already taking shape. This will power a new rise led by the citizen, focused on shining the Diamond.

10

Districts: *The Theatre of Action*

वीर तुम बढ़े चलो! धीर तुम बढ़े चलो!
सामने पहाड़ हो, सिंह की दहाड़ हो तुम निडर डरो नहीं,
तुम निडर डटो वहीं

—द्वारिका प्रसाद माहेश्वरी

(O brave keep moving! O resolute keep moving!
Be it a mountain or the roar of a lion, you must
keep courage, you must hold your ground)

—Dwarika Prasad Maheshwari

Gandhi imagined India as a village republic. Post-Independence, the action shifted in exactly the opposite direction. Large cities such as Calcutta, Mumbai, Chennai, New Delhi and Bangalore, designed to serve the colonial economy, continued to dominate our social and economic landscape. Sandwiched in the middle of a village and a large city lies a district, which is present in India's political consciousness but has been ignored socially and economically. This neglect allowed institutions created in the colonial era to dominate the district and shaped the language of development in the Middle.

Deoria[24], where Jagriti was born, is one such Tier 3 district of the country and has a population of about 40 lakh. Tucked away on the eastern edge of Uttar Pradesh, it borders Bihar to its east and Gorakhpur to its west. It is about 100 km long and 75 km wide. The river Narayani hugs its east, and the holy river of Saryu borders its south. Its name suggests a merging of *Dev*, or god and *Aranya* or forest; an area of sacred groves justified by the ethereal trees that dot its farmland. The Buddha tramped here, passing through this area on his last journey, leaving his mortal body in adjoining Kushinagar. Valmiki penned the Ramayana in the adjoining forests and Kabir's philosophy has a large presence with a number of Kabir Panthis here. The district was home to Devraha Baba and Baba Raghav Das, two sages who had national following, giving it a spiritual aura.

On one visit, the airplane took a wider than normal circle over Gorakhpur airport and I glimpsed the rural surroundings of Deoria. It was a clear day and so the snow-capped peaks of the Himalayas stretching away in the distance up north were also visible. This sheet of ice is responsible for the torrential monsoons that mark this region, called the Terai. In its aerial beauty, the scene was breathtaking, with green fields dotting the countryside and rivers and tributaries snaking south from the white wall up north, with green hedge-like trees on their banks.

Deoria has a quiet intellectualism that is difficult to recognize unless one knows its history and culture, hinted at by the presence of the Nagari Pracharini Sabha, a renowned literary organization. The town of Deoria has dance and music training academies in the dozens, with cultural festivals organized every year. Students from Deoria score high marks in UP board and ICSE examinations and are industrious students at Gorakhpur University. The women of Deoria are aspirational and spunky. This was on display when a young bride, on discovering the absence of any indoor toilet in her husband's home, promptly returned to her parents' place. This led to an equally prompt monetary reward for this act of marital bravery from Dr Pathak of Sulabh International. Over the past few years, new hotels have sprung up, many new dealerships have come to town and one can see a palpable rise in the consumer power in the district. Smaller towns within the area, such as Fazilnagar, Patherdeva, Rampur Karkhana and Tamkuhi Raj, are emerging and in the 1100 villages of the district resides enormous societal energy, something we noticed as we implemented the Internet Saathi programme. The population density of this fertile rural area is one of the highest in the world. The districts of Purvanchal, barring the three Tier 2 districts of Varanasi, Allahabad and Gorakhpur, are very much like Deoria, backward and slow-growing but with rising aspirations, like other districts in the Middle. For example, the widespread use of Facebook, WhatsApp and Instagram takes one by surprise.

From the time of its creation just after Independence, Deoria has grown steadily but in most matters of economic development, it lags behind the country and is a poor part of a backward state like Uttar Pradesh. Purvanchal has twenty-four such districts with 70 million Indians, about the same population as Britain or Gujarat. The region has a per capita income that is lower than that of Uttar

Pradesh[25] and half the national average. That is because there is hardly any industry. The sugarcane mills the district was known for have shut down, reducing from ten to only one. The exchange of value between Deoria and the national economy is one-way, with goods coming in and money, whatever little there is, going out. The last district enterprise report sounded a forlorn note: 'At present there is no report of direct export from the district.'[26] Yes, there are businesspeople who are setting up housing colonies and trying to set up industries. Dealerships are also coming up, but for a district that has more people than the country of Uruguay, the number of industries can be counted on one's fingers. The industrial zone that was set up some decades ago is lacklustre and the few industries that exist are static, with little to show by way of growth. Agriculture is the mainstay of the area, located in a region that is one of the most fertile in India but which has also made Deoria overdependent on agriculture. As a result, per capita income has risen at a rate that is lower than the national average, showing that there is a risk of the gap between the Top and the Middle, on an average, growing larger.

A vibrant society

Society, though, is alive and kicking. A recent Holi spent in Deoria town's by-lanes reminded me of my time in my housing colony in Mumbai. In this case, it was not just a colony—the entire town was out in revelry, creating a riot of colours. As I made my way through its *galis* accompanied by a small van with music blaring at a decibel level that was harming us all, thrice was I the target of balloons filled with water, launched with painful precision from rooftops adjoining the narrow alleys. Bhang was being consumed in steel glasses by older men. There was a general scene of revelry without the social hesitation one feels in public places in large cities.

That is the story of Deoria and many other districts in the Middle. A big heart, energetic citizens, strong communities but making do without industry, employment or helpful governance. A state of economic and social neglect, almost ennui, has remained in these districts from the time of Independence. This is also evident in the divide between the Civil Lines, the administrative part of the town, and the actual town itself. The town is growing but groaning as those from adjoining villages trickle in every year. Many take the harder, emotionally wrenching direct route to Mumbai, Pune or Chennai. In many ways, Deoria is also somewhere in the middle, both in economic terms and in the imagination of its citizens. A place you must go to almost every day from a local village and then one day, you either migrate to it or take a train out to a big city. At its core, the story of districts like Deoria is one of flight, a flight to employment.

In one matter, districts like Deoria get full attention—politics. There is enormous political focus on such Tier 3 districts, with approximately 20 lakh votes in each accounting for 43 per cent nationwide. But social and economic neglect continues, creating fissures in daily lives and an aspirational gap that cannot be papered over. On issues of economic upliftment and bringing people together, these districts have not moved forward much over the past seventy-five years.

The task of building India is the task of building these districts of India, particularly Tier 3 districts like Deoria and Tier 2 districts, the layer above. Of the 740 districts in the country, only 240 are Tier 2 and Tier 3, but with a population of over 800 million Indians, they house most citizens. Focusing on these districts makes sense—doing so for a few districts can address the issues of a major part of our population. Yet, till recently, economically, our nation seemed oblivious to them, jolted only by traumatic incidents like COVID-induced migration. They feature every five years during elections when the campaigning for votes starts and counting ends. They are the political force that waits for five years and explodes on the national stage at the time of elections, toppling or making governments. In the remaining period, the energies, the values and the dreams of these Middle districts go largely unnoticed. Whether in the north, south, east or west, these 240 districts and communities are needed to power our nation forward. It is time we bring out their social and economic potential to match their political relevance.

Discovery of Deoria

To fully understand Deoria, I took a two-day 'mystery shopper' tour of its interiors some years ago. In my normal mode of transportation, an Innova, real conversations are restricted by the car window. I decided to go into the district wearing desi clothes and on a 'tempo', a larger autorickshaw that is used by locals to travel between villages and small towns in the district. The mystery shopper technique is used to test attitudes and approaches to customers. I thought it could give me a social and economic temperature of the district. The exploration would help me understand those who lived in the district through one-to-one conversations. For good measure, I also took along a colleague to help document the experience when key moments of insight arose.

The starting point was the small bus stop below the flyover that is now a major feature of Deoria town. We got there at 7 p.m. and as I stood waiting, a tempo owner came by and asked me to line up for the next batch that was to leave for the town of Tamkuhi Raj, close to the border with Bihar. I got talking to him and like most small-town citizens, he responded immediately with details of his family. He had a son and a daughter, and both were studying in a private school. He seemed passionate about his daughter's education. 'I hope she gets the best opportunities as she is the smarter of the two,' he said. He enthusiastically pointed to the private school across the road where she studied. On asking why a private school, he explained that a free government school would not give his children quality education.

By this time, the tempo had arrived. It was jam-packed. That did not prevent the tempo owner from 'arranging' my colleague, myself and another passenger, a *sanyasi*, into the vehicle, which by then must have had fifteen passengers. The sanyasi, handsome like a Hollywood hero, was travelling with his full kitchen tucked into a bag, pots and pans so tightly squeezed that only a soft jingle betrayed their presence. The sanyasi was making his way to the border where he was to help perform a puja. Detecting a tantric aura about him, I let my conversation drift. Very soon, the conversation was picked up by Ahmed, a young person who clambered on to the tempo at a stop near a nondescript village. Ahmed had one daughter, and like the tempo owner, proceeded to tell me how he did not want another child as he was keen to ensure that his girl got the best of whatever resources he had. His four brothers had left the area in search of work, some working in Kanpur and one working in Muscat as a welder. He was the junior brother who was taking care of their elderly mother and was also, clearly, a dedicated father.

As the tempo moved ahead, a lady with her young daughter clambered aboard. Her mobile was running low on charge. She sought help and was immediately offered support from three passengers with mobile phones. She made a few calls locating the relatives who were to pick her and her daughter up at the next stop. By this time, it was past 9 p.m. and yet, I could sense that she felt safe in the tempo, with her relatives ready to receive her at the next stop. The tempo arrived at Tamkuhi Raj, where we had to change vehicles en route to Sewrahi, where we had decided to spend the night. We thought it best to get a bite to eat before we ventured deeper. At the small *dhaba* where we ate its simple fare, I struck up a conversation with a local teacher who was travelling back from an adjoining district, Mau, where he was posted—this was his weekly commute home. We boarded the next tempo and started our last leg of the journey to Sewrahi, a small town close to the Narayani.

We were told that there was a *dharmshala* where we could sleep and bathe the next morning. It was close to midnight when we entered Sewrahi, and when we saw the familiar silhouette of its train station, we took a snap decision to sleep on its benches, thinking the lullaby of passing trains would help. Just twenty minutes later, we knew we had made a mistake. The quantity and aggression of the mosquitos in Sewrahi was at a new level compared to even Deoria town. A local discotheque had been organized next to the railway station and continued to operate till 4 a.m. Their Bhojpuri songs combined seamlessly with the ravenous buzz of the mosquitoes. Five frustrating hours, ducking vainly under thin sheets brought to cover ourselves, left us mottled with mosquito bites. To make matters worse, at the crack of dawn, we observed that locals wanting to learn driving were using the other side of the railway platform to rev up their cars in Mad Max fashion. This early wake-up call saw us getting up to trudge over to the dharmshala for a bath and a cup of steaming hot tea. This seemed like the edge of the world, but it had character.

On this second day, we travelled to Fazilnagar, another small *kasba*, and went in unannounced to a private school in the main bazaar. The school principal was courteous but asked me to wait as he had to 'ring in' the next class after the interval. The gong sounded and, true to his word, he came back and gave me his full attention with a quick overview of the school and its activities. I asked him his reason for starting the school and how he was thinking of scaling up. His answer was inspiring—he recalled a time when he understood that his own children were not getting a quality education and knowing that a school could solve this. He had rented the premises but sounded positive and committed, full of action. This was soon on display as a lady came in suggesting gently that she was not able to pay this month's school fee. She wore a burqa but had removed her veil to have this conversation with the principal. They negotiated; the principal probed, trying to understand if the need was genuine. Satisfied that this was not a case of the lady asking for a freebie, he relented. You could see the visible relief on the face of the mother as she thanked him and went away.

Spirited citizens, colonial administration

My two-day 'deep Deoria' expedition made me physically uncomfortable but lightened my spirits. Seeing the many ordinary people of Deoria go about their lives in a dignified manner, ever optimistic and wanting to move ahead, surprised and inspired me. They were not putting on a show for the school inspector—these were genuine conversations. The yearning to do something for the family, for society, for the country, for the next generation, for someone else was remarkable. The sense of community, even on that railway station with its roaring cars, was palpable. It was the mark of a society in which members looked after each other. This society, while not particularly rich, was strangely at peace with itself. The societal energies inherent in its citizens are very much required and ready for the nation-building project.

In contrast, the apparatus for governing such districts remains about the same since Lord Cornwallis instituted it back in 1793. From the Patwari to the Kanungo to the Tehsildar to the SDM and District Magistrate, leaders and roles have changed very little for centuries. Post-Independence, the institution of a District Development Officer (DDO) and the Block Development Officer (BDO) created a structure that put development on the agenda too. But the original structure, designed 230 years back, a few decades after the banyan in my village took root, still retains administrative and financial power.

These administrative rules started with British corruption. The first Governor General of India, Warren Hastings, was tried in the British Parliament in 1787 on twenty charges of corruption. This was led famously by the statesman, philosopher and economist Edmund Burke. At that time, the British public and Parliament felt that the imperial project was floundering. British officers in the districts, alongside Hastings, had been accused of mismanagement, corruption and personal gain. Hastings was accused of transferring personal monies to the tune of 2.7 million pounds to England. His wife Marian had been seen in high society circles in Britain bedecked in jewellery worth thousands of pounds, becoming the centre of gossip. Lord Cornwallis, second in command in the Battle of Yorktown in the US, where the British were defeated, replaced Hastings. A trial that ran for seven years finally acquitted Hastings, but it led the British Parliament to rule that the conduct of business, revenue collection and administration would be tightly controlled through processes requiring detailed documentation. As the historian Jon Wilson puts it, 'The new system Cornwallis created replaced the movement of people with the circulation of paper . . . all rights had been reduced to writing.'[27] This is when the administrative system started 'speaking in triplicate'. It was not to stop revenue leakage from citizens. In this first step, it was to protect the East India Company and the British government from *its own officials*. Even then, many civil service officers returned from India rich enough to buy wealthy estates in Britain.

The bigger damage this did was in the rigid application of rules on the peasantry and local landlords. Conversations were substituted with procedures. The face-to-face negotiation that took place in the past, which created a political flow between citizens and the governed, was replaced by paper. To quote Jon Wilson again, 'The new maze of paperwork blocked the creation of the public, reciprocal relationship between the state and local lords.'[28] The requirement of the shareholders and the British government to control its *own* corruption trumped local conditions and relationships.

Some of what prevailed at that time is pictured in the film *Lagaan*, which is more accurate than I originally believed. In the film, even during a drought, the collector collected the same taxes from the landholders as before. To impose this paper and procedure-based administration sans the conversation, the British made themselves even more aloof and imperial, mixing as little as possible with the local population. They created administrative townships mostly around what were previous military camps of the East India Company. These new settlements consisted of a cluster of one-storey brick buildings, the offices of the Kachahari, the collectorate, a treasury, a record room, a court, some official residences and sometimes a cemetery and a church.[29]

Many recent studies have shown that this seemingly organized, hedge-lined apparatus of the British, termed the 'steel frame', was clueless. Its norms were ad hoc and it had no strategic rationale for governance, doing deep damage to Indian society.[30] The British looted India on a massive scale[31] and left in an equally disorganized retreat. Indians were fed the myth of this administrative set-up's efficiency and honesty. I remember my grandfather handing me *Pitt Vs Fox*, a book about the famous rivalry of two eminent British Prime Ministers over a generation. I was dazzled by the arguments in the British Parliament outlined in the book, little understanding that both Pitt and Fox and their rule was neither noble nor stabilizing. Pitt, for instance, defended Hastings's corrupt imperial methods as Prime Minister.[32] As a generation, we were told that post-Independence, the 'steel frame' and these institutions at the district gave India stability. The reality is India continued to grow *despite* bureaucratic overlordship.

A moment arose in the 1920s to change the spirit of this administration, when the Congress started playing a role in provincial governments. The Montagu Chelmsford Reforms of 1919 suggested keeping the district apparatus in charge of policing and finance, while handing over other resources to 'popular control'. Gandhi believed this effort could shape institutions with swadeshi, local, bottom-up values where 'constructive work' was reflected in the approach to managing a district. But in 1928, an important report authored by Motilal Nehru smothered this vision. Asked by the Congress to shape a kind of mock constitution, Motilal's ideas remained colonial, 'retaining the imperial distribution of authority between different tiers of government, in many cases merely replacing British command with Indian deliberation'.[33] Gandhi's vision of our country as a people-led, 'bottom-up' movement was ignored, and the document aimed at 'the ability to command the bureaucratic machinery of state as its end goal . . . to take over instruments of imperial state power and use them for nationalist ends.'[34] The committee that authored this report included the thirty-eight-year-old Jawaharlal Nehru as its secretary.

I see the architecture and thought process of the Cornwallis system still present in Deoria. The Civil Lines locality that consists of bungalows which house senior government officers is cut off from the majority they govern. The 40 lakh citizens of Deoria can vote every five years, but the structure that governs them remains much as it was before Independence. Like British officials 'trying to assert their embattled, isolated sense of power amidst an Indian population they did not trust and could barely communicate with',[35] the district administration of a Tier 3 district remains aloof and imperial. Individuals like a proactive District Magistrate, through personal effort, make themselves accessible if the district is lucky to get people of that mindset.

Numerous administrative reforms have come and gone in the seventy-five years after Indian independence, but at the district level the core ideas and spirit of the system remains inspired by the 'steel frame'. When an entourage of cars with the red light of the district officer comes flashing past, the majority of those in the street still make way hurriedly. The discussion between local leaders and the government officers still requires the bowing and scraping that took place in front of the empire. The 'steel frame' was put to tactical use by our founders in consolidating the nation immediately after Independence, but in these districts, its continuation is throttling the nation-building project.

Local leaders, local institutions

The resilience of such districts is largely due to the structure and network of faith, family and community inherent in Indian society. Young and old, men and women continue to associate with each other to carry on with life. The core of Indian society has remained a community and a network. Their character, as I saw in my 'tempo travels', remains upright. Their aspirations are still fresh, their sights are still on a moral ideal that faith and family instil in them, and which community re-enforces. They deal with the paper-oriented government by going to administrative offices, to the local *thanedar* for succour, to the local *Patwari* for land adjudication, often using whatever money they have, to move their file along. Given a chance, they would rather avoid this encounter. They get a bad rap as the Top of the Diamond sees them as uncouth and incapable of collaboration.

The future of India resides in these districts and the future of a district like Deoria lies in rebuilding the community and putting it to use—a community where 'relationships are felt deeply, when there are histories of trust, a shared sense of mutual belonging, norms of mutual commitments, habits of mutual assistance, and real affection from one heart and soul to another.'[36] This coming together of people must be enabled, championed and encouraged by an updated model of government. The old model of 'controlling' the population must be recognized as the product of a bygone era in which the goal of governance was devoid of development. Its aim was to divide society and the republican energies of our citizens were not available then.

The Banyan Revolution described earlier is one way of addressing the development of these Middle districts. What shape can the Banyan Revolution take in a typical district that will make it meaningful and provide economic and social gains? What are the institutions we can create through societal partnerships and government enablement? What is the shape of the district and local government that will enable this? Can the Swachh Bharat Mission be considered as the first national project enabled by the government at the district level but led by society, as outlined in a later chapter? Can the ongoing Jal Jeevan Mission be counted as the second such effort? At the district level, the Banyan Revolution must start with local leaders. They have a long-term interest in taking their area forward. Parvati Singh, Arjun Sharma, Rahul Mani and R.C. Kushwaha are all udyamis in Deoria and Kushinagar with staying power and a demonstrated commitment to a district. These leaders will have to be part of a 'network of the willing', supported by other leaders in other districts.

What then is required from the government? The government itself should continue to improve its ability to enable a Power On society—providing rule of law through robust policing and judiciary, administering taxes, creating infrastructure, supporting those at the Bottom through schemes and creating platforms for citizens to associate and collaborate for economic and social activities. These require investment to upgrade almost every aspect of the district apparatus. District development can be achieved without creating a welfare model if the local administration is trained and moulded to the reality of New India. The administrative set-up of 'generalists' has to be remodelled as economic activities become important. This will start a more fulfilling and meaningful chapter for the district officers as well, who are burdened by many small issues of the district and do not have time for a planned development effort. Police and judicial reforms are critical so that the thana or the Kachahari in a district like Deoria is a place for getting justice, not another barrier for judicial delays. New institutions at the district level that can enable society must be created. These institutions must be trained for development together with local leaders, creating programmes that need local collaboration.

The government must incentivize and make it easier for leaders and communities to work together. It must create infrastructure and enabling platforms for local services to be delivered throughout the community. The government is already focusing on infrastructure—roads, power and digital. It should now provide platforms that enable the community. One could argue that the project of 'Big Society' in Britain—a concept whereby a significant amount of responsibility for society was devolved to local communities and volunteers— had similar aims but with mixed results.[37] What is different this time is the power of digital technology, networks and the inherent strength of community in smaller towns and districts in India. Fifteen years ago, when 'Big Society' was deemed a partial success, digital connectivity was in its infancy. Today, the opportunities to collaborate through physical and digital networks are enormous. The smartphone revolution is currently being used in a passive manner. In the near future, this can give the district a 'digital uplift', used for a constructive, collective purpose as described by Tom Malone and his investigation of collective intelligence. This movement should be different from the collectivist efforts that led to disasters such as the Great Leap Forward in China, where the state became a naive orchestrator. At its core are the efforts of individuals or teams that work freely and with their own will in a local context, for a local problem, supported by an enabling state.

Building enterprise and institutions for delivering local services such as education, health, water and sanitation is where the community is already taking a lead, and with government enablement, these social enterprises can be strengthened. Services, then, will not be all delivered directly from the government; it will become a community responsibility through local enterprises, both social and economic, with the government acting as an enabler, regulator and a top-up funder. This reduces the cost to the exchequer, involves local citizen groups, creates local buy-in and generates local employment. For instance, the mayor of Deoria is experimenting with a local enterprise that has a new technology and process for segregating waste and will be contracted locally by the Deoria municipality. For such efforts to succeed, more powers must be devolved to the district, block, ward and Gram Panchayats but with government focused even more on governance.

Enabling the community

A congregation space is essential at the district level to foster bottom-up nation-building. Faith brings people together in a mandir, a masjid, a church or a gurudwara; nation-building requires similar local temples for building Middle India as congregation locations. Today, public gatherings are one-way conversations where a political or administrative leader talks down to those gathered. But for leaders gathering to chart out a new future for the district, horizontal conviviality and conversations are important. The town hall in Deoria, where our meeting for Naya Deoria was held, is one such forum, but it is a location for the 15 per cent of the district population that lives in the town. More public places for gathering are required across the district that can improve collaboration between the administration, community leaders and the citizen. The district also needs more stadiums, libraries and theatres that bring people together. These congregation spaces will go beyond building the capabilities of the state; they will build capability for collaboration in society.

Physical connects do matter. Even with the uptick of social media friendships and connections, research shows that more than 60 per cent of such connections were established within a 150 km radius of the person.[38] The place matters as it creates an organic relationship with a location and the society around it. This act of coming together, joint effort and commitment, where positive action can be planned, is almost impossible outside family, caste or religious settings today. Such locations at the district level will elicit suggestions, approaches, volunteers and leaders from among residents, particularly the youth. A district-centric Banyan Revolution based on an ecosystem approach requires a geographic focus where 'you pick a geographic area and throw in everything and the kitchen sink all at once . . . an infinity of positive influences subtly reinforce one another in complex ways . . . It means doing away with the way philanthropy is done now, in which one donor funds one programme that tries to isolate one leverage point to have "impact".'[39] It means creating an ecosystem for action and brokering trust in society. It also believes in something we discovered on Jagriti Yatra—that 'the main way we change our minds on moral issues is by interacting with other people.'[40]

It also means implementing the Panchayati Raj system properly. The Panchayati Raj system was instituted with the 73rd amendment of the Constitution in 1992, as described earlier in the book. Its vision was to create a third layer of governance below the Centre and state, focused on two fulcra of development—village-led and women-led. Each Gram Pradhan was given powers to motivate the local community, understand their issues and solve them with support from the government, and 33 per cent women were to be elected Pradhans.[41] Very quickly, the spirit of this effort was subverted and it became yet another funding pipeline, which often leaks, corrupting local Gram Pradhans. The concept of *Pradhan Pati*, literally, 'husband of the headperson', subverted a key strength of the legislation in bringing women power to the fore, with only a few managing to emerge as independent women leaders.

I attended a meeting of Gram Pradhans in Deoria in November 2018. In a hall full of seventy Pradhans, there was not a single woman. Every one of them, to the last person, was bemoaning the lack of financial authority to do what they wanted to do. But they were focusing on the flow of funding that the government gives them, usually in the range of Rs 15–20 lakh, depending on the size of the village. There was hardly any discussion about bringing the community together. What of the young returnee who wanted to open a school that may need support? Or the night school for women that could do with an assist? Instead of convening village communities to do something together, the focus was on how to get money from the government to make culverts, *naalis* (drains) and *chabootras* (stage) in the village, with the constant grouse that real financial power has not been delegated to them. It had become a smaller version of what happens at the

district with government-funded programmes, where the
energies of society are largely absent and the focus is on
financial flow. When the local leaders were goaded in that
session to seek resources outside government and harness
the societal energies of the village, a different conversation
started to emerge.

A waterway on the Narayani

We tried to create such a narrative by leading one such
community effort. Summoned by local villagers, we
showed up at the edge of the river Narayani on a rainy
monsoon day in August. This region has villages that abut
the mighty Narayani, with lyrical names like Tarya Sujaan,
reflecting its rise and fall. Villagers from Ahirauli Daan
were protesting about how the village had been ignored as
floods chipped away at their homes. Some money had been
allocated by the state government, but it had not reached
the location in time to start constructing a bund. As we
stood by the river, a large building slowly crashed into
the river as the waters ate into its foundation in front of
our very eyes. Rushing to Lucknow, we secured a meeting
with the Irrigation Department, who offered help and
provided relief. But a longer-term solution was needed. If
we were always defending the banks of this mighty river
with fortifications, we may be able save villages from
flooding, but what could bring focus to this area to create
a permanent embankment? This river connects Nepal in
the north to Patna in the south, where it merges with the
Ganga. It has a good draft of water—this is when the idea
of transporting goods downriver from this desolate stretch
of eastern UP and western Bihar came about.

Acting upon this insight, we created a programme and an expedition to highlight the usage of this river as a waterway. When we announced this effort, it caught the attention of the entire area. One push of positivity, and people were first surprised and then engaged. We launched a rafting expedition from near Ahirauli Daan that would take a sample of *haldi* (turmeric) to Patna. When Pundlik and Manish, two Yatris, heard about this plan, they came forward as leaders for this seven-day expedition, with active help from the Inland Waterways authority. We charted the depth of the river at various points with an Inland Waterways sounding boat accompanying the expedition. The rafting expedition was flagged off with over 2000 eager citizens watching and local volunteers taking part as rafters. One small leg also had two women in sarees and life jackets rowing the raft as we knew that women would benefit most from agro-produce and handicrafts going down to Patna. As if by magic, a few days before our expedition, the Varanasi-Haldia leg of the Ganga waterway on National Waterway 1 was also launched in Varanasi. This gave us the confidence that, over time, produce from this backward area can be taken beyond Patna through this waterway. The expedition took 50 kg of haldi and sold it in the Patna market. We brought back currency notes that were earned and displayed them as a small but immediate outcome of our effort. We are now readying a bigger plan to have a water port at Pipra Ghat, the location where Barrister Yadav was born, which is ecologically sustainable and can also transport local produce downriver in large quantities.

We have four or five similar initiatives across the district. The revival of a cold storage and creation of an agro-processing park near Fazilnagar, the creation of *Naya Deoria*, the new township described earlier, the creation of an industrial zone close to Rampur Karkhana, another township and our planned enterprise centre next to the banyan tree. We see other Yatris attempt a similar model in their respective areas across the country. We are keen that our model of district development is copied in the four corners of the country till we have a presence in each of the 240 districts that we term Middle India. For this, early fertilization has started with the Jagriti Ambassador for District Enterprise (JADE), and we have 100 such districts with a JADE already present. If this starts showing success, we believe this network will give a push to the community in each of these districts. Following the success of programmes such as Swachh Bharat and Jal Jeevan Mission, the government is also moving to an enabling mindset. This approach in 240 districts of the Middle can impact the country in a more profound manner than the 1991 reforms affected the Top of the Diamond. We see this sprint centred on districts with citizens, communities and an enabling government, central to national renewal starting from the Middle.

11

Digital: *Human Networks in the Middle*

பயன்மரம் உள்ளூர்ப் பழுத்தற்றால் செல்வம்
நயனுடை யான்கண் படின்.

—திருவள்ளுவர்

(A tree that fruits in the hamlet's central mart,
Is wealth that falls to men of giving heart)

—Thiruvalluvar

The influence of digital on Middle India can re-shape
it, creating a new way of life—one that is decentralized,
networked, sustainable and humane. But digital can create
new imbalances, concentrating wealth and power at the Top
just when the Middle is gaining its voice. It can also control
the Middle, snatching away its agency and engendering
a new colonial extraction, this time centred on data. To
liberate the Middle from this fate, while making full use
of technology, we must yoke digital to the human spirit,

local ecosystems and communities, which will accelerate the nation-building project.

In the past few decades, five digital transitions have already taken place—telephone, computer, mobile, the Internet and now, Artificial Intelligence (AI). In college in the late eighties, when I spoke to my father from a solitary phone in a military hospital in Trivandrum, the telecom revolution was just beginning. The Centre for Development of Telematics (C-DOT) was founded in a hotel close to our campus in Delhi and created telephone exchanges that spawned the yellow booths that dotted rural India. My own career after college, though, started in the opposite direction—searching for oil, which had fuelled the Industrial Age. This quest took me to three continents as a rig manager. I even did a two-year tenure managing an offshore rig, Trident II, in Bombay High, with Pawan Hans helicopters ferrying me from Juhu Heliport to the offshore rig and back. Shortly thereafter, I moved to Nigeria, where oil was being explored in the Niger Delta by our company's swamp barges. The infrastructure needed to drill for oil, refine and transport it was global, and I followed this oil trail faithfully for over seven years.

However, by the mid-nineties, computers had entered a rig manager's life. My Toshiba laptop had a fuzzy green screen but made computing easy. Accustomed to mainframes and long printouts at the freezing computer centre during my college days, I admired the simplicity, elegance and usability of typing Word memos that could be corrected and Lotus Notes spreadsheets that could pivot. The Internet soon began to connect our computers and organize our company very differently. Our reports to our HQ in Paris from Nigeria were now being uploaded on a weak modem line, the only one in our office in Port Harcourt, Nigeria. My French district manager, on returning from one of his visits to Europe, announced that SAP was going to install a companywide system that would give our efforts a digital backbone—from finance to operations. Schlumberger had pioneered the use of data to locate oil seams thousands of metres underground, but the proliferation of computers in our day-to-day life was new and unique. The Information Age was creeping up on us and I wanted to participate.

One evening in sunny Port Harcourt, Gauri saw me come out of the shower, and much like Archimedes, announce with great determination and confidence that I would leave the firm and pursue an MBA to enter the business world afresh with technology as my focus. Leaving the excitement of running drilling rigs in Nigeria, I enrolled in an MBA programme at IMD, a business school in Lausanne near Geneva.

Our business school was then coming to terms with the Internet. As part of a team of five technology enthusiasts in my class, we created 'IMD Online' as a project to convince the institute to install terminals with Internet connections in all rooms and facilities. Geneva is known more for its watches and the hospitality industry than for information technology. However, the French and Swiss governments were operating CERN[1] in underground caverns that spanned both countries. This houses a massive cyclotron that splits atoms using circular tunnels housed below ground. As luck would have it, the inventor of the Internet, Tim Berners-Lee, was employed at CERN at that time. What better way to turn the attention of our institute to the Internet than to ask him to endorse our programme?

We showed up at CERN and discovered that more than its cavernous tunnels splitting the atom, Tim was connecting humans through a digital network that has since girdled the world.

Pervasive digital

When we organized the Azad Bharat Rail Yatra in 1997 on the fiftieth anniversary of India's independence, mobile phones numbered only 5 million, less than half a per cent of the population. We were grateful for this innovation and managed that journey with five such precious devices. I still remember the look on the face of Mohit Joshi, a Yatri in the 1997 Yatra who hailed from Kathgodam, when I asked him to place a call on a mobile phone from the vast lawns of the Rashtrapati Bhawan. For the longest time, he could not comprehend that a phone call was possible without a wire. Just ten years later, in 2007, the sixtieth anniversary of India's independence saw Steve Jobs launch the iPhone. This began a decade-long explosion of smartphones, fuelled subsequently by Google's Android platform and the widespread availability of the Internet. The smartphone was not just voice, it was also a touchscreen that supported visuals, a camera and connectivity via mobile data and the Internet. With the cost of smartphones plummeting, Jio initiated ultra-low-cost mobile data connectivity and the Internet became available to many in the Middle. In recent years Facebook, Instagram and WhatsApp have penetrated these districts, creating a tsunami of content with a 'mobile first' approach. Millions of Indians in the Middle are exploring the world through social media. This is now being usurped by an 'AI first' approach, with Google recently announcing a new chapter focused on AI, opening yet another digital frontier that is disrupting the disruption. Not to be outdone, Facebook renamed itself Meta after the Metaverse, announcing that the World Wide Web 3.0 is now inevitable, and in recent months, ChatGPT has brought both the miracles and dangers of AI into our daily lives.

By 2022, at the soft introduction of 5G, there were 750 million smartphone users in India, a 100-fold increase in twenty-five years, with the most explosive growth in the Middle.[2] Mobile connections are nearing 1.2 billion and fast connectivity will drive AI applications and future technologies such as neural networks to smaller towns and districts. With 50–100 times higher download speeds, 5G will shrink the distance between Middle India and the rest of the world. AI, blockchain, Industry 4.0 and the Internet of Things (IOT) are digital solutions that have started gracing conferences from Davos to Delhi. All five properties of a digital stack—processing power, memory, sensors, connectivity and mobility and software—are now integrated in the cloud. While processing power, memory and sensors remain important, it is at the other end of the technology stack—connectivity, mobility and software— that Middle India stands to benefit most. The explosion, both in processing power and connectivity, is re-shaping the Middle digitally, where values, norms and concepts of distance, relationships, community and enterprise will be impacted. This is also changing economics and society, as the concentration of digital power with those at the Top with access to digital technologies is also concentrating wealth and power.

AI, a term loosely used for different sets of computer intelligence, such as machine learning (ML), deep learning, neural networks, natural processing language and others, is transforming digital technology through big data. This is throwing up both opportunities and risks. The biggest opportunities are where big data is available and can be crunched for a single 'objective function', say, interpreting thousands of radiological reports to come up with a disease pattern that a human eye or mind cannot detect. The risk, though, to India is that large social media giants train their supercomputers on another singular 'objective function'— creating algorithms that keep people on their social media platforms longer to make more money. The platforms then harvest more data with trillion-dollar valuations but at the expense of social cohesion and by seeding a new colonization. Instead of bringing out the best in humanity, to keep people hooked to their platforms, these companies appeal to the least common denominators in humans. By reinforcing egos and spreading salacious and fake news, this process feeds the negative, much like the noise and tumult that creates a pull for news channels.

Thankfully, humans possess both intrinsic social values and 'general intelligence', which requires expertise, cognition, cross-domain circulations and intuition that goes beyond the mathematical equations at the core of AI. In the context of Middle India, digital must enable 800 million people with creative connections. To nurture Middle India, humans, their beliefs and values and a constructive purpose or 'positive freedoms', should be at the core of digital, where computing power and human ethics combine in the manner Tom Malone and Jonathan Haidt described, as outlined in Chapter 7. Both the West and an ageing China are focusing on computing power to automate what humans can do. So far, digital's driving motive is reduction of manpower. India, with her vast reserves of human capital and a predominantly service-oriented economy, should design digital for connecting people, and use technology and design to improve service. This will democratize digital technology instead of dehumanizing it.

Societal networks

If the primary use of digital networks in Middle India is human connectivity, then it requires a focus on human-centric design. Donald Newman at the Design Lab of the University of California says, 'Much of modern technology seems to exist solely for its own sake, oblivious to the needs and concerns of the people around it . . . My goal is to socialize technology, humanize technology.'[3] In this humanization, a building purpose that motivates and gives meaning and positive direction is needed. 'Networks that connect and build' should be the goal of digital in the Middle, anchored in the ethics of local communities rather than in large impersonal platforms.

Thankfully for the Middle, social networks are not the gift of WhatsApp, Facebook, LinkedIn or Twitter. Citizen networks have existed since time immemorial. In smaller towns and districts, societal networks, be it religious, caste, language or geography based, have given society resilience and continue to define citizen associations. These networks are re-emerging and becoming stronger as republican energies rise, bringing the community together with a digital backbone. We can 'extend the yoke' of our republic digitally by networking more and more citizens using digital; the 'longer the yoke, the more horses you can harness to pull your wagon—and the faster and farther you can go'.[4] The wagon of nation-building will accelerate as the yoke is extended by citizen networks in the Middle if the association is driven by positive values.

In Deoria district, I have discovered many such human networks. Praying at a temple a few kilometres from Deoria town, I discovered that this was a network of temples and dharamshalas with twelve regional outposts. This network was created by a sage based in nearby Gazipur, Powhari Maharaj, who had a large following and whose predecessor had been visited by Swami Vivekananda in 1890 during his six years of wandering. On another visit to Sewrahi in Kushinagar, close to Bihar, I saw a neatly kept campus that belonged to the Radha Soami Satsang Beas. I was aware of this religious group, but its presence in a small hamlet on the eastern edge of UP surprised me. The Kabir Panthis have large tracts of land in the region and they continue to follow the egalitarian teachings of Kabir. The association of villagers through marriage criss-crosses the entire district, with strangers in distant villages reminding me about how we were related. Besides these, social organizations, sports associations and women's self-help groups also continue to bring citizens together within and across nearby districts.

Social scientists have stated that an individual can directly associate with people in the 200–5000-person range.[5] Through digital networks, social media, smartphones and connectivity, that association can be extended naturally. The colonial dispensation's hold on the Middle exaggerated and widened divisions in society and disrupted these networks and ties. A modern republic and digital can reverse this. Our networks and supporting institutions must be designed to bring citizens together with a building bias, with citizen builders as its nodes.

Our alumni, the Yatris, have arranged themselves in naturally expanding collaborative networks across the country, with an integrative cause. What brings them together is the shared experience of a national adventure. What keeps them going is the focus on udyamita in ways we never planned for when we initiated the Yatra. These Yatris collaborate with each other, for instance, rallying recently to arrange a distress line during the COVID-19 crisis with national coverage, arranging hospital beds and oxygen concentrators. Our JADE programme is an example of a positive human-centric network design. Here, Yatris understand their local community and districts, and then connect that community to our national 'enterprise cloud'. This enterprise cloud is not just a digital cloud; it consists of market connectors and mentors and connects to money. This is both a human-aided digital effort and a digital-aided human effort. At the district, these networks require supporting actors to make connections. The Internet Saathi programme created a network of women who are now flourishing together thanks to the connections fostered across approximately 8000 villages in the seven districts near Deoria, their confidence enhanced on account of this horizontal network.

Power laws and weak links in networks

Normally, nature throws up a distribution that can be modelled with a bell curve. The height of people in a population or the average IQ of citizens, randomly sampled, comes up with a distribution with the maximum in the middle. In contrast, power laws accentuate the few. In a world where power laws exist, a few people would be 100 feet tall and the vast majority would be dwarves. In a digital and human network, a few hubs or persons have many more connections with the remaining nodes having very few. The growth and strength of the network is based on those hubs or persons having a far greater influence on the remaining nodes of the network. Our intuition in 2008, when we started the Jagriti Yatra, reflected this with a focus on leaders who are connectors and collaborators, including our belief that a few had to be from the Top, a few from the Bottom and some from overseas. Similarly, an udyamita network with udyamis as hubs will create inordinate social and economic impact in any district, influencing other nodes with them.

Network theory also rates links between hubs and nodes as weak or strong. Strong links are part of the core network with frequent interactions with the rest, while a weak link has occasional connects. Counter-intuitively, weak links are *more likely* to solve an issue for the network than strong links. For instance, in the matter of finding a job for another member of the network, weak links serve a bigger role.[6] This is the reason that mentors from across the country can potentially make a greater impact in an udyamita ecosystem located in a small district.

I experienced the power of weak links in Davos while attending the annual World Economic Forum (WEF) conference in 2016. At a dinner event organized one evening, I heard Kofi Annan, the former UN Secretary General, talk of his life experiences. In his baritone, he explained how the world was being reshaped and what businesses could do to create a better society. Senior leaders such as

Chandrababu Naidu, the former CM of Andhra Pradesh, from India and Tony Blair, the former PM of the UK, were also present. After cocktails and dinner, we were ushered into an adjoining room where a band was performing. As I stood on the margins of this crowd, an unfamiliar young person next to me called out my name and reached out to shake hands. He was a Yatri who had been selected by the World Economic Forum's Young Shapers Programme and was attending the conference. I had met him last on the Yatra and now he was in the middle of an influential global community. This was a long weak link that would reach back and inform the strong links within his smaller community network, making the whole stronger.

How can this digitally powered network, fuelled by data, possibly impact Middle India? We can take clues from what took place when Henry Ford's Model T car and the physical network of roads shaped the US 100 years ago. The Model T was 'cheap and easy to maintain with clearance high enough for use near farms and areas without proper roads. Americans began to *believe that cars were for everyone*; they began to understand what this could mean for their families, communities and business'.[7] The Model T and road infrastructure reshaped the life of the ordinary citizen, not just the elite. Malls were built, suburbia grew, cities were concentrated; within half a century, the rural population of the US shrank to 30 per cent[8] and families split as multiple cars offered independent mobility to a family. Community life changed and morphed. The smartphone, digital technology and networks are doing to Middle India what the Model T did to North America, but in a manner that is opposite to the impact of mass-produced cars. If the Model T and the roads it created led to physical centralization, which led to fragmentation, digital can serve to keep people where they are, close to their communities, and drive integration. Over the coming twenty-five years, as the influence of digital technology accelerates, Middle India will see a revolutionary consequence not just in economics but also in society, politics and values. Digital will drive a different urbanization, not one that believes in centralization of the Model T kind but decentralized living in Tier 2 and Tier 3 districts. In my experience, societal memories of an ancient civilization with a 5000-year-old history also creates stronger adhesives to the location, with culture, locality, fauna and flora, like our banyan, acting as emotional magnets.

A strategic decentralization

Digital will play a strategic role in creating this new decentralization that will slow down and over time, stop society from fleeing the Middle. This was tested during COVID-19 with many, some say millions, working from smaller towns such as Bhopal, Bhubaneshwar, Ernakulam and other places, albeit for employers who were in larger cities. My neighbour in Mumbai who works for Reliance moved to Jaipur and told me, 'I would be willing to stay there even if I got 20 per cent less remuneration, as the quality of life is infinitely better than Mumbai and I am closer to my ailing mother.' This proves that amenities and social structure for living are becoming available in smaller towns and districts. What is now required is the use of digital in generating enterprise and local livelihoods in these districts so that migration is slowed down, stopped and even reversed. The rush to a metro destination takes place in search of a job but also in search of better schooling, better entertainment, better healthcare, powerful local social networks and the allure of the 'great traditions' in arts. However, a Tier 3 district headquarters like Deoria can be a viable location if connected with metro and Tier 1 cities digitally, and provided services that can be accessed locally. This is already happening with streaming movies, online coaching classes or hospitals with remote diagnosis. This must be complemented by creating local spaces for community and social gathering—theatres, parks, libraries—'local urbanization' through which the pressure on the metros is released and the local economy is pump-primed. Germany went down a route of decentralized growth where several medium-sized towns continue to thrive, which resulted in a balanced economy with medium-sized companies—Mittlestadt—located in mid-sized towns with small town and village living still in fashion.[9] Things are very different in the US, which marched most of its rural people to megapolises, creating a template other nations started following, thereby creating a modernity that celebrated dislocation.

Digital adoption and a clear national digital strategy allowed South Korea to become the most digitally active nation in the world.[10] It took this on as a national mission and succeeded in establishing a network-centric society over twenty years, albeit with a strong urban orientation. India's small towns and districts can use the new digital network for enterprise creation, community development and decentralized living. India has an opportunity to use a networked society, with recent recognition through the COVID-19 shock, that the Middle can also be digitally enabled. Schools, colleges, retail stores and hospitals started going digital in a matter of weeks. What would have taken a massive effort over perhaps a decade, the pandemic made possible in a few months. Our village *dhobi* in Barpar started educating his children on Zoom during lockdown, becoming a digital citizen within a few months. However, state-held digital power can also create an Orwellian impact, as is occurring in China, where, 'In the near future, every person who enters a public space could be identified instantly by AI matching, including their every text communication, and their body's one-of-a-kind protein construction scheme.'[11]

Liquid Middle

In many facets of life, digital is allowing the Middle to leapfrog the Top, as economy and society are fast becoming liquid. The global economy is de-materializing; for every percentage of GDP increase, the kilogram of input has reduced by half in the last three decades of the twentieth century.[12] Going forward, the economy will become even less tangible. Thomas Friedman likens this to a 'phase change' from solid to liquid catalysed by digital. 'Mobility gives you mass market; broadband gives you access to information digitally and the cloud stores all the software applications so you can use them any time anywhere . . . It is the equivalent of a "phase change" in chemistry from a solid to a liquid . . . it is friction free.'[13] The focus of those in the industrial West or those in metros is to reduce friction in a solid, industrial world, shifting for instance from branch banking to ATM and online cash as a phase change from physical location to a digital process. Without a large industrial and physical base, the Middle can use digital to become liquid from the very beginning, forgoing friction and creating a societal leap. COVID-19 accelerated this phase change with life in the Middle becoming liquid rapidly, with digital cash, remote learning and remote work just a few manifestations of this change. People to people association, as outlined earlier, is becoming easier, and assets that allow physical and human capital to be counted, tracked and resources that were hidden easily mobilized through digital. A district can be mapped accurately so that local assets such as warehouses, cold storage, etc., are fully understood and used. As a digital economy in the Middle creates dematerialized growth, India could aspire to a longer-term goal that would come naturally—the preservation of the environment, covered more fully later in the book.

However, unless digital is used with discipline, this phase of digital growth will become a fad with little impact on the nation-building project. Networked citizens can benefit each other only if motivated by a positive cause of building rather than the passive or perhaps a 'sensational' association. In the absence of a 'purpose framework' to guide digital, the gorier the news, the wider is its circulation within networks such as WhatsApp. This creates a flood of fake news. The only way to neutralize the power of such negative platforms is to create networks and associations that are driven by a positive, collaborative cause. Positive societal networks powered by digital have a glue, a binding sentiment and energy that motivates them for 'freedom to', rather than a passive or reactive negative flavour that leads to 'moronization' of society. Unbridled technology used passively in the hands of those without purpose can lead to ills already visible in Middle India. India has become the third largest downloader of pornography[14] globally. The same device that can enable a young Indian in a small town to take a class on BYJU's to get into a good college also allows access to digital smut. The Linnean system classified plants and animals for exploitation, Cartesian thinking imagined man as an automaton, while Darwin's theory created a culture of fierce competition. Digital, using massive data repositories, can classify and divide humans not just by ethnicity, tastes and values but also in ethical styles, taking control to re-colonize humanity in the name of digital modernity, this time from the inside out. Only a local, societal, spiritual and humanist modernity can counterbalance these tendencies.

Digital value flows

Used with care, digital can connect the Middle directly to the global flow of values. Globally, value continues to shift towards digital. For instance, in 1990, the overall flow of value across borders was pegged at $5 trillion or 24 per cent of global GDP. By 2014, that number had surged to $30 trillion or nearly 40 per cent of global GDP, and digital flows were almost 30 per cent up from 10 per cent in 1991.[15] Smaller enterprises can now participate in this flow. A recent report states that 'globalization, till recently was a one-way affair with large companies dominating this flow. Digital offers an opportunity to make this a two-way flow where the Middle participates equally, with smartphones aiding in this'[16]. Instead of accessing the Net via a computer, millions of Indians simply use a smartphone. Small and medium businesses in a small town or village are benefiting most as 'mobile is . . . allowing emerging market SMEs to leapfrog an entire generation of technology and directly develop business models or operational tools for the mobile platform.'[17] Smaller companies and individuals are putting up their wares on the net and participating in this 'new flow of value', a trend accelerated by COVID-19.

Current approaches make the case for digital penetration so that e-commerce buying can increase in the Middle.[18] The transformative use of digital would be to create platforms that ensure goods and services *from* the Middle are available to the national economy. This requires a local ecosystem that introduces design, quality, marketing, better logistics and connectivity to the market at the click of a button, making the Middle take part as equals. Those from the Middle can then start 'moving value' to the Top of the Diamond and create surplus for themselves.

A vernacular digital economy

To do this, language barriers must be surmounted, as English remains the lingua franca not just of digital but of enterprise too. The number of Indians who understand and speak English is still limited to 10 per cent of the total population.[18] In Middle India, the proportion of fluent English speakers is difficult to measure, but it is probably closer to 3–5 per cent of the population, with some regional variations. The proportion of those who speak Hindi as their first or second language, nationally, is about seven times that of English speakers, with Tamil, Bengali and other languages having significant currency as well.[19] The digital for Bharat must be multilingual, like Bharat herself. Hindi, Tamil, Bengali, Marathi, Gujarati and other vernacular languages will play a critical role if we want digital to be used widely.

Both Parvati Singh and Arvind Rai suffered from a lack of access to knowledge in Hindi. Parvati struggled to get concrete knowledge of designs till she logged into the Internet from her rooftop. But only when Prerna, who spoke fluent English, came to her help was she was able to understand and curate a real rural supply chain. Arvind Rai struggled with Intellectual Property (IP) and innovation when he was assembling his electric cycle. It was only when the Jagriti team introduced him to IP concepts, largely in English, that he considered registering the IP of certain parts of his cycle. The curation of local knowledge and culture is essential for societal confidence, which is only possible in areas like Purvanchal if we document in Hindi or Bhojpuri. The use of vernacular is also increasing nationally, and this will bring the cultural richness of the Middle to those at the Top digitally. We will then not only learn and practise Shakespeare but will look up Kabir or a Thiruvallur with equal facility.

To support such a 'vernacular economy', Jagriti has envisioned a Banyan Digital Library in the Jagriti Enterprise Centre—Purvanchal (JECP). The aim of the library is to promote Hindi literature and knowledge of udyamita. Lack of knowledge of IP and cultural knowledge hinders enterprise and innovation. In the Banyan Digital Library, we envision creating literature that details udyamita and forms a location where local IP can be registered. But we also envision electronic books and videos that document oral traditions, songs and stories that are getting lost in the rush to make English the primary language of the country. Oral 'little traditions', recorded and amplified, will also amplify local pride and self-image. Only by hyphenating vernacular languages with digital and economic growth can the Middle progress and recreate stronger associations. If we want self-confident entrepreneurs from the Middle, we need to make vernacular popular and pervasive, as has happened in Japan and Korea. In Middle India, this 'language levelling' through digital will be critical for udyamita and for our culture.

Digital governance and platforms

Governing a country as diverse, complex and large as India can only be done digitally. In this area, the country has taken commendable steps under Digital India, and during COVID-19, this infrastructure was used fully. The use of electronic funds transfer, the use of digital in supplying food to those most impacted and the pervasive use of applications that track COVID-19 were laudable applications of Digital India. In managing a large and complex democracy, the Electronic Voter Machine (EVM) has ensured free, fair and timely elections, another case where political infrastructure in the Middle is far ahead of economic infrastructure. Partially, technology has managed to lower the burden of a colonial administration by bypassing corruption in the distribution of goods and services and enforcing laws with greater transparency. The use of the Aadhaar card in identification and the recent flowering of UPI in payment methods is bringing finance to the common person. This was the first phase of use of digital in the Middle to create a more transparent state that provides what some call 'wise restraints'[20], and the delivery of goods and services to the last mile. In the private sector, e-commerce and banking are enabled by such infrastructure, which are now penetrating the Middle. However, the strategic use of digital in the Middle is 'citizen to citizen' enablement to support and expand citizen networks and platforms that will create true republican action within the udyamita framework. Digital should also allow the government to segment and differentiate between the Middle, which needs enablement, and the Bottom, which needs direct support from the state.

Government as a platform and government as enablers of local platforms is the next stage of digital governance for the Middle. Here, the focus of digital is not on restraints but on supporting citizens in 'positive freedoms' by switching on the *Power To* function of the state. It allows citizens to come together, to build and grow. In this imagination, instead of serving citizens in welfare mode, the government will *enable* citizens to associate for a positive cause as both customers and suppliers of service, private and public goods through enterprise, examples of which were given earlier. External platforms would pool the resources and talents of citizens, the private sector and the government, reducing the load on the state while making development more local. The 'steel frame' that was designed for extreme *Power On* society went much beyond restraints and actively focused on controlling citizens. This must be remodelled into a 'silicon lattice' that softens the *Power On* function and promotes the *Power To* function in governance, inviting societal involvement, private sector participation and government to work seamlessly, reducing the 'us-and-them' that is evident in local governance. This digital infrastructure should use the *moral capability* in society[21] that uses technology for the good of society and individuals, a capability that exists aplenty in the Middle.

A strong state could still misdirect digital towards control and extraction, as is happening in China.

A positive approach of enablement is already close to becoming a reality in countries such as South Korea. 'Government acting as an intermediary: facilitating collaboration, connecting people and providers, and coordinating ground-breaking public service delivery models of the future'.[22] Such platforms also create collaboration through the exchange of data shared between these entities while keeping privacy intact. While the Swachh Bharat mission was a physical platform, more localized efforts, such as linking of data on health with hospitals, the government and the private sector, can lead to much better societal outcomes.

Digital nations and citizen data flow

Digital is also redefining boundaries of nations, states and the flow of data between nations and between citizens. Nations such as Estonia have issued digital citizenships to those who may not be living in the country but are wanting to work in it remotely.[23] To frame this conundrum, Benjamin Bratton seeks a shifting political imagination of the state, stating, 'Today the authority of states, drawn from the rough consensus of the Westphalian political geographic diagram, is simultaneously never more entrenched and ubiquitous and never more obsolete and brittle.'[24] He outlines six layers of the digital stack— Earth, Cloud, City, Address, Interface and User—that is reimagining the world and blurring hard national boundaries.[25] In his imagination, the flow of data across national boundaries is not like oil, an industrial metaphor

I am only too familiar with. Here, data is not possessed by individuals, corporations or governments but is 'akin to the flow of water in a river, where the riverbed belongs to the nation where it flows, but the data, like water, is difficult to label and control.'[26] Data as nourishing water globally requires each nation and each entity to keep its riverbeds clean and, in the case of emerging countries like India, strengthen the river of data to the Middle. Instead of irrigating our country only through industrial growth, this 'digital Ganga', openly available, protected and accessed, as it is in South Korea, can also irrigate development of society in the Middle.

Data is generated by both machines and humans. Large countries, such as India and China, with populations of more than 1.4 billion each, are rich in human data. This gives such nations an intrinsic advantage in harnessing, processing and using this data for national development, and for creating new sources of national power. However, the dangers of digital colonization of the Middle and of our country by international platforms are also very real. Before Independence, colonization was of land. In this new world, colonization starts by mining India's biggest asset—the data of its 1.4 billion citizens. Networks of citizen, family, society, grounded in nature, powered by digital where data and technology are democratized, is critical to prevent a new de-humanization, a new colonization of the emerging world. We need to be watchful of the naive benevolence that led to 200 years of colonization. Commentators warn of this when they say, 'The East India companies of the Internet have plundered enough data; they have caused enough famines of the truth and plagues of the mind.'[27] A digital strategy that is open, yet understands that the global infrastructure of digital is infiltrated by platforms from developed countries, requires India to protect itself from data-led dominance.

IT and BPO services made up the global brand India started enjoying at the turn of the century. The twin headwinds of automation and trade wars are making offshoring processes increasingly difficult. Today, that confidence has been transferred to unicorns, who are addressing issues in the Indian experience, with India now having the third highest number of unicorns globally.[28] Unicorns are gradually training their technology guns on the real problems of India. Enterprises are 'applying the extraordinary technological advances in IT to do for service what the moving production line did for manufacturing'.[29] The new opportunity for digital is within the vast Middle, where enormous, continental-size issues wait for solutions. Unlike the *efficiency* rationale of the outsourcing industry, digital must make life more *effective* through local innovation and problem solving for the many. As India grows to be a $10 trillion economy, the Middle will need digital methods, not as a back office calling for cost efficiency but to improve quality of life and create new ways of living. It can also be directed to create new technologies to defend our country with the use of non-kinetic warfare.[30]

During this process, citizens will be dislocated as the pace of technology accelerates. Digital will not just impact national reach and economic growth, it will impact concepts of power, liberty, democracy and social justice. Today, 'digital technology is too often designed from the perspective of the powerful and the privileged'.[31] The Banyan Revolution must ensure that digital technology is deployed for the betterment of the Middle, is owned by it, and is moderated with regulation that does not disadvantage the Middle. Societal displacement can be minimized by using vernacular, engaging with and providing the benefits of innovation to many. The culture of India, the humanity inherent in society and the focus on local circumstances with the goal of nation-building will give cohesion to this human digital network.

The idea of an integrative human spirit may seem difficult to reconcile with a digital world. In my experience, as more and more digital gets introduced into our lives, Indians will simultaneously revert to their spiritual selves. The current phase of digital and social media obsession is starting to swing away towards a need for mindfulness. In moments of digital overload, I often retreat to the banyan and look up to the branches that spring from its green foliage, securing a few moments of analog peace. Indians continue to yearn for a centred life, one where the digital network vaguely mirrors our societal memories of an all-pervasive and integrative *brahma*, an inter-connected system with millions of 'give and take' but with a moral centring. Somehow, we must incorporate this in our national digital consciousness. India should use this strength to create an integrated digital *lifeworld* where human connections, values and real networks continue to anchor and stabilize the digital world in the Middle. Thousands of years of spiritual training would allow us to do so.

Part IV

BUILDING: *A New India*

Recognizing a Diamond-shaped India, learning from our history and culture and changing our approach to development, locating it in our Middle, will release a new national energy. This will integrate the Middle, Top and Bottom at our seventy-fifth anniversary, creating an orbit-shifting rise and a new India. A rise that creates prosperity and meaning for 1.4 billion citizens, and in the process creates a new model for development for other emerging countries. This citizen-led rise and development will create national transcendence by connecting and integrating not just citizens but also government and private sector. The resulting sprint of nation-building will be decentralized, sustainable and human-centric, creating a new modernity. This renaissance will see us celebrate the hundredth anniversary of Independence truly free—in body, in mind and in spirit.

12

Integration and Innovation:
A Unified Rise

শুভ্র-জ্যোৎস্না, পুলকিত-যামিনীম্, ফুল্লকুসুমিত, দ্রুমদলশোভিনীম্,
সুহাসিনীং, সুমধুরভাষিণীম্, সুখদাং বরদাং, মাতরম্॥, বন্দে মাতরম্॥

—বঙ্কিমচন্দ্র চট্টোপাধ্যায়

(Her nights rejoicing in the glory of the moonlight,
Her lands clothed in trees with flowering bloom
Sweet of laughter, sweet of speech,
The mother giver of boons, giver of bliss)

—Bankim Chandra Chatterjee

Around 1777, my grandfather's great-grandfather Ram
Mani was born to a family of ordinary farmers in eastern UP.
He grew up to be a learned man, known for his piety.[1] Seven
decades before his birth, in 1707, Aurangzeb had breathed
his last, and in 1739, a weakened Delhi was plundered by
Nader Shah, who attached the peacock throne to his caravan,
and for good measure, also took the Kohinoor with him to
Iran. A mere twenty years before Ram Mani's birth, Clive

had won the Battle of Plassey, commencing British hegemony in India. India at the time was still prosperous, with growth accelerating between 1600 and 1700. In the late 1700s, India pipped Ming China to contribute approximately 20 per cent of the global GDP.[2]

But India was entering a period of rapid decline as the Industrial Revolution picked up pace in Europe and the tentacles of colonialism gripped India. Ram Mani's son Bisheshwar Mani was born in 1810, just after the second Anglo-Maratha War, when any chance of India remaining independent was extinguished. Besides, what is today's eastern UP had been ceded in 1801 by the Nawab of Oudh to the British. Indian GDP as a percentage of the world economy had also declined to 16 per cent.[3] Ram Tahal Mani, the son of Bisheshwar Mani and my grandfather's father, was born in 1842 in my village Barpar, when our share of global GDP had declined to 12 per cent. As a fifteen-year-old youth, he witnessed the revolutionary fervour surrounding India's First War of Independence in 1857. Mangal Pandey from adjoining Ballia, thirteen years his senior, was its prime instigator, and as a result, eastern UP was singled out by the British as the epicentre of the 1857 War of Independence, with retribution to follow for the rest of the time that the British were in India.

My grandfather, Surat Narain Mani, was born in 1900 in an India by then firmly in British chains. India's GDP had crashed to 8 per cent of global GDP.[4] British colonialism had taken a severe toll on the country, having consolidated its power after the bloodbath of 1857. It was also a time of rural distress. My grandfather's mother passed away due to cholera, leaving him, at the age of two, in the care of five elder brothers and his father. Despite this difficult start, my grandfather gave our family a horizon beyond Barpar, although emotionally he never left the village. During his life, India's GDP halved again to 3 per cent of global GDP.[5] When my father, Shri Prakash Mani, started his career as a cadet at the Indian Military Academy a decade after Independence, our GDP began to witness a modest uptick. After 1991, just before my father retired from the army, it started accelerating. It is now nearing 3.5 per cent of global GDP and growing steadily.[6]

Indian GDP as a percentage of global GDP plunged from 20 per cent to just 3 per cent in five generations, when our population doubled from 180 million to 360 million. A 300-year-old banyan tree in my village is a living witness to this decline.

As I peer into the future of my family and our country, there is an opportunity to reverse this decline in two generations. It is likely that Indian GDP will touch 10 per cent of global GDP around 2047, with India becoming a $15 trillion economy.[7] This growth must carry 1.5 billion people along, with India as the largest nation on the planet. My generation will contribute to this upsurge, and Middle India will be central to this effort as more and more citizens participate and national income rises for the Middle. However, this is an intergenerational journey. By 2047, my children will be at their productive prime. Can they and their progeny then take another run at this process so that by the hundred and twenty-fifth anniversary of India's Independence, fifty years from now, we are back to the prosperity levels in which my grandfather's great-grandfather Ram Mani began his life? I hope the banyan tree, that sentient of my village, gets to witness that rise as well.

Orbit shift

The seventy-fifth anniversary of Indian independence is urging us to launch that rise. This moment in our history is not just another turning point; it is an opportunity to put our country into another orbit. This requires a shift in our approach, one in which citizens participate as innovators and builders over the coming twenty-five years, the government as an active enabler and udyamita playing an organizing role. The national baton is being passed to younger runners, but the tracks of the running field itself must be reimagined. The Middle, where the largest number of citizens exist, must be engaged with 'a new toolbox that teach us not what to think but how to think'.[8] That toolbox of udyamita will allow citizens to build in their local circumstances in an integrated manner in which pioneering ideas spring forth from the majority. Local thinking and building will create an orbit-shifting rise, triggering a national renaissance bringing together the energies of the Top and the Middle, which will pull up the Bottom faster and give meaning to millions in the process.

The rise requires innovation, a bold mindset to take the path less travelled, and entails risk. However, in a world that is changing fast, sticking to the old path of an industrial, mechanical, megapolis-led modernity and growth may pose greater risks. With the goals of life and society undergoing rapid change, COVID-19 accelerating those changes, digital reimagining the world, environment demanding attention and millions in the Middle rising, following a path shown by the 'prosperous' West risks a national cul-de-sac. We need to harness energies of our own civilization which can drive societal and economic innovation inside out.

Non-linear growth

The Winning Leap, a report I curated as its lead author, hinted at this non-linearity. Launched back in 2014, it asked the question, 'How can the Indian economy achieve a significantly higher Human Development Index (HDI) and a $10 trillion GDP?'[9] The report analysed ten key sectors that can power Indian growth and improve our HDI so that our citizens are also positively impacted by this growth. It included an analysis of sectors ranging from health, education, finance and infrastructure to digital and physical connectivity, to name a few, and set national targets over twenty years in each sector. A $10 trillion economy over a twenty-year period would bring the per capita income of India to the $7000 per person mark, bringing India's proportion of global GDP to 10 per cent in real terms.[10]

But as twenty-year targets were examined in each sector and the quantum of growth and HDI increases analysed, it became clear that India would not achieve the targets without taking a non-linear approach.[11] Take for instance healthcare, where the vector we sought to shift was 'life expectancy at birth' from the then sixty-six years to eighty years over two decades. An approach using western medicines alone would create a need for additional doctors and nurses the size of a small country, a virtual impossibility, and would pose grave financial burdens on the country. This is when we focused on non-linear solutions combining preventive medicine, home care and telemedicine to create a 'winning leap' for the healthcare sector and the country. Such leaps using innovative approaches are required in all the ten sectors. Together, these non-linear solutions would constitute more than a third of the $10 trillion economy. Only then would growth be resource-efficient, but this would require a greater focus on productivity improvements. A large country such as India, over a twenty-year period with 1.5 billion citizens by then, simply does not have the luxury to take the resource-intensive, linear path that the West adopted. The study concludes that without both non-linear approaches and productivity and innovation, India would not breach the 8 per cent GDP growth mark. Importantly, 240 million jobs required over twenty years will only come with a 9 per cent or higher growth rate.

But our growth rates had started faltering even before COVID-19 struck, and the pandemic forced the economy into the biggest recession since Independence. How does one now think of a rise when even getting back to our previous trajectory looks difficult? Another report, led by me in 2020, outlined the 'slingshot' possibilities of the COVID-19 crisis. While the economic shock was deep,[12] it made visible how 'shallow' and 'narrow' our economy remains more than seventy years after Independence. Massive migrations highlighted a fact well-known to those in the Middle—that economic opportunities, including those for enterprise, remain confined to large cities. The direction of recent migration during COVID-19 to the 'north and east' from the 'south and west' also showcased those states in the north and east that lack economic opportunities and employment. The solution we proposed is to widen the economic canvas, creating more economic volume by 'deepening'—going beyond Tier 1 districts and 'widening'—going north and east, to realize 'full potential revival and growth', giving the study its name.[13] By removing frictions that lead to migration, such as lack of economic infrastructure, formalization and digitalization, instead of a 6–7 per cent growth, India can go to a higher trajectory of 9 per cent GDP growth and a more equitable distribution of that growth. This is echoed in Noble Laureate Edmund Phelps' theory that involvement of more and more people in innovation and production is the very definition of a modern economy.[14] Concerted, collaborative and fearless action at scale can create a bigger bounce-back which could also drive inclusion.

A focus on the Middle through udyamita supports the 'deepening and widening' of the economy naturally. It will co-opt citizen leaders as creators of enterprise and jobs and as pioneers critical for inclusive growth, thereby expanding the frontiers of innovation, production and consumption simultaneously. This requires 'and' thinking where Middle, Top and Bottom as well as the north and the south work together, away from the 'house divided' metaphor that haunted the US at seventy-five. We should celebrate the many millionaires and some billionaires India continues to produce through unicorn success, but we have to celebrate smaller town wealth and job creation—the 'Middle millionaires' who can emerge given the right institutions in the Middle. Instead of a centrally planned rise that pushed China back disastrously during the 'Great Leap Forward', it would be citizen-centric and locally led. Together, the Top and Middle will generate more resources to support the Bottom, a segment requiring a bigger safety net after COVID-19. This will provide new economic rungs for those recently pushed into poverty to start their climb back in an integrated rise that allows a majority to exercise their creative energies. This is different from the zero-sum game of the feudal economy that treated citizens as subjects, or the mercantile economy that seeded colonialism based on a one-way flow of value.

As demonstrated by Edmund Phelps, GDP and employment growth are a result of grassroots indigenous innovation which promotes enterprise and participation.[15] Indigenous innovations result in productivity growth and job creation that statist or corporatist[16] systems are not able to deliver. These systems lack the energy and processes to stimulate and spur experimentation and exploration in the majority and the act of trying new things. Indigenous innovations also result in 'non-material gains' of driving purpose and meaning in the lives of citizens. For a democracy in particular, it will create economic dynamism that is in sync with political and social efforts. For India, with a large population where the service sector dominates our economy, 'it will bring long awaited opportunity for work and career that satisfy "the realization of talent". Post-industrial modernization will spread human development that industrialization never delivered.'[17]

Ecologically sustainable growth

Another reason to create a non-linear but integrative economic and social trajectory is to address the trauma the industrial world is causing to the environment. In recent years, this concern has grown beyond the studies of scientists and economists and entered our daily lives. I realized this when Isha, my younger daughter, sought permission to march with her classmates in the Greta Thunberg-inspired 'School Strike for Climate' held in Mumbai in March 2019. When asked about her motivations, she replied, 'To highlight an issue you all don't seem to care for. Because our generation will see the consequences and by that time you all will be gone.' Her generation is arguing for what philosopher John

Rawls calls intergenerational justice when he says, 'Each generation must not only preserve the gains of culture and civilization, but also put aside . . . a suitable amount of real capital accumulation.'[18] Essentially, while material capital has grown, our children are warning us to stop doing this at the cost of environmental capital. In March 2019, almost 2000 such strikes took place across the world, and 1.4 million young people, including my daughter, took part, aided by digital drums linking schools across the world.

Shaken by recent weather patterns and goaded by the determined voice of our children, the world is waking up to the possibility that the planet we are bequeathing to the next generation is in trouble. The first trend that is causing this is the sheer growth of population, India contributing in a fulsome manner. The world's population has doubled over the past fifty years and will be at the 10 billion mark by 2050.[19] India's population by 2050 will be 1.6 billion, the largest country that has ever existed.[20] The Holocene age has ended and mankind has shaken the planet, creating the Anthropocene age with 'more and more consumption of natural capital, harming rivers, lakes, soils and forests in their countries and beyond'.[21] Man has made such dramatic changes through industrialization that 'planetary boundaries' that keep the earth in equilibrium are being breached, of which CO_2 emissions and global warming is the most obvious crisis.

Drilling through the carbon mountain

A friend and climate warrior, Pavan Sukhdev, introduced a framework that can help visualize the conundrum of economic growth sans CO_2, and guide ecological action.

On a visit to Mumbai, over dinner, he drew the per capita emissions of India, China and the US on a paper napkin, which resembled a sloping mountain. India has a per capita CO_2 emission of 2 tons, China is at 8 tons while the US is at 15 tons.[22] Joining the dots, the graph showed that the US, after reaching the top of the slope at 20 tons per person, had started dropping based on technological solutions such as wind and solar industries for less carbon emissions per unit of energy. Describing this graph as a mountain, Pavan said, 'India has an opportunity to use green development strategies to "drill through the CO_2 mountain".' We can make GDP per capita rise, improving quality of life but still not create as much CO_2 as was done by the US or China. Instead of climbing the mountain and then trying to climb down the other side, India can 'drill through'. This may increase per capita CO_2 emissions but will do so without following the carbon-intensive industrialization path that the West and China had taken till a few years back.

What constitutes the CO_2 mountain, and what can the Middle do while it has the chance to drill through it? A simple way of understanding the mountain is to understand what is causing 51 billion tons of CO_2 emission every year.[23] India at COP 26 agreed to get to net zero by 2070. But this requires innovation so that we increase quality of life for our citizens without increasing CO_2 emissions. Can the answer come from a de-centralized, de-materialized and locally urbanized growth within communities in the Middle? It is a view of life that is opposite to one offered by George Mallory when asked about his motivation to climb Everest in 1923, making him famous as a mountaineer. In an interview with the *New Yorker* magazine, Mallory said, 'Everest's existence is a challenge. The answer, is in part of human's desire to conquer the universe.'[24] That point of view of conquest drove colonialism and communism, damaging our planet, and must be reversed.

We can visualize the process of sustainable living as climbing down a holy mountain—for instance, Kanchenjunga. At a height of 28,000 feet, it is the third highest mountain in the world, located at the borders of Nepal, Bhutan and India, and was first mapped in the mid-nineteenth century by Rinzin Namgyal. Descending it would be a metaphor for climbing down, leaving the pristine heights of our great mountains where they belong, at the apex of an unsullied world where a litter of oxygen tanks should not pollute its spiritual significance to the three countries that surround it.

This descent from an industrial, greenhouse emissive, polluting approach can take place in five stretches. The first climb down would be if we make less cement, steel and plastic by moderating rapid urbanization. This would make us climb down by almost 9000 feet. Today the world adds 'one New York every month',[25] and this is best avoided. A new urbanization in the Middle can help, where small town build-outs such as Naya Deoria, unlike the skyscrapers of New York, Shanghai or Mumbai, can be made with earth works using less cement, steel and plastic.

The second leg of the climb down would be by generating electricity sustainably. Here, India is doing commendable work, with solar already at 8 per cent of total power generation in India, having trebled over the past few years and expected to treble again over the next few years.[26] This would bring us down swiftly by another 8000 feet to a height of 11,000 feet, almost to the base camp of the ascent.

The third element of the CO_2 mountain are 'plants and animals'. A key amelioration here is to prevent erosion of forest cover and organic methods of production which prevent leaching of soil. If this takes place, we will descend by a further 5300 feet to 6000 feet.

Finally, transportation emissions reduction of 4500 feet and heating, cooling and refrigeration reduction of 2000-odd feet can be tackled by living closer to where you belong, and where possible, telecommuting within the country now that Zoom calls are a part of post-COVID life.

In 2021, India contributed only 2.5 billion tons of CO_2, a mere 7 per cent of global emissions for 18 per cent of the population.[27] Cumulatively, India has contributed an even lower number at only 4 per cent of global emissions.[28] By around 2047, with a $15 trillion economy, instead of trebling this load, we should get to a point where we are at a sensible number for our 1.5 billion population while improving their quality of life. This will be achieved not just through technological solutions but through local institutions and by deploying culture. An ecological way of life should emerge from the very basis of society and our approach to udyamita in the Middle. For instance, forestry approaches conceived in the West, and imposed on India as the Forest Act of 1878, segregated forests for 'sustainable timber extraction'.[29] This cultural view of timber as a resource for feeding an industrial machine separated forest dwellers from the forests on which their lives depended in a circular relationship. Middle India has an ability to live with nature, with mini forests and trees as part of rural and semi-rural life. It is marked by a culture of replenishment where life is informed by 'the very nature of consciousness, the apparently consistent unification of an entire set of beliefs about nature and about men in the collective . . .'[30] This must be nurtured from the beginning, rather than resorting to a call to arms once the damage has been done. It should not be a *constraint* as defined by the West which, in a state of ecological exhaustion after climbing the CO_2 mountain, is dictating de-carbonization suited to its own needs. Indian economic growth should rely on cultural *restraint* and circularity with repairing and replenishment being a way of life. The West used an extractive ecology to enrich itself during the colonial period, and post-Communist China moved to focus on unbridled material growth. Instead, life and economic growth in the Middle require a focus on replenishment, 'linear one-way relationships of pure extraction . . . replaced with systems that are circular and reciprocal'.[31]

I remember my paternal grandmother, mostly unlettered, walking slowly after dinner to the cow shed each day to feed a cow, which had given her family milk, two rotis every night. She was following some long-held societal memory of circularity, a return gift to the animal world that had given its milk to her family. Millions of Indians in the Middle live close to nature, experience it first-hand, involve it and have an integrative relationship with it—a cultural gift that will allow us to 'drill through the environmental mountain'.

Cartesian and colonial thinking

This requires us to move beyond an automaton view of the world. India should focus on human spirit, energy, connections and ingenuity as resources for innovation and growth. This will include machines, infrastructure and digital but will not be defined by it. It will focus on human connections that are an important part of our resource pool and interdependent on nature, not just material consumption. A deeper analysis is needed to understand why a human-centric, integrative, environmentally inclusive spiritual growth is needed and why the current environmental crisis is a direct result of extractive, Cartesian and colonial logic.

Thinkers such as Clayton Christensen have proven that successful institutions emerge out of culture.[32] If we follow this logic, a mechanistic culture that believed in automaton created extractive, colonial institutions. This was glorified in Europe and was transposed by immigrants to the US 300 years ago. This exploitation started with what was explained away as a golden 'Age of Reason'. René Descartes (1596–1650) was a key architect of that age, creating a philosophy that separated mind, body and spirit. He gave humans the nomenclature of 'machine', explaining the human body as 'functions, including passion, memory and imagination follow from the mere arrangement of machine organs, every bit as natural as the movement of a clock or another automaton follows from the arrangement of its counterweight and wheel.'[33] Did Cartesian philosophy create the institutions that started with the inhumanities the Dutch armies perpetrated in the islands of Banda in Indonesia when they treated plants, animals and humans as a machine-like resource? Descartes, born in France, spent most of his adult life in Holland and served in the Dutch army for a spell. As Amitav Ghosh has documented, the automaton view of the world gained favour and sealed the fate of fauna, flora and local culture wherever colonies were built, terraforming entire continents in the image of Europe and erasing entire races.[34] It set the 'enlightened West' on a path of material and human extraction including the blight of slavery, often aided by a Church that was co-invested in the conquest of heathen souls. In economics, this manifested itself in that famous diagram most students study, where money is circulated in a hydraulic diagram between producers and workers without any reference to human behaviour or the environment we live in. An automaton world view, aided subsequently by the 'survival of the fittest' theory, led to colonial exploitation and institutions that subjugated Asia, America and Africa. India is just beginning to come out of the shadow of this thinking, now led by a generation that was born free.

This exploitation bankrolled the spread of that world view globally. The colonial enterprise co-opted the elite in colonized states using its illicit surplus, whitewashing crimes and creating a curtain of benevolence. This materialism gave birth to communism, which distracted India's founders through its sister, socialism, in the initial years after Independence. Communism converted China to its cause over two decades of revolutionary war and neutered Chinese civilization, that other original centre of ideas in Asia, extinguishing local traditions, with further damage during the Cultural Revolution in the sixties. In China, a 5000-year historical continuity was sundered by a party that believed in Marx's materialism and perennial class conflict. Global modernity came to be defined by a separation of mind, body and spirit, with progress defined by singular material growth, and with society, life and the natural ecosystem divided for exploitation, making it non-integrative.

This material modernism peaked in the Second World War a few years before Indian independence, where all three parties—a triumphant Western coalition, Communist

Russia and a defeated Germany—remained convinced
about automaton, having just delivered violence on an
unimaginable scale leading, as the story goes, Gandhi to
quip, 'Western civilization would be a good idea.'[35] To end
the Second World War, destructive forces never experienced
by humanity were unleashed on Hiroshima and Nagasaki.
Robert Oppenheimer, the father of the atomic bomb and
the forefather of Jennifer, my rafting companion in Oregon,
quoted words from the Bhagavad Gita to cope with the first
atomic explosion in the Los Alamos desert. He said, 'Now
I become Death, the destroyer of worlds.'[36] The world
still acquiesced in the resulting modernity that continued
to believe in conquest, which seeded the institutions at
Bretton Woods. The success of this modernity was sealed
by a material USA that continued to operate and advertise
an unsustainable myth, in which, if I am to be honest,
I too participated as a drilling rig manager for seven
years. Marxism inspired Leninist and Stalinist thoughts
that through the Cold War created a 'permanent war
economy'[37], which has recently morphed into the rising US-
China confrontation that is re-arming the world. Countries
with large populations and rich organic cultures—India,
Indonesia, Brazil, Nigeria, South Africa, Mexico, etc.—had
no say in the institutions or measures of success that have
guided the world since then. The indigenous economic
cultures of these countries were ignored with western
culture and modernity as the conquering archetype, leading
to a globalization that benefited the Top. Economic Social
and Governance (ESG) is a recent welcome step towards
integration, but it has germinated in the same petri dish
that got us into ecological trouble in the first place. It
offers solutions from 'penitent' nations who are confessing

their sins of ecological extraction, suggesting solutions but discounting the new possibilities of 'drilling through the environmental mountain', for they are already on the top of this environmental heap. Einstein's warning, 'We can't solve problems by using the same thinking we used when we created them,'[38] rings true!

A new modernism from the Middle

Our first response against colonialism post-Independence was tentative as 'it sought to assimilate modern ideas, techniques and institutions—the "secrets" of Western powers—and then turn them against the West itself.'[39] This was a natural response from the post-Independence elite, still convinced about Cartesian logic, Western institutions and pure technological solutions, wanting to imitate them and use them against colonizers. Some, such as Vivekananda and Sri Aurobindo, advocated a more original path that tried to incorporate the human spirit but were not understood, with Sri Aurobindo withdrawing to the seclusion of an ashram in Pondicherry. Others, such as Tilak, Gandhi and Savarkar, succeeded only when they articulated this modernity based on our integrative culture and traditions, but socialism and the statism of the Indian state post-Independence took control and these thought processes were sidelined.

Today, that generation is retiring and the ills of a mechanical world view are there for all to see. It is only now that India can consider a more comprehensive response powered by the originality of the Middle. In this response, a critique of the West or of Marxist China and their exploitative or violent histories is not sufficient. By co-opting the Middle, India must deploy its civilizational energies to offer an alternate modernism. This is not 'lazy modernism' that celebrates ancient India through words and 'tall claims'. Instead, it works hard to discover our scientific, moral and cultural traditions to bring them back to centre-stage. Through research and new institutions, science and innovation, the morality of our own traditions and culture must be re-examined and rejuvenated while we create new traditions through the act of building. In maths, chemistry, physics, agriculture, medicine, engineering and education, there are insights that have been obliterated. For example, the so-called Pythagoras theorem that was discovered in Greece around 300 BCE was solved in 800 BCE by mathematician Baudhyayan and documented in *Sulabhsutra*.[40] Other civilizations too had thought this through, including ancient Mesopotamia and China, but were not given credit. Even René Descartes' famous tenets of coordinate geometry outlined in the 1600s had been postulated by Vachaspati in 850 CE.[41] Closer in time, when Calcutta was 'honoured' as a location named in the *Geography of Genius*, C.V. Raman and Satyen Bose were using the benefits of science that inspired subsequent scientific leaders such as Vikram Sarabhai and A.P.J. Abdul Kalam. Similarly, research and institutions that bring out the originality of our Vedas, Upanishads and Puranas are few and those that exist are underfunded. Many schools in rural areas, such as those outlined in a report by Thomas Munro, the Governor of Madras Presidency in 1822,[42] were obliterated by colonial lethargy and lack of funding. As these traditions are rejuvenated and modernized through research and building new institutions, they are best developed and deployed in the Middle, for culturally this segment still lives an integrated life, less influenced by Cartesian modernity. Only then can the country chart a new path that will give India the rise it seeks and deserves.

This modernism must be both *integrative* and *innovative*. Four values will drive it and make it distinctive from western modernity.

Socially, it will be human-centric, which recognizes and releases the potential in every citizen recognizing the ethics of community and the ethics of divinity. It must integrate with the geographical location, the local fauna and flora, where faith, family and community are housed. While displacement may take place, it should be a pilgrim's journey, like our Yatra, for a return to your station, your karmabhoomi. Economically, it must consider citizens as innovators, producers and consumers in a process that believes in fair competition, circularity and replenishment.

Technologically, it must be driven by science but keeping the human dimension and the human connect topmost in mind. For instance, the singular glorification of medical technology in recent years has been balanced by a view that without the organizing capabilities of human networks, we could not have bested pandemics like COVID-19.[43]

Finally, it should be aligned with the spirit and soul of the country where different classes, castes and creeds blend to create a new nation, moving beyond Westphalian concepts of mere national boundaries by understanding the chitti, the spirit of the country, both to promote innovation and over time, to evolve our culture as this takes place. Vivekananda had an early premonition when he said it was time 'we took our eyes away from this chimera of universal modernity and clear up a space where we might become the creators of our own modernity'[44].

Old colonial-style conquest was done by the twin instruments of violence and proselytization. The mercantile economy of Europe slowly morphed into a modern economy based on innovation, later transported to the US. However, it focused on technology 'prototypes',[45] a certain way of life more interested in 'machine making' rather than 'man making' endorsed and accelerated by the US, a nation with boundless material resources. More vitalist energies like the concept of atman or brahma in Indic life, *dao*, the fundamental way in Chinese memories or *ilam* divinity in Akkadian thought, in contrast, were radiant, sacred forces that are deeper, higher, organic and more fundamental to human existence but were ignored.[46] As outlined earlier in the book, the Santiago theory reasserts this organic viewpoint by suggesting connections which get refreshed and renewed are the basis of life. The CO_2 mountain is an immediate reason for emerging countries in Asia, Africa and Latin America, who are still at the bottom of the mountain, not to commit to a climb that could destroy humanity, but the impact of such an approach will be much broader—socially, economically and politically. A new modernity has to recognize the spiritual connection between humans and all of nature and be humble enough to walk around the industrial mountain, like pilgrims do at Mount Kailash.

Parts of this modernity are already emerging. Yoga, whose definition itself is 'integration', has tasted success both across India and globally—a new discovery of culture that is confident of its own resources, not just because the West sees it like that. That Ayurveda may have cures that are natural, organic and long-lasting is being recognized, alongside an understanding that research institutions in this field are also needed. The idea of a connected human being shaping a new psychology and sociology, as outlined by Deepak Chopra in tomes such as *Meta Human*,[47] is being mainstreamed. The challenge to Western universalism that Indic traditions offer is being outlined by Rajiv Malhotra, among others. The location and purpose of scientific, engineering and digital innovations has to keep the human dimension as a key design principle, a responsibility the largest democracy has to shoulder. This inversion of modernity is symbolized by the *Urdhva Mula* described in the Bhagavad Gita as a banyan with its roots facing skywards and its trunks and branches coming down to earth bringing sustenance[48]—a civilizational belief that an all-pervasive spirit integrates human relationships while keeping the flow of innovation alive, leading to prosperity and meaning.

As we create this modernity, we need to be watchful of at least three risks. The first is that some values and cultures of the Middle need to be modernized. Not all values of the Middle are right, nor are all values of the Top or the West wrong. Women's equality, the removal of narrow caste divisions and the belief that all creeds belong to our motherland are important areas for improvement. The second risk is that machines have made the West so successful, creating an all-powerful 'material matrix', that a new modernity will find difficulty in being accepted in a world fed on material growth, like the incredulity of Neo in the movie *The Matrix*, when asked by Morpheus to swallow the red pill and break out of the make-believe world where machines rule. Today, we are gripped by a material matrix that is all-pervasive. Finally, the power structure of the world is based on Western modernity, defined by material progress and led recently by the US, which used 'manifest destiny' to support its own globalizing mission that was accepted by the elite in emerging nations. China, informed by communism's automaton view of the world, is surfing a large infrastructure wave just north of our border, trying to re-make the world where big buildings, big highways and control on citizens motivates its growth, leaning subconsciously on a 'mandate from heaven' to expand globally. Any suggestion of human centricity or human spirit from India also runs the risk of India being re-labelled mystical and traditional.

India's focus on human connections does not exclude the development of hard structures, technologies and weapon systems. But the purpose of such structures and systems should not be the conquest of nature or of other humans. Instead, it should facilitate collaboration, which can lead to development that is innately democratic. The core experience of India remains service based, and digital is aiding and amplifying that experience fully. This should be seen as a core area of civilizational and national expertise without ignoring material gains and infrastructure build-outs, including a sharp focus on having a world-class defence ecosystem.

A more fundamental objection can be raised by economists and thinkers who argue that 'innovation could be suffocated by a fixation on family and community to the exclusion of the individual'.[49] This objection belies the West's mindset which believes that industrial production, the assembly line and material production, which also spawned the nuclear family, is central to modernity. Eastern traditions, wiser, less obsessed with material goals, with longer traditions of communal and spiritual living, are equally good at innovation but one where integration is key. Indian society is interconnected not just with other humans but with nature, where divinity is defined by an omniscient Brahma. Institutions, innovations and insights are not just those of the physical world and driven by individualism but those of an integrated life that carry a belief in community and divinity.

Buffeted by social stress and recently also by the rising environmental movement, the West is also seeking such an organic, integrative modernity. The fertilization of a material West with humanistic ideas from the East commenced as early as 300 BCE, when Alexander and the Greeks encountered the gymnosophists[50] of India. More recently, it was re-ignited by Vivekananda and others. Western thinkers and philosophers like David Hume had challenged Descartes and his followers.[51] Thinkers such as Giambattista Vico most forcefully supported this by arguing, 'A utilitarian interpretation of the most essential human activities is misleading . . . To sing, to dance, to worship, to speak, to fight and the institutions which embody these activities comprise a vision of the world.'[52] Experience rather than logical wisdom handed down from up top should guide human action. This is a position Vivekananda advocated from the very beginning, culminating in his meditations on the rock in Kanyakumari. Recent focus on behavioural approaches such as Nudge and Design Thinking is an admission that human spirit, local context and connections matter. Design thinking starts not just with the functional needs of humans but with their emotive state as well.[53] Behavioural economics has put human relationships at the top of the economic agenda. Industrial modernity that was centralized and resource-intensive is slowly moving to decentralized living and a search for circularity.

A new Indian modernity by co-opting the Middle will lead to economic, social and environmental integration and innovation for India. The conviction to pursue this modernity will only come by putting the resources, intellect and passion through a democratic process, with the mass in the Middle energized through udyamita. This will give us economic and republican power to take our country forward without mortgaging the future of the next generation. Instead of appealing to 'manifest' forces or a 'mandate' that comes from above, we will start a new national journey appealing to the power in our own 'Middle', a democratic approach that invokes the spirit of our people. Kabir highlighted the possibility of our own centre creating progress from within when he said a 'musk deer roams the forest in search of an aroma that comes from its own navel'[54]. We were misled by a colonial, Western modernity as we roamed the world for ideas when they resided in our own centre. The German philosopher Herder calls it *schwerpunket* or centring, saying, 'Every civilization has its own *Schwerpunket,* and unless we grasp it we cannot understand its character or value . . . Art, morality, custom, religion, national life grow out of immemorial traditions and created by entire societies living an integrated communal life.'[55] This duel between a Cartesian, colonial modernity that seeks to divide, and a homegrown one that seeks to integrate by understanding our own nature, is not just within India— it will take place across the 'Global Middle', where Indian success can become an exemplar. This modernity, explained to others by highlighting the importance of intellectual decolonization using the environmental crisis as literally a 'burning platform', would create relevant innovations, not just in the emerging world but also in the developed world. This may require us to update measures of national success by broadening them to include Gross Environmental Product (GEP), that goes beyond narrow economic measures, given the recent quest to create an 'ecological civilization'.[56] China can also learn from this modernity as it struggles with multiple inconsistencies that comes from borrowing and grafting a model that was used by Mao and the communists tactically for capturing state power, erasing its culture in the process.

That cultural genocide continues in Tibet even today and needs a strategic response from India, which seeded Theravada Buddhism in Tibet to begin with. I heard this story when I met Norgay,[57] who fled Tibet in the early nineties at the age of six and was our tour guide at the Norbulingka Institute in Dharamshala, Himachal Pradesh on a recent visit. Having done his schooling in Dharamshala and higher studies in Chennai, he communicates clandestinely with his parents near the district of Kham in Tibet. In a poignant voice, he described how friends left behind are being groomed by the Chinese for material success when the aim of Tibetan life was 'being a good human'. As we toured the institute and observed young Tibetans painting *thangkas* that preserve Tibetan culture this side of the Himalayas, he described a world in his homeland fast hurtling towards singular material aspirations. Pointing to a map of Tibet and the district of Kham with misty eyes, he knowledgeably described how China is seeking to divert major rivers that originate in this 'rooftop of the world', adversely impacting 1.35 billion people across Asia[58] in a planet already starved of water. China wants to climb down the CO_2 mountain, but it remains imprisoned by its own flush of material progress and a totalitarian polity that continues to placate its restive citizens through material growth. 'Being a good human being' is the new modernity the world seeks instead of one that scrambles for material progress that will cost us our planet.

Economic institutions from the Middle

This modernity will spawn an economics of 'mass flourishing'.[59] Making a case for innovation that involves the masses, Nobel laureate Edmund Phelps suggests that the act of creating and innovating in itself is critical to give humans meaning. The human experience, the thrill of creating something new, in collaboration or alone, is both an ancient tug and a modern urge. Beyond creating a more productive economy, it defines a meaningful life. Its genesis is the aspiration of the human spirit, its goal is the fulfilment of life through 'exploration, creation and exhilaration'.[60] The core of the udyamita experience is a similar process. Udyamita is not just incubating new companies, providing local employment and economic growth. The triple act of inspiration, innovation and incubation[61] drives deeper sources of joy that have merit on their own. This economic link to a new modernity located in the Middle will take forward the ideas of integral humanism and refresh it for the twenty-first century. And this will be adopted more easily in the Middle by people who are least impacted by Western modernity.

New institutions are needed in the Middle to support this modernity and the economics of integration, creating strategic change in the real India. Recent research challenges the practice of foisting institutions from above, arguing that they must emerge from societal action. Clayton Christensen says, 'Successful institutions grow out of culture, not the other way around.'[62] Christensen and his team cite examples from Georgia, Afghanistan, India and other emerging countries to demonstrate that institutional reforms and attempts at nation-building directed from above have consistently failed. Instead, Christensen says, 'Innovations, especially those that create "new markets", typically precede the development and sustenance of good institutions'.[63] He demonstrates that the economic surge seen by Japan and South Korea was created by innovators and institutions which tackled local needs, created local employment and then used this foundation to launch a national and a global effort. Toyota, for instance, first sold and tested its cars on the smaller roads of Japan before taking them international.

Our rise must begin by *pulling* new institutions from within, built in our context, rather than *pushing* institutions from the Top or from overseas.[64] We must guard against colonial institutions that remain unchanged and continue to divide the Middle. Real institutions built through 'shared learning, of people working together to solve problems and figuring out what works'.[65] Starting now, over the coming twenty-five years, effective institutions in the Middle—forms of local governance, financial systems, banking practices, digital best practices, judicial systems, etc.—must be strengthened so that a dynamic ecosystem that believes in driving indigenous innovations and enterprise is built. These will also incorporate centres of congregation, education, libraries and approaches to service with the stamp of our own circumstances to foster joint experiences.

Building these institutions and deploying them in the unexplored Middle will also give purpose to those from metro cities and Non-Resident Indians (NRIs). I saw this echoed by Rajiv Malhotra, a well-known architect who lives overseas, at a talk in Mumbai when he exhorted young architects that instead of 're-designing your mother's friend's kitchen in Mumbai', they needed to address the urgent architectural needs of 2700 small towns that require their talents. The real opportunity for engineers, teachers, designers, architects, technologists, entrepreneurs and others is hardly in the overpopulated and overcompetitive metros. It is in that other India, Bharat, where most Indians are starting their rise and where institution building is most needed.

Topophilia and a modern building

A new modernity suited for our times cannot be prescribed a priori; it will emerge from the Middle over the coming twenty-five years through local innovations and new institutions. The act of building together, joint experiences through enterprise, innovation, digital, inclusion and a sustainable model of growth will give it birth. This will be aided by 'topophilia' or 'love of place'. Ross Baird, the CEO of Village Capital, describes this as 'when people find meaning where they live—both physical location and the ecosystem—they feel the freedom to create.'[66] This is a movement that seeks to stop abandonment of locations as millions of Indians are still living the 'life of elsewhere'. The 'life of elsewhere' dream encourages young people in a small town like Deoria to think that a town like Lucknow is where they are destined for; the person in Lucknow is living a Mumbai dream, and the person in Mumbai, in turn, is hoping to go to Singapore. This not only destroys the spirit of the region but also chips away at the spirit of the person exiting. Colonizing societies valorize this displacement, sometimes forcing it, as the UK did when it established a penal colony in 1788 in Botany Bay in Australia, where today's Sydney is located. American modernity, shaped by immigrants from across the world, paid lip service to location. The appeal of American values, celebrating displacement, are prevalent at the Top with a similar disdain for roots, which justify lives in isolated urban enclaves.

'Love of place', combined with enterprise, innovation, digital and sustainability, are design criteria for four enterprise centres planned nationally by Jagriti, the first being in Deoria. The Deoria centre, named somewhat clumsily as JECP or Jagriti Enterprise Centre—Purvanchal, has been designed by Trupti Doshi, an award-winning sustainability architect and a Yatri who understood our plans when she stayed in Barpar during the Yatra. We have already built Phase I of the centre next to the 300-year-old banyan tree on a 6-acre piece of land in Barpar, in a spiral shape that comes from Trupti's core inspiration—Sri Aurobindo. It signals the possibility of exponential rise—one that is sustainable. Trupti has kept the topmost point of the building lower than the banyan tree, a daily reminder of the spirit and stature of this tree. Two circular arms of the centre will come together paying homage to the banyan, embracing and denoting circularity in our traditions, a direct riposte to Cartesian linearity. Each room of the centre faces the banyan and has a transparent façade, so that each udyami, when they look up, glimpses this centuries-old sentient. A semi-circular amphitheatre sloping down from the central block resembles the ghats of nearby Varanasi. We imagine evenings when this amphitheatre will seat

500 local leaders watching a performance or a business plan competition to showcase how India can be built. The juxtaposition of a curved, modern, digitally armed, people-centric building next to an ancient tree reflects the modernity we seek for the Middle.

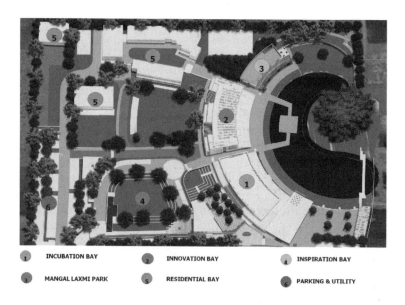

	INCUBATION BAY		INNOVATION BAY		INSPIRATION BAY
	MANGAL LAXMI PARK		RESIDENTIAL BAY		PARKING & UTILITY

We plan similar centres in Kanyakumari, Tamil Nadu, Ganjam, Odisha and Nagpur, Maharashtra, thus creating four *dhams* of enterprise, locating our mission firmly in the cardinal corners of the country. Each of these regional Enterprise Centres will support at least fifteen adjoining districts. In each location, mobile units of Udyam Corps and Udyam Mitra will use the centre as a weekend oasis, while helping 'Middle India udyamis' in their own districts. It will invite local citizens to the centre to gather, converse, educate themselves and use the digital library, creating a congregation space for local innovation and development.

To foster innovation in specific areas that are relevant for our region, six Centres of Excellence, each dealing with a local need, such as agro-processing, handicrafts and apparel, digital, women, health and rural urbanization, are planned in the next phase of building. We seek to bring young students from high school through college so that the youth get exposed to 'positive freedoms' and udyamita early on. They will also get a reminder that the history of our area, and other areas in the Middle, is not about flight. This Middle was the proud protector of our national freedom, sparking Independence and suffering as a result for this display of courage.

Reversing the flow of the Ganga

When I describe the centre to those in large cities, I get questioned on the need for a world-class institution for fifteen-odd Tier 3 and Tier 2 districts. The dominant logic is that those living in these districts will move to large cities, so why bother? Why this 'ulti Ganga', the 'reverse flow of the Ganga', they ask? More damaging is the belief that institutions at the Top, proposing copycat western modernity, should remain the source of leadership and innovation. They borrow from a global narrative that wishes to see India urbanize rapidly and inexorably according to the terms set by Europe and North America. We remind them that at this time, only 15 per cent of India lives in big cities, with 18 per cent of what we call urban India residing in towns like Deoria Sadar, which are spread across the hinterland.[67] And contrary to claims of imminent urbanization, the rate of urbanization over the past six decades has declined from 3.5 per cent to 2.7 per cent per year,[68] even before COVID-19 created another reason to pause. Building ivory towers in large colonial cities such as Delhi, Mumbai, Bengaluru, Chennai or Kolkata is the real 'ulti Ganga'. Crossing the seventy-fifth anniversary of Indian Independence, we must finally turn the river of nation-building in the right direction—to where the majority lives and where our culture remains intact. This is not just a call for rural living, as our founders may have wanted; it includes a call for methodical and sustainable urbanization of smaller towns like Deoria Sadar, as is being attempted in Naya Deoria. It reminds us of what anthropologist Anna Tsing has pointed out: 'Frontiers are not just discovered at the edge; frontiers are places where one goes to see and build the future, and to erase certain pasts.'[69] Even then, some citizens will continue to take a train to the bright lights of a megapolis. However, if we create institutions and enable infrastructure, the majority will stay back to innovate and build locally.

Demands for similar regional development are coming from the Yatri community in other parts of the country. We are only lending a hand if we find a committed local leader who believes in taking udyamita forward, not just over a few years but over a twenty to thirty-year horizon, sometimes entailing an intergenerational effort. National and international governments are also keen and Jagriti has been approached by state governments in India, as well as a recent conversation with a state governor in Nigeria. I am committed to this mission in my region for the next twenty-five years and with luck, my children will follow suit.

To finish my books, I travel to my favourite spot in the world, Kanyakumari. The location is an offshore *sangam* of the Indian Ocean, Arabian Sea and the Bay of Bengal, creating a spiritual vortex that draws me in. In building our four centres of enterprise, we are inspired by the story of Eknath Ranade, who helped envision and built the Rock Memorial as a monument to Vivekananda and to nation-building. We have explored this location many times during the Yatra and did so more deeply through our sea swim in 2017. On finishing that swim, we filled two brass urns of water from Kanyakumari and put it on the train. Alighting in Deoria, we took water from the urns and sprinkled it next to the banyan tree, my family priest uttering shlokas assembled hurriedly that morning, combining an invocation to both the banyan and to our vast seas. As we build the centre at the northernmost point of the Jagriti Yatra, we will link it with the southernmost point, spiritually and intellectually seeking unity for our country. The spirit of Vivekananda and the perseverance of Eknath Ranade is guiding us in this.

As I was writing this book, I ended up in Kanyakumari on 14 August to seek inspiration for the last two chapters. Here, at the edge of our nation, I experienced a moment of spirituality which prompted me to do something I have never done in my life—buy jewellery. As I sat mulling these chapters, waiting for the tide to turn and for the ferry to the Rock Memorial to start, an old man with beads in his hand appeared next to me. He insisted that I buy a necklace of local *motis*, pearls that divers had picked up from the ocean near Kanyakumari. When I declined, he took out a lighter and held the necklace in its flame, suggesting they were real. On asking him the price, he said, 'Rs 100'. Mostly to humour him, I bought the necklace, and as soon as the transaction was done, he disappeared.

That night in my hotel room, this encounter haunted me. As the clock struck midnight and I concluded the first draft of this book, I looked at the necklace on my writing table and wore it, with a vow that I would remove it only when the centre in Deoria was built. The necklace's proximity to my chest became a daily reminder of this responsibility, and I finger it as I type today. On the seventy-fifth anniversary of India's Independence, the first phase of the JECP is being inaugurated. In the foundation of this centre will lie buried a pearl necklace, bought from a mysterious man in a white beard, from the southernmost edge of India—the place where we will build the second centre.

13

Future: *A New Promise*

बाँध लेंगे क्या तुझे यह मोम के बंधन सजीले?
पंथ की बाधा बनेंगे तितलियों के पर रंगीले?
तू न अपनी छाँह को अपने लिये कारा बनाना!
जाग तुझको दूर जाना!

—महादेवी वर्मा

(Will these wax threads capture you with their charms?
Will the colourful wings of butterflies come in
the way of your resolve?
Don't let your shadow confine you!
Awaken, you have to go far!)

—Mahadevi Verma

Many conversations over sixteen Yatras have informed my view of the future. The most poignant of these was in the 1997 Yatra with eighteen-year-old Akhtar, razor sharp and multitalented but blind from birth. In a discussion nearing the end of that journey, he asked, 'Will we continue to be like Columbus, attempting to explore the country, or stay

299

put in one location and build, like Edison?'¹ A few years
after asking this question, Akhtar took his own life in the
blind school where he studied. The reasons for this tragedy
will remain unknown, but in the years that followed, we
answered his question by travelling and discovering the
real India, an India Columbus never managed to reach.
The enterprise effort that commenced five years back in
Purvanchal marked the beginning of our Edison phase.
Through udyamita, we are illuminating these districts,
and this will shine a light on other towns and districts
nationally, a small tribute to Akhtar's two-part question.

My conversations and our experience in Deoria have
confirmed our original thesis—development begins by
releasing the energies of innovation in committed leaders
who work within their context, their communities, so
that local solutions can be found, both small and at scale.
My own experience circling the country over the years
on the Yatra was not so much a discovery of our land
as an exploration of this spirit. The 7500 Yatris who
travelled with us on the journey and the entrepreneurs
in Deoria have given me a window into the real resource
of our nation—its people. I learnt this while circling the
country and in the Edison-like attempt in Purvanchal, in
an action-reflection-action mode, part of the circularity of
Indian life.

That circle of learning commences every year in
November, when the humid Mumbai air turns crisp for a
few months. That change in weather announces the arrival
of the first batch of collaborators for the Jagriti Yatra—a
group of thirty ex-Yatris, endearingly called the Engine
Room Club (ERC), who now want to work behind the
curtains in support of the Yatra. This includes leaders such

as Kshitij Lunkad, who runs his own CA firm with almost thirty employees but breaks away for three weeks for this refresher course in inspiration. He once confided, 'I find reliving the journey with other inspiring people a chance to recharge for the year.' Then, a day before the Yatra, this team is joined by seventy-five facilitators who troop into a hall, hauling their luggage for the fifteen-day journey. This is when spirits shift. The core team and the ERC group feel fortified, like soldiers must feel in battle when an additional regiment joins them. Our learning starts here as each person talks about why they have come on a non-stop fifteen-day adventure where the only surety is hardship.

The core team do not as much listen to their stories as soak in the spirit of that room. Each person, as they relate their life's experience, has a magical effect on all others. In this moment, it is not the singular spirit that rises, it is the plural. It is not the content of what they have done but the *spiritual experience* of connecting with 100 others, that speaks to us at a deeper level. A similar, less intimate spiritual experience takes place the next day, when these facilitators welcome 425 other Yatris in the setting of an auditorium. This connection continues at different moments in the Yatra and recently, in the enterprise ecosystem around Deoria. I saw this change of spirit in Vibha Pandey of Deoria, who got confidence through the Internet Saathi programme, or the comment of R.C. Kushwaha, who told me, 'The mere recognition that I am doing something special came as a blessing', as he proceeded to scale up his sanitary pad distribution business from thirty villages to 900, providing employment to 700 women in the process locally. This is the human spirit unleashed, which can spark a renaissance over the coming twenty-five years.

Inspiring the rise

Will Durant once remarked, 'One cannot conclude the history of India, as one can conclude the history of Egypt, or Babylonia, or Assyria; for this history is still being made, that civilization is still creating.'[2] A civilizational flow that predates the pyramids is 'still creating'! Indian civilization is a flame that burns slowly but burns strong and long. It uses 'pull' marketing that convinces through values and thought processes.[3] To achieve our goal, this civilizational continuity must be given volume through citizen participation, while digital technology will give it pace. If we inspire 1.4 billion citizens to take part in the rise then, like a mighty river formed of tiny water droplets, our country's output will mirror the roaring Brahmaputra in its volume and flow. Settling our democracy over the past seventy-five years has been done. Our historical longevity and our cultural continuity now asks another generation, unburdened by colonial thought, to create an integrated rise. To do this, we must break away from an India typified by a diffident approach, which aped the West. We must continue to collaborate with the world in an equal exchange of ideas but ultimately chart our own path using the deeper resources within our own culture, shaping a new modernity. We must regain our own standing not just in GDP terms but also in demonstrating a new human-centric, environmentally sustainable, spiritually guided path to the world—a duty India has fulfilled from the dawn of history.

This assertion recognizes that other civilizations have their own intelligence and methods. Europe has a strong tradition that originated in the philosophy of Greece and was firmed up through the polity of Rome. Its offspring, the US, has the tradition of a vibrant democracy refreshed by a constant flow of immigrants. The Middle East and North Africa have an Islamic tradition, giving society discipline. The Sinic civilization has a strong state-based intelligence that has been used to navigate tricky political corners as it shifted from Chinese imperial rule to nationalism to communism to state-run capitalism. The Japanese civilization has an ethic of work and detailing that has few equals. Having lived in Africa, I can vouch for its cultural intelligence, a refreshing tour de force which has gone global in music and dance. The Indian civilization has a unique intelligence too, which focuses on the human spirit and potential. It starts with the proposition that the solution to the problems of the world lie within every human, who, when connected with others and nature, can create a new world in wondrous ways.

The essence of our civilizational intelligence remained preserved in the ignored Middle. This intelligence goes beyond traditional binaries, 'living reconciliation of the opposites, manifested in ecological cycles of growth and decay . . . stability and change, order and freedom, tradition and innovation, planning and laissez faire.'[4] A reconciliation of the powers of feminine and masculine, Shakti and Shiv, Prakriti and Purusha, one observes daily in the lived lives of the Middle. Starting now, this can also reconcile both Top-down and Bottom-up development. The Top of the Diamond starts from a method of growth and wealth creation inspired by 'capital' and global flows. The Bottom of the Diamond needs methods of poverty alleviation using the state as a redistributive agent. 'Middle-up' growth and renewal are based on human centricity where our most important asset, the agency of citizens, family and society, are linked to a local context and participation to foster development using udyamita. It will harness citizen power, human potential 'inside to out', creating economic, social, environmental, political activity and a new modernity inspired by the 'heartland'.

The 'heartland' today only comes into focus as elections approach. Till then, it remains a distant place, inhabited by Indians in *dhotis* and *veshtis*. Our approach should make this the substantive heartland of our nation, central to the economic and social imagination of the country. Unlike China, which relied heavily on export-led, consumer goods-based growth and more recently, by exporting infrastructure, we should rely on our own mass of humanity to power our economic growth as innovators, creators and consumers. Socially, the many connects that are taking place horizontally, originating in community-based societal structures, physical and digital connections, will revive societal collaboration and confidence. Civilizational memory and our 'great traditions' will foster national cultural unity, while 'little traditions' can provide local salience. Our culture celebrates the human spirit and a unifying cosmos that includes other forms of life, critical in an environmentally strained world, giving society a broader definition of conviviality. This intelligence will also lead to a strong republican polity that asks citizens to get behind nation-building. This will release two energies beyond democratic freedom—economic energies of citizens as innovators and producers, and the creation of meaning for a fulfilled human spirit.

The first of its kind

A non-linear rise, for a 1.4 billion-strong democracy, will be the first of its kind in the history of nations. Exact pathways for this growth will emerge through 'the act of building' and by creating institutions that support this renaissance. A starting point can be institutions that support udyamita in local communities in the 240 districts of the Middle through a Banyan Revolution. The Banyan Revolution will drive social and economic growth and local innovation in a digitally enabled, ecologically sustainable manner led by young Indians. Women will play a key role in this as balance sheet builders, and they will also be key beneficiaries, for without 50 per cent of India participating and benefiting, we can't be human-centric. Young leaders will create and run enterprises, the bigger players in the private sector will be key to driving market connects, and government will enable this process through policies and platforms. This requires investment in the Banyan Revolution, an investment in the Middle that has been missing so far.

The first investment is to create a strong government as a catalyst and enabler with new capabilities, both nationally and at the district level. Change represented by the horizontal association of citizens in the village Square must be balanced by national discipline through a well-functioning Tower, the government. Nationally, the government must take on projects 'which at present are not done at all'.[5] These projects, such as the Chandrayaan 3 moon mission, will create a cascading set of innovations that will help those downstream.[6] Upgrading the Defence Research and Development Organisation (DRDO) to make it a real enabler for cutting-edge research for the military will also benefit civil applications. Attracting diaspora talent in areas such as AI is critical, an act the Chinese have taken up with great gusto.[7] In such processes, the government may partner with large private sector players to build India, but it will also partner with smaller companies that provide innovations. For instance, the infrastructure capabilities of L&T or the digital capabilities of Jio represent national champions at their best, but the work on mobility, or the stellar work by some of the enterprises seeded by Jagriti Yatra alumni—Socialcops for data gathering in rural areas, GetMyParking for solving the parking problem[8] and others—may also come in handy.

In such a collaboration, culture and attitude often become a hindrance. My father's four decades in the military likely prompted me to take on the role of the aerospace, defence and space leader for a consulting firm. I understood quickly that much like the Banyan Revolution, defence also required collaboration between citizens, government and private sector with a 'whole-of-nation' approach. Our private sector has skills and assets that are critical for our defence forces. This is particularly true in the emerging area of Non-Kinetic Warfare (NKW), which relies on digital expertise, an area where our IT and software industry have much to say and where we undertook industry research. As I reached out to government research establishments to discuss this research, the gruff voice of a scientific administrator who returned my call informed me that 'they knew it all'. To give him credit, when I reminded him that the US military leverages the capabilities of AI and the quantum computing of companies such as Google, Amazon, Microsoft and Palantir, and we may want to consider a similar approach with TCS, Infosys, Wipro and Zoho, he did pause. Similar conversations with private sector leaders in Mumbai indicate that they are reluctant to engage with government given the slow processes and lack of transparency, continuing to believe that they can 'make progress when the government sleeps at night'. In matters of national endeavours, unless both private and public sectors step over an invisible Laxman *rekha* of mutuality and trust, a 'whole-of-nation' approach will remain absent.

In the Middle, at the district level, we need to strengthen the administrative system on at least two levels—to 'regulate' and to 'enable'. If our economy is dominated by titans at the Top, our state is still governed by an industrial era organization that was instituted by the Northcote-Trevelyan reforms of 1854 in Britain,[9] which had a mechanical-industrial conception of the civil service. In recent years, Mission *Karmayogi*, where I had the privilege of playing a role, is a major effort at reforming and upgrading the civil service. To accelerate this effort and support such reforms in a fast-paced developing economy, which has a significant digital content, 'government as an enabler' should become a key tenet of civil service. This will require upgrading the 'Power On' capabilities of our government while creating new 'Power To' systems and capabilities. The first requires improving core functions of law and order, judiciary, infrastructure and better local infrastructure for enterprise. This will strengthen and upgrade a 'standardized model' of governance, including compliance with timelines and budget, a 'better by Friday' culture, where administrative skills and processes are standard and undergo constant, incremental improvement. 'Power On' capabilities mirror the discipline we enforce in the Yatra, where everyone recognizes that they must abide by rules, else they will suffer the *dand* or punishment of deboarding.

But the second capability of enablement needs an alternate governance structure at the district to enable rapid social and economic growth involving citizen leaders. Here, the culture must be 'experimental', 'where every day, every exercise, every piece of new information is evaluated and debated in a culture that resembles an R&D factory',[10] where failure is analysed, not penalized, and sometimes even celebrated. This requires skills in business, innovation and enterprise, along with sector expertise. Existing administration in the districts cannot change into this 'experimental culture'. Instead, we need to create new government institutions fully dedicated to efforts like the Banyan Revolution, trained and manned separately from routine administration, where the focus is on enabling capabilities 'that arm every citizen with the opportunity to build a meaningful life that stirs their passions and engages their talents'.[11] Such complementary institutions at the district level will focus on social and economic enablement and innovation, keeping local realities in mind. If the regulatory function focuses on 'injunctive social norms', most progress has been proven to take place through 'declarative social norms',[12] where citizens do what they see others do around them in an imitative process. In this case, the role of the government resembles that of a gardener who nurtures and prunes plants and trees, rather than a central machinery that seeks to direct from up yonder. In this case, the government will attempt to connect leaders with each other, connect enterprise to the market and assemble sources of knowledge and private innovation—nurture an ecosystem of mass innovation and enterprise. Government servants will then take on the character of Jamavant in the Ramayana, who reminds the citizen Hanuman of his infinite potential—in short, enable local leaders to take the leap that the rise demands.

Integral humanism, indigenous innovation and Swachh Bharat

This effort at the district level requires a new philosophy, new capabilities and missions with a *direct focus* on enabling society. Such capability building can take inspiration from three previous efforts—integral humanism of Deendayal Upadhyaya, indigenous innovation of Edmund Phelps and Swachh Bharat Mission of Narendra Modi.

I studied the philosophy of Deendayal Upadhyaya, who articulated his ideas in a series of lectures in 1964. Born in a poor family and orphaned a few years after his birth, Deendayal's struggles are manifested in this philosophy, which emerged from the genius of the Middle. His philosophy integrated all of humanity and all of nature within a national framework for development. It spoke of the integration of different segments of society, a society that seeks a future which includes plants and animals, evoking the idea of an omniscient brahma, central to Indian traditions. When these ideas were applied to the nation, it led to an important cultural concept—chitti, the soul of a nation having its own salience. Just as Indian kings and rulers were never above dharma, chitti creates a 'meta nation' that breaches Westphalian concepts of nationhood, moving beyond a narrow focus on national boundaries and state symbols. Once citizens grasp that a unifying chitti integrates them, they would address national issues together and from within. Instead of being goaded by law or by a higher authority, they would make a direct connect to a national mission and create transcendence. The upliftment of the common man, *antyodaya*, through this integrative philosophy is then possible through udyamita.

If integral humanism is a philosophy that can prompt an integrative rise, then indigenous innovation at the grassroots, a theory outlined by Edmund Phelps, can give us an economic framework for action. Phelps seeks sources that drive a modern economy, one that can be called dynamic. His magnum opus, *Mass Flourishing*,[13] has two broad theses, both experienced by us as we circled the country and in our work for innovation and enterprise in Deoria. The first thesis is that neither statism nor corporatism can beat the productivity, growth and employment that indigenous grassroots innovation can drive for a country. His second thesis is even more powerful for a democracy, when he speaks to the non-material gains of innovation, which creates a 'good life' or what I call a 'meaningful life'. The starting point of innovation is the human urge to explore and build, with money or material goods a consequence of that process. He suggests this as a widespread human urge, not limited to the elite, as Maslow may have prescribed, which Balagangadharan has challenged in any case. Phelps says that a modern economy 'gets its dynamism and its inclusion by enlisting the imagination and energy of participants from grassroots up . . . craftsmen, day labourers, farmers, traders and factory workers'.[14] These twin theses encourage 'widening' and 'deepening' the innovation and enterprise process, which is core to our focus in Middle India.

Phelps backs his theory through data that proves that the best decades of the US economy lasted from 1890 to 1970, when indigenous innovation was given policy primacy and cultural importance. Productivity growth was high, GDP growth followed and employment remained robust. However, after 1970, corporatist tendencies took hold of the US economy, with collusion between large business houses and governments together with a growing culture of litigation. This slowed indigenous innovation and halved total factor productivity from 2.26 for a century before 1972 to 1.17 since then till 2011, barring a short upward blip around the dotcom boom.[15] This is also when unemployment, social stress and lack of job satisfaction commenced. While Phelps' data does not cover the rise of Donald Trump in 2016 or the tensions of Brexit, the inequality that triggered these political dissents are also the result of lack of innovation, productivity, rising unemployment and resulting inequality. The recent stress in the Chinese economy can also be traced to top-down government control that slows indigenous innovation. Construction-led growth in China can act as a Band-Aid by 'turning on the spigot of capital',[16] while imported innovations, and sometimes stolen ones, can also improve growth, but this does not make the Chinese economy modern or dynamic. Unless indigenous innovation is encouraged and the human potential given space to flourish, productivity will stall, inequality will rise and the citizens will feel stifled. The Tibetan exile I met in Dharamshala instinctively phrased this as lacking a 'good human life'.

Using Phelps' theory, under the philosophy of integral humanism by Deendayal Upadhyaya, a new dynamic Indian economy can be envisaged that is both integrative and innovative. Phelps is inspired by individual achievement and satisfaction, guided by western culture. As outlined in Chapter 7, there is more at work in India than individuality. The innovations that will drive productivity improvements, economic growth and employment go beyond the ethics of autonomy to embrace the ethics of community and the ethics of divinity. In a Zoom call with Prof. Phelps, I articulated this as a point of dissent. To this, he countered, 'Individuality should not be related to selfishness.' In his own way, he was alluding to the search for meaning in individuals that is often associated with solving problems for others. Such a modernity that is integrative should drive Indian economy in an environmentally strained world, aligning with Indian values and culture, making it locally relevant and acceptable. Community ensures circularity in the economy and divinity is defined as a network permeating life itself through connections—physical, digital and spiritual.

For the largest democracy in the world, the theory of grassroots indigenous innovation bridges a gap that was created by statism and corporatism over the past seventy-five years. It aligns the democratic process with a building process naturally: 'grassroots democracy that was in many ways the counterpart of grassroots dynamism.'[17] This marriage of politics and economics will give our nation republican energy that will create both economic freedom for our country and personal meaning for millions. India is starting from a strong base with a seventy-five-year democracy, and thanks to the 'molecular economy' of Gandhi, the success of self-help groups and recent sprouting of farmer producer organizations, India has a foundation on which to build a wider innovation superstructure, Middle-up. This is complemented by a strong start-up culture nationally, supported often by the global Indian diaspora.

Corporate critics of grassroots innovation or die-hard socialists may argue that such an economic approach may create inequality. This is where the theory of justice by John Rawls comes to our rescue. Rawls asserts that while inequality may emerge, it is the 'best inequality' that satisfies the human urge to create while providing 'minimum possible' wage difference without lowering the employment rate.[18] The collectivistic efforts of socialists or a corporatist approach will not be as equitable over the long run. Most jobs and the best possible wages come from indigenous innovations that are widespread. This theory of justice confirms that the approach of pulling up the Bottom faster through Middle India innovation is the most viable one.

The Banyan Revolution will use both these philosophies. Udyamita may create inequality in what is achieved, but it would focus on 'equality of opportunity' in the Middle as citizens serve and collaborate with other citizens. Higher rewards will come to those who serve better and with integrity and those who use their resources more wisely. The bigger and mightier the purpose, the higher and better the service, the more courageous the person or the team, and the harder the team works, the higher the respect and benefit. The more that person or team applies themselves, the more they will gain in self-esteem, societal recognition, monetary reward and meaning. Much like Indian purushartha, which includes *dharma* and *moksha* but also *artha* and *kama*, wealth creation and pleasures remain important. This may create perceived inequality, but that inequality should raise both parties rather than create an 'equal lethargy'. This interdependence through enterprise will keep our society and economy dynamic. Those who succeed at udyamita in the vast Middle and the wealthy Top will create a safety net for those at the Bottom, the weak and the differently abled, to prevent Darwinian reductionism, unleashing antyodaya. Permanent equality for those who are capable of self-progress, which socialism advocated, will weaken the muscles of society to lift itself up.

Finally, to implement the Banyan Revolution, we can learn from the more recent Swachh Bharat Mission. Mission mode thinking has existed since the moon-shot efforts of Kennedy in the 1960s outlined earlier in the book. However, that effort was top-down and technocratic. It was dreamed up, announced and largely executed by a white elite in the US.[19] Swachh Bharat, on the other hand, involved a whole-of-nation approach and delivered impact at a national scale in the largest democracy to an issue we had not managed to solve since Independence—open defecation. At Jagriti, we experienced the guilt of this unsolved problem every year. As we prepared to welcome the 500 Yatris to Barpar village, the team also started feeling uneasy about the messy roads and by-lanes of the village our guests would soon encounter. We would start a mini sanitation drive but with minor and temporary effects. Then, in 2014, Prime Minister Modi announced the Swachh Bharat Mission from the ramparts of the Red Fort, as a time-bound plan to get rid of open defecation across the country.

A few months later, I espied a Yatri, Krishna Ramavat, on his way from Gorakhpur to Deoria. I knew by then that the Swachh Bharat Mission had become a focus, not just of the Prime Minister but of the local administration in Deoria. On asking what he was doing in this region, Krishna said, 'I am conducting training camps for village pradhans who will have to be trained in making toilets and operating them.' There were many behavioural nudges in the mission—focus on dignity of women and citizens shaming those going out for morning ablutions, among others. Soon, we started noticing a difference, and it was not just in infrastructure and hygiene; we could see a new realization emerging in matters of women's dignity, not to mention reducing the adverse impact on health through water-borne diseases.

In the subsequent years, as the Yatris came to Barpar, we saw a palpable difference in the village, although in recent years things seem to be sliding back. This change was difficult when we tried individually, but it was easily catalysed by the government and enabled by an 'ecosystem' that acted nationally in mission mode. The government played the role of an enabler—for instance, paying Krishna to conduct training and involving the private sector to create innovative toilets. This solution was integrative, relational and it empowered the local community to take action. It was *integrative* as it focused on dignity as much as sanitation. It was *relational* as it asked local leaders over a period of time to take the lead, and it *empowered* local families and leaders to construct these toilets themselves, creating ownership.[20] Param Iyer, the then Secretary in charge of the Swachh Bharat Mission, who subsequently attended the Yatra in 2018 and 2019 and spoke to its participants, must also be given credit. He was a leader who had spent much of his life improving sanitation across the world and was brought to lead this mission under the direct and visible sponsorship of the Prime Minister. Passion must be matched by deep expertise for a mission to succeed.

A twenty-five-year rise

The Banyan Revolution would take inspiration from the philosophy of integral humanism and the economics of indigenous innovation, and learn from the execution approach of the Swachh Bharat Mission. The Swachh Bharat Mission tackled an important but specific problem. The Banyan Revolution opens the 'problem aperture' further, tackling the complex problem of promoting udyamita, which has multiple drivers and motivations, including connects to markets that are not in the district. It is also integrative, relational and empowering as it is based on an ecosystem approach. Similar efforts, for instance in improving education, health and urbanization, can be attempted with complementary missions, creating the rise. For instance, the old industrial approach to healthcare that tackles chronic disease with a 'prescription-led' approach can be changed to an approach that is based on well-being and natural care, where patients themselves play a role.[21] The investment in the Banyan Revolution over the coming decade can help other missions as well as the toolkit and institutions of udyamita can be used in other efforts. Think of this in space technology terms— the institutional rocket that puts the udyamita effort into our national orbit can be reused to launch other, similar efforts needed for the rise.

While the Banyan Revolution will be national, it should focus on those 240 districts in the Middle with 58 per cent of Indians who are ripe for enterprise-led development. The government will have to continue with pro-poor schemes in the remaining segment, which makes up the Bottom 33 per cent of our population. Tier 2 and Tier 3 districts in the ten states of the north and the east should be the first geography, as enterprise infrastructure in these states is poor and they have fast-growing demographics. The Banyan Revolution must be a mass movement involving youth, women, farmers, backward classes, Dalits and minorities through a purpose-driven agenda in these districts, creating symbols and campaigns that will impact values and mindsets, creating a culture of innovation in its trail. This may require creating udyamita contests and publicity of early success stories, which would reinforce the movement through networks. It will rely on peer influence and changing behaviours locally rather than through a Top-down plan.

Five multipliers propel the Banyan Revolution. The first—in our experience, capital invested in the enabling infrastructure on average attracts ten times that in investment in the enterprises or innovations that it seeds. If we invest, say, Rs 10 crore in institutions and processes in a particular region for enterprise, it will typically attract Rs 100 crore of capital within a decade. The second multiplier is that the investment thus drawn largely goes towards building assets. A balance sheet investment ensures that the enterprise, once established, will generate revenue and employment over multiple years. For instance, Vyanjanam, a pickle-making company based in Deoria, will keep hundreds of women employed over many years. The third multiplier is of the enterprise leader. Each leader on an average can create between ten and fifty employment opportunities, where personal relationships and mentoring form a bigger value-add, beyond salaries. Finally, the ingenuity and innovation that is triggered will be locally relevant, creating widespread productivity, boosting the national economy from below. The electric utility cycle of Arvind Rai will create an increase in productivity for milk collection and washermen locally, not to mention giving

Arvind, the innovator, new meaning in life that is evident when he talks about his work. An additional multiplier are the 'network effects' of the ecosystem that is created in a district. Once the ecosystem is in place, the flywheel of udyamita will start rotating with minimal extra effort and other efforts can be tagged to that rotation for wider developmental impact. For instance, as we focus on healthcare, our Centre of Excellence can engage with the issues of Primary Health Care centres by asking local entrepreneurs to lease these centres and run them. Early calculations put the amount of investment in the Banyan Revolution at $1 billion nationally over a ten-year period, with an impact that is significant.[22] The bigger benefit is that the latent pioneer in every human would be ignited and energized.

Unlike current approaches, the mission is leader-, market connect- and mentor-intensive, with an ecosystem approach; finance is a follower. Our experience shows that the largest source of capital is the customer, not a bank or a VC. And the best source of connection to a customer is a passion to innovate and serve. By creating a strong market, and subsequent money linkages, both the entrepreneur and the financer are provided more surety of revenue, and once revenue comes in, margins provide money that fuels growth. While some very poor districts may require a 'finance subsidy', an enterprise founded on financial engineering seldom grows sustainably. As our ecosystem has progressed in Deoria and Kushinagar, with the JECP as a permanent beacon, we find that local banks are coming forward as eager partners, for they are also seeking businesses that have a connect to the market. Our focus in Purvanchal has been on local enterprises that have a higher elasticity of employment and where local resources are abundant—apparel, agro-processing, tourism, etc. But technology start-ups in health, education and agriculture are also now being incubated by our team, where innovations play a direct role. Digital can also play a key role in creating non-linearity, enabling collective action through networks, decentralizing development and compressing time for achieving our goals.

To complement and support the four regional centres, we envision a Middle of the Diamond Institute[23] located in Mumbai to answer many questions that will emerge during the Banyan Revolution. For example, while the rough contours of the Diamond have been outlined, what are its precise dimensions? What are the assets and wealth of those in the Middle? What is the shape and quantity of innovative and entrepreneurial human capital and how best can we measure this? What are the specific issues the youth and women face in these smaller districts? What is the state of digital penetration as it relates to enterprise in the Middle? How do we understand the culture of the Middle that has an interdependence with local society and nature, and how do we relate it to the Banyan Revolution? How do we link enterprise and environment, so that we can 'drill through the environmental mountain'? Can Udyam Corps and Udyam Mitra be a truly nationwide service, and how do we architect it so that it remains local and flexible? Can we create a national Udyamita Index for different regions and districts? These questions are likely to have regional or even district-level answers. The institute will build on a network of entrepreneurs anchored by the four centres planned across the country, which will operationalize udyamita.

Exporting the Banyan Revolution

The Banyan Revolution can inspire other emerging countries with their own Middle. Many African, south-east Asian and Latin American nations are a few years ahead or a few years behind the Diamond-shaped demography of India. I remember the words of Ghanaian participant Joseph Kenneth Otchere when he came on board the Jagriti Yatra in 2012: 'I can relate to the problems of India as our situation is much like yours; a similar expedition in Europe or the US would have left us cold.' These countries have also been patronized by the West through a 'grant and aid' treatment that ignores local talent, culture and solutions.[24]

The BRICS nomenclature did classify some countries as emerging, but there are significant differences between a Russia and an India. A more accurate and meaningful classification would be the 'global Middle', which has broadly similar issues and aspirations. India has the opportunity to demonstrate success in its Middle through the Banyan Revolution and seed a strategic development model that supports udyamita for the Middle of other developing countries. It should create finance, mentorship and market connects across global emerging markets that aid this internationally, which will also give Indian companies an opportunity to lead innovations in the Global Middle. In this, it should collaborate with both Japan and South Korea as two large Asian democracies interested in the emerging economies of Asia and Africa. India is already one of the largest peacekeeping force contributors to the UN. Its enterprise brand can extend that positioning by providing training, mentorship, market connects and techniques to bring about an entrepreneurial rise in the

Middle of other developing countries—an udyamita *sans
frontières* globally which will accelerate its own economy
and make it relevant globally on its own terms.

At the end of the Second World War, the US launched
a major initiative internally with the GI Joe bill to re-
train and place returning solders in universities.[25] It also
launched the Marshall Plan externally to revive Europe
and formed institutions at Bretton Woods to establish its
presence internationally. India, over the next twenty-five
years, has an opportunity for a similar double act, through
the Banyan Revolution internally and an external thrust
to support the Global Middle, where our innovations
and entrepreneurial brand can inspire global prosperity.
India has relevant innovations, what some call frugal
innovations. In addition, as a large and diverse geography,
India has proven the case for digital innovations which can
be taken to other parts of the world. Many innovations and
enterprises from here can be taken to the global Middle.
This is also globalization but of a different type, where the
majority in the Middle takes part from the beginning.

The previous rise of great powers were material, through
colonial conquest or institutions like those created at the
Bretton Woods, based on the Atlantic Charter of Western
dominance thrashed out by Roosevelt and Churchill.
In recent years, the rise of China is similarly oriented—
Deng Xiaoping initiated a process where China was intent
on 'beating the West at its own game', copying western
modernity through Marxist methods while proclaiming 'it
is glorious to be rich'.[26] India's rise has to be different in
being human-centric by involving citizens in the process of
innovation and enterprise. Not just India, but the world
can embrace this approach and create a new modernity.

322 Middle of Diamond India

The growth of GDP would remain important, but it would be informed by the involvement of humans in a meaningful pursuit. The well-being, both physical and spiritual, of 8 billion people would be its goal, not the enrichment of a few. America and China are engaged in a global geopolitical contest, both using the Cartesian theory of exploitation with corporatism[27] and communism, respectively, as its instruments. The Middle of the Diamond approach can create a different entry point by invoking the human spirit and potential for innovation. The Anthropocene age would belong to humans but where they relate to each other and with nature materially, socially and spiritually. Such a rise would contrast with and respond in particular to China's Belt and Road Initiative (BRI), which is opposite in its top-down intent and continues to promote Marxist materialism.

The political schism today is no longer between the left and the right. It is in the division in thinking, economic, social and cultural stance of the elite at the Top and the vast majority in the Middle. This was evident with Trump and the US, it was also evident in Brexit, and in a more subterranean form it is emerging in China where prosperous coastal areas and inner China are divided by growing disparity.[28] It also remains in India between the Top and the rest. The institutional cycle of roughly seventy-five years after Bretton Woods, when many Asian countries gained independence from colonial powers, coincides with this schism. These countries, mostly in the 'Global Middle', with a cumulative population of over 4 billion, are now experiencing the rise of the Middle. For these nations, the US, that other large democracy, may not be the right example for democratic inspiration. The US's location in an uncomplicated neighbourhood, with two oceans on each side, a benign Canada and a reasonable Mexico to its north and south, not to mention its history of 'settling' the continent that gave it almost infinite resources, makes it a democratic outlier rather than the norm. India, born as a bloody caesarean section baby after 200 years of imperial onslaught, in a hostile neighbourhood, with a population that is both diverse and large, remains a unique democratic success story and a better exemplar for these nations. As the largest democracy of the world, and now the largest nation on the planet, India is well positioned to lead an economic, political and social surge by taking innovation and enterprise to its Middle and inspiring other parts of the Global Middle with this approach.

Our last chance

Cocktail conversations about nation-building in a typical south Mumbai setting draw surprised looks. Most assume that someone, somewhere, will undertake this—the bureaucracy, politicians, the Ramakrishna Mission, a charitable organization—anyone but them. They believe the task of the private sector is to generate profits, which when taxed will be used to distribute that profit to those in need. Private sector leaders are now changing their views through ESG, and through their experience in COVID-19, that mere *re-distribution* of tax is insufficient. There is a realization that supporting their suppliers, their employees and a deeper understanding of the customer is critical for innovation and value creation. Leaders are shifting their gaze upstream, from minding profit pools to *pre-distribution*, where 'the very process of production or service can give economic value to a wide section of society'.[29] By taking this view of business as inclusive, '. . . giving many people a say in decision-making, unlike extractive ones that privilege the voice of the few',[30] a new approach is emerging, which could make the economy deeper, wider, more innovative and more productive when private effort is expanded, and nation-building is brought to the centre of our drawing rooms. This involvement is sorely needed as the private sector exemplifies the best in management and talent, including the recent growth in Indian unicorns that are the fruits of the organizational and technological capability of venture capitalists and the start-up ecosystem. Our daily lives will then be informed by a national mission to create: a better industry, a better company, a better office, a better leader, and that will, in turn, build a better country.

This will create national transcendence that includes the Top, Middle and Bottom, the private sector, the public sector and civil society. Such transcendence was once created by our founders just before Independence. Those who marched with Gandhi to Dandi knew they were creating a narrative of freedom that would impact them, their children and millions who would follow. Those who took blows with Sarojini Naidu at Dharsana Mines in wave after sickening wave believed in the story of Independence, not just for themselves but for India's destiny and future generations. Soldiers such as Mangal Pandey and Subhash Chandra Bose or freedom fighters such as Bhagat Singh, Chandra Shekhar Azad and Veer Savarkar understood that when they put their lives on the line, the lives of those who came after them would finally be free. Similarly, the meta story of the Banyan Revolution reminds udyamis that their current sacrifice, honesty, discipline and creativity will not only benefit them but create a prosperous India for future generations.

This opportunity will not wait forever. By around 2040, our population will start to age, and it will be much more difficult to start the rise then. The moment for urgent, bold action is now. Netaji Subhash Chandra Bose had encouraged a local plus national approach when he said, 'Pride in the progress of one's village, one's city, one's district, one's province should co-exist with a feeling of pride in the progress made by one's country.'[31] In 1942, when freedom was within our grasp, Gandhi used the words 'do or die'. He said, 'We shall either free India or die in the attempt. Let every man and woman live every moment of his or her life hereafter in the consciousness that he or she eats and lives for achieving freedom and will die if need be.'[32] Our generation's 'do or die' moment has arrived, except in this case it is for the much harder task of building.

Seventy-five years of democracy have provided ample evidence that large democracies can flourish, but slowly. India's story demonstrates that the 'cruel choice' of democracy versus development, highlighted by economist Jagdish Bhagwati, can be reconciled.[33] The birth of the Middle is a direct result of that labour. Whether our future will be glorious or bleak depends entirely on how we frame, engage, build and nurture it. As the youngest large democracy in the world, we remain the country of the future within an ageing world. Yet, a casual walk outside a village, small town or the many slums of India shows many youth are unemployed. We are blessed with an ancient civilization that gives our society gravity, but that very gravity often weighs us down. We are a digitally enabled society, smartphones visible in every hand, and yet large swathes of society use them for frivolous purposes, spreading fake news that create divisions rather than collaboration. We are blessed with seas, rivers, mountains, forests, flora and fauna that would be the envy of any nation, yet, if we are not careful, the ecological sanctity of our land is at risk. We are seventy-five years old and a successful democracy that emanates from 'the experience of action in concert'[34] and yet, that action has been confined to the few at the Top. This must change.

Roving learners

The Yatra began as a vehicle to wander. By wandering, we connected with our country and its culture in the Middle. The JECP and our vision of four dhams is designed to give our mission permanency in that Middle. Unlike Columbus, our land itself is defined by pilgrims who, after their Yatras, return to their regions in an Edison-like fashion to innovate and build. The modern-day monk who personified this spirit was the itinerant Swami Vivekananda. Before his awakening in 1892 at the southernmost point of mainland India on a rock off the coast of Kanyakumari, he travelled non-stop for six years. Our own Yatris follow that tradition in an abbreviated form. The Yatra tugs at the *ghumakkad* dharma of young Indians, a key reason for its success. But the transformative gifts of wandering can be acquired only through a 'coming back'—in the case of the Swami to the Belur Math in Bengal, where he set up the Ramakrishna Mission. Vivekananda said after his wanderings: 'The history of the world is the history of a few who had faith in themselves.'[35] He went on to say, 'He alone serves God who serves all other beings.'[36] This comes from a monk who, in his spirit of exploration and inquiry, did not take himself too seriously, naming himself 'the Fat Maharaj'.[37] The lesson we have learnt as we travelled is that service is an act of equals. It is to partner with others to innovate and create with a 'joy of building' that Vivekananda would have also advocated. With the vast majority in India no longer 'in poverty', we need a collaborative process to build, shedding an extractive mindset that damages the environment or the palliatives of aid that create dependency. This service is of a higher order as its fruits are not visible immediately, in contrast to the temporary 'high' of alms giving. It requires 'tough love', which needs patience—asking those who are capable to stand up and join the mainstream to build. In doing this, it is sensitive to the fact that 250 million may not be able to stand up on their own, yet.

Celebrating the chitti of India

The youngest large nation in the world is revved up for action. The spirit of those 5 billion cumulative votes over seventeen general elections have time and again steered our democracy back on the right path. These seventy-five years of independence celebrate the chitti, the soul of our nation; its continuity and innovation would make our forefathers proud.

This ancient continuity was spotted by my daughter Isha when she blurted out, 'Who coordinated all this?' We were stepping away from the Ajanta caves on a drizzly July afternoon, where our tour guide had explained how these thirty caves had been hewn across 700 years from 200

BCE to 500 CE. The next day, we would visit Ellora, where 30,00,000 cubic feet of rock were excavated to create one temple, Kailash, over the reign of six Rashtrakuta rulers starting from Dantidurga in the seventh century CE and ending with Krishna II in the ninth century. The answer to Isha's question of coordination, I believe, lies in chitti, which has played this role for centuries. This chitti was not just in the architectural monuments we admire, or the artistic innovations they house but in the culture that is stored in our citizens, passed down through civilizational memories that, in my case, started at least with Ram Mani in 1777, not to mention the spirit of a 300-year-old banyan tree. Chitti forged our civilization through cultural connections between the human spirit, creating intergenerational handovers, which will continue to guide Tarini and Isha's generation and those after them. I am also confident that chitti is a creative She, an incandescent mother, like mine and that of Shankaracharya and Vivekananda and other leaders who were shaped most by their mothers[38] whom, as a nation, we revere in the image of Bharat Mata.

The chitti of our nation started taking shape approximately 5000 years ago, around 2900 BCE, when Indian civilization flourished amid the neatly laid bathing tanks of Mohenjo-daro, Harappa and Dholavira. Viewed in the light of that timespan, our country, along with China, has an extraordinary continuity and flexibility. This continuity saw the emergence of thoughts that have inspired thinkers globally, leading to the birth of the Vedas and Upanishads, Buddhism and Jainism, not to mention the statecraft of Kautilya. Rulers such as Chandragupta, Ashoka, Harsha, Krishnadeva Raya, Raja Raja Chola, Akbar, Shivaji and Ranjit Singh, among others, gave our polity discipline and stability. Thinkers, teachers and writers such as Shankara, Kalidasa, Valmiki, Tulsidas, Kabir, Thiruvalluvar, Nanak and others continued to renew and refresh our moral framing. Kautilya had given an early warning in the second century BCE and is said to have opined, 'There are two ways to deal with thorns and wicked people. One is to crush them, and the other is to stay away from them.' We did neither. Indian civilization, under attack from Turks, Persians, Afghans and later Mongols, innovated at the end of the first millennium to survive when it propelled the Bhakti movement, which decentralized our culture and kept it alive. When monasteries and temples were under attack, our civilization survived in the *bhajans* of the Alvar poets, Mira's verses and the cultural innovations of a Kabir and a Nanak with a direct connect to the Almighty, which no sword could crush.[39] In the late eighteenth century, military raids on Delhi by Nader Shah weakened the country again and taught us a lesson we must never forget: the need for military strength and internal unity. Later, when Europeans came to our shores, Indian rulers, ignoring Kautilya a second time, gave them *firmans* and taking advantage of our weakness, India was easily colonized by a merchant company in 1757, starting a precipitous decline. This conquest and rule were accomplished when the military might of these conquerors was complemented by co-opting the elite and by denigrating our culture, sowing doubts in our own minds. The First War of Independence in 1857 started our journey to freedom with leaders, mostly from the Middle, challenging that world view. Mangal Pandey, Rani Laxmibai, Vivekananda, Aurobindo, Tilak, Gokhale, Tagore, Gandhi, Patel, Nehru, Azad, Sarojini and others worked over ninety years to secure our freedom. But by the time the chains were broken, Bharat Mata was poor, uneducated and divided, with the majority in the Middle drained of resources and a mindset of colonialism still intact at the Top. As every citizen got to vote, we democratized our polity, releasing republican energies, signalled by a rising Middle. In this duration, our smaller villages, towns and districts, mostly neglected, continued that civilizational flow, with millions holding on to our sanskriti. This mass and its hidden culture must be tapped now to create our rise. Instead of *survival*, our second freedom at seventy-five asks us to *thrive*, using social, economic and political *integration* and *innovation* aligned with our inherent genius.

Return as renaissance

Renaissances get triggered when two cultures encounter each other and challenge each other, fostering new methods, new thought processes and technologies, aided by societal and national purpose.[40] Ironically, in India, the Middle and Top are 'encountering' each other within our own geography— like twin sisters meeting after seventy-five years of separation. Led by the rise of the Middle, that encounter is creating a new modernity, which will see another civilizational curve in that ancient flow defined by a refreshed chitti. Indian civilization has a long continuity of 'being'. Today, with the republican energies of 1.4 billion citizen builders, it can take on the earnest process of 'becoming'. 'Not an uncritical revival or unthinking reaction, rather a new birth, a true and far-ranging renaissance'.[41] Such renaissances have occurred before, shaped by stories of early hardships, followed by journeys of discovery that entailed risks, with a subsequent return.

Ram's fortitude was shaped, against the wishes of his father Dasharatha, by Guru Vishwamitra in the dense forests of Purvanchal across the Sarayu River near Ayodhya. This early initiation helped him, Sita and Laxman in their wanderings across India for fourteen years, which became a moral story of sacrifice, filiality and valour not just for India but for large parts of south-east Asia too. He returned to establish Ram Rajya, which became a global exemplar of benevolent rule. Similarly, Buddha, born a prince in the Sakya principality of Terai, shielded by his family, had an awakening only when he stepped out of his palace and saw the realities of his realm. 'One day he went forth from his palace into the streets among the people, and saw an old man, and on another day a sick man and on another day a dead man',[42] sparking his enlightenment. When he left his palace at the dead of night mounted on Kanthaka, his favourite horse, he discarded his clothes, shaved his head and became an ascetic or a *shraman* when he crossed the Aumi river, which continues to flow through Purvanchal. In that crossing, he burnt the bridge to his privileged life, creating the seeds of Buddhist thought.

Both Ram and Buddha are civilizational heroes who had early exposure to hardships and went out, only to return. The stone carvings of Angkor Vat, the stupas of Thailand and the Zen philosophy of Japan carry the spirit of this circularity. Both narratives carried the story of India to south-east Asia, China, Japan and Tibet. Both stories originated and ended in Purvanchal, an area blessed by the Himalayas to its north, and cuddled by the Sarayu and the Narayani rivers to its south and east. Subconsciously, our inspiration for the Yatra and the location of the first Enterprise Centre under the banyan are also inspired by the 'sacred geography'[43] of an ancient tree. Other regions of India are also replete with this civilizational strength that rises from our land and culture. This call of the land prompted Mangal Pandey and Rani Laxmibai in Purvanchal, Birsa Munda in Jharkhand, Chhatrapati Shivaji Maharaj in Maharashtra, Guru Gobind Singh in Punjab, Rani Chenamma in Karnataka, Pazhassi Raja in Kerala, Veerapandiya Kattabomman from Tamil Nadu and many more, who took inspiration from the land, nurturing and protecting it. Very often, we have ignored these local inspirations and borrowed from a Western narrative that has captured the Top. This must change as we adopt the true civilizational forces of our nation to create a new modernity at seventy-five. This will start a renaissance leading up to the hundredth year of our independence.

At the end of his life, the Buddha too returned close to the location he set out from. The year was 483 BCE, in the month of May on a full moon night, when he travelled to Kushinagar, a few kilometres from the banyan in Barpar, not far from the Aumi. He was eighty years of age. In the true traditions of ghumakkadi, he had spent almost forty years in constant wandering from the time he became an ascetic—initially to Gaya, where he meditated under the Bodhi tree, and then to Sarnath, where he preached his first sermon in a deer park. In the years after his passage, his message of the 'Middle path' would spread through wandering monks to the farthest corners of Asia, including China, Korea, Thailand, Burma, Japan, Sri Lanka and Tibet. Falling ill from food poisoning that day, he encouraged Ananda, his favourite disciple, with a final promise: 'Press on with due care.' Amid an unseasonal shower of forest flowers, he lay on his right side, between two sal trees, entered a profound meditative state and passed away. A thirty-foot-long reclining statue in the same pose, at the same place in Kushinagar where he attained *paranirvana*, has kept that message alive for more than 2500 years.

Today, the civilizational flow of India, the memories of those who fought and gave us freedom, a proven seventy-five-year democracy and the energies of the Middle are seeking a renewed promise—to 'press on'. With the citizen leader at its helm, not only can we do so by shining the Indian Diamond, we can also provide inspiration for other nations to attempt this across the world. In this journey, we must recognize what John Rawls once said, 'The life of a people is conceived as a scheme of cooperation spread out in historical time.'[44] Such a narrative will create an intergenerational movement where every citizen is involved in fulfilling Swami Vivekananda's dream of 'building an India yet greater than what she has been':[45] a moment of 'national transcendence' over the coming twenty-five years where individually and as a group, we experience the awe of nation-building. Of being part of a phenomenon that is rarely, if ever, experienced in the history of nations. The experience of a 1.4 billion strong humanity which has decided to lift itself up.

Committing to the Banyan Revolution in the *Amrit Kaal*

A few months before completing this book, I attended the Independence Day celebrations on 15 August 2022 at Red Fort. I left my job that day to focus on Middle of Diamond India over the Amrit Kaal starting with the development of Deoria and Kushinagar by seeding the Banyan Revolution. This broadly coincides with the *Vanaprasta* ashram of my life, and I hope to work for my region over the coming twenty-five years, an act named *Kshetra Sanyas* by Ashutosh Kumar, Jagriti's CEO in his recent TEDx talk.

Those who want to commit to developing their own area through a similar process can connect with me at shashank@shashankmani.in and follow the progress of the Banyan Revolution on www.shashankmani.in, or on my Facebook (Shashank Mani), page, to support this cause. You can also associate directly with Jagriti by coming on the Yatra by applying on www.jagritiyatra.com or by visiting us in Deoria at the JECP with details on www.jecp.in.

I outline below how Yatris, Individuals, Women, Corporates, Government Institutions, Political leaders, Non-Governmental Organizations, Academic Institutions, Non-Resident Indians (NRIs), and international well-wishers can support this movement.

Yatris: are ambassadors of this book, for they have experienced much of what I have written here. They should spread the word on the Banyan Revolution, educating others to come on the Yatra, and join as JADE, while using the JECP as a second home to refine and hone their ideas on udyamita.

Individuals: can adopt a region where they support local enterprise, become entrepreneurs, support policies that drive udyamita and volunteer time as mentors, support through finance, experience the real India through efforts such as the Jagriti Yatra or JECP.

Women: have a special responsibility to give support to each other to take the path of udyamita and realize their full potential. They can join the Yatra, create enterprise locally, and support each other as entrepreneurs, mentors, market connectors, and financiers.

Corporates: as entities closest to national and international markets can support the movement through value chain integration, use CSR money for creating an enabling environment, and extend mentoring and volunteering opportunities for employees.

Government: should create an enabling environment and policy by understanding the movement, sending officers to the JECP and to the Jagriti Yatra to experience udyamita, and create infrastructure in the Middle to enable udyamis and the Banyan Revolution.

Political leaders: are closest to the citizen in the Middle and can support by helping propagate the values of udyamita among their constituents and by supporting enterprise infrastructure. They can challenge voters for *sabka prayas* by asking them to become builders and creators, not just voters.

Non-Governmental Organizations (NGOs): should examine the multiplier impact of udyamita and contribute through partnerships, and through supporting social entrepreneurs to scale up their efforts entrepreneurially, and in backing enterprise clusters and institutions.

Academic Institutions: shape minds and attitudes early and should examine out-of-class and out of off-campus opportunities, such as Jagriti Yatra and JECP, encouraging students to learn by wandering and inviting them to look beyond the surface to explore the Middle

Non-Resident Indians (NRIs): are naturally tuned to enterprise and can contribute by understanding the Middle by visiting the JECs and travelling on the Jagriti Yatra. They should send their children to the Jagriti Yatra and the JECs to experience the real India.

International supporters: bring the rational perspective of an outsider and can contribute by understanding the real India, challenge Indian assumptions while helping support the movement by offering market linkages and finance. Some may want to replicate this movement in their own countries.

The Amrit Kaal needs the energies, ideas, resources, and commitment of every person interested in the development of India. This is an act needing urgent attention, for this is our last chance, as well as a glorious opportunity.

For those wanting to visit Shashankmani.in, please scan this barcode

Those wanting to visit JECP.in, may please scan this barcode

Those wanting to visit Jagritiyatra.com, please scan this barcode

Acknowledgements

A book documenting a movement has numerous co-authors. But to bring a book to life requires inordinate support from a select few who go the extra mile. In this long list, Samir Mody features at the top, as he devoted many weekends editing the manuscript, and keeping me on track. Many others read the manuscript and gave me thoughtful feedback—Annaswamy Vaidheesh, Sudhanshu Pandey, Pradeep Mishra, Kushal Sinha, Sudhanshu Bohra, Shraddha Kalani, Kaushik Banerjee, Sarita Vijayan, Punit Modhgil, Pallavi Tak, Yashraj Akashi, Madhu Gopinath, Dinesh Raja, Sameer Ahluwalia, Stella Lau, Udayan Kelkar, Rahul Garg, Manoj Motwani, Rama Raghunathan, M.S. Raghunathan, Shoaib Ahmed, Shilpi Singh, Anusuya Das, Pranchal Joshi, Anubha Sinha, Ravi Pokharan, Hemang Jani, Mudit Yadav, Patrick Dowd, Meera Kaushik, Deepak Sahajwala, Vijaya Sahajwala, Virat Tandon, Shivani Tripathi, Raju Shete, Gopal Jain, Pankaj Bansal, Vanita Viswanath, Lt Gen. Shamsher Mehta, Dr R. Mashelkar, both gurus to me. There are many others who gave suggestions and I apologize if I am not able to name all of them here.

My editor Karthik Venkatesh at Penguin was simultaneously patient, encouraging and creative. Having understood the core of the book, he helped me nurse out its true essence. Special thanks to Disha Nawani who first introduced me to Karthik.

My father, Lt Gen. (retd) Shri Prakash Mani, read the manuscript early, and I was relieved when he liked it. My mother, Shashi Mani, is an inspiration not just to me but to the women of Deoria through her role as the founder of Jagriti Sewa Sansthan, and continues to support Jagriti in Deoria. My father-in-law, Surendra Sharma, and my mother-in-law, Padma Sharma, have been a constant source of support to me and my family. The book is dedicated to these four who have influenced me through their values and the love they shower on me. My wider family, Shipra, Anindya, Reva, Pushkar, Mrigank, Neha, Suryansh, Shaurya, Sanjay, Aradhana, Anshuman, Aradhya, Shri Vilas Mani Chacha, Vidya Bua, Suruchi, Vivek, Gaurav, Ranjana Bhabhi, Parikshit and my extended family remain a source of wisdom for me.

The full-time team at Jagriti and those who are now part of the Jagriti ecosystem have a special place both in this book and in my life. Our chairman Sharat Bansal, our CEO Ashutosh Kumar, our COO Anurag Dixit, and other leaders like Raj Krishnamurthy, Rewati Prabhu, Swapnil Dixit, Gitanjali Banerjee who were present when Jagriti Yatra started in 2008. In recent years, Madhu Gopinath, Vanita Viswanath, Sunil Pangarkar, Ramanan Ramanathan, Nikhil Bhatia, Manish Jain, Sarita Vijayan, Shoaib Ahmed, Annaswamy Vaidheesh, Anant Krishnan, Kirti Poonia and others have helped this movement. Seema Saili, Chinmay Vadnere, Pragati Baheti, Pankaj Mane, Archana Bohra, Lalitha Prakash, Akash Gosavi and others hold the Yatra aloft. Local work in Deoria and Kushinagar would not be possible without the support of Udyam Corps and Udyam Mitra and CoE team and the JECP construction that includes Gaurav Srivastava, Ashutosh Kumar Mishra, Vishwas Pandey, Anand Singh, Shilpi Singh, Abhishek Bharadwaj, Satyasha Rajput, Shahana Hussain, Manoj Verma, Manish Bajaj, M.D. Tripathi, Manoj Tiwari, Priti Pandey, Dhirendra Yadav, Saddam Ansari, Rajeev Rai, Naina Verma, Vikash Shahi, Shubham Tripathi, Nandita Giri, Vivek Vishwakarma, Ashish Mani Tripathi, Prashant Yadav, Durgesh Rai, Manish Kumar Tiwari, Ashwini Tiwari, Abhishek Bajaj, Ganesh Singh, Suvarna Tapkir, Vibhuti Sharma, Saqib Hussain, Zuber Tomer, Dheeraj Singh, Babish Chaturvedi and others. There were many others who took part in the Jagriti story, not least the twelve inspiring role models, the Engine Room Club, and many others who joined the Yatra or the JECP in Deoria at our Independence Day celebrations, with many as characters in the book. All the 7500 yatris and many udyamis from Purvanchal are named at the back of this book. Their commitment to Building India through Enterprise is the core of this story. A special call out to Patrick Dowd and Mattew Dardaillon who started similar enterprise journeys in the US and France seeding an international element, with many joining a Jagriti G20 Startup 20 Yatra planned later this year.

The role of Deoria and Kushinagar as districts and the banyan tree in my village which inspired this book must be acknowledged, even if this is a case of acknowledging a 'location'. To do that I have named the 1000-odd villages that constitute the area where I work most, and from where many characters emerge. Apart from people from these districts who feature in the book, I want to thank Dr Ramapati Ram Tripathi, MP from Deoria, Shri

Manoj Sinha, Lt Gov., J & K, Shri Shiv Pratap Shukla, Governor, Himachal Pradesh, Shri Suresh Prabhu, former Minister of Commerce, Ms Kiran Bedi, former Lt Gov., Puducherry, Shri Kashmiri Lal ji, Sundaram ji, Bhagavati Prasad ji, Satish ji, Jeetendra ji, Archana ji, Dr Rajiv ji, and others with whom I have worked in recent month for the Swavalambi Bharat Abhiyan. A core team that works with me in Deoria continues to provide ideas and suggestions— Sarvajot Singh, Nihal Sharma, Prince Chaturvedi, Taufiq Ali, Keshav Roy, Manish Mani, Dheeraj Tiwari, Prabhakar Tiwari, Karan Tripathi, Sanjay Rao and others. Others in that region who have provided ideas, and hail from Middle India deserve a mention—Antaryami Singh, Vijay Bahadur Dubey, Hemant Mishra, Rajesh Mishra, Bhupendra Singh, Arun Singh, Girjesh Mani, Ravindar Mall, Ajay Shahi, Sanjay Singh Saithwar, Mantan Singh, Pappu Singh, Durgesh Nath Tripathi, Mukul Tiwari, Sanjay Rai, Markandey Tiwari, Nagesh Pati, Ramashish Prasad, Ajay Tiwari, Sandeep Tiwari, Pramod Singh, Vijendra Kushwaha, Satya Prakash Pandey, Vivekanand Yadav, Sanjay Kushwaha, Yogeshwar Upadhyay, Ambuj Shahi, Satyam Shukla, Alka Singh, Sarita Pandey, Bharati Sharma, Vibha Pandey, Sandeep Tiwari, Mukul Tiwari, Ojaswi Mishra, Anand Mani Tripathi, Ved Tiwari, Dharmendra Chouhan, among others.

The ten years I spent in PwC India as a partner and strategy leader, and later as the government strategy and aerospace, defence and space leader were years when I firmed up my views on a 'whole-of-nation' collaboration for national growth. In this duration PwC chairman Sanjeev Krishnan, previous chairmen Deepak Kapoor and Shyamal

Mukherjee, senior partners and friends, Sanjay Tolia, Arnab Basu, Vivek Prasad, Satyavati Berera, Padmaja Alagnandan, Sudhir Dungarpur, Kameswar Rao, Ranen Banerjee, Girish Shirodkar, David Wijeratne, Akshaya Kapoor, Vishal Kanwar, Nipun Agarwal, Nikarrika Puri, Mansi Kapoor, Hardik Vig, Sandipan Maiti, Sandeep P.M., and former colleagues Deepankar Sanwalka, N.V. Sivakumar, Sanjay Dhawan, Dhiraj Mathur, Neel Ratan, Chaitali Mukerjee, Nikita Jain, Aditi Namdeo, Anurag Garg and Sam Waller shaped my thoughts and the themes in this book.

My friends from both my school and colleges have been emotional and intellectual supporters of the Jagriti movement and have shaped me, mostly through the constant banter that continues, most recently on WhatsApp. Jayant Krishnan, Samarth Narain from Colvin, Rahul Dhir, Vineet Khosla, Raghav Mehra, Samir Seth, Rohit Bhagat, Umesh Baveja, Udayan Kelkar, Rajiv Arora, Deepak Verma, Sanju Agarwal, Pawan Rewari, Ajay Kaul, D.K. Goel, Atul Srivastava, Ashok Singh, Arvind Kumar, Somesh Khanna, Sanjeev Gupta, Mukul Goel, Arvind Goel, Saurabh Garg, Rajiv Bansal, among others from IIT Delhi deserve mention.

In writing the book, I have been influenced by the thinking of a number of stalwarts who are quoted in the book, but a few names deserve to be acknowledged more formally. The thinking of Pandit Deendayal Upadhyaya, S.N. Balagangadhara, Prof. P.L. Dhar, Prof. Edmund Phelps, Prof. Tom Malone, Jonathan Haidt, David Brooks and Arthur Brooks stands out. The coaching of Art Kleiner, previous editor of *Strategy + Business* magazine helped with key insights as I wrote the book.

Finally, the author's family carries a heavy burden as a book is given birth. I want to thank Gauri, Tarini and Isha, the 'three Devis' in my life in for being patient, as I tackled the task of writing this book. All three play a cameo role in the narrative and will continue to inspire my life's work.

Shifts for Middle of Diamond Paradigm

Sections	Chapters	Shifts	Previous Paradigm	Middle of Diamond Paradigm
Framing	Awakening	1	Learning through Classroom	Learning through Exploration
	Diamond	2	Growth dependent on Trickle Down	Growth fuelled by Middle, includes Top & Bottom
	Youth	3	Protest to force Change	Purposeful Building for National Renewal
	Women	4	Women as Beneficiaries	Women Led Development
Learning	Revolutions	5	Colonial Values and Institutions	Citizen Centric Values and Institutions
	Democracy	6	Rights of Citizens	Responsibilities of Citizens
	Culture	7	Values driven by Industrial approach	Values driven by the Human Spirit
Changing	Udyamita	8	Enterprise focused on Wealth	Wealth an outcome of Building and Giving
	Citizen	9	Vertical, Extractive Association	Horizontal and Collaborative Association
	Districts	10	Directive, Control and Paper based	Platform based for Empowerment and Enablement
	Digital	11	Automation through Technology	Citizen Collaboration through Technology
Building	Integration	12	Aping Western Modernity for Copycat growth	New Modernity for Humanist Rise
	Future	13	Borders, Boundaries and Laws define Nation	*Chitti* as National Soul defines National Identity

Appendix 1

Banyan Revolution:
Definition, Ingredients, Resources, Application and Impact

Definition: *Banyan Revolution as creating a garden*

The Banyan Revolution seeks to create a national udyamita ecosystem, resembling a garden. An ecosystem that has many efforts that simultaneously support creation and destruction, different from a formal planning process. Such an ecosystem will have regional and district level locations where udyamis are given support within its nourishing environment. Such an ecosystem links the spiritual and human energies of citizens to associate, exchange and grow in Middle India.

Ingredients: *For setting up the ecosystem*

To create this ecosystem we have to invest in providing the right soil, manure, space and gardeners for udyamis to flourish. The most critical resource is the citizen leader, the udyami, to seed this movement. The ecosystem needs congregation spaces, market connects, enabling policy, digital connections and platforms, as well as enabling gardeners like our Udyam Corps and Udyam Mitra. The garden has to be given institutional support, so that udyamis get confidence that support will exist over a long period. The ecosystem will have networks that connect

347

them to larger companies and mentors, who guide and connect them to markets.

Resources: *A billion-dollar investment*

Jagriti has quantified a $1 billion, or Rs 8000 crore investment to power this movement across the Middle over a ten-year period. This will create four *Dhams* of enterprise starting with the one in Deoria, one Middle of Diamond Institute, network offices in 240 Middle of Diamond districts as well as operating costs of having gardeners who support last mile udyamis. Once this garden is established, it will create its own microclimate and sustain itself after the first ten years through a revenue model Jagriti is trialling. Such an ecosystem will attract an estimated $10 billion in the form of enterprise capital for these enterprises.

Application: *Five primary uses of resource*

There are five primary uses of $1 billion investment in creating the ecosystem. The first is creating physical infrastructure in four cardinal corners of the country to support udyamis by giving them a congregation space for peer-to-peer collaboration and offices in fifteen adjoining districts with suitable hiring of last-mile connectors. Secondly, to build network offices in the remaining 180 districts with suitable franchises of the network office model to local JADE and other leaders to curate this in their district. The third is creation of a Middle of Diamond Institute to foster research into udyamita in Middle India. Fourth, to create digital platforms that can connect udyamis to each other and to markets, mentors and money. Finally, suitable investment in marketing this movement to make udyamita aspirational to those in the Middle.

Impact: *Inclusive growth that creates meaning*

Early estimates show that enabling investments will attract ten times the enterprise investment improving national GDP significantly. More importantly, the ecosystem created will continue to nurture entrepreneurs, creating growth in the hinterland of India, where it is urgently needed. It will also provide meaning to citizens who take part in the Banyan Revolution. This double act of inclusive economic growth and creation of meaning is the *Amrit* that will come out of this *Manthan*.

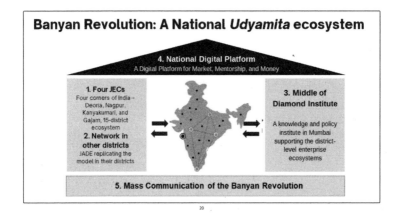

Appendix 2

New Modernity for Environmental Sustainability: An Investigation

This book's core purpose is to reveal the social and economic potential of Middle India using the tool of udyamita. In the process of writing it, however, an additional, related prize became visible—environmental sustainability, featured in Chapter 12. Given the urgency of this issue, I elaborate here on some key concepts, the shifts that are needed for these to be emerge, and the mode of inquiry required to investigate how the Middle of Diamond India can drive environmental sustainability to start a specific dialogue on this important subject.

Framing of development as 'conquest of nature'

As a number of authors and thinkers—Jeremy Lent[1], Amitav Ghosh[2], Karen Armstrong[3], Siddarth Shrikanth[4], et al.—have argued, philosophically and culturally, Western civilization's success in colonizing the world stems from a mental model that believes in 'conquest of nature', very different from Eastern thought on this subject. The genesis of this divergence between the West and the East goes back to Greek philosophy, which gave supremacy to the exercise of reason, a faculty possessed by man alone. This was then adopted by Christian theology, envisaging a benevolent God in heaven who bestows exclusive, discriminatory rights over nature to man. Sixteenth-century philosophers, such as Francis Bacon and

René Descartes, perpetuated this thought process by framing an automaton view of life. In this imagination, reason was supreme with its control over matter, and man was supreme supported by a God who had given him authority and power that justified subordinating nature. As Karen Armstrong writes, 'In Descartes's writings, there is none of the awe that had informed traditional views of the sacred. Indeed, it was the task of science to dispel such reverence.' This framework led to colonization and a materialistic culture that is at the heart of Western modernity. No doubt numerous technical innovations emerged, but at an existential cost to mother earth. Institutions, creating and sustaining this flawed modernity, continue to dominate global narratives, unsustainable for a planet now hosting 8 billion humans.

Framing development as a 'web of life'

Eastern traditions, both Indic and Chinese, that survived or avoided colonial conquest, sustained a world view where meaning and purpose are derived from a 'web of life'. Indic traditions symbolized this through as an interconnected, infinite *Brahman* and a personal *Atman*. *Tao* pointed to a connected life with the fundamental 'way' transcending all material realities, with *qi* representing the essence of 'being' in Confucian thought. In the ancient Middle East, *ilam* in Akkadian was a radiant power that transcended any singular deity. Under attack from colonial forces, industrial technology, control of trade, abetted by an overreaching church, these ancient traditions were eclipsed. Today, there is a growing realization that an adversarial relationship with nature will lead to extinction of earthly life; unless we revive these traditions through a new modernity.

'Web of life' drives a connected modernity

A generation after colonial institutions were created, extractive thinking is being seen as having failed society, and as destructive of the environment. This is why there is an urge, both in the East and the West, to investigate a 'web of life' framework, which can become the foundation of a new modernity. The Santiago theory of cognition highlighted in this book in Chapter 8 lays the foundation for this. The Internet is fostering new connections in the Middle, and COVID-19 created a temporary, forced experiment, where decentralized living was seen as less environmentally-destructive. The use of technology in this Middle is not to automate and divide, but to integrate and make connections. This is important as with Artificial Intelligence (AI), techno elites are becoming even more powerful and will encourage pure technological solutions that could reinstate and reinforce the 'conquest over nature' mindset, this time turbocharged by technology. It is my belief that the necessary shifts in our mindset and consequent framework will neither come from the West, nor from the Top, for they are vested in those very structures of extraction that have benefited this segment for centuries now.

Lessons in sustainability from the Middle?

As outlined in this book, Middle of Diamond India continues to live with traditions that have respect for other forms of life. As has been argued, this segment can drive inclusive development through udyamita, using technology that is locally relevant, integrative and environmentally sustainable. Other traditions, like those of Chinese *Tao* and *qi*, and the beliefs of indigenous people in the Americas, Africa and Australia, can also inform such a framing. Communism suppressed such thinking in China through Marxist materialism, with Mao's cultural revolution another nail in that coffin. Colonial efforts in other geographies erased indigenous thought processes, with pagan traditions branded as backward. Indic traditions, via Hinduism, Buddhism, Jainism and Sikhism, survived this onslaught, with the first war of independence in 1857 playing a key role in this process. Based on this heritage, Indian thinkers, such as Pandit Deendayal Upadhyaya, brought this philosophy back through *integral humanism*, outlining both the role of human potential as well as our fundamental integration with nature. Other societies in Asia, the Americas and Africa are also re-thinking the prevailing framing. However, unless the largest democracy and the largest nation steps forward, using the power of the Middle, the framework of conquest is unlikely to change.

Further investigation of this model of sustainable growth

This book proposes the revival of an *integrative* and *innovative* life that will trigger an Indian national renaissance over the Amrit Kaal. Innovation believes in improvements, including technological ones, but where integration with other humans and the rest of nature is the primary goal. The 800 million citizens who broadly define India's Middle can create a ballast and credibility to such modernity, and lead to an environmentally sustainable model of development, which treats nature on par with humans. But this model can and must be extended to 4–5 billion citizens globally, the Middle of Diamond World, which can be encouraged to adopt this thought process, using their own values and culture. Instead of convincing the West or our elites to change their behaviour, the global Middle can lead and drive this change by building institutions showcasing social, economic and environmental sustainability from the Middle up. This is proposed in this book through the Banyan Revolution in India, but it can be extended to countries such as Indonesia, Nigeria, Brazil, Mexico, South Africa, and other middle-income countries that will impact the majority of the global population. I believe such a thought process will inspire the Chinese people to reject communism by rediscovering their own Taoist and Buddhist culture and history. This will be India's Belt and Road equivalent, not by proposing polluting highways and dams that perpetuate the conquest of nature, but a rise where humanity and nature work interdependently, often using mutually beneficial technology.

Investigating five shifts for creating a new modernity

I recommend the following five shifts as the starting point of research work to support this environmentally sustainable new modernity.

Shift	From	To	Research Questions
1	**Happiness:** that seeks pleasures that result from the satisfaction of desires, leading to bigger desires, and a perpetual restlessness on a hedonistic treadmill	**Meaning:** that seeks a frame of cognition that identifies oneself within the wider construct of life through purposeful actions in the service of others	What drives human life? How does one find true joy? Does purposeful service of others generate satisfaction and meaning? What sacrifices is one willing to make?
2	**Automaton:** that visualizes life as a number of mechanical moving parts, leading to a view that drives material consumption	**Web of Life:** that views life in the context of relationships and networks with other humans and the rest of the natural world, where such connections define the essence of life	How do ecosystems define economics? How are human and environmental networks enmeshed? Does 'live and let live' apply equally to non-human life forms?
3	**Materialism:** that relentlessly seeks material wealth, and craves status and position as defined by economic factors driven by narrow personal gain	**Relationships:** that seeks experiences through interaction with other humans and with the rest of nature, that views status as driven through the quality of relationships and connects	What defines value and growth in life? What is the scope of material and experiential factors in life? How do we re-establish our broken relationship with nature?

Shift	From	To	Research Questions
4	**Machine:** that views life's objective as the creation of better machines that ease the burdens of physical and mental work for humans	**Humans:** that seeks a moral, physical and spiritual betterment through relationships, confining machines to a supporting role	What ought to be the balance between machine, humans and the rest of nature? What are brand images that convey this modernity? Other questions . . .
5	**Displacement:** that seeks to venture out in the conquest of nature and other humans, and to establish dominance, control over and extraction of resources for selfish material gain	**Rootedness:** that is satisfied with one's lot and seeks local salience, connectedness in growth and that nurtures the locality and its people, driving prosperity through collaboration	What are the new idioms of local development? What technologies will realize sustainable decentralized living? Is reverse migration at scale possible?

Those institutions and individuals who are keen to support or explore this line of thinking should write to shashank@shashankmani.in, and support Jagriti's Middle of Diamond Institute to undertake this research.

Appendix 3
Names of Yatris, Udyamis and Villages

Those who participated in Jagriti Yatra and the enterprise ecosystem of Jagriti Enterprise Centre (JEC)—Purvanchal are named below. All names are engraved in a marble plaque in Barpar village, Deoria. The 1000 villages of the district are named here as they form the locus of our first JEC.

Jagriti Yatra 2008

Abhishek Goyal, Aashish Sharma, Abdul Qadir, Abdul Nazar, Abdullah E.R., Abhijit Mhaske, Abhijit Dhada, Abhishek Sonavane, Abhishek Seth, Achin Bansal, Aditi Gupta, Aditya Relangi, Aditya Vardhan Gupta, Agni A S, Ajay Deo, Ajaya Mishra, Akash Patki, Akhilesh Kedawat, Akshay Kant, Amal B, Amar Deep Gupta, Amia Mishi, Amit Kalukhe, Amit Beriya, Amitosh Gautam, Amol Kadam, Amrut Kale, Amruta Shirpurkar, Anand Namjoshi, Anand Kumar, Anand Jodhani, Anbarasi Kanniah, Ancy David, Anirudh Bindage, Anita Kulkarni, Anjali Kumar, Ankit Dhankad, Ankit Dubey, Ankit Bajaj, Ankit Sabharwal, Ankur Dholakia, Ankur Sethi, Anupreet Kaur Dhody, Anutosh Kanoria, Anvesha Khandelwal, Aparna Iyer, Aravind K C, Archana R, Arnab Banerjee, Arun Kumar, Arun Sharma, Aruna Ramnathan, Arvind Kulkarni, Arvind Sridharan, Ashesh Dayal Srivastava, Ashish Garg, Ashish Singh, Ashvini Ghuge, Ashwin Chandrasekar, Ashwin Garlapati, Ashwin Krishna, Ashwini Ramanisankar, Asif Hussain, Asokan Chakravarthy, Atik Jain, Aurobii Mitra, Avani Joshi, Avi Jain, Avinash Saoji, Avinash Adhav, Ayush Goyal, Bavya Sivashree, Beena Parmar, Bhaiyuraje Deshmukh, Bhavin Panchasara, Bijlee Deshmukh, Bilal Khan, Chandrashekhar Patil, Charan Chaudary, Chetan Malhotra, Chetan Garg, Chinmay Vadnere, Chintan Siriya, Devavrat Shah, Devesh Bhimsaria, Dipti Tambe, Disha Pinge, Dr Satish Kulkarni, Ganesh Talekar, Gargi Rajawat, Gaurav Jha, Gaurav Sharma, Gaurav Sharma, Gaurav Agarwal, Gnana Deepan, Gourav Srivastava, Gurunath Bhide, Harinath Chandrasekaran, Harisharnam Rastogi, Harsh Chitlangia, Harshad Patil, Hemant Mehta, Himanshu Gothwal, Hitesh Kataria, Hrishikesh Gaikwad, I. S. Vijayalakshmi , Ilyas Kadri, Imayavaramban Gs, Jaideep Dewani, Javed Alam Khan, Jaydeep Jhaveri, Jitendra Rathore, Jivan Biradar, Jogashish Chowdhury, K Priyanth Rachamadugu, K Rama Krishna Reddy, Kalyani Vartak, Kalyani Khodke, Kamal Rathi, Kanishk Vedantham, Kapil Daga , Kaushal Sarda, Keshav Kshirsagar, Keyur Patel, Kiran S, Kirti Ekbote, Krishika Rajkumar, Krunal Doshi, Kshitij Bajaj, Kshitiz Sharma, Lakshman Charan, Lakshmi Kanth Mannem, Leo Mavely, Lewitt Somarajan, Llewelyn Dmello, Mahaboob Shaik, Maithili Desai, Maitreyee Mujumdar, Mamtesh Sugla, Mangkhenlal Gualnam, Manish Kanadje, Manish Yadav, Mathew Jose, Mayank Rungta, Mayank Gupta, Md. Sirajul Alam Barbhuiya, Meera Bhat, Mendon Hemraj, Mohammad Jakeer, Mohit Sureka, Mohit Chopra, Muthumanigandan Duraibabu, Nagumalli Srikanth, Naidu Lekha, Namesh Killemsetty, Nandkumar Kalate, Narendra Patil , Naveed Ks, Naveen Goyal, Navneen Jha, Neerja Srinivasan, Neetu Sharma, Neha Parikh, Neha Khond, Nidheesh Joseph, Niha Masih, Nikhil Bhagia, Nikhil Garg, Nikhil Golchha, Nilesh Gadle, Nilesh Gudape, Nilesh Kotalwar, Nitin Singal, Nitin Jathar, Nitin Nagori, Pallavi Bhatia, Parag Awasthi, Paritosh Mukhija, Pavan Kumar, Paveethra R, Phani Kumar Kadambari, Piyush Agarwal, Prabal Bhardwaj, Prabhu Swaminathan, Pradepan Thangaraj, Prajkta Thube, Pranav K, Prashant Zaveri, Pratik Doshi, Prem Addala, Pritee Jinturkar, Priyanka Sareen, Priyanka K, Pundlik Wagh, Rachana Malpani, Rahul Kapoor, Rahul Mankar, Rahul Buddala, Raja Sekhar, Rajendra Meena, Rajesh Golani, Rajesh Patidar, Ramana Killi, Ramya Mohan, Rana Golder, Rani Priyanka Vasireddy, Rashmi Gupta, Ravi Agarwala, Ravivarman Rajendiran, Rishikesh Rai, Ritu Jain, Rizat Tangvah, Rm Nagappan, Rohini Chandrashekharan, Rohit Khirapate, Rujuta Patil, Rupesh Manne, Sampad Sahu, Samuel Fernandes, Sandeep Kirpalani, Sandeep Soni, Sandeep Vedantam, Sandeep Bansal, Sandip Adling, Sandip Ramnath Andhale, Sanjay Lakhotia, Sanjay Bajaj, Sanket Tondare, Santhosh Subramaniam, Sarabjeet Singh, Sasha Dcosta, Sasi Kumar, Sathish Nagarajan, Satwinder Singh, Saurav Garg, Seema Mulay, Shalini Malhotra, Shashwat Roy, Shikhar Dubey, Shivani Ghaisas, Shivani Karkhanis, Shobhit Gupta, Shrikant Gabale, Shripad Buddhisagar, Shruti Veenam, Shruti Raheja, Shubhada Naik, Shubham Goyal, Sidarth Balasundaram, Siddhant Pattanaik, Siddhartha Gupta, Siddhesh Ware, Silky Kedawat, Simranpreet Singh Oberoi, Sindhu Ponguru, Sindhu Priyadharsini

357

Sankar, Siri Yar, Smriti Kedia, Sneh Dugar, Sontu Mandal:, Soonrita Sahasrabuddhe, Soumya Inumella, Srinivasan Iyengar, Suchitra Deshpande, Sudhyasheel Sen, Suhas Phadnis, Sujeet Bhamre, Sujeetkumar Kulkarni, Sulabh Chhabra, Suman Chennamaneni, Sumit Bhosale, Sunil Goyal, Sunita Thanekar, Sunita Kumari, Supriya Mudaliar, Surekha Bhange, Suyogkumar Bhavare, Swapnil Sawant, Swathi Jain, Swati Malik, Tanuj Poddar, Tanya Sikororia, Tejasa Khambete, Tirumaladevi Medarametla, Tranzita Dsouza, Ujjawal Bothra, Umesh Bora, Umesh Kumar Getta, V.R. Shankarendhra Gurunath, Vaibhav Aggarwal, Varshini Visweswaran, Varun Miglani, Varun Jain, Varun Gupta, Varun Patodia, Varun Kashyap, Veeranjaneyulu Pokala, Vidyadhar Prabhudesai, Vijay Mardhekar, Vijay Chavan, Vijay Anirudh, Vijay Mardhekar, Vijaypal Bishnoi, Vikram Undre, Vinay Bhaskar Pendurthy, Vineeth Patapati, Vinod Kumar, Vinod Jadhav , Vipin Jain, Vipul Shaha, Viren Naralkar, Vivek Kabra, Vivek Khandelwal, Vivek Kumar, Vivek Pawar, Yeshwant Limaye, Zainab Kalal

Jagriti Yatra 2009

Abhay Sarawgi, Abhinand Parthasarathy, Abhinandan Kohli, Abhinandan Kavale, Abhinav Kumar Gupta, Abhisek Mittal, Abhishant Pant, Abhishek Gupta, Abhishek Jindal, Abhishek Kumar Jha, Abinash Panigrahi, Adhiraj Deshpande, Adithya Prakash, Aditi Desai, Akash Jain, Akram Feroze. Md, Alok Arunam, Alok Kulkarni, Altaf Ul Rehman, Alysha Tharani, Amandeep Singh Hora, Amber Jain, Ambuj Anand, Amina Ahuja, Amit Kataria, Amit Rupnawar, Amitabh Mishra, Amresh Sinha, Anamika Kirad, Anand Datla, Anand Deshpande, Anchal _, Animesh Kumar, Anish Tiwary, Anitha Pai, Anjusha Lohakare, Ankan Pal, Ankit Desai, Ankit Madhogaria, Ankit Tulsyan, Ankita Kukreja, Ankur Chaudhary, Anupam Kumar, Anvesh Chinthala, Aparajita Bharti, Aparna Iyer, Arati Chavan, Ariya Bala Sadaiappan, Arjun Goyal, Arnab Dasgupta, Arun Ganesan, Arvind Palanisamy, Arvind Mani Tripathi, Asha Sawale, Ashish Nawale, Ashoka Varshini G, Asif Mohammed, Augustine George, Avinash Sharma, Avinash Mirge, Avril Picardo, Ayas Thazhvara, Bakar Ali Datrelia, Balaji Ingole, Balram Molwane, Barkha Kedia, Barsa, Bharti Mulchandani, Bhausaheb Dhokale, Bhavani Ravindran, Bhumika Saini, Chaitanya Wingkar, Chaitra Kurlageri, Chanchal Agrawal, Chandrika Maheshwari, Darshan Raut, Darshna Ganapathy, Deepak Kadam, Deepan Chakravarthy, Deepika Rn, Deepti Badve, Dhanraj Pardeshi, Dhawal Shah, Dheeraj Bansal, Dhiraj Kumar Singh, Dipika Prasad, Diptee Kolhatkar, Divya Jain, Dr Rizwan Ghasura, Dr Kamlesh Pathak, Dr Mahendra Khilari, Dr Suyogkumar Bhavare, Elita Almeida, Fazana Tamboli, First Name Last Name, Gaurav Bhadoria, Gaurav Nagalia, Gaurav Saxena, Gaurav Kullarkar, Gaurav Gupta, Gaurav Bhatt, Gaurav Bajaj, Gausiya Khan, Gautam Chopra, George Abraham, Ghanshyam Kanani, Gourav Jaiswal, Gunvant Jain, Hardik Vara, Hari Shanker R., Haripriya Madhavan, Harita Perla, Harjot Singh, Harmandeep Bhandal, Harriet Jemima Velpula, Harsh Khadloya, Harsh Agarwal, Harsha Vardhan Reddy K, Harshal Shewale, Hemakshi Meghani, Himanshu Kumar, Hita Unnikrishnan, Hitesh Shadija, Ilyas Kadri, Indira Priyadarsini.B, Isha Gupta, James Lama, Jatin Thacker, Jaya Shree, Jayanthi Cv, Jayasri Vadali, Jaydeep Punglia, Jerin Jose, Jyotsna ., K Chendu, K Rama Krishna Reddy, K. Prasad Rao, Kailash Chandak, Kalagara Divya Krishna, Kanika Thakrani, Karan Shah, Karthik P.N, Kaustubh. Itkurkar, Kavita Mandale, Keats Sukumar, Ketan Nandha, Khamir Purohit, Khom Raj Sharma, Kinjal Mehta, Koch Janardan, Komal Kankariya, Kuldeep Dantewadia, Kunal Chatterjee, Kushal Agrawal, Kushal Singh, Kushal Suhasaria, Lavanya Keshavamurthy, Lucky Singh, Luv Kalra, M.D Mahadev, Madhav Sanatan, Madhav Shile, Madhavi Nalluri, Mahendra Pyati, Mahendra Gupta, Mahesh Nayak, Major Rajesh Ranjit, Manas Gajare, Manas Tripathi, Manasi Dhawale, Manish K, Manish Sehgal, Manish Agarwal, Manisha Dandge, Manjunath Ganeshan, Manoj Sharma, Manu Gupta, Mayur Palod, Megha Mandavia, Megha Raut, Mithun Gangadharan, Monali Shelke, Monica Pande, Muthu Raman, Nagabhushana S, Nagam Karthya, Naji Naji, Namrata Arora, Namrata Bhandarkar, Nandini Joshi, Nandita Dhindsa, Nashvia Alvi, Naveen Damle, Navjot Singh Saini, Nayantara Mb, Nazir Ahmad Dar, Neeraj Pandey, Neeti Bandodker, Neha Jain, Neha Arha, Neil Parmar, Niju Mohan, Nikhil Ket, Nikhil Sobti, Nikunj Jain, Nilesh Ghodke, Nilesh Lodha, Nithin Nemani, Nitin Mangal, Nitish Suri, Nitisha Jain, Nupur Ligade, Omkar Pardeshi, Pankaj Rana, Pankaj Pansari, Pavitra Prabhanjan, Phani Kumar Yadavilli, Piyush Pranay, Pooja Mutha, Poonam Golani, Poonam Bhagia, Pradeep Mittal, Prakash Kumar, Pranadhika Sinha, Prasanth Prahladan, Prashant Mehta, Prashant Singh, Pratibha Pal, Pratik Poddar, Pratik Sawal, Praveen Bhanjdeo, Pravesh Dudani, Prithvi Ts, Priti Parekh, Priya Gopalakrishnan, Priya Agarwal, Priyadarshi Hem, Priyadarsini G.Phanindra, Priyanka Bhagat, Priyanka Singh, Pynhoi Tang, Rachana Kapadia, Radhakrishna Nayak, Raghubir Kumar, Rahi Kachole, Raja Sekahr Mamillapalli, Rajat Sharma, Rajiv Ratna Panda, Rajni Sharma, Rakhi Trust, Ramalakshmi Subramanian, Ranphoa Ngowa, Rashmi Sandilya, Rashmi Agrawal, Ravi Khatri, Ravi Ranjan, Ravi Kumar, Ravindra Vaidya, Richa Tiwari, Richa Choudhary, Richa Mani Tripathi, Rishupreet Oberoi, Rita Shetiya, Ritesh Maheshwari, Rithu Gopalan, Ritika Gwalani, Ritu ..., Rohin Mittal, Rohini Vaswani, Ruhani Singh, Ruhi Khanna, Rupali Patil, Rutunjay Singh, Sachin Bhosale, Sagar Gadekar, Sahil Arora, Sai Sudha, Sanchita Bhalwankar, Sandeep Hegde, Sandeep Kothawade, Sangeeta Garve, Sangram Chavan, Sankalp Khanna, Sarada V, Sarat Chandra Prasad, Seetha Srikanth, Seshagiri Gudipudi, Shahid Khan, Shailesh Kumar, Shailini Suave, Shareek Kammadtah, Sharvari Patil, Shashank Agrawal, Shekhar Korde, Shilpa Bisht, Shridhar Samant, Shubham Agrawal, Shveta Suneja, Shweta Pawar, Shweta Shetkar, Shweta Agrawal, Siddharth , Siddharth Biyani, Siddhartha Jain, Sidhartha Jatar, Sindhu Priyadharsini Sankar, Sivadarsheni Ravindran, Sivaji Bobbili, Smira Rao, Sneha Kupekar, Sonali Shah, Soraisham Okendro, Soumya Harapanahalli, Srishti Shridhar, Subodh Rathore, Suchita Mate, Sudarshana Gede, Sudeep Phase, Suhaas Kaul, Sujeeth Ramakrishnan, Sumit Chavan, Sunil Kumar Yadav, Supriya Balaji Ramachandran, Surajmal Chandak, Suvarna Tapkir, Swapnil Barai, Swathi Addala, Swati Garg, Swati Seshadri, Swati Rastogi, Syed Mohammed Peershavali, Tanpreet Sehgal, Tarun Agarwal, Thangzamang Hatlang, Tshering Lhamu Bhutia, Utkarsh Mehta, Uttpal Bhattacharjya, Vaishali Gandhi, Vallepalli Yonithya, Vandana Kamthe, Vansh Tahliyani, Varun Sood, Varun Jain, Venkatesh Gogineni, Vignesh.J Jayachandran, Vijay Chavhan, Vijayeta Singh, Vijeta Shrivastava, Vijita Mistry, Vinay Agrawal, Viraj Mahadik, Vivek B S, Vivek Pai, Yatin Suri, Yogendra Singh, Yogesh Deshpande, Yogesh Bhong, Yogita Kalra, Yuvaraj Galada

Jagriti Yatra 2010

Abhimanyu Kasliwal, Abhishek Sharma, Akash Jain, Akhilesh Kumar, Akshata Bhat, Amit Singh, Anand Kumbhalkar, Anand Deo Tamrakar, Anil Mahamulkar, Anjali Ambekar, Ankit Agrawal, Arpit Mehta, Aruna Kulkarni, Arvind Garimella, Ashish Poddar, Ashish Kumar, Ashish Changole, Ashmeet Kapoor, Ashok Kumar, Ashutosh Bachchhav, Ashwini Lahane, Aswin Yogesh, Atul Kulkarni, Ayush Bansal, Balasaheb Ghuge, Baleshwar Prasad, Basur Kiran, Bharat Prasad, Bharat Varshney, Bhargavi Gogula, Bhumish Khudkhudia, Bhuvi Kathpalia, Biswajeet Panda, Bothaina Qamar, Chandana Raizada, Chandikaprasad Udke, Chandni Goel, Charnita Arora, Chhitup Lama, Dayanand Kumar, Deepak Thakrar, Deepali Sharma, Devika ., Dhanush Kuttuva, Dileep Sn, Divya Gaitonde, Divya Sornaraja, Divya Gupta, Dnyaneshwar Jadhawar, Dr G.Narasima Rao, Dr Prashant Kuchankar, Dwijo Goswami, Ekta

Agarwal, Eliza Paul, Eswaran Sivaraman, Fernando Tamayo Grados, First Name Last Name, Ganesh Pawar, Ganesh Jangir, Gargeyee Iyengar, Gautam Palukuri, Gayatri Deshpande, Girija Periasamy, Gulzar Hussain, Gunjan Rathod, Hareram Dubey, Harish Mohan, Harshada Karnik, Harshal Joshi, Harshila Suri, Heena Jethanandani, Heena Chauhan, Himanshu Nihalani, Hitesh Kumar Kyal, Ish Jindal, Ithadi Subba Rao, Jaya Arya, Jayantraj Bhagyawant, Jayasharadha Chandrakalatharan, Jayasudha Arunachalam, Jhansi Rani Nuthanakanti, Jitendra Sahu, Jithin Paul Varghese, John Basumatary, Jyoti Mani, Jyotsna Taparia, Kaminee Ranga, Kanav Nayyar, Kanchana Kathiresan, Kanupriya Bansal, Kapil Agrawal, Karan Choudhary, Karan Jagani, Karthik Ram, Karuna Ahuja, Kathleen Wagner, Kaustubh Ibitkar, Kaustubh Joshi, Kavi Bharathi, Kavya Thelakkat, Keshav Krishnamani, Ketan Bhongle, Ketan Parmar, Kirti Jadhav, Kirti Poonia, Komal Chowbay, Krishna Kumar, Krithika Dutta Narayana, Kriti Mittal, Krushnali Taori, Kshitij Garg, Kshitij Bhotika, Kumar Ankit Sarawgi, Kumari Parijat, Kunjan Gandhi, Kunwar Rajeev Singh, Kushagra Alankar, Lalit Varshney, Lalith Kumar Vemali, Lav Mehta, Laxmi Nair, Lipika Salaye, Madhura Dange, Mahadeo Karande, Mahesh Shejal, Mahesh Pawar, Manan Saraiya, Manish Makhija, Manish Bajaj, Manjit Nath, Manoj M, Manvi Goel, Mayank Gupta, Mayank Jain, Mebaailin Blah, Mederametla Sandeep, Meenakshi Vashist, Meghan Mahajan, Midhu K Mohan, Mihir Singh, Mihir Deshpande, Miss. Aarti Zambare, Mithilesh Kandalkar, Mithun Sundar Raj, Mohammed Saifu, Mohan Raj, Mohd Irfan, Mohit Tiwari, Ms.Vidya Yadav, Muhammed Rafi Ap, Mukesh Bhavsar, Mukta Darera, Nagajyothi Nookula, Nakul Arora, Namrata Deshmukh, Nandkishor Boddu, Narendra Singh Thakur, Natasha Mistry, Nauman Sharif, Naveen Mortha, Naya Nandargi, Neelohit Prakash Tripathi, Neeraj Kuletha, Neerav Kumar, Neha Gupta, Nihar Todupunoori, Nikesh Murjani, Nikhil Nair, Nikhil Bhandare, Nikhil Kumar, Nikita Bharadia, Nilesh Sharma, Nirupama Murali, Nitish Kumar, Nitisha Popat, Nivedita Ghonge, Nowfal Abdul Khadar, Nupur Jain, Nutan Paliwal, Om Prakash Jat, Oojwal Manglik, Pallavi Salunkhe, Pankaj Kumar Jain, Paromita Nath, Parvathi Devi, Pavan Evsr, Payal Tak, Peeyush Nathani, Pooja Mishra, Poonam Kumar, Poonam Singh, Poornima Sardana, Prabhat Kumar, Pragya Mishra, Prahalathan Kk, Prajakta Jadhav, Prakhar Mishra, Pramod Jindal, Pranay Jivrajka, Pranjal Jain, Prasanta Biswal, Prashant Agarwal, Prathamesh Chavan, Pratik Hakay, Priya Nair, Priya Krishnamoorthy, Priya Poddar, Priyadarshi Bhattacharya, Priyanka Ahuja, Priyanka Bajaj, Priyanka Lonkar, Puneet Goyal, Punita Mittal, Raghuraj Singh Ueke, Rahul Gupta, Rahul Nair, Rahul Saini, Rahul Shah, Rajamurugan R, Rajani Wagh, Rajesh Thazhapallil Radhakrishnan, Raju Smg, Rakesh Bunkar, Ram Nath Raman, Raman Agrawalla, Ramesh Kohane, Rammohan Reddy, Ramya Gayar, Ramyaswati Metlapalli, Ranjan Kumar, Rashmi Mehta, Rashmi Raut, Raushan Thakur, Ravi Darda, Ravi Kumar Sharma, Ravi Ranjan Singh, Ravindra Rapeti, Ravish Vasan, Rekha Gajendran, Renju Rajan, Revanti P Wadhwa, Rijul Jain, Rishabh Jain, Ritish Reddy, Rohan Handa, Rohit Kanthale, Roshan Raja, Roshni Wanode, Ruchi Parikh, Sahil Patwa, Sakshat Kapoor, Saloni Gupta, Samar Agrawal, Samrawit Biyazin, Sana Kadri, Sandeep Shelke, Sandhya Pandey, Sanjeevanee Vaidya, Santosh Kumar, Santosh Lakshman M, Sarika Gaikwad, Satendra Kumar Singh, Satyapal Patil, Saurabh Jain, Saurabh Thakur, Sayali Borole, Sebin John Mathew, Shaifali Gupta, Shaik Mohammed Samdani, Shailendra Singh Gautam, Shaji B, Shambhavi Tambulwadkar, Shankar Barve, Shankar Kumar, Shantanu Gupta, Shashank Pathak, Shashi Bhushan Singh, Shefali Bajpai, Shikhar Gupta, Shilpa Billur, Shilpi Tripathi, Shimolee Sheth, Shiny Cyriac, Shital Nade, Shivaji Kad, Shraddha Shanbhag, Shraddha Gupta, Shravanthy Krishnamurthy, Shriya Sk, Shubangini Naidu, Shuvashree Mohapatra, Sibi Saseendran, Sidharth Mahajan, Sindhoor Hegde, Smita Vahadane, Sonali Arote, Sonali Bhojwani, Sonali Shivale, Soori Babu, Soumya Gupta, Sourabh Jain, Sreepriya , Srilakshmi Reddy, Sujit Dharmpatre, Sujith Eranezhath, Suman Nala, Sumit Rao, Sumit Khude, Sumit Deshmukh, Sunita Kumari, Sunney Fotedar, Sunny Bharani, Surabhi Bhatnagar, Suraj Deshmukh, Suruchi Kumari, Sushanth Vasuki, Swaroop Gorajala, Swati Chawla, Swetha Stotra Bhashyam, Tanya Saxena, Tejashree Mokashi, Tilkesh Bhatia, Trishma Pinto, Tushar Madage, Udit Bansal, Unnati Narang, Usha Pillai, Utkarsh Narain, Uzair Fahmi, Vaibhav Karwa, Vallabh Munshi, Vidur Khanna, Vidyun Goel, Vikas Vimal, Vikas Jadhav, Vikramjeet Singh, Vinay Mishra, Vinisha Handa, Vinod Bachhav, Vipin Handa, Vishakha Modi, Vishwanath Malla, Yash Chaudhary, Yatish Lalwani, Yogesh Kansal, Yogesh Raut, , Garima Garg, Harshie Wahie, Megha Vyas, Anmol Chopra, Ashutosh Kumar Mishra, Damini Gupta, Gaurav Dahake, K Durga Prasad, Md Zeeshan, Parul Vig, Priya Dhanuka, Ravi Agarwal, Sandip Rajpopat, Sayana Dutta, Somnath Meher, Vikram Kadam

Jagriti Yatra 2011

Aafreen Hasnain, Aakanksha Mehta, Aakash Saha, Aarati Rao, Abdul Kaleem, Abhay Yadav, Abhijit Gadewar, Abhishek Saha, Abhishek Sinha, Abhishek Mangla, Abhishek Shrivastava, Abhishek Choudhary, Adil Azeem, Aditi Prakash, Aditya Kumar, Aditya Rathi, Aditya Maheswaran, Ahmed Choudhary, Ajay Chokhani, Ajinkya Tambe, Ajit Bombatkar, Ajit Singh, Akshay Kumar, Akshay Tiwari, Aliaksandr Hudzilin, Althea Carbon, Ameed Hashmi, Ameeti Mishra, Amit Kumbhar, Amit Maurya, Amit Kumar, Amit Sharan Singh, Amrita Agnihotri, Ana Maria Araos Casas, Anagha Todalbagi, Anand Gupta, Anant Goenka, Anchal Goel, Andi Dwi Putra, Anil Chaturwedy, Anil Kumar, Anitha Lakshmanan, Anjali Singh, Anjana Choudhary, Ankit Manchanda, Ankit Kapoor, Ankit Jain, Ankita Chauhan, Ankur Phadnis, Ankur Singh, Ankush Saraff, Anmol Gupta, Anna Mori, Anubhav Modi, Anup Sheshadri, Apoorva Reddy, Apurva Mudliar, Aravind Thumbur, Aravind R, Archana Mohankumar, Areum Kim, Arpita Chakraborty, Arvind Iyengar, Ashish Agarwal, Ashish Anand, Ashish Bhutada, Ashish Pal, Ashish Bhonde, Ashish Mutha, Ashish Tripathy, Ashok Sekar, Ashwarya Pratap Singh, Ashwini H Sridhar, Asmita Misra, Aswath Sampath, Avirneni Basanth, Bethun Bhowmik, Bhawanngal Manda, Bhaskar Chattoraj, Bhavya Sharma, Bhumi Purohit, Bibhu Parida, Bikash Sahoo, Binay Neekhra, Biswajeet Panda, Braj Bhushan Pandey, Brian Abel, Burhan Hussain, Chaitanya Goyal, Chanchal Kumari, Chandershekhar Meena, Chandra Rekha Gunji, Chandu Sasidharan, Chinthala Saikumar Reddy, Chirag Garg, Darshana Dave, Debarati Rakshit, Deeksha Ahuja, Deepak K, Deepan Chakravarthy, Deepti P. Bhat, Deewesh Prasad, Devendra Singh, Devina Sharma, Dheeraj Dhingra, Dhruba Jyoti Kalita, Dhwani Desai, Digvijay Dhanorkar, Dilip Mishra, Dilip Singh Palsaniya, Dinesh Mohata, Dipak Adak, Dipak Sonawane, Dipika Panchbhai, Divya Datta, Divya Goel, Divya S, Divyani Mishra, Divyanjali Sharma, Dr Sanjiv Mishra, Eeshanpriya Ms, Erika Funck, First Name Last Name, Frank Arnold Okyere, Gabriel Weinstein, Gaee Kim, Gajanan Bhale, Ganesh Motkar, Garima Gupta Kapila, Garima Maheshwari, Garv Manchanda, Gaurav Sehgal, Gaurav Mohta, Gaurav Garg, Gauri Sawant, Gayathri Balan, Gayathri Swaminathan, Ghanapriya Nagarajan, Giriraj Sirohi, Gobinda Dalai, Gopi Krishnan, Govind Rajput, Gracelyne Fernando, H T Srinivas, Hamsini Ravi, Hang Dao, Hannah Bird, Hardik Thakker, Hariharan Suresh, Harish D, Harish Lohar, Harsh Dhankani, Harsh Bansal, Harsha Vardhan, Harshal Lodha, Harsimran Singh, Hasmeet Singh, Hemant Agrawal, Hemanta Mahanta, Henri Combrink, Himanchal Sahu, Himanshu Gupta, Hirenkumar Umaraviya, Inga Chen, Isaac Abeiku Otoo, Ishan Kawley, Ishani Mehta, Israel Sadovitch, Jamshadali Tt, Jasmine Goel, Jay Khattar, Jaya Prakash Jain, Jinesh Parakh, Jitendra Agrawal, Jithin Emmanuel, Joanita Britto, Joel Modestus, Johnson Dsouza, Jonathan Greener, Joseph Mirro Macatangay, Julie Zarka, Justin Francis, Jyothirmayi Dakkumalla, Jyoti Kakati, Jyotismita Devi, K Kranthi Kumar, Kalpana Prajapati, Karishma Rafferty, Karishma Kotwani, Kashimbi Limata, Kaushik Kishore, Keta

Shah, Khamarudheen K.P, Kimberly Lapaglia, Kiran Patil, Kiran Patil, Komal , Komal Savla, Koushiki Banerjee, Kripa Ramachandran, Kritivasas Shukla, Krupala Nune, Kshitij Patil, Kumar Abhishek, Kuntal Barman, Lakshmi R. Nair, Lavanya Jagannathan, Leena Bansal, Leigh Potter, Leila Mucarsel, Madhav Rajgarhia, Madhura Nanivadekar, Makakmayum Salman Khurshid, Malika Whitley, Mangesh Patil, Manish Sharma, Manoj Sharma, Martice Sutton, Marty Pollak, Maya Beaucasin, Meera Saujani, Milan Jain, Minal Ingale, Mishaal Sarawgi, Mitali Agarwal, Mogili Vijender, Mohammad Alishan Mustafa, Mohit Lohani, Mohith Kumar·Kanoj, Monal Rohankar, Moumita Majumdar, Mrinalini Sardar, Mudit Vijayvergiya, Mukesh Kumar, Muskan Bamnia, Nabajit Saikia, Nafeesa Gupta, Naheda Parvin Kadri, Namrata Ganguly, Nana Ama Tima Boakye, Nancy Aggarwal, Nandkishor Lohot, Naresh Raj Goyal, Natasha Correa, Naval Tayal, Navalkishore Shinde, Naveen Rander, Naveen Tiwari, Navendu Mishra, Neha Thakrar, Neha Kamra, Neha Zade, Nehal Sapre, Neilesh Chorakhalikar, Nickolai Kinny, Nidhi Anarkat, Niharika Drolia, Niharika B, Nikhila Kanakamedala, Nikita Gupta, Nikita Lalwani, Nilesh Patil, Nilesh Deshmukh, Niraj Bhatt, Nirmal Brar, Nirpesh Agrawal, Nishtha Singh, Nitesh Agrawal, Niti Shree, Olga Usachova, Orpita Majumdar, Padma Hoge, Pallavi Gandhalikar, Pankaj Gortyal, Pankaj Agrawal, Pannala Navadeep, Papisetty Manoj, Paryushan Jain, Pavan Karwa, Pavithra Kl, Pavithra Kannan, Pavneet Kaur, Pawan Gupta, Pitamber Kumar, Poem Kabra, Prachi Pawar, Pradeep Kumar Hial, Pragyan Dubey, Prakash Chittoor, Prakhar Jain, Pranali Sisodiya, Pranoti Regoti, Prasun Chokshi, Prathamesh Advilkar, Pravesh Gupta, Premanku Chakraborty, Prerit Tiwari, Priyanka Peeramsetty, Priyanka Agrawal, Priyanka M, Priyanka Cherekar, Pulkit Jain, Quinton Fivelman, R Praveen Kumar, Radheshyam Nayak, Radhika Bhongale, Ragini Rastogi, Rahul Pawa, Rajashri Sai, Rajat Agrawal, Rajen Makhijani, Rajesh Kvr, Rajvihar Reddy, Rakesh Gadewar, Ravi Agarwal, Ravi , Ravi Chandan Ray, Reshu Pratik, Richard Russell, Ridim Agarwal, Rishi Garg, Ritwik Sahoo, Ritwik Chatterjee, Robin Ravi, Rohit Kandalkar, Rohit Aggarwal, Rohit Saffar, Rohit Shah, Ruchi Choudhary, Ruhi Kumari, Rupali Tuse, Ryker Labbee, S.N.Keerthi Sagar, Saahil Narang, Sachin Patil, Sachin Kasera, Sagar Manglani, Sahil Jagnani, Sahil Garg, Sai Sharan, Sakshi Chadha, Sandip Garg, Sangram Kakad, Sanket Wadte, Satnam Wadhwa, Satyam Kumar, Satyapraksash Pareek, Saumendra Swain, Saumya Saumya, Saurabh Sable, Savan Vachhani, Sayli Walke, Seela Srikanth, Senthilkumar Govindarajulu, Shabana Tamboli, Shachi Madhogaria, Shailendra Mahani, Shakeela K.T., Shalini Menon, Sharad Goenka, Shatakshi Gawade, Shay Eyal, Shikha Pandey, Shiva Charan Raj Kasu, Shivangi Narayan, Shivya Nath, Shradha Iyer, Shradha Sharma, Shrish Biyani, Shruthi Iyer, Shruti Bansal, Shruti Subramanian, Shubhangi Gupta, Shubhanshu Bansal, Shweta Narula, Shweta Rao, Siddharth Chandrasekar, Sidharth Mahajan, Smriti Shyamal, Sneha Jain, Sonal Singh, Soo Im Shin, Sowmya Bharathi Bhuram, Sreedevi Prasannan, Sreelal S, Sriraj Reddy, Srujith Lingala, Stella Lee, Subham Sahu, Subodh Chandra Subedi, Sudam Batule, Sujeet Kumar Yadav, Sukhdev Singh, Sumi Roy, Sunil Gupta, Sunil Pawar, Sunil Kumar, Supriya Sharma, Supriya Sharma, Suvarna Bagal, Swapnil Hadpe, Sweta Chandramouli, Syed Faizan Haider, Tabassum Husain, Tanuja Malla, Tanvi Randhar, Tarun Bansal, Tathagata Basu, Trisha Roy, Tushar Bansal, Tushar Handa, Uday Krishna, Udayan Banerjee, Uma Shunmuganathan, Utkarsh Agrawal, V.L.V.Vamsi Krishna, Vaishnavi Bala, Valeria Vizuete, Vanya Saxena, Varsha Sutrave, Varun Deshpande, Varun Sharma, Vayavya Mishra, Veerender Lavudi, Venkata Swaroop, Vijay Khanna, Vikas Kumar, Vikas Ranga, Vikrant Mahajan, Vinay Goel, Vineet Chirania, Vini Khabya, Vinod Nannaware, Vinutha N, Vipul Patil, Vipul Garg, Vishakha Pant, Vishal Shah, Vishal Ramaswamy, Vishal Vachani, Vivek Kumar, Vivek Mandowara, Yammanuru Dharma Teja Reddy, Yogi Agarwal, Zim Ugochukwu, Zubiabegum Saiyed

Jagriti Yatra 2012

Aakanksha Gupta, Aakriti Goel, Aarya Palsule, Aashima Madaan, Aashlesha Ghanekar, Abha Gupta, Abhay Nandan, Abhijeet Anand, Abhijeet Oza, Abhijit Tiwari, Abhijit Gundawar, Abhijoy Sarkar, Abhinav Singh, Abhinav Kasliwal, Abhinav Kapoor, Abhishek Kumar, Abhudai Beohar, Aboli Kadam, Achal Garg, Adarsh Bhat, Aditya Kansal, Aditya Agrawal, Aishwarya Tipnis, Ajay Jain, Akanksha Bapna, Akanksha Srivastava, Akhil Bhiwal, Akshay Jain, Akshay Koli, Akshaya Sundaresan, Alan Miranda, Alexander Harmsen, Aliakbar Shafi, Alok·Kumar, Alpaxee Kashyap, Aman Raj, Amit Monga, Amir Saurabh, Amit Dalmia, Amruta Pund, Amruta Sheth, Amrutha Varshini, Amuktha Naraparaju, Anand Choudhary, Anandh Ramachandran, Angarayan Sundarakalatharan, Aniket Patil, Anil Kumar, Ankit Kanani, Ankit Kedia, Ankit Agarwal, Ankush Kumari, Annesha Dutta, Anshum Kocher, Anuj Bheda, Anuja Chavan, Anuradha Mahajan, Anurag Priyedarshi, Aparna Arun, Apoorva Anand Conjeevaram, Archana Rao, Archit Kumar, Archit Rathi, Arihant Daga, Arjun Arora, Arjun Sundar Raj, Arpan Koirala, Arpit Sarin, Arthi Gomathinayagam, Arun Sumant, Aruna Arora, Arunadeepthi Ravada, Asha Jomis, Asheeque Nasim.C , Ashesh Rajhans, Ashis Dash, Ashish Agarwal, Ashraful Islam, Ashutosh Tiwari, Ashvini Kumar, Ashwin Ravichandran, Ashwini Krishna, Ashwini Patil, Ashwini Shinde, Ashwini Pawar, Avinash Veeramachaneni, Baikunthanath Dwibedi, Banoth Hussain, Bhabani Mallick, Bhabya Singh, Bhagyashree Suryawanshi, Bharat Kunduru, Bharath Kumar M, Bharathi Gutta, Bhargav Chandrababu, Bhargavi Sakthivel, Bhaskar Singh, Bhushan Phirke, Bhushan Taskar, Binod Poudel, Braz-Vieira C Chloé, Chaitali Kathale, Charneet Singh, Chetan Raut, Chirag Jain, Chockalingam G, Danish Mir, Darshan Mundada, Deepa Sai Avula, Deepti Somani, Dev Chundi, Devanshee Deepak, Devika Lal, Dhairyashil Patil, Dhanashri Yadav, Dhara Manek, Dip Jung Thapa, Disha Shroff, Divya Khandelwal, Dnyanesh Magar, Dnyaneshwar Borse, Dr Atul Jaiswal, Ekta Yadav, Elizabeth Mathew, Eric Dadson, Falguni Parekh, Freshta Karim, Gala Soler, Gaurav Thakrar, Gautam Kumar Agrawal, Geet Srivastava, Girish Sampath, Gitanjali Roy, Gourav Mohata, Govind Kumar, Gowtham Guttuls, Gurram Ashok, Hanna Paulose, Harchand Sundeshaa, Harish Bhavsar, Harish Kumar, Harish Reddy M, Harsh Snehanshu, Harshita Mehta, Hemali Chothani, Himani Baru, Isha Zade, Ishaan Bhola, Jaghvi Mehta, Jasmeet Khanuja, Jatin Garg, Jay Prakash, Jeevan Paudel, Jishnu T Mekkara, Joseph Kenneth Otchere, Jyothi Mehta, Kailash Chandra, Kanakamedala Deepthi, Karan Bajaj, Karmvir Tiwari, Karthik Pedduri, Karthik Thomas, Kes , Keshav Singhal, Khalid Jaffrey, Kiran Vadalasetti, Koustubh Sinkar, Krishna Mohan.P.S, Krishna Ramavat, Kristen Neymarc, Kriti Taneja, Kumar Gourav, Kumari Pushpa, Kunal Goel, Kunduru Sanjana Reddy, Lipi Goyal, Lucile , Mallika Galani, Mandeep Singh, Mangesh Lalge, Manish Choudhury, Manish Meena, Manish Barnwal, Manish S Sugandhi, Manju Shree Vyas, Manohar Gupta, Manoj Savekar, Masha Nazeem, Masood Adil, Matthieu Dardaillon, Mayank Bhatia, Mayur Kurhadę, Meenali Sharma, Megha Yadav, Mohit Kumar, Mohit Verma, Mohneesh Patel, Monalisha Mohta, Monica C, Monika Choudhary, Mridul Kumar, Mrunal Pagnis, Mude Jayaprakash Naik, Muhammed Shafi, Mukesh Darshan, Muralikrishnan Chandrasenan, Murukan Pareparambil, Narayan Singh, Navak Gupta, Navdeep Aggarwal, Naveen Agrawal, Naveen Kumar, Navnath Kad, Neeha Neeha, Neha Kaur, Neha Rai, Neha Rai, Neha Nogia, Neha Gugale, Neha Sharma, Neha Singh, Netra Jere, Nidhi Gupta, Nikhil Raju, Nikhil Kulkarni, Nikhil Tuse, Nilam Muzaffari, Nilotpal Jha, Nimish Khandelwal, Nishank Varshney, Nishant Gupta, Nishigandha Bawdhankar, Nitesh Sardana, Nitin Tayal, Nitin Kayande, Nivedita Peddi, Orrie Johan, Padma Karri, Padmapriya Nirmalkumar, Pakhi Mahawar, Palak Sinha, Pallavi Verma, Pallavi Kesarwani, Pankaj Nanda, Parabal Singh, Parag Verma, Paras Mehendiratta, Partha Pati, Pavan Ananth, Pavitraa P, Pintu Kumar, Piyush Goyal, Piyusha Jagtap, Pooja Thakur, Poornima Srinivasan, Pournima

Barhate, Prachur Tayal, Pragati Singh, Pragati Khabiya, Pramod Jadhav, Praneet Kumat, Pranjal Modi, Pranjal Singh, Pranjal Koranne, Pranshu Sugara, Prashant Kadam, Prashant Kumar Sharma, Pratik Munot, Pratik Chaudhari, Praveen Selvasekaran, Pravin Agrawal, Pravin Yadav, Pritesh Gupta, Pritesh Mittal, Prithvik Kankappa, Priya Singh, Priya Ratnam, Priyanandhan Rajendhiran, Priyanka Shylendra, Priyanka Bhille, Prukalpa Sankar, Purnima Kesavan, Rachit Murarka, Rachna Chopra, Rahul Garg, Rahul Singh, Rahul Gaadhe, Raj Anmol Singh Garg, Raj Kumarr Solanki, Rajat Mahajan, Rajeev Rajeshuni, Ram Manohar, Ramachandran Narayanan, Ramesh Babu M, Ranjeet Kumar Khatri, Rashmita Mohanty, Rasik Pansare, Ratandeep Dhody, Ravi Jha, Ravi Ranjan, Ravi Goyal, Ravi Bhan Singh Bhati, Rebecca Millward, Rehana Razack, Richa Ranwaka, Rinchal Gawali, Ritesh Kayal, Ritika Jaiswal, Robin Chaurasiya, Rohan Singh, Rohit Vyas, Roshan Kumar, Ruben Mascarenhas, Rucha Vakhariya, Ruchi Junnarkar, Sachin Damekar, Sadique Mohammad Iqbal, Sagar Prabhudev, Sagar Chandra Reddy L, Sagar Mahapatra, Sagnik Chakraborty, Sai Upalekar, Sai Krishna Sujith Kumar.S, Sai Sharan Bandi, Saikat Chakrabarty, Sajal Bansal, Sakshi Sangwan, Sakshi Mohan, Samarth Batra, Samarth Mahajan, Samkit Jain, Sammy Agrawal, Sangeet Ranjan, Sangeeta Kumari, Sanjay Rathore, Sanoop K V, Sanya Chawla, Satomi Yokoo, Satyamurthy K R, Saumya Ranjan Nath, Saurabh Nayak, Saurabh Kumar, Saurabh Jindal, Saurabh Wakhare, Savita Mundhe, Savitha Jvn, Shadab Hassan Shahid, Shahin Makandar, Shailaja Shah, Shailesh Verma, Shalini Dwivedi, Shantanu Pandharkar, Sharan Girdhani, Sharath R, Sharique Usman, Shashank Kalra, Shashank Shekhar Pandey, Shipra Agarwal, Shital Birajdar, Shivam Kesari, Shivam Arora, Shivam Kumar Choubey, Shivkumar Channagire, Shrikant Yerule, Shristy Gupta, Shruti Parmar, Shubham Shivani, Shubham Agarwal, Shubham Sharma, Shwetal Karade, Siddarudha Singadi, Siddharth Naidu, Siddharth Karnavat, Siddharth Agarwal, Siva Karthik Valaparla, Sivagnanavathy Ksk, Sneh Ganjoo, Snehal Lokhande, Snehal Adsod, Sonali Porwal, Sparsh Choudhary, Spriha Saggar, Srikanth Chebolu Shankara, Sudheendra Chilappagari, Sudhir Keshri, Suhani Mohan, Suma Swaminathan, Sumangal Saxena, Sumit Kumar, Sumit Sahu, Sunay Gupta, Suneet Sharma, Sunil Prakash, Surabhi Yadav, Suraj Pardeshi, Surbhi Jain, Surbhi Singh, Surendra Bishnoi, Sushil Balan, Susmita Das, Swapnil Munde, Swarna Ramineni, Syed Wajahath Ali, Tanu Rawat, Tanvi Pritmani, Tanvi Kulkarni, Tejashri Kamble, Tejaswini Jayanthy, Thingnam Romila, Tomasz Kozakiewicz, Trupti Upadhye, Urvi Malviya, Utkarsh Tiwari, Vaibhav Kumar, Vamsi Krishna, Varalaxmi Pillai, Vartika Bansal, Varun Bhojvaid, Vatsal Bajoria, Vibhav Joshi, Vibhuti Aggarwal, Vijay Adhitya S K, Vijesh Kumar Raju B, Vijin V, Vikesh Gusain, Vikram Rebala, Vinita Negi, Vinod Babu.V, Vipul Goel, Vishesh Sharma, Vrashali Khandelwal, William Swashnick, Yamini Singh, Yashaswini K S, Yashwant Thakur, Yassine Redissi, Yeshoda Prashanti Kalyan, Yogeshkumar Motwani

Jagriti Yatra 2013

Aarti Devi, Abhijeet Singh, Abhijit Sachdeva, Abhijit Katkade, Abhinandan Singh, Abhinav Saxena, Adithya Pasupuleti, Aditi Gupta, Aditi Pohekar, Aditya Ranjan, Aditya Charegaonkar, Aishwarya Sharma, Aishwarya Arun, Ajay Mittal, Ajeet Bharti, Ajeetha Triplicane, Akanksha Naygandhi, Akhalya N, Akshay Palande, Alok Misra, Aman Kumar, Amandeep Saluja, Amar Kumar, Amarnath Shetkar, Amit , Amit Saraogi, Amit Gupta, Amol Mane, Amulya Kalangi, Anand Mishra, Anandita Kumar, Anant Deep, Ananya Rawat, Ananya Sanchita Sharma, Aniket Patole, Aniruddh Jain, Aniruddha Dhage, Anirudh Kumar, Anirudh Rao, Anita Taral, Anju Kumari, Ankit Pansari, Ankit Gupta, Ankit Mittal, Ankur Gupta, Ankur Golwa, Ankur Jhunjhunwala, Ankush Gupta, Anmol Kaur, Anoop Garg, Anoop Kumar Agarwal, Anshu Kujur, Anuj Gahoi, Anupama Kalgudi, Anupriya Inumella, Anurag Nema, Anurag Satpathy, Anurag Agarwala, Anusmita Nikam, Anvita Dixit, Aparna Lomte, Apoorva Vyas, Apoorva Tapas, Apratim Ganguli, Arjit Raj, Arnav Malik, Arpita Bhojane, Artatrana Tandi, Arti Bhandari, Asha Dhondkar, Ashvin Yadav, Ashwanth M P, Ashwini Kumar, Ashwini Agrawal, Asmit Hisaria, Avinash Bhakta, Avishma Matta, Avnika , Baidurya Sen, Balaji Sundeep V, Barath Balachandran, Barkha Bansal, Bharat Bylappa, Bhavna Gupta, Bhawna Arora, Bhushan Reddy, Bidisha Kalita, Bikram Nayak, Bimal Raturi, Bipin Patil, Boddu Naresh Goud, Brajesh Kumar, Chahat Abrol, Chaitanya Pathak, Chaitanya Reddy Bokka, Chandan Agarwal, Chandni Gupta, Chandra Prakash Bhakuni, Chandrahas Muvvala, Charu Deshmukh, Charumathy R K, Chetan Jadhav, Chi Hao Wong, Chintamani Pawar, Damini Nenawati, Deeksha Wattamwar, Deepak Kumar Deo, Deepanshi Jain, Deepjyoti Deb, Deepshikha Bhardwaj, Deepti Khurana, Devayani Borse, Devendra Tayade, Dharmendra Kumar Singh, Dhiraj Singh, Dnyaneshwar Kaulwar, Dr Shraddha Tendulkar, Dr Saurabh Patle, Dr Ravindra Chhabile, Eklavya Singh, Ekta Aswal, Elise Westphalen, Emmanuelle Pecoux, Esha Gupta, Farish C V, Ganesh Walunj, Gaurang Agrawal, Gaurav Agrawal, Gaurav Sood, Gaurav Agrawal, Gaurav Ketkar, Gaurav Singhal, Gayathri Devi, Gayatri Khairnar, Geeta Patil, Geetika Goyal, Gokul Ravikumar, Gokul Krishna, Gopagani Vijaychander, Govind Moghekar, Harbeer Singh Sidana, Hardik Shah, Hari Haran, Hari Chandana Andipakula, Haridas Kalbhor, Harsh Gupta, Harshal Dalvi, Harshita Kumra, Himanshu Joshi, Hina Shah, Hunaid Shakkarwala, Ian Kwong, Ishan Padgotra, Ishwarya Bhaskaran, Jay Megotia, Jean Haag, Jiaul Haq, Jignesh Talasila, Jitendra Markad, Josephine Mary D, Juhi Shah, Jyotsna Dedha, Kajori Das, Kannika Iyengar, Karan Ambwani, Karanjeet Verma, Karjan Sharma, Karthick Anandaraman, Keerthana Balasubramani, Keerti Bhandary, Keshav Aggarwal, Keshav Pratap Singh Champawat, Ketan Shahade, Khushboo Rathore, Kiran Dumbre, Komal Goyal, Krishna Agarwal, Krishna Kumar Ajjarapu, Ksenia Semenova, Kshitiz Anand, Kumaraguru K, Kumari Neeraj, Kushaal Devanahalli, Lokesh Rai, Lucie Argeliès, Malay Milan Choudhury, Manish Bansal, Manish K. Gupta, Manmath Matake, Manorma Kashyap, Mansi Kashatria, Mayur Charde, Medha Bankhwal, Medha Dixit, Megha Todi, Megha Gholap, Minakshi Holgunde, Miranda Edner, Mital Gondaliya, Mithilesh Bhakre, Mohammed Jani Pasha, Mohd Abdul Qadir, Mohit Raghav, Mr Bhooshan Kokare, Mrinalini Garg, Mrunal Kamble, Mrunmayi Sahasrabudhe, Muhammad Aslam, Muhammad Tabish Parray, Muhammed Fabari, Muhammed Shereef K, Naina Kansal, Nandhakumar Natarajan, Narendra Singh, Naveen Malpani, Navneeth Prasanna Kumar, Navya Sree, Neha Lahoti, Neil Merchant, Nihal Rustgi, Niharika Sharma, Niharika Swaroop, Nilanjana Bhattacharya, Niraj Mani Chourasia, Niranjani Elango, Nisanth Issac, Nistha Lahoti, Nithin Paul Cherian, Nithya Subramanian, Nitin Tailor, Nitin Gupta, Nitin Tripathi, Nitish Rajpurohit, Nitish Midha, Nitya Bhutani, Nivedita Sharma, Norat Mal Jat, Olutayo Ajayi, Padmavathi Bareddy, Palamasi Vipru Chanukya, Pallavi Gaur, Pallavi Nahata, Pallavi Todi, Pallavi Gulati, Pankaj Mane, Parag Shinde, Parth Saxena, Parth Mehta, Parth J Dave, Piyush Agrawal, Pokhar Mal, Pooja Rani, Poorva Joshi, Prabhakar Gautam, Pradeep Gupta, Prakul Agarwal, Pranav Nandu, Pranav Vashistha, Pranjal Kalita, Pranshu Bhutra, Prarthita Biswas, Prasad Jadhav, Prasanna Kapoor, Prasanth Garapati, Prashant Kumar, Prashant Kumar Singh, Prateek Jain, Prateek Kasat, Pratik Palod, Preet Angad Singh, Preeti Saraf, Pritesh Kodgire, Prithvi Reddy, Priya Singh, Priya , Priyanka Rajawat, Priyanka Khairnar, Priyanka Garg, Priyanka Agrawal, Priyanka Khandelwal, Priyanka Barve, Pulkit Mehrotra, Puneet Jain, Puppala Raviteja, Purvi Jain, Purvika Sharma, Pushpawati Waykule, Pushpendra Dwivedi, Rachna Iyer, Rahul Goyal, Rahul Ghosh, Rahul Jaisingh, Rajesh Bonawate, Raju Kendre, Rakshit Monga, Ram Babu, Ram Prasad, Ramakrishna , Raman Kumar, Ramesh Ballid, Ramyamanasa Kada, Rashmi Akode, Rashmi Shankar, Rashmita Mohanty, Ratan Guha, Raunak Mittal, Ravikiran Reddy, Rina Singh, Ritesh Kumar, Ritesh Shahi, Ritika Chawla, Rohit Gupta, Rosetta Mendes, Rupak Som, Rupesh

Badkhal, Rushikesh Kirtikar, Rutuja Chhajed, Rutwik Shah, S Harigovind, Sachin Lohare, Sadanand Kurukwad, Sagar Gangurde, Sagar Unde, Sai Spurthy, Sai Uday Kumar S, Sainath Kad, Salini Kyal, Sampada Bhusare, Samrat Dey, Sandeep Nardele, Sandeep Bhavsar, Sangeeta Devi, Sanket Gupta, Santosh Sukhadeve, Santosh Gawale, Sanvar Lal, Sapna Bist, Sarah Fraser, Sarah Thomas Broome, Sarang Jewlikar, Sarayu Agarwal, Sathvik Reddy Junutula, Sathwik Akula, Sathwik Reddy, Satya Komal Gutta, Saurabh Narute, Saurabh Raj, Seema Garg, Senthil Prabhu, Serdeesh Kv, Shalini Pathi, Shantanu Garg, Sharad Dombe, Sharada Raparthi, Sharwari Hole, Shashank Tulsyan, Shashikant Pathak, Sheetal Nagare, Sheryl Abraham, Shilpa Malge, Shilpa Roy, Shipra Singh, Shivam Gupta, Shivani Arora, Shivdas Ashtekar, Shrenik Daklia, Shreya Khedia, Shreyans Sekhani, Shreyansh Chamaria, Shreyas Chavan, Shrikant Ganjre, Shrish Aute, Shruti Sharma, Shruti Choudhary, Shruti Sekhsaria, Shubham Gortyal, Shubham Gupta, Shubhra Mittal, Shweta Wankhede, Shweta Kabade, Shyama Muralidharan, Siddha Jain, Siddharth Rajpal, Siddharth Chatwal, Siddharth Arora, Siddharth Jindal, Simran Rana, Siva Rama Krishna Kuntamukkala, Siva Theja Maguluri, Smriti Nagpal, Sneha Barman, Snehal Hursad, Sonali Gandigude, Sonam Dubey, Soumya Kavi, Sourav Shaw, Srajan Gupta, Sri Harshith Rajam, Srichandana Nagoji, Srujana Chillala, Subhro Sengupta, Suchi Smita Mahato, Sumit Kumar Sharma, Sunil Baffna, Sunil Mekale, Sunil Kumar, Sunita Tarlekar, Surabhi Bhandari, Surbhi Verma, Sushil Bari, Suwarna Deshpande, Swapnil Chapate, Swati Reddy Chitteti, Tabish Hussain, Tamsin Buchan, Tanmay Arora, Tanya Gupta, Tarun Choubisa, Tarun Vijay Bonthu, Tarush Jain, Tejal Kamble, Theertha Menon, Timmanna Waddar, Toral Parmar, Tushar Joshi, Tushar Gupta, Vaibhav Sisinty, Vallari Shah, Vani Karikalan, Vani Thakur, Varun Jain, Varun Gupta, Varun Gupta, Vasanth Gopal, Venkata Prasanth Tummala, Venkatesh Sittula, Vidit Aggarwal, Vihang Patil, Vijay Kawade, Vijayaragavan Prabakaran, Vijeta Vani Verma, Vimmi Surti, Vinayak Kulkarni, Vineela Yegireddi, Vipul Mehta, Visakh R J, Vishal Chowdri, Vishal Agarwal, Vishnu Vinjam, Vishnusri Tannamala, Yamini Yadla, Yash Modi, Yashaswi Dwivedi, Yogita Muttha, Zoe Hamilton

Jagriti Yatra 2014

Aakash Mishra, Aastha Wadhwa, Abdul Nazar, Abhilasha Sachan, Abhimanyu Prakash, Abhishek Jagtap, Abhitosh Goyal, Abodh Kumar, Aditi Soni, Aditya Patni, Aditya Sakhuja, Aditya Narayan Patnaik, Adnan Ansari, Afrin Mujawar, Aishraj Dahal, Ajinkya Kulkarni, Ajinkya Jadhav, Akanksha Modani, Akanksha Kestwal, Akash Naoghare, Akhil Sikri, Akhil Satheesh, Akiraa Ps, Akshat Kohli, Alekhya Valleru, Altaf Fakir, Aman Tomar, Aman Pratap Singh, Ambika Ghuge, Amit Prabhu, Amit Raj, Amit Karda, Amit Gaiki, Amit Khanna, Amrita Jhunjhunwala, Amrita Sukumar, Anand Reddy, Ananya Tiwari, Anchal Ojha, Aniket Korabu, Anil Kumar Reddy, Anirudh Goel, Anisha Jalan, Anjali Merchant, Ankit Batheja, Ankit Rathi, Ankit Saigal, Ankit Agrawal, Ankur Bang`, Ankur Jain, Annapoorni , Anshul Garg, Anugrah Agrawal, Anup Kumar, Anurag Bansal, Anushka Rajan, Aparna Sawant, Aparna Rani, Apurba Barman, Arati Adsule, Archana Gwari, Archana Stalin, Archana Takte, Archana Nair, Arjun Arora, Arpit Abhishekgupta_31@ Yahoo.Co.In, Arpita Bhagat, Artika Shah, Arun Raman, Ashish Vaya, Ashwani Tiwari, Ashwini Bambal, , Atul Dukale, Avinash Pandey, Ayush Agarwal, Ayush Rai, Azam Nathaniel, Babeeta Faujdar, Beerelli Kalyani, Bérengère Daviaud, Bhagyashri Hulpalle, Bhavesh Neekhra, Bhawna Mishra, Brad Vanderford, Chaitali Kamble, Chaitra Yadavar, Chanchal Agrawal, Chandni Aggarwal, Chandrabhan Singh Nathawat, Charan Gp, Charen Koneti, Chayan Laddha, Chetan Soni, Darshil Parikh, Dawa Sherpa, Deepak Agarwal, Deepak A. Sangama, Deepak Wagh, Deepak Sharma, Devansh Mittal, Devendar Mittal, Devika Rege, Dewal Sawarkar, Dheeraj Jha, Dilip Pawara, Dilip Radkar, Dinesh Lahoti, Dipankar Trehan, Divas Vats, Divya Paluri, Divya Joseph, Diwanshu Bhutani, Emani V S Nanda Kishore, Eric Kalapura, Faizan Khan, Gargi Vasthava, Garima Varshney, Garima Saxena, Garima Gupta, Gaurav Gattani, Gaurav Agrawal, Gaurav Pawar, Geetanjali Dumbare, Gokoulane Ravi, Govind , Hanuman Gurjar, Hardik Shah, Hari Shekhar, Hari Prasad Koppineni, Harinder Yadav, Harun Raaj, Helene Reinhardt, Hersh Shah, Hetansh Desai, Himanshu Aggrawal, Himanshu Batra, Indrajit Sinha, Intissar Bouftaim, Irfan Mohammad, Irum Raza, Isha Hambarde, Jagdish Repaswal, Jagruti Bhikha, Janani Subhashini Umamaheswaran, Jatin Garg, Jayashree Sakthivel, Jaytirth Ahya, Jeh Krishna Agarwal, Jyoti Dahiya, Kalpana Gite, Kalyani Shintre, Kamya Batra, Kanchan Dhonnar, Kanchan Bhagat, Kannav Chadha, Karumanchi Bala Rama Krishna Sai, Katariya Dharmishtha Jitubhai, Kaushal Agarwalla, Kaushank Khandwala, Kaustubh Prabhu, Kaustubh Pawar, Kavish Seth, Kavitha Rajendran, Keshav Parthasarathy, Kirtika Singh, Kishan Gehlot, Kishori Pawar, Komal Madhav, Koshank Pratik, Krishna Pradeep, Kshitiz Jamer, Kumar Manish, Kunj Vaidya, Kunjal Gandhi, Lakshmi Prabhakaran, Lalasa Mukku, Lalit Jamdade, Liliane Cheung, Lohit Lingam, Madhusmita Brahma, Mahanthesha H, Mahavir Jat, Mahesh Lade, Manali Kulkarni, Manikandan Sivaramakrishnan, Manisha Mohan, Manohar B, Mansi Srivastava, Marketa Strakova, Mathieu Renaud, Mayuri Shah, Megha Nikam, Megharaj Mantri, Mittu Tigi, Mohamed Asif, Mohammed Ameen Ec, Mohini Choudhary, Mohit Arora, Mohit Garg, Molka Majdoub, Monika Tiwari, Mounika Kancheti, Moupiya Ukil, Mridula Maddukuri, Mukesh Choudhary, Munna Kumar, Murali Talasila, Mustafa Baqari, Naga Madhusudhan Battala, Nageshwar Panchal, Namit Gvalani, Nanda Nithin Sreedharala, Nayeem Ahmed, Neel Tamhane, Neha Arora, Neha Zade, Nehal Modak, Nikhil Gampa, Nikhita Agrawal, Nilesh Kakad, Nilesh Gaurav, Nilesh Kolharkar, Nilophar , Niraj Agarwal, Nisha Alavandi, Nisha Kanwar Rathore, Nishanth Neeli, Om Prakash Shah, Onkar Deshpande, Padmaja Jonnalagedda, Padmavati Rajpanke, Parag Maheshwari, Piyush Anand, Pooja Bhoir, Pooja Sethiya, Pooja Verulkar, Prabash Kumar Rath, Prachi Kulkarni, Prachi Mantri, Pradeep Joshi, Pradeep Kumar, Pragati Pritmani, Prakash Jha, Prakash Kumar, Prakhar Maheshwari, Pramod Bhagat, Pranay Patil, Prashant Tripathi, Prashant Karande, Prashant Singh Garhwaliya, Prathamesh Kadolkar, Pratik Jain, Pravin Ingawale, Pritha Khetan, Priya Shukla, Priya Muralidharan, Priyanka Nanda, Pulkit Garg, Puneet Melwani, Punit Bopche, Pushpa Kumari, Rahul Patidar, Rahul Dolas, Rahul Shah, Raja Mettu, Rajiv Agarwal, Rajkeshwar Kumar, Rakhi Reddy Bommineni, Ram Sharma, Ram Narayan Tiwari, Ramkrishan Sharma, Ranjani Ramamoorthy, Rashmi Rajgarhia, Ravi Teja, Ravi Kumar Kolla, Ravikant Ganjre, Ravindra Vikram Singh, Reena Lokadiya, Revathi Gorijavolu, Rhythima Shinde, Richa Minglani, Richa Shah, Rifa Sanbaq, Rishabh Sood, Rishabh Jhol, Rishi Mehan, Rishi Dutta, Rohinee Misal, Rohit Kulkarni, Rohit Nyati, Sachin Gaikwad, Sagar Jadhav, Sai Kulkarni, Sai Srinivas Kotni, Saikiran Devatha, Sailaja Vadlamani, Sajal Chakravarty, Sakshi Jain, Saloni Gandhi, Sandeep Sharma, Sandeep Anirudhan, Sandesh Rawat, Sandipan Shinde, Sangharsha Kelzare, Sanjana Teje, Santosh Toge, Santosh Nandurkar, Satish Patil, Satyajeet Kanetkar, Satyam Dudwewala, Saurabh Maurya, Saurabh Rautela, Saurabh Dawrani, Sayali Shah, Shah Riya, Shailendra Nangalia, Shailesh Zambad, Shailja Mishra, Shalki Agarwal, Shalvi Sinha, Sharada Baichbal, Sharans Kabra, Shashank Mishra, Sheetal Patel, Shifali Thakkur, Shilpa Malviya, Shivika Bansal, Shradha Agarwal, Shreya Mazumdar, Shrihari Jadhav, Shrikant Kadam, Shrikant Wagh, Shriya Garg, Shruthi Shetty, Shruti Choudhury, Shubham Goyal, Siddharth Jain, Sidharth K Varma, Snehitha Avirneni, Sonal Jain, Sonia Parekh, Sonu Kumar, Soumya Patro, Sourabh Narsaria, Spandana Varun, Spriha Atray, Sreejit Ramakumar, Sri Lakshmi Anumolu, Sriharsha Ganti, Srikanth Pasam, Srinivas Patil, Srinivas Santhosh Praveen Chandra Buddha, Srujana Enduri, Subrat Tripathy, Suchendra Kadam, Sudarshan Reddy Thummalapally, Suhaas Kaul, Suhani Parekh,

Suman Ghimiray, Suman Kumar, Sumit Chandani, Sunayana Tulsian, Sundeep Agarwal, Sunita Mekale, Supriya Deshmukh, Supriya Jadhav, Surekha Vijay Kalel, Sushant Chavan, Sushilkumar Kharat, Sushree Jena, Swati Prasad, Swmdwn Basumatary, Tanuj Kumar Singh, Tanvi Mathur, Tanvi Singhal, Tapak Dagam, Tapas Mani Shyam, Tarachand Dhaygude, Taylor Quinn, Thomas Zachariah, Trupti Doshi, Tulunga Basumatary, Udit Hinduja, Utkarsh Mishra, Uttam Byragoni, Vaishali Jethava, Vaishnavi Amrutwad, Vandita Kamath, Varsha Pagar, Varsha Raina, Varun Trivedi, Varunesh Dwivedi, Vedanti Shah, Venkat Ram Kommineni, Venkata Naveen Indala, Vidhu Saxena, Vidita Kochar, Vidya Sanap, Vidyut Varkhedkar, Vijaya Tarigoppala, Vikas Pandey, Vikas Kashyap, Vikash Madduri, Vinay Prabhakar, Vinay Kanchanapally, Vinay Kancherla, Vindya Sivaram Ayyar, Vinod Kumar Lokku, Viral Shah, Visalam Narayanan, Vishal Kumar, Vishal Jain, Vishal Shinkar, Vishesh Gupta, Vivek Belgavi, Vivek Aditya Tangirala, Vrundan Bawankar, Vyshali Tummala, Xiaoyue Gu, Yashee Mathur Mathur, Yogesh Gaikwad, Yogesh Bhete, Zubin Sharma

Jagriti Yatra 2015

Aakash Doshi, Aayush Kedia, Aayush Baid, Abdulla Munna, Abhinaav Singh, Abhinav Jain, Abhirat Shinde, Abhishek Ghosh, Abinaya Rangarajan, Adhavan P.R, Aditi Tiwari, Aditi Soni, Aditya Jain, Aditya Singhania, Aditya Sakhare, Aditya Patni, Afnan Hannan, Ahirnish Pareek, Aishwarya Patwari, Aiswarya Baskaran, Ajita Shukla, Akash Desai, Akash Pandey, Alay Naik, Albin Mathew, Ali Asgar Attar, Alok Jain, Amandeep Singh, Amar Kumar, Amel Zenagui, Amey Mundada, Amisha Tirthani, Amod Ghodake, Amogh Bhongale, Amruta Pagariya, Anjana Telang, Ankit Aggarwal, Ankita Kar, Ankita Garg, Ankur Saxena, Anmol Agarwal, Anna Korepanova, Ansad Ahmad, Antara Choudhury, Antony Thomas, Anuj Khandelwal, Anuj Kumar Dwivedi, Anum Raza, Anuradha Subramanian, Anurag Shukla, Anurodh Sachdeva, Aparna K I, Apoorva Mani, Apurva Agrawal, Apurwa Raghuvanshi, Archana Bora, Archit Puri, Arpit Gupta, Arpit Agrawal, Arpita Srivastava, Arti Palnitkar, Aruna Jyothi Patapati, Arunava Mitra, Asheesh Mor, Ashirwad Gupta, Ashwin Swaminathan, Ashwin Chandra, Asit Kumar Sahoo, Avadhoot Dixit, Avinash Kaur, Avisha Sati, Awais Hussain, Ayan S R, Ayush Rathi, Ayushi Shukla, Ayushmi Soni, Aziz Husain, B.Shruti Rao, Bapanapalli Srinivasulu, Batul Hafizji, Bhairava Prasad Lokayyagari, Bhargava Sajjala, Bhaumik Shah, Bhavana Ravella, Bhavya Mahendra, Brendan Baker, Brijesh Prasad, Carol Rajala, Cassandra Bui, Chaitanya Suri, Chandra Shekar D P, Chirag Mehta, Daniel Scott, Darshini M H, Datta Pagar, Davis Cutter, Deepak Kumar Jha, Deepali Sanpurkar, Deepika Goyal, Deepti Khera, Devashish Raut, Dhanalakshmi Padmanabhan, Dhanashri Patke, Dhanesh Dhoot, Dhruv Sanghvi, Dhruvin Mehta, Dhvani Parekh, Dhwani Rathi, Digant Kapoor, Dilip Kumar Akula, Dinesh Kumar Sonti, Divija Lahe, Divyanshi Chugh, Diwakar Sing, Dwarakanath Atchutuni, Ekta Raj, Elliot Bromley, Eloi Bitterlin, Eshwar Agarwal, Etienne David, Eureka Khong, Gaurav Totla, Gauri Kulkarni, Gazal Arora, Geeta Madiraju, Gitan Shah, Gokul Krishna Pothuri, Gopikrishna B, Gowtham Pitchuka, Greeshma Balabhadra, Gunjan Pahuja, Gurkiran , Harish Nair, Harishchandra Babu, Harmandeep Kaur, Harpalsinh Vaghela, Harsh Mehta, Harshit Singhania, Harshita Poddar, Hemanth Kumar Virothi, Hemanth Kumar Sandireddy, Honey Parekh, Hosherdar Polad, Ilya Kutsenko, Ina Jain, Ishank Singh, Ishita Chatterjee, Ishtaarth Dalmia, Ivan Damnjanovic, Jagniwas Tripathi, Jagmanjeet Singh Gill, Jared Perry, Jhanvi Patel, Jigar Patel, Jinish Kataria, Jitendra Kewalramani, Joohi Bairoliya, Jyoti Vaghani, Jyoti Dahiya, K. Balaji Krishnamoorthi, Kalpesh Nawandar, Kamal Bhattarai, Kanika Kohli, Karan Sinha, Karan Chhabra, Karan Bandi, Karthik Vadlamani V S S, Kartik Singla, Kasula Jhansi Lakshmi, Kathiresan Kulandayan, Kavita Joshi, Kavita Wankhde, Kedar Ubhaykar, Keerthi Reddy Narra, Keshav Kudale, Keshav Sharma, Keshav Daga, Khushboo Jha, Khushbu Maheshwari, Kinjal Vora, Kiran Patil, Kiran Kotwal, Krati Gahlot, Krishan Anand, Krishna Varshney, Kriti Jain, Krunal Kapadia, Kshitij Sharan, Kulukuru Sneha, Kumar Akshay, Kushal Jasoria, Lakshmi Kamal Sanjay Romala, Lamia Mamoon, Lavina Amesar, Lavina Amesar, Leena Shekhar, Lourdes Soares, Maansi Shah, Manasa Buddharaju, Mancy Sanghavi, Mandar Joshi, Manisha Tiwari, Manoj Kumar, Mansi Dhawan, Manudeep Aavula, Markandey Dayal, Mayur Parmar, Mayuri Kherde, Md Adil Hussain, Meeti Mandani, Megha Madan, Meghana S Belavadi, Meghna Mittal, Meha Upadhyay, Mehak Aggarwal, Milind Chindarkar, Minakshi Punekar, Mitali Gupta, Mohit Gupta, Mridul Dhar, Mrunalini Pol, Mudit Gandhi, Muhammed Jaseel, Mukesh Panwar, Murali Mallikarjunan, Nabila Amarsy, Namrata Thacker, Nandni Rana, Narayan Chapke, Narendra Doot, Nasif N M, Nataliya Chertkova, Navneet Maheshwari, Neelam Akhil, Neeti Jain, Neha Mahajan, Neha Agrawal, Nicole Culp, Nidhi Saraf, Nidhiya V Raj, Niharika Gujela, Nikhil Lohia, Nilakshi Dalia, Nilmadhab Mondal, Nipun Jain, Nirpendra Kumar, Nisha Bhatia, Noel Raj Sagi, Nupur Patil, Om Marathe, Om Prakash Ram, Oriana Pound, Owen Priestley, Padma Uma, Padmanikant Khurana, Pankaj Prashant, Pankti Agarwal, Parth Davda, Paul Mathew, Pawan A, Payal Tiwari, Pooja S Kulkarni, Prabhasa K L, Prabhu Murugesan, Prakash Sahoo, Prakash Tripathi, Pratap Tiwari, Prateek Gupta, Prateek Bansal, Prathamesh Kapote, Pratibha Shivnani, Pratik Shetty, Pratyush Devliyal, Pravin Dube, Preetam Dhengle, Preethi Ashok, Prem Singh Dangi, Pritesh Shrivastava, Priya Dharshini, Priyanka Parle, Priyanka Kulkarni, Priyanka Modi, Priyanka Shah, Priyanka Thorat, Prodip Chatterjee, Pulkit Malpani, Puneet Choudhary, Puneet Singh, Punit Jain, Punit Gandhi, Punj Rajan, Purvi Vora, Rachana Shah, Rachit Jaggi, Radhika Biyani, Raghav Sarda, Raghav Gupta, Raghavi P, Rahul Jain, Rahul Kulkarni, Rahul Das, Rahul Krishna, Rahul Wadhwani, Rahul Kumar, Rahul Koppula, Rahul Tripathi, Raj Kumar, Rajat Chakraborty, Rajat Agrawal, Rajesh Haldipur, Rajesh Kumar Sahu, Rakesh P Vinay, Ram Agarwal, Ram Prakash, Ram Sharma, Ram Prakash Krishnan, Ramachandran Thandapany, Ranjeet Kumar Singh, Ranjith Pandranki, Ratna Sagar Agrawal, Raunak Kohli, Raushan Kumar, Raviteja Koneru, Reety Wadhwa, Riddhi Shah, Riddhi Saboo, Rishabh Jain, Riti Shah, Ritika Chawla, Ritul Kakar, Riya Garg, Rohan Gugale, Rohith Salim, Ruchi Patel, Ruchika Dandale, Rupal Pareek, Rutuja Pagaria, Saakshi Sharma, Saanya Gulati, Saawan Balavai, Sachin Satpute, Sagar Agarwal, Sagar Zole, Sagar Prasad Babu, Sahanraj Shridhara, Sahil Bagwan, Sahil Mittal, Sai Prabhu Konchada, Sai Tharun Nadipally, Sailesh Singhal, Sakshi Agrawal, Sakshina Bhatt, Saloni Garg, Samartha Balgude, Sameer A Krishnamurthy, Samu Thomas John, Sanam Budhrani, Sandheep Kumar Vurukkara Boopal, Sanjay Meena, Sanket Yamgar, Sargam Sharma, Sarvesh Kumar Singh, Sathya Narayana, Satish Kumar, Saurabh Sharma, Saurabh Satyam, Sethuraman T A, Shagun Setia, Shalini Pandey, Shantanu Katkar, Shantanu Garg, Shantanu Rawat, Sharad Dhore, Sharath Koona, Shashank Agrawal, Shashank Shekhar, Shashank Lunkad, Sheetal Chavan, Sheshnath Mishra, Shifa Thobani, Shiv Shankar Mishra, Shivangi Bhaduri, Shivani Shah, Shivani Gandhi, Shivani Parasnis, Shivasharana Biradar, Shraddha Kalani, Shraddha Pandey, Shreekar Suryawanshi, Shreya Chandak, Shreya Singhal, Shreyansh Chandak, Shreyas Vatsa, Shreyas Prakash, Shrikant Giradkar, Shruthi Vinod, Shruti Shukla, Shruti Jargad, Shubhada Kasle, Shubham Choudhary, Shubham Jejani, Shubham Nagargoje, Siddhartha Vadlamudi, Sindhujarajan Sounthrarajan, Sindhura Cheruku, Sivam Subramanian, Sneha Gokhale, Sneha Sumam, Snigdha Bairagi, Somnath Asati, Somya Jain, Sonali Ingle, Sonali Deshmukh, Soumya Sharma, Soundera Rajan, Sreemathy Surender, Srikanth Prabhu, Srilata Bharadwaj, Srinitha Reddy Barla, Srinivas Morramreddy, Srinivasa Chary Maheshwaram, Subhashini Vinod Baghel, Subhasree Jain, Suchi Agrawal, Suchitha Kakulamarri, Sudarshan Srinivasa Ramanujam, Sudeep Mishra, Sugavanesh B, Suhaib Kawish, Sujata Jadhav, Surabhi Bhardwaj, Surshree Meshram, Sushma Dongare, Susmeet Jain, Swapan Mahajan, Swati Gupta, Swetha Tibrewal,

Tanmay Musale, Tanvi Bhalerao, Tarun Malhotra, Thomas Gibert, Tooshan Srivastava, Tui Williams, Ujjyaini Mitra, Uma Shah, Uma Devi, Upasana Shah, Urvi Shah, Usha Gehlot, Utsav Gudhaka, Vaibhav Garg, Vaibhav Menkudle, Vaibhav Tamrakar, Vaibhav Gupta, Vamsi Seemakurthi, Vandana Tripathi, Vani Chandra, Vareesha Sachan, Varnica Arora, Varsha Lalwani, Varun Gampa, Vedika Mittal, Venkata Dileep Nalli, Venkata Kamesh Motamarry, Venkata Subramanian Ramesan, Venkatesh Chennakesavula, Vibhor Kalra, Vidhi Shetty, Vigil J Vijayan, Vikram Thakur, Vikul Aggarwal, Vilas Shinde, Vinoth Kumar Durairajan, Virendra Tuwar, Vishaka Ayalur, Vivek Piddempally, Vivek Bharti, Vrundan Shah, Vuppala Vikas, Xenia Raynaud, Xintian Zhang, Yadukrishnan S, Yash Mehta, Yash Agarwal, Yashaswi P N, Yeshwantlal Chakka, Yogesh Karnam, Yogeshwar Reddy Airala

Jagriti Yatra 2016

A. K, Yogesh Chandra, Aakil Mehta, Aanchal Sadarangani, Aaruni Shrivastava, Aashank Ambe, Aashima Singh, Aastha Kapoor, Aayush Agrawal, Aayushi Bairoliya, Abhay Mahipal, Abhishek Jhawar, Abhishek Juneja, Abhishek Bhatnagar, Abhishek Jain, Abhisht Vepa, Achuth Rs, Aditya Tibrewal, Aditya Rane, Aditya Ganti G. N. S., Aditya Valli Kollimarla, Afrah Muzayen, Aishwarya Pokuri, Aishwarya Pawar, Aishwarya Saxena, Ajinkyakumar Gadhave, Akash Desai, Akhil Bharampuram, Akhil Reddy Ramolla, Akshaia Kumar Ramanan, Akshat ., Akshay , Ali Hasni, Alok Sharma, Aman Agrawal, Amar Penta, Amara Mahendra Babu, Amit Gupta, Amit Jain, Amita Dokhale, Amol Dhakadey, Amrutha Balachandran, Anagha K.P., Ananta Badil, Anchit Patni, Anchit Jain, Aniruddha Bhatt, Anirudh Madhavan, Anjalee Bhanusali, Ankit Agarwal, Ankit Jain, Ankit Gupta, Ankita Aggarwal, Ankita Sahay, Ankur Podder, Anshul Agrawal, Antoine Maudinet, Anubha Nagawat, Anuj Gangwal, Anujraaj Goel, Anurag Barde, Anurag Gupta, Anurag Khetawat, Anush D, Anushmita Roy Choudhury, Anushree Parasrampuria, Aparna M.P, Aparna H, Apoorva Srivastava, Apoorve Jain, Archana , Archit Patel, Arunima Bindal, Arya Murali, Ashish Negi, Aswitha Visvesvaran, Avanti Misal, Avijit Verma, Ayushi Mittal, Betha.Praveen Kumar, Bharati Das, Bharti Singh, Bharti Singh Chauhan, Bijal Bharwad, Bijal Gandhi, C R Narendra Babu, C V Bhargava, Catharine Roy P, Chaitanya Kunkulol, Chaitanya Marwaha, Chaitanya Dhruv, Chandan Kumar Mohanty, Chandra Maloo, Chandra Bhushan Singh, Charlotte Hoefman, Charlotte Guan, Charu Sukheja, Charu Jain, Clament John, Darshan Gor, Darshan M Pathak, Deeksha Hegde, Deepak Jatav, Dhanya Balasubramanian, Dhawal Patel, Dhruv Batra, Digantika Mitra, Dilip Kumar, Dipen Patel, Donatella Basdereff, Dr Surendra Singh Choudhary, Drashti Thakrar, Durgaprasad Bandi, Durgesh Rawat, Edward Yee, Ekta Sapra, Elvina Das, Erdinc Koc, Faisal Bashir, Falguni Bhushan, Fatima Zaidi, Franziska Roettger, Fredy James Joseph, Gargi Kucheria, Gaurang Varshney, Gaurav Jambhalkar, Gaurav Kumar, Gaurav Pahuja, Gaurvit Saluja, Gautam Singh, Gautam Shah, Gautham Ramamoorthy, Gauthamraj Elango, Ghatna Trivedi, Girish Jayaraman, Greeshma Gopidas, Hafis Muhammed T, Hanane Boukhalfa, Hardik Shah, Hari Kishan Sudheer, Harish Venkataraman, Harmeet Vohra, Hars Saraf, Harsheita Choudhary, Harshit Mandiya, Harshvardhan Choudhary, Hemant Jain, Herold P C, Himanshu Mittal, Hira Jethanandani, Irwan Malhotra, Ishaan Kapoor, Ishita Chawla, Jahanara Rabia Raza, Jaidev Gurjar, Jaime Costa Centena, Janak Bathija, Janvi Vadher, Jatan Bawa, Javier Canas, Jayson Ganatra, Jeeva Mathew, Jes Thomas Mathew, Jisha Krishnan, Joao Duarte, Joseph J Ponnezhath, Joshi Bhavaniprasad, Jyotirmayee Mhetre, Jyotsna Singh, K Chaitanya Reddy, Kanchan Modak, Kannan Venkataramanujam, Kannan Sethuraman, Karan Doshi, Karthik Shenoy, Kartik Bansal, Kartik Kutmutia, Kaushik Bhakat, Kavya Kannekanti, Ketan Gupta, Kokkiligedda Mojesh Kumar, Konark Sharma, Krati Gahlot, Krishna Todi, Krishna Khandelwal, Krishna Murari, Kshitij Lunkad, Kumar Nimitt, Kumarapuram Gopalakrishnan, Kunal Dakhane, Lavanya Babu, Lokesh Reddy, M P Srivignesh, M.Sathiya Meera Meera, Madhav Patel, Madhulika Harkare, Madiyas Mali, Mahathi Gandi, Mahaveer Rana, Mahavir Kumawat, Maheshwari Palleti, Malhar Patil, Manicka Sevugan Velan, Manideep Kanagala, Manish Tapadiya, Manmeet Kaur, Manoj Karthik, Manoj Kumar, Manu Joseph, Matthew Wolf, Mayank Kasera, Mayank Gupta, Mayank Gulati, Mayuresh Huchche, Md Saif Ali, Meenakshi Sangal, Meera Parthasarathy, Megha Maheshwari, Mena Mankeshwar, Mimansa Shastri, Minal Pednekar, Mital Chhadva, Mithilesh Mantri, Mohit Raj, Mohsin Gulam, Monabili Basumatary, Mudit Kucheria, Mukesh Solanki, Murali Krishna, Naman Bhatia, Nandini Sharma, Naresh Sijapti, Natasha Yadav, Naveen Kumar Kori, Navjivan Pawar, Neha Sipani, Neha Gupta, Nidhi Prajapati, Nidhi Nasiar, Nihar Thakkar, Nikhil Mannan, Nikhil Yandapalle, Nikhil Goel, Nikhil Mukkawar, Nikhilesh Rochlani, Nilisha Wandile, Nimesh Jain, Nirav Thacker, Nishi Saxena, Nitesh Chandnani, Nithin Gudisa, Nithin Thomas, Nitisha Pandey, Nivedittha Varma, Om Naik, Om Prakash Choudhary, Pallavi Tak, Pankaj Gangwani, Papari Saikia, Pawan Sharma, Phani Krishna, Pooja Rai, Poonam Pal, Pragya Gandhi, Prajit Gorentla, Prajwal Gupta, Prakhar Ojha, Prakhar Joshi, Pranav Koshal, Pranav Kulkarni, Pranav Mathur, Pranav Jain, Pranav Khattri, Pranav Kumar Sampath, Prashant Gupta, Pratik Agarwal, Pratika Khinvesara, Pratish Goel, Praveen Selvam, Preethi Lr, Prerak Chitnis, Prince Diwakar, Pritishree Dash, Priya Taneja, Priya Maheshwari, Priyam Kaushal, Priyanka Dalvi, Puja Pritmani, Puneet Choudhury, Purnasneha Sundaramahalingam, Purvi Jain, Pushkar Deshpande, Radha Bordia, Radhika Nair, Rafael Barreto, Raghunath Reddy Koilakonda, Rahul Maurya, Rahul Pancholi, Rahul Heda, Rahul Tulsiani, Rahul Ratan Kumar Racha, Raj Shah, Raj Vora, Rajat Arora, Rajat Agrawal, Rajkumari , Rajul Khinvasara, Rakshith Bhagavath, Ramakrishna Naidu Koppisetti, Ramkrishan Sahu, Rashid Khan, Raunak Maheshwari, Ravichandhra Palla, Raviraj Pawar, Reeti Pal, Rekha Devi, Rishabh Rateria, Rishika Reddy, Riyas Kamarudeen, Rodrigo Ferreira, Rohit Sarda, Rohit Ahuja, Rohit Jhunjhunwala, Rohit Lahoti, Rohit Ahuja, Rony Tom, Roshnee Sundararaman, Rucha Deshpande, Rushi Rajeshkumar Agrawal, Sachit Batra, Saheba Arora, Sai Li, Sai Raja Veera, Saketh Kothamasu, Sakshi Garg, Sambhav Jain, Sameer Rastogi, Sameer Singh Solanki, Sanchit Malhotra, Sangamithra M. A., Sanidhya Yadav, Sanjana Srivastava, Sanjay Nagarajan, Sankalp Pasricha, Sankalp Sodhani, Sankalp W, Sanskriti Mittal, Santhosh Kumar S V, Saran Shivarajan, Sarang Pusdekar, Sarang Juthani, Saransh Mehta, Sarika Panwar, Saroj , Sarvajot Singh, Satish Bhonagiri, Saurabh Chopra, Saurav Arora, Sayali Gokhale, Sergey Larionov, Setika Gupta, Shaista Porbanderwala, Shakti Pratap, Shalini Gnansekaran, Shalu Kumari, Sharada Mourya, Shardul Dabir, Sharmishtha Balwan, Shashank Jasrapuria, Shashwat Shandilya, Shashwat Goel, Shefali Golecha, Shekhar Jain, Shikha Gupta, Shikhar Mittal, Shikhar Bhargava, Shiv Anekar, Shivam Gupta, Shivam Kapoor, Shivam Singhania, Shivani Pant, Shivraj Nirmal, Shreyas Bhalerao, Shreyash Sarode, Shrushti Runwal, Shruthi Y, Shruthi Tk, Shrutika Patil, Shubham Gupta, Shubhangini Patel, Shweta Chavan, Shwetabh Suman, Siddhant Chowdhary, Siddharth Prabhu, Siddharth Yedgaonkar, Simran Malhotra, Sindhu Lavanya Nandikunta, Sitanshu Shekhar, Siva Chaitanya V, Sivaprrasath Meenakshisundaram, Snehil Agarwal, Somnath Nabajja, Somya Jain, Sonali Patwe, Sonali Kadam, Sourav Mishra, Sourav Gattani, Sowmya Dontharaboina, Sree Pruthvi , Srikanth Kolasani, Srikanth Katikala, Srikar Mokkapati, Srishti Attri, Srishti Ramaprasad, Stephanie Saab, Subbalakshmi Kasiviswanathan, Sudhanshu Poddar, Sujatha Bharadwaj, Sujeet Kumar, Sujina S Babu, Sulbha Jadhav, Sumegha Singhania, Sunil Prajapati, Sunitha N, Suraj Raman, Surbhi Mundra, Susanti Prithika Vijaykumar, Swapnika Vajrapu, Tanvi Mittal, Tanya Gupta, Tarang Mehrotra, Tathagat Gupta, Tejas Shah, Tejinder Singh Sidhu, Thuy-Anh Nguyen, Tushar Khurana, Ujjwal Anand, Uma Shah, Umang Palan, Utsav Sachdeva, V S M Prasad Kancharla, Vaibhav Mehta, Vaibhav Dahiphale, Vaibhav Mehndiratta, Vanditha Sai, Vani Gupta, Varun Sanghavi, Vibhooti Kayastha, Vidya Madhavan, Vigil J Vijayan, Vikas Kashyap, Vikram Donkeshwara, Vikram Borade, Vinay Kumar, Vipul , Vishnu Kayande, Vivek A, Yash Tomar, Yash Kumar Jain, Yash Roongta, Yesha Kapadia, Yeshwanth Sonnathi, Yogesh Dandekar, Yoheswaran Gnanavel, Yugandhara Katkar, Yuvika Gupta, Mellacheruvu

Jagriti Yatra 2017

Aanchal Gupta, Aashi Bhaiji, Abdulla Shafi, Abhas Kumat, Abhishek Nagekar, Abhishek Sharma, Abhishek Singh, Adiba Ahmed, Aditi Belsare, Advait Raval, Aishwariya Sarawgi, Ajay Mori, Akanksha Singh, Akanksha Dokania, Akash Vispute, Akash Sawant, Akhil Shah, Akhil Aravapalli, Akhil Tumpudi Venkata, Akshat Jain, Akshay Wadhwa, Akshita Sahni, Alakanandalal Paliyil, Alex Mitchell, Alice Schan, Alok Kumar, Ambika Anil, Ambili Raghavan, Amit Nandwana, Amit Godse, Anand Bhargava, Anandha Raj Narayanasamy, Anant Baweja, Anant Sanjeev Doogar, Anarkali Rajput, Aniketh Mendonca, Anish Chandra Prakash, Anjineyulu Chagaleti, Anju Mathew, Ankita Tirthani, Ankur Banerjee, Anshul Garg, Antariksh Tiwari, Anukriti Jain, Anupam Rani, Anush Porwal, Aparajita Singh, Apoorva Nalam, Aradhya Gupta, Archana Chillala, Archana Kumari Sahu, Aritri Roy, Arnav Mishra, Arnav Bhattacharya, Arpit Agarwal, Arpita Mehta, Arti Singh, Aru Mangla, Arunima Raghavan, Arush Bahuguna, Arvind Kumar, Arvind Kumar, Aseem Kayastha, Asha Devi, Ashish Gupta, Ashish Phophaliya, Ashish Bhosale, Ashlesha Kshirsagar, Ashok Shah, Ashwin Kumar Erode Natarajan, Asiya Yunis Gavandi, Atmakur Susmitha, Aviral Shah, Ayush Batra, Ayushi Jain, Babalu Gupta, Baldip Singh Kohli, Banalata Sengupta, Barkavi Mageshkumaar, Beautiqueen Shylla, Bharathi Thiyagarajan, Bhargavi Mahajan, Bhavin Chhaya, Bibhishan Bagal, Bidit Roy, Brahmadatha M R, Buddappagari Manaswini, Celestine Schorlemer, Chandani Vishwakarma, Chetan Singh Solanki, Chetna Sureka, Chhoti Kumari, Chirag Sarawagi, Chirag Mehta, Datt Chapke, David Argumosa, Debia Nana, Devanshu Chaudhary, Devi Malhotra, Devidas Bachhav, Devkanya Jagdale, Dhanush K P, Dharmil Bavishi, Diksha Adukia, Dilip Gehlot, Dinh-Long Pham, Dipti Deswal, Divya Bharti, Divyansh Mathur, Dori Lal, Drishti Jain, Ejya Singh Sharma, Ekta Tirthani, Fausya Amalh, Garima Dahiya, Gaurav Chordia, Gaurav Singh, Gokul Koushik, Govardhan Kunchapu, Hardika Sharma, Hari Krishna Upadhyayula, Harikrishnan P, Harkirat Singh, Harsh Vardhan Shukla, Harshad Tathed, Harshikha Gupta, Harshitha Ch, Hemalatha T.P T.P, Hemanth Reddy K, Himali Gupta, Himani Tapdiya, Himanshu Kumar Gupta, Hitesh Solanky, Hussain Bhavnagarwala, Iccha Kohli, J Cathrine, Jashodaben Solanki, Jeevan Potdar, Jess Raphey, Jia Chakma, Jitendra Choudhary, John Peter, Joseph Jagan, Jyosthna Gaikwad, K Sruthi, Kailashben Taral, Kalyan Reddy, Kalyani Jagtap, Kalyani Ananda Mane, Kamal Dharewa, Kamalesh Nuthi, Kamna Aggarwalla, Kamna Kakar, Kanika Khurana, Kareena Fagwani, Karima Kishore Verma, Kashfa Haque, Kashish Aggarwal, Kaviarasi Mariappan, Khandoba Lokhande, Kiran Devi, Kislaya Dubey, Komal Thakkar, Kornica Jain, Krisha Shah, Krishnachandran Bm, Kritika Jain, Kushal Agarwal, Lalita Maurya, Laxmi Yadav, Leena Radjibaly, Leena Borhade, Linh Do, Lissy Babu, Lohith Reddy, Lokesh Reddy, Lokesh Rao Jadav, Maathuriyaa Venkatesan, Madhuri Putrevu, Mahendra Gupta, Mallika Goenka, Manek Parmar, Manideep Tummalapudi, Manisha Singh, Manisha , Mansha Yadav, Mansi Gala, Manvi Kansal, Manvitha S L S V, Marie Chkaiban, Mary K.K, Maya Kamble, Maya Amruthakumar, Mayank Agrawal, Mayur Dhande, Md Tauseefur Rahman, Meena Gupta, Meenakshi Kothari, Meera Bharadwaj, Meera Rathod, Meera Bhatt, Mehul Totla, Milli Vikamshi, Mithlesh , Mithlesh Devi, Mk Maqbool Qutub, Mohamed Imran Gaffur, Mohammad Taashif Iraib, Mohan Krishna Dadala, Mohit Garg, Mudit Yadav, Mukul Agarwal, Naga Sri Pravallika Golla, Nagender Pratap Singh, Nallasivam T, Nasir Iqbal, Nasmina Mp, Naveen Kumar Dayam, Navnath Singh, Neeraj Hasija, Neha Nikam, Neha Yadav, Neha Gupta, Nehpal Singh Rathore, Nidhi Aggarwal, Nidhi Dwivedi, Nihal Sharma, Nikhil Aggarwal, Nikunj Chandak, Nilesh Choudhary, Nilesh Jaybhaye, Niqat Patel, Nisha Nahata, Nishant Sharma, Nishigandha Raut, Nishkarsh Swarnkar, Nishta Shri, Nithun Raj Periasamy, Nitisha Sancheti, Nitul Shah, Nitya Samuel, Nivedita Todi, Nivetha Maheshkumar, Nivitha Ann Paul, Niwas Kumar, Nupur Kumari, Oshin Dhawan, Palak Tiwari, Pallavi Sangle, Pallavi Radheshyam, Pallavi Girhepunje, Pavani Peddadarpally, Piyush Lanjewar, Po Fong Chiu, Pooja Deshmukh, Pooja Grover, Poonam Mishra, Pothana Kavya Vatti, Prabeesha Pradhapan, Pragati Baheti, Prajeeth Prabhu, Prajwal Puthane, Pranadhika Sinha, Pranav Dedhia, Pranav Gaidhani, Pranav Patki, Pranjal Aneja, Prapti Lohi, Prasanth Babu, Prashant Bhansali, Pratap Tiwari, Pratima Chandra, Pratiti Shah, Pratyusha Simharaju, Praveen Uniyal, Praveen Vootla, Pravin Kavitake, Premlata Parihar, Prerna Ajitsaria, Pretty Priyadarshini, Pritam Shinde, Priyalakshmi Kanotra, Priyanka Thomake, Puneet Singh, Purva Khanna, Pushpa , Raashi Saxena, Rachna Tripathy, Rachna Singh, Radhika Agarwala, Radhir Kothuri, Rahul Jain, Rahul Sharma, Rahul Kumar, Raj Kumar, Raj Choudhary, Rajat Arya, Rajendra Awate, Rajiv Menon, Rajiv Karade, Raju Chirutha, Ram Dulari, Ramashankar Chauhan, Ravi Gautam, Ravi Kumar Choudhary, Reena Patel, Renuka Vetal, Richa Saxena, Rilina Ghosh (Chatterjee), Ripan Dutta, Rishabh Vishwakarma, Rishav Agrawal, Rithwik Singh, Ritika Zatakia, Ritika Chokhani, Rivika Bisht, Rohit Singh, Ronak Sanklecha, Ronik Patel, Rony Koonthanam, Rubi Vishwakarma, Ruchi Arora, Rupali Madan, Rupali Chowdhary, Ruplali Avdhute, Rushikesh Andhalkar, Rutuja Chaphekar, Rutuja Chougale, Sabina Laskar, Sachi Shah, Sachin Padale, Sadasiva Reddy Dharmavaram, Sagar Chandni, Sagar Sutar, Saiprasad Poyarekar, Saiyasodharan Rajendran, Sajan Kedia, Sakshi Choraria, Sakshi Agarwal, Sameer Dixit, Sameer Kumar Singh, Samim Sultana, Samina Taj Shaikh, Samuzal Bhuyan, Sana Kalim, Sanchit Tuli, Sangeeta Bhatt, Sangram Pisat, Sanjali Suryawanshi, Sanjay Khare, Sankalp Nandanwar, Sanket Temani, Santhan C, Sarumathi N, Sathvika Iragavarapu, Satyavati , Saurya Velagapudi, Savyasachi Kandule, Selvakumar Varadharajan, Senthil Kumar Gowri Sankar, Shaan Kumar, Shailendrasingh Rajput, Shakshi Katoch, Shakuntala Palapure, Sharv Godhamgaonkar, Shashank Madhukar, Shashank Rai, Sheetal Banchariya, Shenbakam Natarajan, Sherly Shaiju, Shivali Kapoor, Shivam Saini, Shivam Joshi, Shivani Rana, Shlomoh Divekar, Shradha Venkataramanan, Shreeyash Dharmadhikari, Shreya Koona, Shreyas Nevse, Shrishail Birajdar, Shristi Gupta, Shriya Agarwal, Shruti Raman, Shruti Boddu, Shruti Sridhar Murthy, Shubham Singh, Shubham Rathod, Shubham Mishra, Shubhendra Sachan, Shubhesh Verma, Shweta Singh, Shweta Malik, Shwetambari Ahire, Shyam Kalantri, Shyam Prasanth Thangavelu, Siddarth Korakanchi, Siddhartha Agarwal, Siddhi Malpani, Sisira K, Sita Devi, Smriti Mittal, Somya Tibrewal, Soumya Khanna, Sourav Agarwal, Sparsh Yadav, Sreehari R.K., Sreenivasan Ac, Sri Lalitha Sarada Poduri, Srishti Sinha, Sudha Sundaram, Sudha Surendran, Suguna Manasa Ramamohan, Suhas Mane, Suman Luthra, Sundar Venkatakrishnan, Sunny Vishwakarma, Suraj Nair, Suraj Mbv, Susheela Jakhar, Swati Kamble, Swati Singh, Tarun Chintam, Tharun Reddy Pesara, Thiruvenkadam Rajasekaran, Tonje Fjagesund, Tushar Tyagi, Tushar Kukreja, Udita Nawal, Unnati Joshi, Unnati Shah, Urvi Singh, Usha Thomas, Vaibhav Shah, Varada Ranjane, Varsha V, Varsha Thanooj Byrapaneni, Vedanth B, Venkata Manikanta, Venkata Harshavardhan Nagalla, Venkata Siva Prasad Gali, Venkatesh Kandimalla, Venkatesh Chunduru, Vidhi Dedhia, Vidhya K, Vijai Kanth Panthail, Vijay Kanthale, Vineeth Nelakuduru, Vineetha Devu Kanisetti, Vinoth R, Vipul Sharan, Vishnu Prasath Devarajan, Vishwas Dalwani, Vitthal Chavan, Vivek Mapari, Vivek Kumar, Vivek A, Vivek Vishwakarma, Vivek Kr. Chandra, Vyasa Raj Pasakanti, Yasaswini Kovela, Yash Raj Singh, Yash Mehta, Yashovardhan Ganeriwala, Zahir Khan

Jagriti Yatra 2018

Aaditya Agrawal, Aashini Goyal, Aashish Aggarwal, Abadh Bihari, Abhay Juneja, Abhi Gawri, Abhilash Khobragade, Abhishek Kumar, Abhishek Maheshwari, Abhishek Dhangar, Abhishek Singhania, Abhishek Agrawal, Abhishek Chandra Oraon, Aboobacker Haris, Adarsh Kumar, Aditya Aggarwal, Aditya Kulshrestha, Aditya Dave, Aditya Murarka, Aditya Shukla, Aditya Ketkar, Agrata Sharma, Aishwarya Maheshwari, Ajay Menon, Ajinkya Bhalchandra, Akhil Swaminathan, Akhila Puvvada, Akil Mohammad, Akli

Tudu, Akriti Sharma, Akshat Surana, Akshat Garg, Akshat Kedia, Akshay Kumar, Akshay Bhorde, Akshay V, Akshita Kanumury, Akula Pavani, Amal Joe George Palliparambil, Aman Lohiya, Aman Mittal, Ambuj Kumar, Amirthavarshini Jagadish, Amod Patule, Amol Ganjare, Amol Chitalkar, Amrita Sarkar, Anagha Basu, Anantkumar Najan, Anil Bukna, Anirudh Khandelwal, Anisha Pooja, Anka Rajkumar Mekala, Ankit Baranwal, Ankit Mudpe, Ankita Toppo, Anshu Thakur, Anuja Dwivedi, Anukriti Garg, Anupama Jaiswal, Anuradha Kumari, Apeksha Dixit, Apoorv Anand, Apoorva Pathak, Aravindhan M , Armaan Hatwal, Arunita Mitash, Arya Arun, Arzoo Shakir, Aseem Shendye, Asha M, Ashish Godya, Ashish Sahuji, Ashutosh Sharma, Ashwani Pandey, Ashwini Nair, Astha Sangal, Avani Tavargeri, Ayush Kanoria, Ayush Gandhi, Ayushi Mittal, Beena Gupta, Bhagyashree Balapure, Bharat Aggarwal, Bharat Bommena, Bhargav Thakkar, Bhavana Salvi, Bhavya Gorji, Bhoya Vinaben Sureshbhai Sureshbhai, Boryana Dzhivdzhanova, Brien Rodrigues, Chadrrakalee Markam, Chanda Devi, Chanesh Babu, Chinmay Mahajan, Chinmaya Dhiman, Chirag Mahawar, Chirra Jagadeshwar Reddy, Deep Kulkarni, Deepak Babar, Deepak Malani, Deepali Barapatre, Deepanjali Srivastava, Deepanshu Rathee, Devang Kusumgar, Devanshu Rastogi, Dewanshi Patil, Dhananjay Suthar, Dhanashri Virkar, Dhriti Dey, Dileep Kumar Sakkimsetti, Dinesh Kumar Mandavi, Dinh-Long Pham, Diptiman Chowdhury, Disha Unadkat, Divyanshu Raj, Divyasha Arora, Dori Lal, Drishti Kahnani, Ekashmi Rathore, Elluru Anurag, Fatema Attar, Fatima Rathod, Ganesh Chappalwar, Gargi Sachdev, Garima Shukla, Gaurav Oswal, Gaurav Kumar, Gazal Aggarwal, Geeta Shelke, Geetika Bagaria, Ghanta Bhavana, Gitanjali Pillai, Gnyanee Kandukuri, Gopalbhai Charaniya, Gopinadh Tiyyagura, Gopisairam Tanneeru, Gourav Tayal, Gyander Kumar, Hardik Sachdeva, Harrshini V B, Harsha Naga Vardhan Poloju, Harshad Munshettiwar, Harshala Jambhulkar, Harshil Bhadra, Harshit Brahmvanshi, Harshvardhan Shukla, Harshveer Shrimal, Havyas K S, Hemant Agarwal, Hemanth Kumar V, Hercules Munda, Himanshu Shekhar, Hitesh Agarwal, Hrishikesh Topale, Imtiyaz Ansari, Ishan Jhunjhunwala, Jabir Karat, Jahan Zaveri, Jainam Gandhi, Jasdeep Singh, Jatin Gulia, Jayasree Racha, Jeet Patel, Jeetendra Ajmera, Jefin Thachil, Jitendra Karji, Jolly , Jose Tom, Josephine Bouchez, Justine Lerche, Jyotish Chaudhari, Kalyani Tidke, Kamlaben Damor, Kamlawati Devi, Kanaga V, Kanhaiya Ningwal, Karan Singh Chhabra, Kartik Agarwal, Kartik Agarwal, Kartikay Kumar, Kasif Iqbal, Kaushal Ladhad, Kavit Shah, Kavita Nag, Kedarnath Pandugayula, Keerthana Kumares, Keerthi Chandana, Keshav Bagla, Kherunnisha Fakir, Khushbu Kumari, Kiran Kava, Krishna Jaiswal, Krishna Kanth Joga Venkata, Kumar Akhil, Kumari Komal, Kunal Bhatia, Kushal Pancholi, Lalit Rathi, Lalit Kumar Yadu, Laura Tschümperlin, Lola Jutta, M.S.Shree Harini, Madhuri Bandla, Madhusmita Majhi, Madhusudhan Naik, Mahima Chawla, Mamta Priyanka Lugun, Manas Aggarwal, Manjunath Jamathi, Manjunath Ranganatha, Manoj Kumar Soy, Meera Poladia, Mekala Sumanth, Melanie Mossard, Midhun Noble, Mitali Gupta, Mitesh Patel, Mohanapriya Srinivasan, Mohit Parmar, Monika Rajwani, Mudita Bapat, Mugdha Shah, Mukat Jain, Nabin Sil, Naimil Shah, Naina Gupta, Nainika Shah Rathore, Najuka Sawant, Naman Jain, Namrata Rajagopal, Narayan Prasad Tiwari, Nataraj Tunuguntla, Navaz Mannan, Navnath Karande, Nawrath Minda, Nayan Thakare, Neha Kumari, Nidhi Thawal, Nikhil Gorkhe, Nikhil Mutha, Nikhil Rakhecha, Nikita Dattani, Nikunj Bansal, Nimish Goyal, Niraj Kumar, Niraja Chopade, Nirala Kumar Pandey, Nischai Leo, Nishant Randhir, Nishigandha Raut, Nitin Barhate, Nivedita Arumugasamy, Nivedita Bansal, Niyati Saxena, Nupur Kumari, Ojas O, P Jagajit Prusty, P.Santhosh Reddy, Paras Pundir, Pawan Sahu, Peddi Shreni, Peyush Karel, Pinki Patel, Pooja Rautela, Pooja Kulkarni, Pooja Soni, Pooja Patil, Poonam Devi, Poornima Pandita, Prachi Turakhia, Pradnya Patil, Pragyan Deep Agarwal, Prajkta Chavan, Pramila Uttam, Pramod Satish Rapeti, Pramodh Yellapu, Pranav Pathak, Pranav Ravi Kumar, Praneet Devliyal, Pranitha Kandra, Pranoti Shinde, Prashant Luhana, Prashant Madhukar, Prashanth Reddy, Pratap Singh, Pratyush Raj, Pravin Kale, Prerak Baheti, Prince Kumar Tiwari, Priyanka Vaidya, Priyanka Yadav, Priyanka Karande, Priyanshi Goyal, Priyanshu Goyal, Purvika Kejriwal, Pushkar Tripati, Rachana Nakil, Rachit Mehta, Radhika Kishore, Radhika Gupta, Radhika Mohta, Rahol Rajan, Rahul Rahangdale, Rahul Marri, Rahul Tiwari, Rahul Kumar, Rahul Merchant, Rahul Kumar, Raj Shah, Rajat Raghatwan, Rajdip Roy, Rajesh Velpandian, Rajiv Jha, Raju Jat, Rammohan Gunapati, Ramo Soren, Ramya Balakrishna, Ranadheer Reddy, Ranjeet Mishra, Rashida Husaini, Rashmi Raja V.R, Ravi Surana, Ravi Motwani, Ravineet Yadav, Renuka Anand, Retul Pillai, Rishabh Gupta, Rishabh Shetty, Rohit Kumar, Roy Keshav Sharma, Rudraj Mehta, Rudraksh Pathak, Rupali Londhe, Saanchi Marwaha, Sagar Shinde, Sahithya Sreenath, Sai Phani Raghupatruni, Sakshi Banjhal, Samanta Pai T, Samir Mody, Sampath Reddy, Sampreet Gupta, Samveg Singhi, Sandeep Mishra, Sanika Godse, Sanjana Barthakur, Sanjeevan M, Sanket Oswal, Santosh Kumar Manusannipally, Sarang Raghatate, Sarthak Garkhel, Sarthak Sharma, Sarthak Chhabra, Satendra Singh, Saumitra Khanwalker, Seema Jaiswal, Shahin Bano, Shaik Mohammad Irfan, Shambhav Shandilya, Shardul Nanivadekar, Shaunak Handa, Sheela Kanwar, Sheetal Jagtap, Shilpi Singh, Shivam Sahu, Shivani Reddy, Shraddha Bagul, Shravan Mantri, Shravani M, Shreyas Ugemuge, Shria Goel, Shruti Mishra, Shruti Rudrawar, Shubham Gaba, Shubham Agarwal, Shubham Naik, Shubhi Singh, Siddhant Prabhu, Sima Dahale, Sindhuja Penumarty, Siripuram Sagar Krishna, Sirisha Velugula, Sishir Suresh Mohammed, Siya Marathe, Sneha B, Snehal Pawar, Snehal Borle, Snehal Naik, Snehith Budime, Somshekhar Badkar, Sona Chand, Sonali Bhusare, Sony Joy, Sourabh Maheshwary, Sourabh , Sourjya Singh, Sree Teja Deeti, Sreshtha Jupudi, Srishti Chawla, Sriya Musunuru, Subhash Budati, Sudarshan Sawra, Sudhir Jain, Sumanti Devi, Sunaina Srivastava, Surbhi Jain, Surya Teja Kollipara, Sushmitha Yadav, Swapnil Bagchi, Swathi R S, Tanmay Sharma, Tanvi Sinha, Tanya Thourani, Tarif Abbas, Tarini Dalal, Tarun Chand, Taufique Ali, Thajudeen Aboobaker, Trisha Reddy, Ushaben Dineshbhai Vasava, Utkarsh Baru, Utsav Agrawal, Vaidehi Mittal, Vani Khanna, Varsha Rahase, Varshit Ratna, Varun Behani, Vasundhara Arya, Vattikonda Jagadeesh, Vedika Padwal, Vendhan Psd, Vignan Kintukuri, Vikas Chaparwal, Vikas Singh, Vishal Kapoor, Vishesh Harnal, Vishnupriya Gundreddy, Vishram Puri, Vivek Kayande, Vivek Singh, Waras Singh, Yash Jalan, Zachary Wolff, Zarnain Fatima, Zhong Han Lee

Jagriti Yatra 2019

Aashima Gogia, Aastha Choudhary, Abdul Shaik, Abdul Ahad Malla, Abhilash Nune, Abhilasha Bhartee, Abhimanyu Kumar, Abhinav Sinha, Abhishek Vaidya, Abhishek Pipaliya, Abhishek Jaiswal, Achyut Todi, Adithya A, Aditi Bhat, Aditya Singh, Aditya Garg, Aditya Ajit, Aditya Bali, Advait Mohan, Afsal Mohammed B, Akash Joshi, Akash Singh, Akashmika Nayak, Akhila Bandam, Akshata Birajdar, Akshay Awari, Akshay Kumar Cheedalla, Alankrit Mahajan, Alok Ratre, Aman Gupta, Amit Nair, Amit Raj, Amit Dubey, Amol Deshmukh, Amrutha Varshini, Amy Johnson, Anaj Antony, Anand Jadhav, Angad Sakhare, Aniruddha Bagchi, Anish Malpani, Ankit Bajaj, Ankul Sharma, Ankush Goyal, Anshika Singhal, Anuj Satya Matta, Anuja Kulkarni, Anurag Goswami, Anushka Joshi, Apoorva Jaiswal, Appy Parikh, Arohi Pendharkar, Arpan Singh Rajput, Arun Singh, Arvind Shroff, Aryalaxmi Elkunchwar, Aseem Sindwani, Ashikha K K, Ashok Maurya, Ashok Lingesan, Ashutosh Bandekar, Ashutosh Patra, Ashwin Nilleri, Aurelia Nguessan, Avani Reddy, Avanthika Musipatla, Avinash Kumar, Ayush Mehta, B B Bharadwaj, Bapathu Sasidhar Reddy, Basit Ali Khandey, Bharadwaj Chukkala, Bharath Raja, Bhat Sulail Mushtaq, Bhavana Garlapati, Bhawna Solanki, Bhupesh Gunapati, Bikash Hela, Birmohit Bathla, Biswajit Mahanta, Biswajit Muduli, Boyina Rajesh, Cathy Guo, Chaitanya Punwatkar, Chaitanya

Pamunugundla, Chaitanya Kumar Ganjhu, Chanda Kumari, Chandamma Ambalgi, Chandan Kumar, Chandni Gupta, Charlotte Cotton, Chetana Amrute, Chhaya Sharma, Daniel Lemer, Debasis Mahanta, Deboprasad Das, Deepak Kumar, Deepak Kuamr Naik, Deepansh Daryani, Deepanshu Jindal, Deepti Chukkapalli, Devika Kawle, Dhananjay Thigale, Dhaval Jirge, Dhrub Kumar, Dhruv Bansal, Digvijay Shitole, Dipali Murumkar, Dipali Khandelwal, Divya Mehta, Divyarani Kulkarni, Dr Nitika Tiwari, Faizul Rehana S, Gade Sreeja, Ganesh Annamareddy, Garima Dhar, Gaurav Singh Chaudhary, Gauri Gandhi, Gaus Sayyad, Gokulnath G P, Gopika Kumaran, Govind Bharadia, Govind Krishnamani, Govinda Daga, Gowri Priya Ac, Gunti Sahiti Ragaleena, Guru Likhith Kumar Achyutha, Harish Saiju, Harish Bawaskar, Harsh Didwania, Harsh Kothari, Harsha Jhunjhunwala, Harshita Keswani, Heet Ghodasara, Hemanth Pamidimalla, Himal Jung Thapa, Himanshu Raizada, Himansu Sekhar Panda, Idrees Ahmad Dar, Ikwinder Kaur, Imtiyaz Ahmad Lone, Irfan Mushtaq Parray, Ishmeet Kaur Sethi, Jagadish Mishra, Jasir Tp, Jayesh Bhave, Jeevan Patil, Jenifa Ahmed, Jogendra Randhari, Juhi Dhruva, Júlia Flores, Justina Prusinskaite, Jyoti Sanap, Jyotsna Priyadarshini, Kabir Ahmed, Kalyani Kolhe, Kameya Dhanure, Kamlakant Pathak, Kamma Sai Janardhan, Kanchan Sharma, Karan Mantri, Karthik Yadagiri, Kartikay Agarwal, Kashinath Padhan, Kaushal Ishwar, Kavvampelli Prashanth, Keshav Sureka, Keshav Garg, Khalid Jabbar, Khushboo Singhal, Khushbu Gupta, Khyati Sheth, Kishan Mahipal, Kishinchand Poornima Wasdani, Konapur Rahul, Krishna Kamdi, Krisna Koundinya, Kshitij Kucheria, Kuldeep Malla, Kunal Bhatia, Kushal Sarawgi, Laad Lohar, Lakshay Sharma, Laxmikant Nadiwade, Likhit Unadkat, Lovish Singla Vijay Kumar, Lu Xu, Malik Abdul Hai, Mallesh Kumar K S, Manas Sikri, Manav Chandak, Mandaji Narsimha Chary Narsimha Chary, Mangesh Ghadge, Manish Jain, Manisha Patel, Manisha Parpiani, Manjunath Ranganatha, Manoranjan Behera, Mariyam Siddiqui, Masarat Kawsar, Mathpal Singh, Mayank Jain, Mayank Jadhao, Mayur Pawar, Md Saharukh Khan, Meet Gada, Megha Suresh, Minaz Memon, Mohammad Siraj, Mohan Prabhu Desai, Mohana Priya Rcm, Monika Sharma, Mrutyunjaya Sahu, Mudasir Ahmad Kochay, Mugdha Shah, Muhammad Ovais, Muhammed Faris O C, Mukul Barmecha, Mukund Maheshwari, Murugesh Munaswamy, Mussarat Fayaz, Nalla Prannay Kumar, Navaneeth Ganesh, Naveen Kumar Adicharla, Nazia Ali, Neel Gugale, Neeraj Gupta, Neha Devapuja, Niaz Ahmed, Nidhi Thakkar, Nikita Ladda, Nimesh Jain, Nirupama Mohankumar, Nithin Lalachan, Niveditha Mathad, Ojas Khurana, Pabitra Kumar Panda, Palak Oswal, Pallavi Joshi, Pallavi Choudhary, Paras Jain, Parmar Chandrika, Parth Joshi, Pavani Konda, Pavankumar Yadav, Pawan Agarwal, Pawan Tripathi, Pinki Goyal, Prabhasini Mathur, Pradeep Kumar, Praful Patle, Prahllad Mittal, Prakalp Lohiya, Pramila Chouhan, Pranav Gupta, Pranav Bhosale, Pranay Didwania, Pranita Shinde, Pranjal Chokhani, Pranjal Maheshwari, Pranoti Vaidya, Prasan Dutt, Prashant Jadhav, Prashant Dadhich, Prathyusha Ponnam, Pritismita Rout, Priya Kumari, Priyal Bohra, Priyanka Chandak, Priyanka Singh, Priyanka Singh, Pruthvi Pullicherla, Pulkit Karwa, Pulkit Mantri, Punam Bang, Rabina Jaiswal, Raghunandan Sriram, Rahisuddien , Rahul Goyal, Rahul Bajaj, Rahul Garg, Rahul Rautela, Rajat Sharma, Rajendar Choudhary, Rakesa Kumar Sahu, Rama Choudhary, Ramesh Chandra Biswal, Ramkran Meghwanshi, Randheer Gautam, Ranjani Raghavan, Ranjani Kumari, Raphaël Masvigner, Rashmi Sharma, Rashmi Bathal, Ratan Rajpal, Ravishankar Nilegar, Riddhika Bhandari, Rishabh Sheth, Rishabh Agrawal, Rishi Garg, Ritu Sharma, Ritu Gautam, Rohan Bhowmick, Rohit Shrivastva, Rohit Kumar, Ronak Agarwal, Rounak Bhatia, Ruchika Jain, Rujuta Kulkarni, Rupal Singhvi, Rupesh Mittal, Rushi Shah, Rutuja Runwal, Rutvi Chafekar, Sabbisetti Gowtham Kumar, Sachin Kumar, Sadai Eeswaran, Sagar Salunkhe, Sahiti Agarwal, Sai Akhil Godavarthi, Sai Manikanth Panditaradhyula, Saiprasad Shelke, Saksham Bhalla, Samar Sisodia, Sameer Alam, Samidha Patil, Samiksha Goyal, Samiksha Jichkar, Samrat Kanade, Samruddhi Lakade, Sandeep Bansal, Sandesh Nagare, Sangavi Ramesh, Sanket Pingale, Santosh Dhakne, Saraswati Munda, Sarika Duggal, Sarthak Agrawal, Saswat Pattnaik, Sathvik Reddy Vemunuri, Saurabh Chauhan, Saurabh Gupta, Shalu Jain, Shantanu Jain, Sharad Nagpal, Sharon Manu, Shashank Srivastava, Shaunak Handa, Shital Rajput, Shivam Mantri, Shivani Anandhakumar, Shivraj Singh, Shoven Mehta, Shraddha Panicker, Shraddha Kadam, Shraddha Ankamwar, Shraddha Mehta, Shresth Rateria, Shreyansh Chopra, Shubham Shinde, Shubham Gotmare, Shubham Khetan, Siddhali Phule, Siddhant Dwivedi, Siddharth Muthu, Siddhesh Khot, Siddhi Mutha, Siraj U Din Ganie, Smitesh Desale, Sneha Jain, Snehasis Majumdar, Sonal Nagwani, Sonika Sharma, Soumya Turakhia, Sourabh Khandelwal, Sreenidhi Veluswamy, Srinath Namburi Gnvv Satya Sai, Sruthi Sodum, Srutika Raut, Subhransu Sekhar, Subrata Khuntia, Sudha Rajesh, Sudheer Varma, Sudipta Saikia, Suhana Tahaseen Shaik, Sujit Bidawe, Sulekha , Sumayya Farvi, Sumit Gandhi, Sunita Alagi, Sushma Gupta Batchu, Suyash Yadav, Swapnil Jain, Swapnil Bagad, Swati , Syed Asadullah, Tejas Bhawsar, Tousif Shah, Uday Girish Maradana, Ujeshkumar Nada, Umika S Padia, Ushma Goswami, Utkarsh Srivastava, Utsarga Mondal, Vaibhav Virkar, Vaibhav Arora, Vaishnavi Bhartia, Vama Rungta, Vama Pugalia, Vandana Mishra, Vansh Nanda, Varalakshmi Somarouthu, Varun Singhal, Vasavi Elluru, Vedant Mehta, Venkatesh Kodukula, Vibhuti Choudhary, Vidisha Sukhwani, Vidit Shah, Vidya Bommisetti, Vijay Lohchab, Vipesh Singh, Vipul Singhania, Vipul Goyal, Vishal Pinto, Vishnu Raj Saravanan, Yashaswi Tapadia, Yashwwanth Tunikipati, Yasmeen Bhati, Yogarajan Rajavel, Yogita Deokate, Yugandhar Nathe, Zahid Hussain, Zeenat Bandukwala

Jagriti Digital Yatra 2020

Aabha Pimprikar, Aakash Deep, Aanchal Choudhary, Aarohi Trivedi, Aarti Thanki, Aaushi Sharma, Aayu Kharbanda, Abdul Salam Syed, Abhay Vashishth, Abhay Mishra, Abhijeet Shukla, Abhilasha Priyadarshini, Abhishek Saha, Abhishek Shetty, Abhishek Deshpande, Abhishek Garg, Abhishek Salunke, Abhishek Sharma, Adapa Sai Sandeep, Adarsh J, Adarsh George, Adil Sha, Aditya Rahate, Aditya Sharma, Agata Rundo, Ahil Prasanth, Aishwary Agrawal, Aishwarya Mishra, Aishwarya Settipalli, Aishwarya Shinde, Aishwarya Bansal, Ajay Kirti, Akanksha Jain, Akarsh Mishra, Akhil Subramanian, Aklank Jain, Akshansh Shrivastav, Akshatha Nayak, Akshay Kakkar, Akshita Rathore, Alark Thakkar, Alekh Bansal, Alexia Gaube, Alpana Pandey, Amar Deep Kumar, Ambica Ghai, Ameer Sohail Khan, Amey Jain, Amey Walvekar, Amilsha Mathews, Amish Ralhan, Amiya Vidit, Amruta Bhalerao, Anamika Suresh, Anamika Kumari, Ancy Siraj, Anirudh Mohan T P, Anirudha Mulgund, Anish Kumar, Anish Ghogare, Anitha M, Anjali Gupta, Anjali Agarwala, Ankit Sinha, Ankita Bodhwani, Ankur Srivastava, Ankur Jadhav, Ankuri Bose, Ann Maria Sabu, Anna George K., Annapoorna Polavarapu, Annapoorna Devi A, Anshika Jain, Anshu Kumar, Anuj Piplani, Anuja Roy Chowdhury, Anuja Salwatkar, Anuja Bali Karthikeyan, Anupama Kalgudi, Anuradha Tripathi, Anurag Datta Roy, Anushka H, Apoorva Sarkar, Apoorva Upadhyay, Aprameya Joshi, Arati D Gite, Aravind Nayar, Archis Bodkhe, Arijit Goswami, Arvind Totre, Ashi Choudhary, Ashish Anand, Ashish Agarwal, Ashutosh Bhardwaj, Ashutosha Panda, Asif Ayoob, Asif Iqbal, Atharva Otavanekar, Atushi ., Avijit , Avinash K, Balaji Ejjada, Bhagyashree Lodha, Bhagyashri Patil, Bharat Gupta, Bhumisha Goyal, Bikash Kumar Agrawal, Binal Dave, Bipul Chatterjee, Bv Pradeep, Chandraneel Polavarapu, Charu Tiwari, Cheshta Naval, Datrika Shivani, Debashis Saha, Dedeepya Peeramsetty, Deepesh Kumar, Devang Chauhan, Devendra Deshpande, Dhaarna Bhardwaj, Dharmesh Chaudhari, Dhinesh Kumar, Dhwani Shah, Dipesh Singh, Divija Kavuri, Divya Diwan, Divya Mishra, Divyabharathi Koneti, Diwakar Mishra, Dr Hema Thorat, Dr Mrudula Talekar, Dr Sunita Tank, Dr Munish Jindal, Dr Pallabi Roy, Dr Tanushree Jain, Dr Nanthini Saravanan, Ekta Aggarwal,

Fayaz Ahamad Shaik, Fnu Salwan, Ganesh Satav, Ganesh Lipane, Ganpati Goel, Gargi Bachal, Gauri Sonar, Gayatre Viswaja Goda Venkata Surya, Gayatri Borkar, Gitesh Aggarwal, Gk Shravya Rao, Gopal Shah, Govardhan Sai Pinni, Govind Jadhav, Gurpreet Singh, Hanan Binth Basheer, Hareesh Kumar, Harichandana Cherukuri, Harsh Singh, Harsh Agarwal, Harsh Agarwal, Harsh Kumar Shah, Harshabardhan H, Harshaditya Singh Chauhan, Harshal Sonwane, Harshita Shivhare, Hemanth Kg, Hemanth Kumar Kotha, Henna T, Hillori Desai, Hudha M K, Ila Sharma, Isha Mishra, Isha Bhattacharyya, Ishani Kumari, Itishree Behera, J Tamal Atab, Jagruti Chamle, Jairaj Gambhir, Jayati Agrawal, Jaydeep Chachria, Jeevan Porwal, Jesna Joseph, Julekha Sheik, Juliana Amado, Jyothsna Bolleddu, Jyoti Bodhak, Jyoti Verma, Jyotsna Mehta, Kalpesh Bagal, Kamalesh T, Kamlesh Yadav, Kanchan Thoke, Kanishka Sharma, Kapil Kumar, Karan Dumbre, Karan Dhir, Kaustubh Sudhakar, Keshav Agrawal, Keshav Mishra, Khalid Anwer, Khyati Kapoor, Kimngaihoi Vaiphei, Kirti Khade, Kiruthika Adhi, Kislay Barve, Kotla Akshitha, Koushik Bandari, Koustubh Ubhegaonker, Krishana Murari, Kriti Behal, Kuldeep Ram, Kumar Amit, Kumari Neha, Kunal Kumar, Kunal Gupta, Kushagra Srivastava, Kushal Gorti, Lakshya Poddar, Lavrez Chaudhary, Linu V Cheeran, Lokap Sahu, Lubna Khan, Madhavi Dharankar, Mahmood Alam Syed, Mallika Mathur, Manam Srilakshmi Prasanna, Manan Mathur, Manasa Reddy, Manav Kishor, Manisa Mondal, Manish Kumar Thakur, Manita Sharma, Manjunath A U, Manjushri Gulve, Manoj , Mansvi Ahuja, Mayur Dhawale, Mayuri Singhal, Medha Mehta, Meena Pharande, Meenal Shah, Meet Thacker, Meghna Jain, Mihika Mehta, Mira K Desai, Misba Sayyed, Mohammed Arshath Parvez Murthuja, Mohammed Zeeshan Jamadar, Mohit Dahiya, Mohit Kamra, Mohit Maheshwari, Mokka Naresh, Monik Raj Behera, Monu , Mrigank Gupta, Mudassir Ali Sayyed, Mudit Garg, Mugdha Sonwane, Mugdha Shah, Muhammed Irfan Ali C T, Munni Bhatta Mishra, Muralikrishna M Kulkarni, Myneni Siddhartha, Naman Gupta, Namrata Shingote, Navpreet Singh, Navya Regode, Neeraj Alavelli, Neeresh Jain, Neha Sabu, Nidhi Sabale, Nikhil Gunagi, Nikhil Rai, Nikhil Bhat, Nirzaree Vadgama, Nisha Karamchandani, Nishant Tiwari, Nithin Balaaji D V, Niti Singhal, Nitin , Niyanta Vashisth, Nupur Gohri, Ogireddy Sai Lahari, Ogireddy Nagaramya, Omkar Balel, Oshin Koul, Pallavi Nitin Yelekar, Pankaj Sanodiya, Pankaj Kumar, Paoni Patidar, Parul Goyal, Parul Goyal, Pavithra Rajagopal, Pawan Kumar Singh, Pooja Parameswaran, Pooja Yadav, Poonam Mor, Poonam Saini, Poonam Chawla, Prabalya Kumar, Prachi Shevgaonkar, Prachi Mandil, Pragnesh Jogadiya, Prakash Kumar Gupta, Prakhar Agrawal, Prakhar Srivastava, Pranchal Joshi, Pranjal Maheshwari, Pranshu Jain, Prasad Devdatta Joshi, Prasanth Lagudu, Prashant Tambe, Prateek Jain, Prateek Awate, Pratibha Ghogare, Pratikshit Sharma, Praveen Kumar G R S, Pravin Mali, Preeti Kamble, Preeti Jain, Priya Magar, Priya Kumari, Priyamveda Mathur, Priyanga Thirugnanam, Priyanka Kharche, Priyanka Achhpeliya, Priyanka Thigale, Priyanshu Agrawal, Purvi Asthana, Pushpa Rajawat, Puste Bindu, Rachana Sahu, Radhakrishnamurthy Chunduri, Raghav Ajitsaria, Raghul Sakaravarthi, Raghvendra Gupta, Rahul Sonke, Rahul Dhamane, Rahul Vatsa, Rahul Ranjan, Raja Mohiddin Shaik, Raja Sekhar Satyavada, Rajanya Dey, Rajat Khurana, Rajat Kedia, Rajat Gupta, Rajiv Sahu, Ram Kumar, Rama Gondu, Ramprasad Subramanian, Rana Qamar, Rana Qamar, Ranjana Suresh Ingale, Ravi Kapoor, Ravi Kumar Meena, Ravi Teja Komma, Rekha Kumari, Rekha Bhatt, Reshwin Washington, Riddhi Bhatt, Robin Kumar, Rohan Jadhav, Rohini Sudhakar, Rohit Kumar, Rucha Mare, Ruchika Goyal, Ruchira Sawant, Ruchita Barhate, Ruchita Pedram, Rudresh Jayaram, Rutal Deshmukh, Rutuja Nawale, Rutuja Thorat, Sachin Dhumal, Sachin Sahani, Sadhana Mudigonda, Sai Nikam, Sai Harshini, Sai Madhav Patakota, Sai Prakash Veeram, Saitejaswi Gillela, Sakshi Shah, Sakshi Dhiman, Saloni Sacheti, Samiksha Jain, Samikshakiran Agham, Sana Hazari, Sandeep Kumar, Sanjay Sahu, Sanju Pandey, Sanmita Kamat, Sannihitha Gangina, Satyam Bhandari, Satyasha Rajput, Saurabh Gupta, Saurav Pattanaik, Savani Nerlekar, Savita Shinde, Sayali Pawar, Sayali Deshpande, Seema Sali, Shabanabi Shaha, Shadwal , Shailesh Bhagwat, Sharanya Ojha, Sharda Diwnale, Sharvari Shinde, Shashank Prabhu, Shashank Singh, Shashank Mishra, Shashwat Agarwal, Shaunak Handa, Shilka Agarwal, Shilpa Hattiangadi, Shital Gujarkar, Shiv Santra, Shivangi Singh, Shivani Sisodia, Shivani Chaudhary, Shonglian Wang, Shounak Kulkarni, Shravanee Shinde, Shreeharee Chinchkhedkar, Shreeya Hattekar, Shreya , Shreya Deep Bansod, Shrikant Patel, Shriya Maini, Shruti Dhawan, Shruti Kulkarni, Shubham Kumar, Shubham Gupta, Shubham Khanna, Shubhangi Mishra, Shubhasish Chakraborty, Shweta Azad, Shweta Chaudhari, Siddharth Devarakonda, Siddharth ., Siddharth Jain, Siddhi Thakur, Sindhura Kandipati, Smriti Singh, Sneha Nimbarte, Sneha Dwivedi, Sneha Raman, Sneha Sharma, Snehal Patil, Snehal Khatavkar, Snigdha Bhandari, Soumita Roy, Soumya S, Sri Sowmya Sunkara, Srinivasa Chavali, Srividya Amireddy, Suchita Aswar, Sudarshan Murali, Sujitha Reddy, Sukanya Lande, Suman Bharati, Sumanyu Sharma, Sunilkumar Mohandas, Sunita Lande, Sunita Borse, Suporna Noronha, Supriya Jaiswal, Surabhi Hazra, Suresh Dodwe Karam Singh Dodwe, Susheel Chaitanya, Suyashi Dwivedi, Suyog Bhatte, Swapna Nixon, Swapnil Singh, Swati Deskar, Swati Jain, Swati , Swati Singh, Tanaya Unhale, Tanuj Shinde, Tanushree Keshan, Tanvi Shende, Taslish Chadha, Tatsat Shah, Tejasvi Baviskar, Trisha Rajpurohit, Trupti Bhattad, Tushar Garg, Ubaid Nasir, Ujin Prabu A, Ujjwal Katiyar, Urmila Jadhav, Vaibhav Rautela, Vaibhav Karn, Vaibhav Sharma, Vaidehi Agrawal, Vaidehi Kulkarni, Vaishali Gawade, Vaishnavi Kushare, Vaishnavi Jamdade, Vaishnavi Sammanu, Vaishnavi T, Vani Prashamsa Aldas, Vanita Satpute, Vasundhara Kanoria, Vedasri Akuthota, Veeramachaneni Manasa, Vibhanshu Kumar, Vibhanshu Garg, Vibhuti Choudhary, Vidhi Goel, Vidya Desai, Vidya Anekar, Vijay Velpula, Vikas S Badami, Vikrum Srivastava, Vimal Shelke, Vineesh U S, Vinita Kokate, Vinitha I, Vishesh Tripathi, Vishnu Manoharan, Wageesh Shukla, Yogita Dineshrao Zilpe, Yojana Varkhede, Zaid Mehraj

Jagriti Digital Yatra 2021

Aakanksha Dutta, Aashna Basotia, Abhijit Das, Abhimanyu Vhanamane, Abhishek Bharadwaj, Abhishek Kumar, Abhishek Maurya, Abhishek Prosad, Abhishek Salian, Aditi B Madaan, Aditya Pandey, Aditya Raja, Aishwarya Maruvada, Ajay Grandhi, Ajay Ravidas, Ajay Yadav, Ajim Maniyar, Akanksha Maheshwari, Akanksha Vale, Akhilesh Chobey, Akshada Kharade, Akshata Ghadge, Akshatha Haganoor, Akshay Kedia, Akshay Paigude, Akshay Poudel, Akshi Singhvi, Aldrin Jenson, Amar Kumar Singh, Amar Shinde, Ameer Ali Madari Porkundil, Amol Sonavane, Amrutha Girish, Anamika Goyal, Anand Devsharma, Anand Kumar Singh, Anant Vyas, Ananth Vedantham, Ananya Dey, Ananya Richa, Aniket Saraf, Anil Krishna Makam, Anil Kumar Giri, Anima Agarwal, Anirudh Kesharwani, Anisha Das, Anisha Gaikwad, Anita Dhebe, Anita Kumari, Anjali Patil, Ankesh Harmukh, Ankit Jajoo, Ankit Kumar Chaudhary, Ankita Sonkar, Ankur Lamba, Anshuman Atroley, Anuj Asawa, Anuj Goyal, Anuja Pharate, Anupam Sahu, Anupam Shrivastava, Anuradha Rajbir, Anurag Gangwar, Anurag Pandey, Anurag Wasnik, Anushka Bramhankar, Anvita Viswanathan, Apurba Chatterjee, Apurva Kengar, Archana Rai, Arun Prabhakar S, Ashish Mani Tripathi, Ashish Pandya, Ashwin Agarwal, Ashwin Shenoy, Ashwini Pawar, Ashwini Sartape, Asmita Shinde, Atul Dubey, Atul Kumar, Atul Kumar, Atushi , Avanish Singh Chandel, Ayesha Shaikh, Ayush Jain, Ayush Singh, Ayushi Pundir, Baksheesh Sachar, Basant Manjhi, Beauty Kumari, Bela Joshi, Benazeer Baig, Bhanu Prakash, Bharat Bhandkoli, Bharat Lal Patel, Bhola Prasad Vaishya, Bibhu Prasad Hota, Bonita Bairagi, Ca Anand Yadav, Chaitanya Belhekar, Chaitanya Ram Chandu Garikapati, Chandrakant Thombare, Chirag Patil, Christopher N, Cleeta D Souza, Darshan Gala, Debasish Patnaik, Deep Gundecha, Deepak Goyal, Deepmala Kesarwani, Desam Geethikaa, Dhammpali Chavan, Dhananjay Pal, Dhanshree

Dusane, Dheeraj Kumar, Dheeraj Mor, Dhirendra Yadav, Dhruva Anantha Datta, Dhwani Purohit, Digambar Sutar, Dimple , Disha Goyal, Disha Varshney, Ditya Chawla, Divya Alapati, Divya Sarmalkar, Dr Bhaskar Igawe, Dr Khushboo Makhija, Dr Prabhakar Chavan, Dr Darshana Vithalani, Dr Meera Singh, Dr Tashu Garg, Durgaprasad Bandi, Ekta Khaire, Ekta Lahoti, Faiza Momin, Fathima Shajahan, G Sumitra Priyamvada, G. Renuka Jahnavi, Gadiparthi Revanth, Gargi Sinha Sarkar, Garima, Gaurav Gupta, Gaurav Sahni, Gaurav Singh Rajawat, Gauri Gayatri, Gauri Saluja, Gauri Yeram, Geeta Gawade, Geeta Shukla, Girish Dhumal, Gopal Gawande, Gorakshanath More, Gowri Anil, Hari Narayana Swame Ravi Chandran, Hari Priya Vangaru, Harsh Shukla, Harsh Veer Singh, Harsha Ravi Karjagi, Harshad Batule, Harshavardhan Dhulipalla, Himanshu Dua, Himanshu Jindal, Huda Hameed, Insha Mir, Isak Shaikh, Isha Samant, Ishan Anjay, Ishan Malik, Jacinth Angelina, Jagarapu Kasi Siva Suryarao, Jagriti Gupta, Jewel Joshy, Jignisha Solanki, Jogendra Kuanr, John Mathew, Jyoti Singh, Jyoti Tiwari, Kaavya Rajaram, Kallolini Patro, Kalpesh Mhase, Kamla Mahakhud, Kanchan Kamble, Kartik Charan Lenka, Kavya Gustala, Ketaki Patil, Khaleed Basha Shaik, Kirti Kadam, Kisun Kumar Hansdah, Komal Arya, Krishita Raj, Kritika Baldi, Krushna Taur, Kshitij Pal, Kuldeep Kumar, Kumar Rishav, Kundan Kumar, Kushagra Bansal, Lakkaraju Vishnu Dattu, Lakshmi Setty, Lalit Kamal Zode, Latha Sabbam, Lubhanshi Jain, Madankumar Thirumalai, Madhavi Shah, Madhukar Lengare, Madhukiran Kulkarni, Madhumita Bhaskar, Madhura Jawalikar, Madhurima Agarwal, Madhusmita Dehury, Mahasweta Chakravarty, Mahesh Bharatula, Maitri Shah, Majeti Satya Mohana Krishna, Manasa Sunkara, Manoj Kumar, Manoj Tatikonda, Manoj Tiwari, Maria Francis, Meena Pawar, Meghavati Korda, Mehak Jain, Mexson Fernandes, Mohammed Abdul Noman, Mohammed Feroz, Mohan Chandrabhan Ghode, Mohan Manavta, Mohit Kamra, Monanki Pathak, Monika Kharivale, Monira Chaudhari, Motamarry Krishna Keerthan, Mrudula Ganapuram, Muhammad Nihal C V, Muhammad Umer Farooq, Naman Agarwal, Naman Soni, Nanda Naik, Nandkumar , Naveen Vadde, Navendu Nimare, Nayan Satghare, Neelakshi Undavalli, Neenu Rathin, Neha, Neha Sharma, Nidhi Singh, Nilima Jadhav, Nimisha Pathak, Nirmal Sagar, Nisha Kumari, Nisha Vinod, Nishita Tudu, Niteen Katariya, Nithish Kumar S, Niyati Shukla, Nupur Tripathi, Om Bonde, Paardhiv Sarakam, Pabla Iraz, Pachu Kumar, Padma Raj Keshri, Panthdeep Singh, Parmeet Kaur Bindra, Pavan Kale, Pavan Kumar Sudarsanam, Pehimidai Kamei, Periyarthambi S P, Peter J Pulikkunnel, Piyush R Golecha, Pooja Agarwal, Pooja Bhalerao, Pooja Ghanagale, Pooja Reddy, Pooja Tonge, Poorvaj Hinge, Prabakar S, Prabhas Raj Panigrahi, Pragathi Manohar, Pragati Verma, Pragya Gupta, Pragya Maheshwari, Prakhar Kumar Srivastava, Prakhar Mishra, Pramiti Saxena, Pranchal Joshi, Praneet Srivastava, Pranit Thakare, Pranjal Mishra, Pranjay Gupta, Prashant Agrawal, Prashant Kushwaha, Prastuti Sonowal, Pratheeksha K R, Pratik Kumar, Pratiksha Kalpraj, Pratima Gupta, Preeti Singh, Prem Swaroop Arisetty, Prerana Mohite, Priti Pandey, Prity Burande, Priya Maria, Priya Maurya, Priya Tewary, Priya Tiwari, Priyal Goyal, Priyanshi Baheti, Purna Gope, Qureshi Sayma Mohd Rizwan, Rahul Anand, Rahul Galphat, Rahul Kumar, Raj Madankar, Rajat Srivastava , Rajeev Ranjan, Rajnish Kumar, Rajput Minakshikanvar Premsinh, Rakesh Paswan, Ram Prasad Yamsani, Rameshwar Walkikar, Ratanpal Singh, Ravi Rawat, Ravi Teja Paluvadi, Ravina Raibole, Reshma Kinake, Rishu Goenka, Ritik Jain, Ritika Mazumdar, Riya Elizabeth, Ronak Shaikh, Roselin Kiro, Roshan Shahi, Roshini Ankushkar, Rucha Deshpande, Ruchita Dhamne, Rukmini Iyer, Rupesh R, Rutuja Pawar, Sabrin Khan, Sachii Tripathii, Sachin Urkude, Sadashiba Sahu, Sai Mohit Kapila, Sai Priyanka Sajja, Saiakash Konidena, Saiprasad Balasubramanian, Sakshi Dangi, Sakshi Dhaigude, Salman Shah, Saloni Saraff, Samrat Pawar, Sandhya Karpe, Sanjana Jadhav, Sanjay Kumar Runthala, Sanjeev Kumar Srivastava, Sanjeevani Awasthi, Sanju Pandey, Sanket Aher, Santhoshi Gardas, Saorav Kumar, Sapana Abhang, Sarita Pasi, Satya Batchu, Satyasha Rajput, Satyawati Sardar, Saurabh Kalyani, Saurabh Kumar, Saurabh Nanda, Saurabh Singh, Sayali Pange, Shaheda Shaik, Shailendra Upadhyay, Shameena Khatoon, Sharbani Sengupta, Shashank, Shashank B, Shashikant Panchal, Sheeba Sayyed, Sheikh Ziaur Rahaman, Shilpi Singh, Shipra Dogra, Shivashish Kulshreshtha, Shraddha Pokharkar, Shradha Agrawal, Shristi Banerjee, Shruti Sinha, Shruti Wankhade, Shubham Maurya, Shubham Rajak, Shubham Sachdeva, Shubhangi Gaikwad, Shweta Padher, Shweta Patel, Shweta Patil, Shweta Sharma, Shyam Sundar Kumar, Siddharth Prakash, Siddhi Hire, Siddhi Mohite, Siddhi Pingat, Simran Yadav, Siva Prasath T R, Smita Tatewar, Sneha Agarwal, Sneha Bhosale, Sonu Kumar, Soudamini Barik, Soumendra Patnaik, Soumyaranjan Sahoo, Sowjanya Vangalapudi, Sri Lakshmi Vattigunta, Srini Rao, Srinivasan, Sriparna Das Chakraborty, Srishti Gupta, Srishti Jupudi, Subbitsha S, Sudarsan M S, Sudhanshu Kumar Bhagat, Sukant Maharana, Sumedh Kolwadkar, Sumit Khanna, Suneel Kumar, Sunidhi Tiwari, Sunil Shinde, Sunny Kumar Singh, Supriya Bathineni, Suraj Rajabhau Late, Surapu Naidu Chandaka, Surendra Jued, Suresh Kumar Ananthakumar, Suryakanta Padhan, Sushmita Basak, Sushmita Suresh Katkar, Susmit Raut, Suyash Mahajan, Swapnil Masalkar, Swati Jadhav, Sweta Kanavaje, Swetha Mehta, Tammanna , Tammineedi Nirmala Devi, Tanay Kurapa, Tanjima Ahmed, Tanzeela Wajid, Thatikonda Srilekha, Thrilokesh Boggarapu, Uday Purandare, Urvashi Vasishtha, Uttkarsh Agarwal, Vaibhav Kulkarni, Vaibhav Sharma, Vakul Gupta, Varsha Hile, Varun Jayaraman, Vatsal Sanghvi, Vedanti Saxena, Venktesh Mirdode, Venky Datla, Vibhu Thakur, Vidhya Gaddam, Vidya Kedar, Vijaya More, Vijayakrishna Acharya, Vijayan Ramesh, Vijaykumar Dandavatimath, Vikas Kumar, Vikash Shahi, Vikrum Srivastava, Vinay Kumar, Vinayak Mali, Vishnu Thite, Vishwadip Yewale, Vishwas Pandey , Vivek Vishwakarma, Yamini Ulhalkar, Yash Vora, Yashica Arora, Yeshaswini Bheemreddy, Yogita Ahlawat, Yogita Bhargav, Yojana Vanjare, Zainab Ansari

Jagriti Yatra 2022

A Maruthi Rao, Aaditi Kharade, Aaroh Jain, Aayu Kharbanda, Abhijeet Bhoyar, Abhijeet Shinde, Abhishek V.t, Abhishek Mishra, Abhishek Jakkannavar, Abhishek Kumar, Abhishek Kumar, Abisheik Aravindan, Adepu Madhukar, Aditi Tibarewal, Aditi Popli, Aditi Kochatta, Aditya Iyer, Aditya Shanker Raghuwanshi, Adityakumar Shrimali, Advaith Madhukar, Ahammed Rizvan K, Aiswarya Bose P V, Ajendra Neeraj, Ajim Maniyar, Ajith Kumar, Ajuma Tk, Akanksha Malaiya, Akanksha Nagdeve, Akarsh Shroff, Akash Nema, Akash Kumar Sahu, Akashdeep Saxena, Akhilesh Gaur , Akshaf Kumar, Akshat Rajan, Akshi Singhvi, Alisha , Allati Rajesh, Aman Ranjan, Aman Kumar Paswan, Amar , Amogh Aradhya, Amritha , Anamika M P, Ananjan Basu, Anant Seth, Angela Honegger, Anila Mathew V, Animesh Jain, Anindita Debroy Kalita, Anirudh Kesharwani, Anisha , Anjali Singh, Anjali Bagade, Ankit Varma, Ankit Mishra, Ankit Sahu, Ankit Gadiya, Ankita Verma, Ankur Anpat, Anmol Agrawal, Anmol Agrawal, Anmol Misra, Anne-maryse Van Der Slikke, Anoushka Jain, Anubhav Kaushik, Anuj Jain, Anupam Agrawal, Anuradha Rajbir, Anurag Bhatkar, Anurag Jain, Anushka Gokhale, Anuska Agarwal, Anwar R, Anwesh Patel, Aradhana Neelakantan, Archit Mangal, Arihant Jain, Arnav Jena, Arpit Goyal, Arpit Aggarwal, Arya Kumar Shaw, Aryan Purohit, Ashay Shrivastav, Ashish Pal, Ashish Parmar, Ashish Kolarkar, Ashitha Kp, Ashwat Sehgal, Astha Delvadia, Astha Garg, Aswin Chandra, Atul Yadav, Atul Anand, Avadhesh Sharma, Avani Ajikumar, Ayush Kuchiya, Ayush Agarwal, Ayushi Shukla, Azim Dinani, Balaji Mahalingam, Balaraju Bhusaveni, Balkrishna Karma, Basil Eldhose, Benee Prasad Kushwha, Bhargavi K S, Bhawani Kumari, Bhawna Sharma, Bhonjo Singh Banra, Bhrugu Pandya, Bidyadhar Pradhan, Bikram Biruli, Camille Fitoussi, Chaitanya Inge, Chaithanya Chittapur, Chaitrali Kale, Chaitya Shah, Chenab Chavan, Cheshta Naval, Chetan Murarka, Chethankumar Gs, Chinmay Phatak, Chintan Parekh, Chirag R, Cibi Chakravarthy, Daksh Singhal, Daksha Dixit,

Damini Haresh Teckchandani, Daniel Jacobsson, Deeksha Parashar, Deepak Bokaria, Deepak Paranthaman, Deepali Shedge, Deepanshi Gupta, Deepika Singh , Deepmala Kesarwani, Deepthi S, Devesh Chauhan, Devesh Vashishtha, Dhanya Vangalapudi, Dheeraj Chellaramani, Dhriti Sharma, Dinesh Raja, Disha Varshney, Dishikesh Jadhav, Divyansh Arora, Dr Mool Chandra Gupta, Dr Nina Singh, Drishtant Kaushal, Durga M, Farakh Abbas, Ganesh Garg, Ganesh R, Gantavya, Gargie Bahuguna, Gaurav ., Gaurav Srivastava, Gauri Dhokale, Geetam Jain, Gitapremnath Raja, Gnyana Shri Chenna, Gopal Shah, Gorakshanath More, Gouri Jayasurya, Hardik Babariya, Harsh Veer Singh, Harshad Batule, Harshit Goyal, Harshit Jain, Harshita Dhiman, Harshkumar Parakh, Harsimran Passi, Hemangini Rathod, Hemanth Varma, Heramb Verma, Himalay Thakkar, Hriday Sahni, Hrithik Ravuri, Hrudyesh Pankhania, Ikhshvakh Kalla, Isak Shaikh, Isika Agarwal, Ismail Shaikh, Jacob Jose, Jagriti Khanna, Jahanavi Divate, Jai Vardhan Dabriwal, Jalendra Tripathy, Jalshree Bhatt, Jamsheed Valiyakath Karakkatt, Jasiya Gomango, Jay Lakhotiya, Jayaram Prusty, Jayati Agrawal, Jayati Modi, Jeetkumar Namha, Jitendra Tripathy, Joséphine Magnière, Jyothi Kandregula, Kakku Kumar, Kali Babu, Kalyani Nevase, Kalyani Kirti Singh , Kanchan Thoke, Kanwar Ujjwaldeep Singh, Kapil Jayant, Karishma Jain, Karthik Varghese, Kartik Saini, Kartikey Singh Yadav, Kavil Rawat, Kavya Murugan, Kawalpreet Singh Judge, Keshav Khandelwal, Keyur Konkani, Khaja Reddy Koncha, Khanak Gupta, Khushboo Jain, Khushi Shah, Khushi Golecha, Kirti Gupta, Kishor Kumar Sutar, Koen Deweer, Kranthi Kiran Sodem, Krishikesh Khairnar, Krishna Joshi, Krishna Raghav A C, Krithish Kumar C, Krunal Jagtap, Krushna Taur, Kumar Satyam, Kumar Shaurya, Kunal Marian, Kunal Ostwal, Lakshay Kapoor, Lakshmi Narayana Kopparapu, Lavish Motani, Laxmi Sijapati, laxmi , Lokesh Garg, Maharudrappa Mirji, Mahesh Chillakuru, Mahesh Magar, Maitreyee Suravajjula, Maleka Rangwala, Mamata Kumari Choudhary, Mamta Kumari, Manasi Kabra, Mangala Shenoy, Mangesh Mali, Mangesh Dharmal, Mangesh Pol, Mangesh Ghadge, Manika Jain, Manish Bhakuni, Manish Jaiswal, Manish Sharma, Manjusha Aware, Mansi Shinde, Manvi Ahuja, Manvitha Saragadam, Mayank Jain, Mayank Virmani, Mayur Vyawahare, Mayur A, Md Danish Raja, Meet Kachhara, Megha Gupta, Megha Belgundkar, Megha Sharma, Meher Prabhu, Mohamed Imthadullah, Mohammad Shayan, Mohammed Nadeem, Mohit Pandey, Monil Gada, Mritunjoy Bhattacharjee, Mrunali Dupare, Mudit Baid, Munjabhau Mane, Muralidhar Teppala, Muralikrishna M Kulkarni, Murkuri Sahit Kumar, Muskaan Toshniwal, Muskan Agrawal, Naman Jain, Nandani , Naveen Raj S M, Navneet Singh, Nayan Gurav, Netala Vinay, Nidhi Vispute, Nidhi Sharma, Nikhil Jain, Nikita Abhang, Nikunj Agrawal, Nilesh Isswani, Nimisha Pandey, Niranth D, Nirmala ., Nishant Raj, Nishka Mishra, Nitesh Kumar, Nitesh Pandey , Nithyananda Bhat, Nitin Kumar, Ojus Tyagi, Om Jee Pal, Om Prasad Patro, Pabla Iraz, Pankaj Sanodiya, Parag Kumar Walde, Parshuram Jarhad, Parth Chabhadiya, Pauwel Casimir Delhaas, Pavitjot Singh, Pitambar Sahu, Piyush Lohia, Pooja George, Pooja Tendulkar, Pooja Mehta, Poonam , Poorna Krishna, Pornima Mohite, Prachi Paranjpe, Prafull Wathore, Prakalya B, Prakash Chand, Prakash Kumar Gupta, Prakhar Gupta, Pranali Chikte, Praneeth Venkatesa Sambathkumar, Pranit Roy, Pranjay Gupta, Prasad Chakor, Prasanna Kumari J K, Pratibha Jain, Pratik Agrawal, pratiksha Prosad, Pratiksha Kalpraj, Pratyush Tawani, Pratyush Sahoo, Pravin Kumar, Pravin Khale, Pravin Mitkar, Preethy F, Prem Anand Chandrasekar, Prerna Rani, Prerna Jhunjhunwala, Priyajan , Priyanka G, Priyanka Mishra, Priyanka Chabukswar, Priyanka Kumari, Priyanka ., Priyanshi Baheti, Pushpa Devi , Rabindra Gilua, Rahul Khatri, Rahul Sharma, Rahul Maram, Rahul Sharan, Rahul Ghaste, Rajat Kathotia, Rajvi Mehta, Raksha Choudhary, Ram K V S, Ramakrishna Reddy Nelaturi, Ramalingam Natarajan, Ranjana Srivastav , Rautan Singh Kushwah, Reetika Srivastava, Revan Tiwatane, Rinkesh Patel, Rishi Kashyap, Rishika Tibrewal, Ritik Jain, Ritu Pandram, Robin Kanattu Thomas, Rohan Pandit, Ronak Subudhi, Rupak Ravuri, Rupesh Pawar, Rythm Agrawal, Saathwik Chandan Nune, Sachin Korla, Sachin Jain, Sagar Tapadiya, Sagarikka Sivakumar, Sagrika Shah, Sahana Ravikumar, Sahil Islam, Sai Ram, Sai Priya Veerabomma, Sai Sampath Dangeti, Saifi Khan, Sairam Patil, Saishyam Balaji, Saketh Ram Bozza, Sakshi Yadav, Salhanti , Samriddhi Sakshi, Sanam Primalani, Sanchit Aggarwal, Sanchit Agarwal, Sandeep Sinha, Sandeep Kumar, Sandeep Kishore Satpathy, Sanjana Gupta, Sanjana Sawant, Sanjay Singh, Sanket Aher, Sanmat Choudhury, Santhosh Sivan Venkatesan, Santosh Garje, Santosh Kumar, Sarwat Bagwan, Saswati Pradhan, Saswati Dash, Satish Aghav, Satwinder Singh, Satyam Dubey, Satyen Khashu, Saurabh Dwivedi, Sauransh Bhardwaj, Saurav Malve, Saurav Jha, Sayali Pange, Seema Gupta, Shakti Bansal, Shamal Ingle, Shamyuktha San, Shilpa Kollari, Shilpa Mangesh Doiphode, Shirish Auti, Shivank Joshi, Shivansh Sagar, Shraddha Nawandar, Shraddha Nagane, Shravan S K, Shreeman Misurya, Shrenik Jain, Shrenik Gundecha, Shrest Gupta, Shreyasi Patil, Shriya Singh, Shriya Arora, Shruti Mehata, Shruti Bhargava, Shubham Kadam, Shubham Saw, Shubham Kumar, Shubham Arora, Shweta Sharma, Siddhi Patel, Siddhraj Mahurkar, Sidharth Padhy, Snigdharani Patra, Somashekar Divate, Sonal Singh , Soumya Jha, Sparsh Agarwal, Sri Ram Deepak Chivukula, Steven Thomas, Subham Pradhan, Subhashree Rout, Sucheendra M C, Suhail Ahmed, Suhas S Gowda, Sujeeshlal K Santhosh, Suma R, Sumandhar Kamble, Sumer Singh Badole, Sunder Singh, Sunita Maurya , Suprabath Sai Chadalavada, Sushmita Kaneri, Swamy A, Swattik Chakraborty, Sweta Jhunjhunwala, tanaya , Tanmay Jain, Tanvi Pradeep Muragundi, Tara Singh , Tejashree Munot, Tejasvi H Y, Thennarassu Sundaram, Toshi Kumawat, Triparna Barthakur, Triveni S, umang jain , Umesh Dugani, V Sreehari, Vaibhav Sharma, Vaidya Pankaj Vishnoi, Vaishnavi Tikotakar, Vanya Grant, Varsha Shah, Varsha Jha, Vasudev Vangara, Vedangi Rahane, Vedant Tapadiya, Vedant Sharma, Vedula Sai Siva, Venkat Manjunath Boganatham, Vidya Kirave, Vignesh Vadivel, Vijay Samraj Balasubramanian, Vikas Verma, Vikas Golhar, Vikas Kumar, Vikram Kumar, Vinamra Gandhi, Vinamra Harkar, Vinay Magdum, Vinay Kumar Gaddam, Vinayak Mali, Vinod Kumar, Virendrakumar Munnalal Uikey, Vishad Ranka, Vishal Avhale, Viviana , Vrushali Gaurkar, Yash Jain, Yash Tyagi, Yash Maru, Yash Sharma, Yash Mishra, Yashika Chugh, Yashwant Khandagale, Yeroen Van Der Leer, Yogeshwar Rathi, Yugandhara Dange

Udyamis Supported in Purvanchal by Jagriti

RC Kushwaha (Freedom Care Sanitary Pad), Rahul Mani (Rural Shores), Hakik Khan (Zoya Brooms), Pushpa Devi (Broom Manufacturing), Asha Devi (Broom Manufacturing), Malti Devi (RPF Foods), Ajay Sharma(Mushroom), Sunita Kushwaha (Moonj), Ghanshyam Mishra (Samadhan Telemedicine), Sachin Verma (Santosh Masala), Ajit Singh (Kushinara – Consumer Products), Avinash (AE Enterprises-Apparel), Bhupendra Singh (K & K Enterprises-Eatable cups), Pooja Shahi (Arjan Crafts), Shiv Tiwari (Shiv Foods & Dairy), Ramesh Chandra Pandey (Vasundhara Organics), Tafseer Alam (Manav Swasthyacare), Vikas Maddheshiya (Kishor Sweets), Narendra Yadav (Honey), ARC Foods (Abhishek Dwivedi), Asha Kushwaha (Handicraft), Kautuki Milk (Vikas Misra), Ashish Mishra (Durga Foundation), Bhism Yadav (Vermi Compost), Prashant Tripathi (Dynamic Academy-Self Defence), Sacchida Nand Shahi (Sarvadev Agro Foods), Gufran Khan (SKFK Beverages), Manikya Chaturvedi (GDPM Enterprises), Beerbali Prasad (Mangalam Namkeen), Pawan Kushwaha (Kadaknath), Shah ALam (Kadaknath), Gyaneshwar Singh (Pragatisheel Kishan FPO), Ganga Achar(Pankaj Sonkar), Asha Kushwaha (Cow Dung Products), Kanti Yadav (Jhapi-Moonj), Deepmala Mishra (Community Haat), Sunita & Kusum (Waste Management), Arvind Rai (Electric Bycycle), Abhishek Shukla (Banana Fiber), Bam Bahadur (Banana Fiber), Ram Naresh Gupta (K S Fashion), Jai Singh (Medicinal Plants)

Villages of Deoria and Kushinagar

Belwa Pandey, Savana Parashurama, Savana Lakshmana, Baria, Bharia, Pipradhanni, Chorkhari, Bakhra, Madarsan, Pipravari, Kataura, Charianav Bujurg, Labkani, Rasauli, Tandubari, Babhnauli, Chariyav Khas, Khaira Banua, Narayanpur Tiwari, Bansahia, Dummarbhiswa, Pandey Bhiswa, Karajahi, Budhra, Ratanpur, Kakaval, Vishunpura, Kuaar Bakhra, Bhanratapatti, Tangergadhi, Gopalpur, Devataha, Harpur, Chilouuna, Mundera, Karamhan, Mathia, Vinayak, Rashree, Kharatia, Bhatauli Bujurg, Gauri Bujurg, Gauri Khurd, Harerampur, Karamajijitpur, Kalaban, Bhatauli Khurd, Paanan Kunda, Rampur, Patharhat, Sanhar, Usri Bujurg, Sanda, Parasia, Pokhrabinda, Nagrauli, Devagaon, Umbhav, Devakuva, Keshavbari, Lakhanchand, Karaudi, Laxipur, Sohasa, Chiriha, Bhanda, Sirjamdei, Sirjam, Balua, Baitalpur, Goodri, Itwa, Bhaguva, Sopari Bujurg, Badhya, Udhopur, Jagdishpur, Mukundpur, Govindpur, Belhi Tiwari, Tenduhi, Dhatura Khas, Belderia, Dhatura khurd, Vikrampur Baspar, Bourdih, Batulahi, Jungle thukrahi, Banki, Bhelapar, Dila, Khoraram, Bodia Sultan, Jungle Sahajouli, Mahuwan pratham, Ruchhapar, Aurachouri, Bodia Anant, Mehada, Moodadih, Babhni, Raghwapur, Dhanauti khurd, Gobarai Special, Pidra, Paparpati, Deoria Khas, Parasia Aka Kharjarwa, Tilai Belava, Parasia Miskari , Borwa Gayasthan, Sonda, Danopur, Kathinhiya, Parasia Ahir, Katarari, Mohnidei, Saroura, Bahorwa, Malakouli, Haraiya, Kolhuua, Israhi, Barsha, Singahi, Majhgawa, Chhitaruaa, Aagaya, Surouli, Pakauli, Baida, Baspar, Bhatjmuava, Fulvaria Lchal, Phulwaria Karan, Agast Par, Dhamur Parashuram, Ranighat, Saujouli, Mastodargir, hata, Rohuar Vishunpur, Rohuar Dhirjan, Banuadih, Chaumukha, Sirsia, Sirsia Pandey, Arjun Deha, Babhnauli Math, Bagapar, Ananpur, Parasia, Bhudipakad, Karaj, Kanhauli, Narayanpur, Mukundpur, Rampur, Chainpur, Vikram Vishunpur, Samogar, Balakua, Jaswali, Chiuraha Khas, Harkauli, Pipra Nayak, Amarjgaa, Gotha Rasulpur, Deoria, Surchak, Pahadpur, Dhanauti, Sonadhi, Haraiya Vantpur, Vishunpur Murar, Lying, Rampur Dullah, Mahawa, Dhamur, Barwan Mansingh, Sahava, Jangalbelwa, Jigni, Shampur, Paparhia, Bhagwanpur, Nerui Ama, Barawa, Kar Jahan, Mahuva, Barari, Mahuadih, Rampur Dubey, Belwa, Tilatali, Pipra Madan Gopal, Rampur Hiraman, Deoria Budhu Khan, Tawakalpur, Savreji Money, Grabbed Bujurg, Savreji Kharg, Baltikara, Khadaich, Sekhuna, Bharwaliya, Araipar, Israki mafi, Jamuna, Chartubhujpur, Sakrapar Khurd, Sakrapar Bujurg, Parsauna, Rampur Chandrabhan, Vishunpura, Banakata, Barnai, Basantpur, Sajhava, Belawar Dubawar, Rampur Lala, Pandychak, Jaitpura, Suryapura, Baliywan, Baspar Elderly, Mundera, Parsabarwa, Narayanpur, Gour, Pokhrabinda, Bahorpur, Banakat Bahadurpur, Bhujuli, Hatimpur, Dumri Ekhlas, Kotwa, Sadohar Patti, Rampur Jagdish Alias Siswa, Mundera Chand, Bhutni Bujurg, Haraiya, Avarahi, Bhatni Dadan, Akatahia, Rampur Shripal, Gopalpur, Nautan Hathiagarh, Deoria Nakchhed, Phulehra, Chakia, Pipra Daula Kadam, Madapaa, Sonbarsa, Pakrivirbhadra, Shahjahanpur, Mundera aka Deurwa, Imilia aka Bhagwanpur, Deshi Deoria, Purani, Dubouli, Nebibarwan, Bhardhapatti, Dighwa Potwa, Baijnathpur, Madrapali Bari, Kaulachhapar, Hariyarpar, Baravameer Chhapar, Pauhari Chhapar, Semri, Mushari, Dwarika, Asi Tola alias Mainpur, Tarkulwa, Balpur Srinagar, Alakichhapar alias Lakshmipur, Barwa Semra, Rampur Jagdish alias Brindavan, Konhwalia Baburai, Konhwalia Bhartharay, Bhiswa, Mahuva Bajratar, Rampur Khas, Derawa, Mahua Patan, Mahuari, Mathyartti, Bharouta, Siswa, Mathia Mahawal, Sohanaria, Amava, Jalua, Mahuva Khurd, Sonula Ramnagar, Barath, Jamuni, Parsauni, Kanakpura, Kavalachak, Banhanarhar Patti, Saraini, Babupatti, Sitapatti, Bellhi, Pagra, Rampur Dhowatal, Baripatti, Sakatui, Saktua elderly, Farendha, Vrukshapatti, Pathardeva, Bhelipati, Sindhawe, Dharmagatpati, Chitouni, Devaghat, Pipradaud, Ghudikund khurd, Ghudikund Kala, Kuchaiya, Machaila, Kurmitati, Koyarpatti, Olipatti, Dharmachaura, Kharat, Harpur, Banjariya, Deela Jaddhuri, Turkapatti, Dela Manuddin, Motipur, Amwa Dubey, Medipatti, Noniapatti, Malsi Special, Jaitapatti, Kanthipatti, Murarchapar, Neruari, Shahpur Shukla, Shahpur Bhikham, Garamha, Masjidia, Dularpatti, Ghoratap alias Anandagar, Bindahi, Pakadiyar, Rampur Mahuwari, Mehahahahangpur, Baghouchachat, Sakhani, Pandipur, Mundera, Sundarpur, Koaripatti, Harimhuva, Tirma Sahun, Malwabar, Ramnagar, Koilswa Khurd, Pakaha, Chamanpura, Madrapali Bulaki, Pokhrabinda Ishwari Prasad, Vishunpur Bhartharay, Sabbazpur, Dighwa, Rustampur, Kesharpur, Karamha, Sarangpur, Hiranandpur, Madhopur, Mundera, Karanpur alias Pachfeda, Vishunpura, Raghopur, Dumri, Rampur Karakhana, Khadechapar, Govindpur, Madrapali, Harpur, Baripur, Seemapatti, Pipperhia Bharatra, Vishunpur alias Chikihwa, Ahirauli, Mogalpura, Mohanmundera, Parasakhad, Kathwalia, Sirsia Patti Hussain, Vishunpur Bhupat, Madria, Sirsia Ghota, Patkhouli, Pakdichhapar Patkhauli, Harpur Nizam, Gopalpur, Rampur Shukla, Pakadibabu, Pachaukhia, Ratanpura, Kanchanpur, Siravniya, Konhwalia, Kamdhenwa, Mathurachapar, Kotwa, Pokhrabinda, Sirsia, Babhnauli, Bhimpur, Barari, Bhagautipur, Bibtanthpur, Purushottampur, Bhagwanpur, Shahpur, Belwa, Sidhu, Gautamchak Mathia, Mathia Khurd, Mundera Mishra, Harpurkala, Chodpur, Manikpur aka Nandalatar, Kishunpali, Belvania Tola, Vishunpurkala, Gorya, Bindwalia, Chakajagbandhan alias mishrauli, Baghda Mahuari, Kalamundera, Buffalo, Mundera Jagdish, Pipra, Majdhir Viracha, Shahpur Purani, Bhikhampur, Kushari, Mahuva Khurd, Mujahna Lala, Gaura, Semerahwa, Garibpatti, Mahuvo Bujurg, Lohrauli, Vishunpura Bazar, Pipra Kanak, Rampur Awasthi, Dhuswa, Bhajouli, Udaipur, Dalan, Nautan, Lagda, Guddizor, Mujhanaghat, Khajuria, Sohniipar, Rampur Tari, Pandipur, Mahuapatan, Dihanant, Mehrauna, Chakbandi alias Pranpur, Dung Raid, Noniachhapar, Lahilpar alias Ratanpura, Lahilpar, Baspar, Chakbudhan alias Singhpu, Dhanauti Art, Pipraich, Kusmaha Belwa, Dambarpur alias Jatmalpur, Pagra alias Parasia, Budhra, Pakadi Bujurg, Grabbed elderly, Ghatalagaji, Chakarvadhus, Gambhirpur, Madipar elderly, Chakmadho alias mathia, Bhulua, Asna, Dulhu, Buffalo, Mujahna alias Bhatpurwa, Dhobi Chhapar, Pakadi khas, Batrauli, Babhni, Harpur Khurd, Rawatpar, Varuadih, Kishunpali, Baikunthpur, Bhawaninpur, Barsha, Chubariapatti, Amghat, Belvania alias Hasimachak, Siswa, Saroura, Mahui, Karaundi, Parasia, Khajuri Karauta, Nunkhar, Narulikhem, Dila, Naroli Khem, Naroli Sangram, Naroli Bhikham, Tenua, Bahadurpur, Khukundu, Khursear, Siswar, Surha, Sazhwar, Jaitpura, Itching, Mangraich, Dhanauti, Sisai, Bardiha, Pawanar, Pipra Shukla, Rupai, Majhgawa, Sathianv, Aghila, Pipra Devraj, Jiraso, Belwa Babu, Amava, Purana Chhapar, Parsauni, Sallahpur, Deoria, Fatehpur, Tagra, Khoribari, Laxipur, Shivrajpur, Mahuravan, Rampur, Chakur Tiwari, Banakata Shiva, Dumri, Pipra Dakshit, Jigna Dixit, Mishrauli Dixit, Birsinghpur, Ekdanga, Sahopar, Barsha, Rajwal, Bahorwa, Mujuri Khurd, Kamhariya, Baidauli, Mangrachi, Padri Pandey, Kola, Padri Membrane, Bharauli, Dubouli, Chakarwa, Majhawalia, Purani, Mahui Pandey, Padri Banmali, Penetration, Kodara Thakur, Badhporva, Pivkol, Khurdhar Khor, Mujuri Bujurg, Chandpur, Madria, Sakrapar, Devaghat, Chapia Jaydev, Jagini Mishra, Kurmouta Thakur, Gaonaria, Bharhechaura, Chandauli, Behra Dabur, Uska, Savreji, Danur, Nonapar, Bhatni Khas, Singhaidih, Babhnauli Kala, Vandalia Mishra, Madpahi, Chauthia, Putri, Barathi, Banakata Dixit, Pyasi, Bagusara, Bansgaon, Gauri Shriram, Manjharia, Ganesha Strip, Gagalwa, Pande Patti, Sikatia, Dhokarha, Dashavaha, Amavakhas, Bichwatwa, Amava Digar, Rampur Barhan, Chaubaya Patkhauli, Gauri Shukla, Rampur Janunia, Blessing Bujurg, Rampurpatti, Gauri Jagdish, Tiwaripatti, Rakbadulma Patti, Shirktiya Karapatti, Babhnauli, Banaraha Purab patti, Pakadiyaar Purabpatti, Kataura, Turkavalia Sahabganj, Sumahi Mohan Singh, Harkhauli, Contaminating Tola, Sumahi Saint Strip, Gauri Ibrahim, Tasting unhappy Mishra, Gauri Narottam, Davanha, Ahiruli Mishra, Ahiruli Hanuman Singh, Dhumpatti, Vishunpura, Dhuria Imlia, Hata, Dhuria coat, Bhatavaliya, Tamkuhi Raj, Labania, Makhua, Majhouwa, Furnace, Harpur, Purana Kataya, Bihar elderly, Balua Shamsher Shahi,

Parsauni Khurd, Mungari strip, Mir Bihar, Banabira, Lakshia Deoria, Narahwa, Kotwa, Tikampar, Bihar Khurd, Gangua, Pipra Baghel, Laxmipur Bujurg, Saraya Bujurg, Dubha, Rakaba Raja, Hardiya, Hata, Pansarva, Basadila Khurd, Parsauni Bujurg, Ghazipur, Banbaria, Laxmipur Raja, Hariharpur, Koindi Bujurg, Koindi Gosaipatti, Koindi Bariyarpur, Chakhani khas, Gosaipatti, Mathia Khurd, Morvan, Munnipatti, Pandey Pur, Black Patti, Madhopur Bujurg, Rampur Raja, Dibani Banjarawa, Saraya Khurd, Latwa Muralidhar, Chhapra Ahirauli, Latwa Jit, Khudura, Nainpahru, Bahadurpur, Salemgarh, Basadila Bujurg, Madhopur Khurd, Goda Shriram, Pathrva, Bahirabari, Karanpatti, Ramchanderpur, Mathouli, Parsoun, Pipra Muskil Agarwa, Sumahi Bu Aka Mahediya, Sumhi Sangram, Pandepur, Jagdishpur, Mishrauli, Rajpur Bagaha, Pipraghat Muktil, Pipraghat eh, Pirozha, Parsa alias Sirsiya Moo., Parsa alias Sirsia eh, Rakba Jangli Patti, Ghaghwa Jagdish Mustakil, Ghaghwa Jagdish Ehtamali, Bhagwanpur, Gadhiya Chintaman, Domath, Zadawa, Baijupatti, Mathia, Bhavpur, Bhumiya Agarwa, Taraya Sujan, Basadila Gunakar, Mohan Basadila, Mukundpur, Hafua Chaturbhuj, Hafua jivan, Hafua Balaram, Marwa, Dumariya, Tinfedia, Jamsadia, Jamsada, Taraya Lakshiram, Taraya Harkesh, Kathwalia alias Habibpur, Taraya Baikuth, Tarya Sunder, Gadhia Pathak, Gadhia Mohan, Gopalpur, Jawahi Narendra, Jawahi Dayal, Jawahi Malahi Ehtamali, Jawahi Malahi Mustakil, Pipra Mishra, Chopradal Ray, Jawahi Harvallabh, Daniadi, Koindha, Chamapathia, Rampur Bangra, Malho, Siswa Bujurg, Tulsipatti, Mathia Shriram Mustakil, Mathia Shriram Eh, Siswa Digar, Siswa Awwal, Bedupar Muskil, Bedupar Eh, Bihetar Konhawalia, Bank Khas, Baghachaur, Fagu Chhapar, Ahiruli Dan, Jungle Siswa, Jungle Luthha, Jungle Naugawa, Babhnauli, Bhula Patti, Narhwadih, Maila Narhava, Kiratpatti, Narwa Acharaj Dubey, Govind Patti, Kokilpatti, Baikunthpur, Ahirauli, Mathia Kartagiri, Barhra Vrutt, Chirkutha, Loharpatti, Matia Mafi, Godaria, Jungle Vishunapura, Jungle Lalachhapra, Chaf, Batrauli, Shahpur Khalwapatti, Shahpur Uchkipatti, Shahpur mafi, Sorhawa, Jungle Shankarpur, Fisherman Basant Bharti, Jungle Ghorat, Thadhibhar, Mishrauli, Dudahi, Padaron Madurahi, Vishunpur Bariya Patti, Prithvipur, Mathia Bhokariya, Dumahi, Barwa Rajapakad, Retail Ahiruli, Bagra Rambax Rai, Rajapakad, Barampur, Dharampur, Vijaypur Uttarpatti, Vijaypur Dakhsinpatti, Gurwalia, Mathia, Sariswa, Maheshpur, Machria Daljeet Kunwar, Khiriya, Doghra, Wire Vishunpur, Semra Hardo Strip, Pagra Prasad Fall, Saphi, Pagra Padri, Basantpur Haricharan, Naugawa, Amarvau Khurd, Padri Tilak Rai, Padri Vishundayal, Amarva Bujurg, Pakadi gosai, Saphi Khurd, Khalwapatti, Saphi Bujurg, Javar, Bhaisha, Lohlangadi, Gagalwa, Mathouli, Rajavatiya, Bughi, Narayanpur Ramsahay, Baluaa Takiya, Patherwa, Pipra Kanak, Pakhihwa alias Kar Jahan, Karamaha, Jogia Sumali Strip, Jogia Hazoric, Bardha Pandey, Basadila Mahanth, Parsauni, Ahladpur, Mahuva, Senduriya bujurg, Mogalpura, Karmanini, Chandrauta, Bhelaya, Tirma Sahun, Koriya Bhelhi, Sendiya Bujurg, Batrauli, Sapha, Bhaluhi, Kishundas Patti, Mahuva Khurd, Gagitikar, Padri, Devpokhar, Lavkush Purba, Mahuva Bujurg, Srirampatti, Turkapatti, Koriya, Parsauni Khurd, Tejavaliya, Nakatha Basadila, Amava bujurg, Singha, Jamunia Mahuvow, Dhanauji, Sirpatkhar, Kurmouta, Rudwalia, Amava, Belwa Khurd, Chhahu, Jinkul, Tenua, Rautpar, Basadila, Belwa Sukdev, Belwa Bujarg, Fursatpur, Mahasone, Lavkush Paschim Patti, Huta, Gaurakhor, Dehwapatti, Kuppaptii, Dhunwalia, Sohang, Jokwa Khurd, Gaid, Bairagi patti, Avarava Sofiganj, Auva Sofiganj, Kuchaya, Dhanauji kala, Belvachittu alias Kazipur, Fazilnagar, Sathiav, Pipra Razjab, Patkhouli, Jokwa Bujurg, Madhuria, Daharipatti, Saraiya Mahanth Strip, Dhaurahra, Kotwa, Karajahi, Mystery, Kanaura, Vishnapura, Jauramnarkhan, Noniapatti, Amwa Sridube, Dhanha, Beili, Matihinia, Laxipur, Bakulhar art, Bakulhar Khurd, Nadwa Vishunpur, Madhopur, Basadila Durjan, Dhekulia alias Dubouli, Devichak, Ashogava bujurg, Budhra, Bardha Market, Vishunpur Raja, Belwa Kala, Kataya Manudin, Pokhrabinda, Taruvanwa, Bhatavaliya, Chaura Ramatvakal Shahi, Chaura Khas, Shankarpatti, Shankarpatti, Sasturba, Pachaukhia, Bhadarwa, Kharatia, Bhatwan, Narayanpur, Chakia, Sumahi elderly, Sumahi Khurd, Rampur Khushihal Tola, Vishunpur Sheikhajralli, Darjiya, Arranwan, Usmanpur, Chhathu Kateya, Mundera, Bhathi Dariyav Tola, Nakatha alias Hariharchapra, Bhanpur, Farendha, Badurao, Nathapatti, Loharwalia, Baliwa, Bhatahi Bujurg, Bhard Khurd, Belwa Alamdas, Duldulia, Sherpur Barhara, Chainpur, Banakata market, Koilsawa Bujurg.

Appendix 4

Translation of Some Sanskrit Words

The theory of Sanskrit Non-Translatables[1] suggests that many Sanskrit or derived Hindi words have to be explained to retain their original meaning

Sankhya: is one of the schools of ancient Indian Hindu philosophy whose foundation is attributed to sage Kapila, regarded as the system's primary proponent. According to Sankhya, the universe is composed of two fundamental realities: Purusha (the spirit or consciousness) and Prakriti (the material world). It seeks to explain the nature of existence, the origin of the universe and the relationship between the individual Self (Purusha) and Prakriti. Purusha represents pure consciousness—eternal, infinite, unchangeable and devoid of any attributes. Prakriti refers to nature, comprising three fundamental gunas (qualities) that govern all aspects of the material world, including the mind and senses, and are detailed later.

Upanayan: also known as the sacred thread ceremony or the initiation ceremony, is a significant rite of passage in Hinduism, particularly for boys. It marks the formal beginning of their education and spiritual journey. The Upanayan ceremony typically takes place during the early teenage years, although the specific age can vary. It involves the investiture of a sacred thread (Yajnopavita) around the boy's left shoulder, symbolizing his readiness to study the holy Vedas and engage in spiritual and religious practices. After the Upanayan ceremony, he is expected to receive formal education in Vedic scriptures, philosophy and other subjects under the guidance of a Guru.

Guru: is considered an enlightened being; revered as someone who has attained a high level of spiritual realization and has the ability to guide others on their spiritual path. Hence, Guru cannot be loosely translated as 'teacher'. A Guru possesses deep knowledge and insight into spiritual practices, scriptures and philosophies. The Guru's role extends well beyond mere intellectual teaching and involves a transformative and personal relationship with their disciples. They provide guidance, support and practical instructions to help individuals overcome obstacles; they cultivate spiritual virtues and deepen the disciples' understanding of the divine.

Laxmi: is a prominent Hindu goddess associated with wealth, prosperity, abundance and good fortune. She is considered the embodiment of beauty, grace and auspiciousness. Laxmi is often depicted as a radiant and benevolent goddess, adorned with jewellery and seated on a lotus flower, symbolizing purity and divine consciousness. Laxmi's association with wealth extends beyond mere material prosperity to the spiritual domain. She is seen as the bestower of inner virtues, such as love, compassion, generosity and humility. Her blessings are sought after not only for material abundance but also for spiritual growth, harmony and overall well-being.

Ardhanarishvara: is a composite form of the Hindu God Shiva, wherein half of the body represents Shiva (masculine aspect) and the other half represents his consort Parvati (feminine aspect). The term 'Ardhanarishvara' is derived from the Sanskrit words 'Ardha', meaning 'half', 'Nari', meaning 'woman', and 'Ishvara', meaning 'Lord' or 'God'. Therefore, Ardhanarishvara can be translated as 'the Lord Who is Half Woman'. The Ardhanarishvara form represents the divine union of the masculine and feminine energies within the universe. It symbolizes the idea that Shiva and Parvati are inseparable and complementary aspects of the same divine consciousness. The form evokes the concept of the non-duality of existence, where the male and female energies are in balance and harmony.

Purabia: derived from the Hindi word 'purab' meaning 'east', is a term that highlights the cultural, social, linguistic and regional identity of eastern India and its diverse traditions and practices. Purabia is used to refer to someone or something associated with the particular regions of eastern Uttar Pradesh, Bihar, Jharkhand, Odisha and parts of West Bengal. The Purabia culture is known for its rich heritage, including folk music and dance forms, languages such as Bhojpuri, and distinct culinary specialities.

Tirth: (also spelled 'tirtha' or 'teerth') refers to a sacred place or pilgrimage site that holds religious and spiritual significance. Tirths are typically associated with rivers, mountains, temples and other locations believed to be infused with divine energy and blessings, and represent a new crossing. It is believed that tirths are imbued with the presence of gods, goddesses, saints and spiritual energies. Many tirths are associated with specific deities or religious events, and visiting these sites is believed to grant devotees spiritual merit (punya), bringing them closer to the divine. Tirths are often characterized by India's sacred rivers, such as the Ganges (Ganga), Yamuna, Godavari, Brahmaputra and others.

Ahimsa: The traditional Hindu concept of ahimsa emphasizes the quality of kindness and harmlessness, but not absolutely nor unreservedly. Hence, the typical, but excessively loose, translation of ahimsa as some form of universal 'non-violence' is inaccurate.

Satyagraha: a term coined by Mahatma Gandhi, is derived from two Sanskrit words: 'satya', meaning 'truth', and 'agraha', meaning 'insistence' or 'holding firmly'. Satyagraha is a philosophy and method of non-violent resistance or civil disobedience, based on the principle of relentlessly seeking truth and justice through moral, peaceful means. Satyagraha embodies the belief that non-violence is a powerful tool to confront injustice and challenge oppressive systems, and to create positive social change based on truth, justice and human dignity.

Sarvodaya: is a term that translates to 'welfare of all' or 'upliftment of all'. It is a concept and philosophy that advocates for the well-being and progress of all individuals and communities, with a focus on social and economic equality, justice, harmony, sense of community and mutual respect. Hence, it goes beyond mere economic development and encompasses the broader aspects of human well-being.

Dharma: is a Sanskrit term that has multiple interpretations and applications across different religious and philosophical traditions, particularly in Hinduism, Buddhism and Jainism. Its meaning varies depending on the context, but it generally refers to one's moral and ethical duty, righteousness and the divine cosmic order that upholds and sustains the universe. Dharma is derived from the Sanskrit root 'dhar', which means 'to support' or 'sustain'; hence dharma means 'that which supports or upholds the worlds and its beings', but should not be indifferently interpreted as 'religion' or 'duty', without context, as is often done through English translations.

Shastras: are a collection of ancient Hindu scriptures that serve as authoritative texts on various aspects of spirituality, philosophy, rituals, life and social conduct. The word 'shastra' is derived from the Sanskrit root 'shas', which means 'to teach' or 'to instruct'. Shastras are considered sacred and are regarded as the revealed knowledge or wisdom passed down by sages, seers and divine beings. They are written in Sanskrit and cover a wide range of subjects, including theology, philosophy, law, governance, astrology, medicine, architecture, music and dance.

Sanskriti: is a Sanskrit term that encompasses customs, traditions, beliefs, values, arts and social practices that define a particular society or community. It is an essential element of the cultural identity of a group of people and shapes their way of life. Sanskriti often refers to the diverse cultural heritage and traditions of the Indian Subcontinent, and extends to a wide range of aspects, including language, literature, music, dance, art, architecture, cuisine, rituals, festivals, social norms and religious practices, reflecting the accumulated wisdom, creativity and expressions of a society over time. Sanskriti acts as a vehicle for transmitting values, knowledge and social norms from one generation to the next, fostering a sense of collective identity and continuity.

Gharanas: are traditional schools or lineages of classical music and dance in India. They represent distinct styles and approaches to music rendition and dance style, and each Gharana has its own unique characteristics, techniques and repertoire. These Gharanas have been instrumental in preserving and passing down the rich musical and dancing traditions of India from one generation to another. Gharanas originated during the mediaeval period and were traditionally associated with particular regions, cities or royal courts. The teachings and practices of these Gharanas were passed down through an intimate guru–disciple (guru–shishya) relationship, ensuring generational continuity and authenticity of a style.

Atman: a Sanskrit term, is a central concept in Hindu philosophy and spirituality. It refers to the eternal, unchanging, pure essence that is believed to exist within each living being. Atman is considered to be the innermost core, the Self, of a person's being and is believed to be identical to Brahman, the ultimate pervasive reality or cosmic consciousness. According to Hindu philosophy, the Atman is eternal and transcends the temporary nature of the physical body and the fluctuations of the mind. The realization of Atman and its unity with Brahman is considered the supreme goal of human existence, and is associated with self-discovery, self-realization and spiritual liberation (see 'Moksha' described later).

Sila: is a Pali term commonly used in Buddhism, particularly in the Theravada tradition, and it translates to 'virtue' or 'moral conduct'. It refers to the ethical principles and guidelines that Buddhists follow to cultivate wholesome actions and behaviours. Sila forms an integral part of the Noble Eightfold Path, which is a fundamental framework for Buddhist practice. It is one of the three components of the path known as the 'Threefold Training', alongside samadhi (concentration) and panna (wisdom). Sila serves as the foundation for mental purification and spiritual development, and its practice involves the observance of precepts or moral guidelines that vary in number depending on tradition or individual commitment.

Guna: refers to the three fundamental qualities or attributes that are believed to pervade all of creation. These gunas are considered intrinsic qualities that govern the behaviour, nature and perception (of the mind and the senses) of beings and objects in the universe. Prakriti (described earlier under 'Sankhya') is composed of three constituent gunas: Sattva, Rajas and Tamas.

Sattva: represents the quality of purity, harmony and balance. It is associated with qualities such as wisdom, clarity, knowledge, peace, equanimity and spiritual upliftment. When the sattva guna is dominant, individuals tend to exhibit virtues such as compassion, selflessness and a calm and peaceful demeanour.

Rajas: is associated with the quality of activity, passion and dynamism. It represents the energy and drive that propel individuals into action and achievement. It is characterized by restlessness, desire, ambition and attachment. When the rajas guna dominates, individuals display traits such as ambition, competitiveness, a strong desire for success and anger/aggression when it fails to manifest.

Tamas: represents the quality of inertia, darkness and ignorance. It is associated with dullness, laziness, confusion and a lack of clarity (about what is right and wrong, etc.). When tamas is predominant, individuals exhibit lethargy, ignorance and a lack of motivation or initiative.

Dana: is a Sanskrit term that translates to 'generosity' or 'charitable giving'. It is a concept and practice that holds great significance in various Indian spiritual traditions, including Hinduism, Buddhism and Jainism. In Buddhism, dana is one of the foundational virtues and is considered an essential part of the path to enlightenment. It is one of the three pillars of Buddhist practice, known as the 'Threefold Training', alongside sila (ethical conduct) and bhavana (meditation). Dana involves the act of selflessly giving or offering support, with a belief that ultimately goodwill will return through an interconnected world.

Daya: is a Sanskrit term that translates to 'compassion' or 'sympathy'. It refers to a deep feeling of empathy, care and concern for the suffering or well-being of others. Daya is considered a noble virtue and an essential aspect of ethical conduct in many spiritual and philosophical traditions. In Hinduism, daya is regarded as one of the fundamental qualities of a virtuous and compassionate individual. It is considered an expression of divine love and an important principle in relating to all beings with kindness and understanding.

Dama: is a Sanskrit term that translates to 'self-control' or 'restraint'. It refers to the practice of controlling one's senses, desires and impulses, i.e. one's mind, in order to cultivate inner discipline, harmony and spiritual growth. Dama is considered an important virtue in various spiritual and philosophical traditions. In Hinduism, dama is one of the nine fundamental virtues known as the 'Nava-Nyaya', which are qualities that are essential for leading a righteous and virtuous life.

Brahmacharya: is a Sanskrit term that has multiple meanings depending on the context. In general, it refers to a lifestyle or practice characterized by celibacy, self-restraint and moderation. However, the term is also interpreted in broader ways beyond its traditional association with celibacy. In Hinduism, Brahmacharya is one of the four stages of life (ashramas) prescribed in the ancient scriptures known as the Vedas. It is the stage of studenthood involving the practice of abstaining from sexual activity and maintaining purity of thought, speech and actions, with utmost reverence for the Guru.

Grihastha: is a Sanskrit term that refers to the second stage of life in Hinduism, known as the 'householder' stage. It is one of the four traditional stages of life, or ashramas, prescribed in Hindu philosophy. Grihastha is the stage in which an individual accepts the responsibilities of married life, establishes a household and engages in worldly pursuits. It is the stage of life associated with family, social engagement and the fulfilment of worldly duties and responsibilities. In the Grihastha ashrama, individuals are expected to fulfil their duties towards their spouse, children, parents, extended family and society.

Vanaprashta: is a Sanskrit term that represents the third stage of life in Hindu philosophy. It is one of the four traditional stages of life, or ashramas, prescribed in Hinduism. Vanaprastha, also known as the 'forest dweller' stage, follows the Grihastha (householder) stage, and precedes the final stage of Sanyasa (renunciation). In the Vanaprastha stage, individuals gradually withdraw from their active worldly engagements and responsibilities, and start preparing for a life of contemplation, self-discovery and giving back to society.

Sanyasa: is a Sanskrit term that refers to the fourth and final stage of life in Hindu philosophy. It is one of the four traditional stages of life, or ashramas, prescribed in Hinduism. Sanyasa is the stage of renunciation wherein individuals voluntarily detach themselves from worldly attachments and dedicate themselves exclusively towards spiritual pursuits and the path to liberation (see 'Moksha' described later). It is a stage of complete renunciation of material desires and attachments, and social roles and responsibilities. In the Sanyasa stage, individuals leave behind their familial and societal ties, including their possessions, social status and relationships.

Kalpavriksha: is a term from Hindu mythology that translates to 'wish-fulfilling tree' or 'tree of abundance'. It is a mythical tree that is believed to grant any desired object or wish to those who approach it with reverence and purity of heart. In Hindu mythology, the Kalpavriksha is often associated with the celestial abode of the gods, specifically in the mythical forest called Nandana Vanam. It is described as a divine tree that symbolizes material prosperity, abundance and fulfilment. The tree is said to possess extraordinary magical powers, capable of fulfilling any wish or desire.

Mahaul: is a term from Hindi that translates to 'environment' or 'atmosphere'. It refers to the overall ambience, mood or atmosphere of a particular place, situation or setting. The word 'mahaul' is often used to describe the collective feeling, vibe or energy present in a social gathering, event or environment. It encompasses the combined influence of various factors, such as the physical surroundings, the people present, their behaviour, interactions and the general atmosphere prevailing at that moment.

Sangham: is a term that has different meanings in different contexts. The term originates from the Buddhist congregations that were part of the Gangetic plains in the years following the birth of the Buddha. It is also used in ancient Tamil literature to refer to gatherings or assemblies of Tamil poets and scholars who engaged in literary discussions, composed poetry and contributed to the development of Tamil literary works. Sangham also denotes a cultural, social or professional group that brings together individuals with shared interests or objectives.

Sanyasi: is an individual who has embraced the stage of 'Sanyasa' (see earlier description of Sanyasa) in Hindu philosophy.

Dharmshala: is a term commonly used to refer to a shelter or accommodation facility that provides lodging and basic amenities for pilgrims, travellers or individuals seeking temporary residence. Dharmshala is derived from the Sanskrit word 'dharma', which has various meanings, including righteousness, duty and moral principles (as described earlier). In this context, a dharmshala is a place that upholds the principles of hospitality, charity and service.

Kachahari: also spelled 'Kacheri' or 'Kachari', is a term used in South Asia, particularly in India, Bangladesh and Nepal, to refer to a courthouse or administrative office. Kachahari originates from the Persian word 'kachahri', which means a place for holding official or legal proceedings. It typically denotes a government office or a judicial building where administrative matters, legal hearings, settlement of disputes and public meetings take place, involving the participation of officials, lawyers, judges and the public.

Urdhva Mula: is a term derived from Sanskrit, where 'Urdhva' means 'upward' or 'ascending', and 'Mula' means 'root' or 'base'. It is a concept commonly found in yogic and spiritual practices, particularly in the context of energy centres or chakras. In yogic philosophy, the human body is believed to have several energy centres, known as chakras, which are responsible for the flow of vital energy or prana. The chakras are thought to be located along the central channel of the body, which runs from the base of the spine to the crown of the head.

The term 'Urdhva Mula' specifically refers to the energy or life force that is directed upwards.

Dham: is a term commonly used in Hinduism to refer to a pilgrimage site or sacred place of spiritual significance. These places are considered highly auspicious and are believed to have a divine presence or connection to the divine.

Karmayogi: is a term commonly used in Hindu philosophy to describe individuals who perform their duties and responsibilities with a selfless and dedicated attitude. The term is derived from two Sanskrit words: 'karma', meaning 'action' or 'duty', and 'yogi', referring to a practitioner of yoga or one who seeks spiritual union. In Hinduism, the concept of karmayogi emphasizes the importance of performing one's duties and actions without attachment to the results or personal desires in order to, thus, cleanse one's mind and prepare for a yet higher spiritual path.

Chitti: is a concept outlined by Pandit Deendayal Upadhyay as part of his philosophy of Integral Humanism. It refers to an integrated 'atma' of a country, which transcends personal motivations and combines these within a transcendental personal for a nation.

Purushartha: is a concept from ancient Indian philosophy that refers to the four fundamental goals or pursuits of human life. These goals are considered essential for the well-being and fulfilment of an individual. The four purusharthas are: Dharma, Artha, Kama and Moksha.

Moksha: represents the ultimate, the supreme goal of liberation, spiritual enlightenment and self-realization. It is the pursuit of transcendence and liberation from the cycle of births and deaths (Samsara). Moksha involves seeking spiritual truth, self-discovery and union with the divine or the ultimate reality. It is the highest aim of human existence, where one realizes one's true nature as inherently divine, unified with Brahman and, thus, attains liberation from rebirth and suffering.

Artha: pertains to material well-being and prosperity. It encompasses the pursuit of wealth, success and economic security. Artha includes efforts to acquire resources, establish financial stability and fulfil one's material desires in a responsible and ethical manner, with concomitant benefits for society.

Kama: refers to the pursuit of pleasure, desires and aesthetic enjoyments. It encompasses the fulfilment of sensual and emotional desires, including those related to love, relationships, art, music and other forms of aesthetic enjoyment. Kama recognizes the importance of experiencing pleasure and finding joy in life.

Shramana: also spelled Śramaṇa, is a term used in ancient Indian religions to refer to spiritual seekers or ascetics who renounce worldly attachments and dedicate themselves to the pursuit of spiritual liberation (moksha). The term originated in the ancient Vedic period and was later adopted by various religious traditions, including Jainism and Buddhism. Shramanas are individuals who follow a path of self-discipline, meditation and renunciation of material possessions.

Paranirvana: also known as Mahaparinirvana, is a term primarily used in Buddhism to refer to the final nirvana or liberation attained by a fully enlightened being, usually a Buddha. It represents the ultimate state of transcendence and liberation from the cycle of birth, death and rebirth. Paranirvana is considered the complete and final release from all forms of suffering and the end of the cycle of life and death. It is the state of absolute peace, wisdom and freedom from the limitations of existence.

Notes

Introduction: A New Beginning at Seventy-Five

1. Deoria is a Tier 3 district, which is one of approximately 164 districts that reside below Tier 2 districts, and comprise approximately 43 per cent of India's population. The tiering is based on size and socio-economic parameters of the district outlined further in Chapter 2.
2. Isaiah Berlin, *The Proper Study of Mankind: An Anthology of Essays*, edited by Henry Hardy and Roger Hausheer, Vintage Classic, 2013; carries some of the author's best essays, which illuminate the past and offer a key to the burning issues of today. The anthology shines a light on his most distinctive doctrine—pluralism as well as the principal movements that characterize the modern age: romanticism, historicism, fascism, relativism, irrationalism and nationalism. He states this quote in reference to his reading of Giambatista Vico's work on page 7 of the book.
3. 'Bottom of the Pyramid' is a phrase made famous by Professor C.K. Prahalad in a book by the same name, and is detailed further in Chapter 2. It has been subsequently modified to be 'Base of the Pyramid', denoting a large majority of those who were economically poor when the book was written approximately two decades ago.
4. The total number of citizens who can be considered Middle India is explained in Chapter 2 and total approximately 800 million, residing largely in Tier 2 and Tier 3 districts. This is further detailed in Chapter 2.
5. President Ramnath Kovind hosted approximately 600 participants and organizers at Rashtrapati Bhawan on 5 January 2018, when he gave a keynote speech to encourage the assembled Yatris. In this he articulated his desire that the organizers of the Jagriti Yatra convert the journey into a national movement. This speech can be seen on YouTube, (78) President Kovind meets over 600 participants of Jagriti Yatra-2017—YouTube.

Chapter 1: Awakening: A Journey into the Middle

1. Diane Eck, *India: A Sacred Geography* (New York: Three River Press, 2012), is a book based on the premise that from the earliest times, the geography of India has been based on sacred spots. Millions of pilgrims crisscrossed this geography and created the India that we know today, much before modern democracy gave it its current boundary.
2. Shashank Mani, *India: A Journey through a Healing Civilization* (HarperCollins India, 2007). An earlier book by the author that describes the Azad Bharat

Rail Yatra, a train journey executed by him with collaborators to celebrate the golden jubilee of India's Independence.

3. Shimon Peres, *No Room for Small Dreams: Courage, Imagination and the Making of Modern Israel* (Weidenfeld & Nicolson, 2017), which outlines the audacious goals a small country such as Israel crafted at its birth and then through courageous leadership achieved them, recounted through the life story of Shimon Peres, a President of Israel.

4. Shashi Tharoor, *An Era of Darkness: The British Empire in India* (Aleph, 2016), describes the plunder and loot of India and the cover-up of that extractive economy by the British. He examines the many ways in which the colonizers exploited India, ranging from the drain of national resources to Britain, the destruction of the Indian textile, steel-making and shipping industries, and the negative transformation of agriculture, and counters the supposed benefits of western-style democracy and political freedom, the rule of law and the railways.

5. The Jagriti Yatra was announced at a press conference in Mumbai in August 2008, which was led from the Tata Group by R. Gopalakrishnan, then a board member at Tata Sons, Romit Chaterjee of Tata Sons, Shashank Mani, founder of Jagriti Yatra and Swapnil Dixit, the then executive director at Jagriti. The phrase comes from the speech of R. Gopalkrishnan from the press conference.

6. The Jagriti Yatra and Jagriti Enterprise Centre–Purvanchal (JECP) are part of Jagriti, a registered charity under the Section Societies Registration Act 1860. It has focused on skills and enterprise-led development since 2001. Its flagship programme, Jagriti Yatra, has been in existence since 2008, and the JECP is being constructed in Barpar village of Deoria district since January 2021. www.jagritiyatra.com, www.jecp.in.

7. Names have been changed for confidentiality.

8. Tiago Forte, in *The Future of Learning is Community: The Rise of Cohort-Based Courses*, describes three waves of learning methodology. The author likens cohort-based as the fourth wave 'which has taken on the name "Cohort-Based Courses", referring to a group of learners who join an online course together and then move through it at the same pace', https://fortelabs.co/blog/the-rise-of-cohort-based-courses/.

9. Jonathan Haidt, *The Righteous Mind: How Good People Are Divided by Politics and Religion* (Penguin, 13 March 2012). Haidt seeks to enrich liberalism and political discourse with a deeper awareness of human nature. Haidt argues that people are fundamentally intuitive, not rational, and illustrates this with learning that comes from emotional peer influence.

10. Lt. Col Suresh Patil is a retired army colonel who helped the journey in 1997 as the train in-charge, and has subsequently been the train in-charge on at least ten of the sixteen Jagriti Yatras after it was started in 2008. A person who took part in action during the 1965 war, he continues to contribute to his region in Pune by working on water conservation issues through his charitable organization Green Thumb.

11. Ticket for Change is an organization in France founded by Matthew Dardieu, a Yatri from the 2013 Jagriti Yatra, which takes a group of entrepreneurs on a journey in France, encouraging their business ideas and forming a network in his area of entrepreneurs. https://www.ticketforchange.org/

12. Sudhanshu Palsule and Michael Chavez, *Rehumanizing Leadership: Putting Purpose and Meaning Back into Business* (LID Publication, 2020), is a book on leadership, where the authors make a compelling case for rehumanizing leadership for the twenty-first century. The concept of 'going out of your context and then having the courage to come back to transform' came about in conversations with Sudhanshu around 2008 and 2009.

13. Reference the Impact Report by Impactree which investigated the impact of the Yatra by polling Yatris over an eight-year period. Almost all Yatris said they were transformed by the Yatra: 28 per cent of those surveyed had started an enterprise, 49 per cent had done something for the country and the remaining had gone about their life with a more rounded view of India.

14. Teach for India is a national organization that believes that education has a severe deficit of people at all levels and it seeks to find leaders who are committed to working together to improve the capacity and quality of India's schools. The core Teach for India fellowship invites young leaders to spend time in schools supporting the education process, in collaboration with different stakeholders. https://www.teachforindia.org/.

15. The Gandhi Fellowship is an initiative by the Piramal Foundation and was born from Gandhi's statement, 'Be the change you wish to see in this world'. The Fellowship is a platform established in 2008 for every self-motivated Indian youth with a dream of seeing a thriving India by discovering and building on the leader within. It is an experiential, residential two-year Fellowship. This immersive journey, undertaken at the grassroots of India, provides an in-depth experience across areas of public health, education and water.

16. Margaret Mead, American anthropologist and author of *Male and Female*, is credited with the quote 'Never doubt that a small group of thoughtful, committed citizens can change the world. Indeed, it is the only thing that ever has.' I have shortened the quote here for brevity. Some commentators have argued that the word 'organized' should be inserted before citizens so that long-term commitment is also recognized. https://leandroherrero.com/the-missing-word-in-the-famous-margaret-mead-quote/

17. Pablo Neruda won the Nobel Prize for literature in 1971 and this quote is taken from his acceptance speech given on 13 December 1971. The quote can be found in the sixth-last paragraph in the speech Pablo Neruda – Nobel Lecture—NobelPrize.org, https://www.nobelprize.org/prizes/literature/1971/neruda/lecture/.

Chapter 2: Diamond: A New Metaphor

1. C.K. Prahalad, Stuart L. Hart, 'The Fortune at the Bottom of the Pyramid', which first featured as an article in *Strategy + Business* magazine in 2002, urged leaders to imagine the world's 4 billion poorest people as potential consumers—and described how they could engage them profitably. The article was followed by the bestselling book *Fortune at the Bottom of the Pyramid: Eradicating Poverty through Profits* (Pearson Education, 2004) and created the phrase 'Bottom of the Pyramid', which was subsequently changed to Base of the Pyramid. https://www.strategy-business.com/article/11518?gko=9b3b4.

2. World Bank 2010, recast in *Profitable Growth Strategies for the Emerging Middle: Learning from Next 4 Billion Markets* (PwC, 2011), p. 4, talks of four broad segments of countries: those countries with per capita GDP of $12,000 and greater, which had countries like the US, the UK, France, Japan and others with a total population of 1 billion, another group of countries with a total population of 1 billion with a per capita GDP in the range of $12,000 and $4000, with countries like Brazil and Russia, followed by the 'next 4 billion' cluster with a population of 4 billion, including India, China and others, and the last 1 billion segment of countries with less than $1000 per capita GDP.

3. *From Middle India to the Middle Class: Inclusive Growth as a Path to Success* (2017) elaborates on the difference in middle class and Middle India, and charts a path where today's Middle India will rise to be tomorrow's middle class. The

report makes an important distinction between Middle India and middle class and gives statistics on the average per capita income of those in the Middle relative to those at the Top and the Bottom. The reference to the Top being 2.6 times higher economic status from the Middle comes from a chart on p. 10 of the report. https://www.mastercardcenter.org/content/dam/public/mc-cig/uploads/From-Middle-India-to-Middle-Class-of-India.pdf.

4. The classification of metro, Tier 1, Tier 2 and Tier 3 districts is based on a combination of size and economic status as expressed in district GDP. This is reported on the website www.jep.in and has been discussed with different experts. The exact dimensions of the Middle will be further investigated in the Middle of the Diamond Institute. This detailing takes the help of the Mastercard Report (https://www.mastercardcenter.org/content/dam/public/mc-cig/uploads/From-Middle-India-to-Middle-Class-of-India.pdf) as well as recent works such as *Winning Middle India: The Story of India's New Age Entrepreneurs* by Bala Srinivasa and T.N. Hari (Penguin, 2022).

5. Edward Humes, *Over Here: How the GI Bill Transformed the American Dream* (Harcourt Inn, 2006). The book outlined how the GI Bill was conceived by the US administration to create a positive channel for the 16 million citizens returning after the Second World War. Initially conceived as a modest bill, it got rechristened as the GI Joe bill and played a key role in transforming US economy and society after the Second World War. Quote referred from p. 55.

6. The 'soft bigotry of low expectations' was first used in a speech by George W. Bush while speaking at a NAACP, the National Association for Advancement of Colored People, in July 2000. It has been used thereafter for race and the notion that the Americans of African or Latin descent are not quite up to par when it comes to intellectual achievement. There is less of a demand or expectation for these people to achieve. Educational and social philosophy simply reinforces that stereotype, which in turn further slows their advancement.

7. *Profitable Growth Strategies for the Emerging Middle: Learning from Next 4 Billion markets* (PwC, 2011), outlines different strategies which can be employed to understand the needs of and supply goods and services to the emerging middle. There are three key areas of exploration, and the one related to value proposition outlines how the emerging middle is aspirational.

8. Tyler Cowen, *The Complacent Class: The Self-Defeating Quest for the American Dream* (St Martin's Press, 2017), outlines how prosperity has sapped the energies of those who rise, decreasing their ability to take risks and reducing the productivity of the economy as a result. While the Top of the Indian Diamond is not at the same level of absolute prosperity in purchasing power terms, and relative to the rest of the country its position can be considered like the situation described by Tyler.

9. Eric Liu, *You're More Powerful than You Think: A Citizen's Guide to Making Change* (Public Affairs New York, 2017), p. 8, makes a powerful case for community-based action. He argues that the recent success of many movements, ranging from LGBT to Arab Spring, are the product of citizens understanding their power and rising in an organized manner. His thesis of the recognition of your own power is a growing realization in Middle India.

10. Ananya Vajpeyi, *Righteous Republic: The Political Foundations of Modern India* (Harvard University Press, 2012), studies the lives of five founding fathers—Gandhi, Rabindranath and Abanindranath Tagore, Nehru and Ambedkar, to outline the core foundation of their personal philosophy as we constructed our republic. This was influenced by the deep cultural streams

of India, creating an originality in our founding philosophy. Reference the Page 47.

11. Names of Parvati and Prerna changed for confidentiality.

12. Arthur C. Brooks, *The Conservative Heart: How to Build a Fairer, Happier and More Prosperous America* (Broadside Books, 2015), describes faith, family, community and meaningful work as key tenets of a compassionate, conservative movement, which is not based on material success but founded on moral principles. P. 30 is where the book refers to these four tenets, what Brooks calls a 'happiness portfolio'.

13. Rajiv Malhotra, *Being Different: An Indian Challenge to Western Universalism* (HarperCollins Publishers India, 2011), documents the difference in Indic faiths and Judeo-Christian faiths through diagrams and illustrations. It points out that faith in Indic traditions commences from an understanding of '*Aham Brahmasmi*'—the cosmos is within yourself. This leads to a different approach to spirituality and religion relative to Judeo-Christian traditions, which start with a god in heaven and flow down from there.

14. Alvin Toffler, *The Third Wave: A Classic Study of Tomorrow* (Bantam Books, 1980), created a discussion much before the digital economy became current on what a post-industrial world would look like. The 'non-nuclear family' was a phrase that originated in this book and subsequent discourse by Tofflers, both Alvin and Heidi, to cope with a world where greater customization would lead to the uprooting of standard, impersonal societies.

15. Educate Girls, https://www.educategirls.ngo/, is a charitable organization with its head office in Mumbai, founded by Safeena Husain, working in different parts of the country to educate girls at scale. They have a system that uses local helpers from within society to identify girl students who are falling behind and seek to enrol or support them in education. Educate Girls also pioneered a development bond linked to outcomes. The quote refers to a conversation with Safeena in 2017.

16. Arthur C. Brooks, *The Conservative Heart: How to Build a Fairer, Happier and More Prosperous America*, (HarperCollins Publishers, 2015) p. 97, details earned success, where the worth of work goes much beyond poverty alleviation or economic gain. Meaningful work creates transcendental value, that fulfils the human urge for self-worth.

17. Arthur C. Brooks, *The Conservative Heart: How to Build a Fairer, Happier and More Prosperous America* (Broadside Books).

18. https://www.thehindubusinessline.com/opinion/why-agriculture-sectors-share-in-employment-is-declining-in-rural-india/article32900228.ece. Over the years, rural households' dependency on agriculture has declined to 50 per cent as per the Periodic Labour Force Survey (PLFS) for 2018–19. In addition, the agriculture sector's contribution to national GDP has declined from 34 per cent in 1983–84 to 16 per cent in 2018–19.

19. James Plunkett, *End State: 9 Ways Society Is Broken and How We Fix It* (Trapeze, 2021), p. 146. Quoting Wright, he discusses how, in a high-growth economy, those with high skills and high-paying jobs benefit and on the other extreme, low-paid jobs requiring low skills also grow, leaving the Middle to sag, with lower employment rates.

20. William Dalrymple and Anita Anand, *Kohinoor: The Story of the World's Most Infamous Diamond* (Juggernaut Books, 2016) tells the story of how the diamond was taken from India by Nader Shah in 1749, and how, after Maharaja Ranjit Singh had brought it back to Punjab, it was transferred to the British as part of the Treaty of Lahore in 1849.

Chapter 3: Youth: Our Growth Engine

1. *State of the Urban Youth, India 2012: Employment, Livelihoods, Skills,* a report published by IRIS Knowledge Foundation in collaboration with UN-HABITAT. The report traces the rise of the youth population in India. The population in the age group of fifteen to thirty-four increased from 353 million in 2001 to 430 million in 2011. Current predictions suggest a steady increase in the youth population to 464 million by 2021 and finally a decline to 458 million by 2026.
2. Somini Sengupta, *The End of Karma: Hope and Fury among India's Young* (W.W. Norton & Company, 2016), p. 20. The book explores India through the lens of young people from different backgrounds. Driven by aspiration—and thwarted by state and society—they are making new demands on India's democracy for equality of opportunity, dignity for girls and civil liberties.
3. David Brooks, *The Second Mountain: The Quest for a Moral Life* (Allen Lane, 2019), p. 58. He says, 'Our commitments allow us to move to a higher level of freedom. That's freedom from. But there is another and higher kind of freedom. You must chain yourself to a certain set of virtuous habits, so you don't become slave to your destructive desires.'
4. Tom Keller, *The Reason for God: In an Age of Scepticism* (Penguin, 2009), says, 'In many areas of life, freedom is not so much the absence of restrictions as finding the right ones, the liberating restrictions. Those that fit with the reality of our nature and the world produce greater power and scope for our abilities and a deeper joy and fulfilment.' This quote is from David Brooks' quotation, p. 58 in the book referenced earlier.
5. UN Population Division, data from 1950 to projections till 2100. Total dependency ratio is the population of the dependents, the number of people below fifteen and those above sixty-five as a ratio of those who are working, that is, people between fifteen and sixty-five. India's dependency ratio was 81 per cent in 1965. It declined to 75 per cent in 1980, to 71 per cent in 1990 and to 63 per cent in 2010 and a faster decline to 54 per cent by 2020. Some economists link this to a higher growth trajectory in that decade, although this is debatable. Today, India's dependency ratio is 49 per cent, still higher than China. It will level with China around 2030, at around 47 per cent, and will remain at 48 per cent till 2050. China, with a fast-ageing population, will shoot up to 63 per cent.
6. Total population of India in 2020 was 1.391 billion, of which those in the fifteen to twenty-nine age bracket were 27.5 per cent, based on a 2016 estimate and extrapolated to 2020. This results in a youth population of 381 million, https://en.wikipedia.org/wiki/Demographics_of_India.
7. Makarand Sahastrabudhe, *Swami Vivekanand: Hinduism, and India's Road to Modernity* (HarperCollins Publishers, 2020), where the author describes how Tesla heard Vivekananda at a lecture in New York in 1892, where he was staying. Nikola Tesla, a Hungarian-born scientist, had already made discoveries in arc lighting (1886), alternating current power system transmission (1888) and Tesla coil transformer (1891). They met for dinner at Corbins House, a mansion on Fifth Avenue, New York City, on 5 February 1892, and Tesla invited Vivekananda to visit his lab on 45 East Houston Street by letter.
8. From its soft launch in December 2015 to a full plan of its fibre network in 2019, Jio has rolled out a countrywide network in all the twenty-two circles of India. The laying out of the fibre across the country at speed, creating a new brand in the market, different from the mother brand, and then launching the service was done at a rapid speed, and created a telecom platform business

that is now one of the three dominant telecom businesses in India. https:// en.wikipedia.org/wiki/Jio.

9. Interview with Eric Wiesner, author of *The Geography of Genius: Lessons from the World's Most Creative Places*, talks of the process and the ecology that produced genius across the world and over time. These remarks are taken from his interview which is given on https://www.youtube.com/ watch?v=4dBed7Ry9Nk.

10. Ibid.

11. Sourced from https://www.archives.gov/founding-docs/declaration-transcript which gives this quotation as part of the Declaration of Independence.

12. Arthur C. Brooks, *The Conservative Heart: How to Build a Fairer, Happier and More Prosperous America* (Broadside Books, 2015), analyses the typical activities linked to happiness, such as wealth, pride and sexual activity, which have little relationship to happiness compared to earned success. He quotes Daniel Kahneman and discusses the marginal utility of wealth as it relates to happiness, with a 'hedonic treadmill' where expectations speed up almost seamlessly to match our resources.

13. Fritjof Capra, *The Hidden Connections: A Science for Sustainable Living* (Flamingo, 2003), p. 45, The book posits that in order to sustain life, the principles underlying our social institutions must be consistent with the broader organization of nature. Discussing pertinent contemporary issues ranging from the controversial practices of the World Trade Organization (WTO) to the Human Genome Project, he concludes with an authoritative, often provocative plan for designing ecologically sustainable communities and technologies as alternatives to the current economic globalization.

14. Emily Esfahani Smith, *The Power of Meaning: Crafting a Life That Matters* (2017), where the author explores how we can craft lives of meaning. Analysing psychologists, sociologists, philosophers, neuroscientists and individuals such as George Eliot, Viktor Frankl, Aristotle and the Buddha, the book shows how cultivating connections to others, identifying and working towards a purpose, telling stories about our place in the world and seeking out mystery can deepen our lives.

15. Earthrise is a photograph of Earth and some of the Moon's surface that was taken from lunar orbit by astronaut William Anders on 24 December 1968, during the Apollo 8 mission. Nature photographer Galen Rowell declared it 'the most influential environmental photograph ever taken', and it is credited with accelerating the environmental movement. https://en.wikipedia.org/wiki/ Earthrise.

16. This definition of transcendence is from the Oxford English Dictionary.

17. Dr Govindappa Venkataswamy or Dr V. founded Aravind Eye Care in 1976 at the age of fifty-eight, after retiring from government service at the mandatory retirement age. He founded the hospital in Madurai, Tamil Nadu, with his four siblings, G. Nallakrishnan, R. Janaky, G. Srinivasan and G. Natchiar, and their respective spouses, Meenakshi, R.S. Ramasamy, Lalitha S. and P. Namperumalsamy. They defined Aravind's mission—to eliminate needless blindness by providing high-quality and compassionate eye care affordable for all. https://en.wikipedia.org/wiki/Govindappa_Venkataswamy.

18. Jonathan Haidt, *The Righteous Mind: Why Good People are Divided by Politics and Religion* (Penguin, 2013), where he defines moral systems as interlocking sets of values, virtues, norms, practices, identities, institutions, technologies and evolved psychological mechanisms that work together to suppress self-interest and make cooperative societies possible. Western democratic societies, he suggests, are much more individualistic than most other cultures, where

morality focuses on protecting individuals rather than protecting groups or social order.

19. https://belurmath.org/swami-vivekananda-speeches-at-the-parliament-of-religions-chicago-1893/ where he declaimed and outlined the religion of India at the Chicago World Parliament of Religions.

20. The Bhakti movement was a significant religious movement in medieval Hinduism that sought to bring religious reforms to all strata of society by adopting the method of devotion to achieve salvation. Bhakti movement – Wikipedia, https://en.wikipedia.org/wiki/Bhakti_movement.

Chapter 4: Women: Creative Force Multipliers

1. Quote from the speech of Mahatma Gandhi at the Gujarat Political Conference in Godhara, November 1917. https://yourstory.com/herstory/2020/07/women-labour-force-it-stem.

2. *Stree Darpan* is a historic feminine Hindi magazine that focused on women's rights and was published in the pre-Independence era from 1909 to 1929 in Allahabad. It was part of India's urgent concern for recasting its own identity and historical consciousness from the early nineteenth century onwards. It sought to anchor India in its past while testing the validity of new constructs and ideologies produced by cultural and ideological encounters between India and England. Women's place in society was a key constituent of reconstructing historical consciousness and the search for a golden age.

3. Henri Nouwen, *Life of the Beloved: Spiritual Living in a Secular World* (USA: Crossroad Publishing Co., 2002), p. 72. The book asks how one can live a spiritual life in a completely secular culture. The book is a classic essay on death and how to die well. This comes directly out of Nouwen's personal experience of being with the dying and asks, 'How can my death become fruitful in the lives of others?'

4. World Bank, 'World Development Report: Gender Equality and Development', World Bank, 2012, p. 6. The report argues for better opportunities and conditions for women and girls, which can raise productivity, improve outcomes for children, make institutions more representative and advance development prospects for all. The report details big strides in narrowing gender gaps but shows that disparities remain in many areas. The worst disparity is the rate at which girls and women die relative to men in developing countries: globally, excess female mortality after birth and 'missing' girls at birth account for an estimated 3.9 million women each year in low- and middle-income countries. About two-fifths are never born due to a preference for sons, a sixth die in early childhood, and over a third die in their reproductive years.

5. Nicholas D. Kristof and Sheryl Wudunn, *Half the Sky: Turning Oppression into Opportunity for Women Worldwide* (Vintage, 2010). Through stories of women in Africa and Asia and their struggles, and drawing on a wide breadth of reporting experience, the book shows how a little help can transform the lives of women and girls globally. These stories demonstrate that the key to economic progress lies in unleashing women's potential. It posits that throughout much of the world, the greatest unexploited economic resource is the female half of the population. It outlines how countries such as China have prospered because they emancipated women and brought them into the formal economy. Unleashing that process globally is not only the right thing to do, it's also the best strategy for fighting poverty.

6. ILO Report, 'World Bank Statistics'. The Labour Force Participation Ratio (LFPR) is the number of people who are seeking jobs, over the total number

of people in the working age population. In the case of India, the women's LFPR has been falling over the past few decades. According to an ILO report of 2014, the fall in LFPR is due to four key factors. Some are positive, linked to increased attendance in education and higher household income levels, and indicate development on the whole. An ILO report also indicates that the survey methodology is likely to have contributed to the estimated decline in female participation, due to the difficulty of differentiating between domestic duties and contributing to family work. The key long-run issue is the lack of employment opportunities for India's women, owing to factors such as occupational segregation.

7. David Halpern, *Inside the Nudge Unit: How Small Changes Can Make a Big Difference* (Penguin, 2016). The author, a behavioural scientist and head of the UK government's Behavioural Insights Team, or Nudge Unit, outlines the unconventional, multi-million-pound saving initiative that makes a difference through influencing small, simple changes in our behaviour. Using the application of psychology to the challenges we face in the world today, and in particular in government, the Nudge thesis allows behavioural changes beyond legislation and process-driven action. P. 121 refers to Robert Caldini's explanation of the Big Mistake, when the pervasive use of a negative that government seeks to eliminate, itself gives it new life.

8. The 'soft bigotry of low expectations' was first used in a speech by George W. Bush while speaking at a NAACP, the National Association for Advancement of Colored People, in July 2000.

9. John Gerzman and Michael D' Antonio, *The Athena Doctrine: How Women (and the Men Who Think Like Them) Will Rule the Future* (Wiley, 2013). Through a survey of 64,000 people in thirteen nations, the authors point out that two-thirds feel the world would be a better place if men thought more like women. This is a global trend away from the winner-takes-all, masculine approach to getting things done. The authors draw from interviews at innovative organizations in eighteen nations and at Fortune 500 boardrooms, revealing how men and women alike are recognizing significant value in traits commonly associated with women, such as nurturing, cooperation, communication and sharing. The Athena Doctrine shows why femininity is the operating system of the twenty-first century, post-industrial world's prosperity.

10. Nicholas D. Kristof and Sheryl Wudunn, *Half the Sky: Turning Oppression into Opportunity for Women Worldwide* (Vintage, 2010).

11. World Bank, 'World Development Report: Gender Equality and Development', World Bank, 2012, p. 125.

12. World Bank, 'World Development Report: Gender equality and development', World Bank, 2012.

13. Sheryl Sandberg, *Lean In: Women, Work and the Will to Lead* (2013) looks at what women can do to help themselves, and make the small changes in their life that can effect change on a more universal scale. She draws on her own experiences working in some of the world's most successful businesses, as well as academic research, to find practical answers to the problems facing women in the workplace. Learning to 'lean in' is about tackling the anxieties and preconceptions that stop women from reaching the top—taking a place at the table and making yourself a part of the debate.

14. Shaheen Mistry is the founder of Teach for India, an organization focused on improving education. Madhura Chatrapati is a leader from Hyderabad who has devoted her life to strengthening women.

15. 'Women Voters in India: Changing Patterns Over The Last Decade' (womenforpolitics.com), indicates that from the 2004 elections, where the

difference in women and men voters was 8.4 per cent. It has consistently decreased to a point where it is equal to men in 2019, and this is being called a silent revolution.

16. Milan Vaishnav, https://carnegieendowment.org/2018/11/08/indian-women-are-voting-more-than-ever.-will-they-change-indian-society-pub-77677, argues that despite a skewed gender ratio of 943 per 1000 men and an ever more skewed registered voter ratio of 908 per 1000 men, the votes polled by women is now the same as that for men.

17. Harsha Singh, 'Lok Sabha Election 2019: Highest Number of Women MPs', Timesofindia.com, 1 February 2020, https://timesofindia.indiatimes.com/india/lok-sabha-elections-results-bjp-wins-first-seat-in-karnataka/articleshow/69463310.cms.

Chapter 5: Revolutions: Lessons from the Middle

1. Dr Surat Narain Mani, *A Commoner's Struggles in Life*, second edition (Pioneer Printing Press, 2013), p. 23. A book that outlines the struggles of Dr Surat Narain Mani, the grandfather of the author and an eminent educationist who was the founder of the Gorakhpur University and served as the vice chancellor of the Banaras Sanskrit University. The author traces the family history in his ancestral village of Barpar as well as memories growing up in Purvanchal, where he studied in Gorakhpur, qualified for the civil services and served in different districts of the United Provinces, becoming the first Indian district magistrate of Gorakhpur in 1952 shortly after Independence.

2. Jon Wilson, *India Conquered: Britain's Raj and the Chaos of Empire* (Simon & Schuster India, 2016) is a general history of British India which shows how British rule oscillated between paranoid paralysis and moments of extreme violence, and was beset with chaos and chronic weakness. The author argues that this contradictory character was a consequence of the Raj's failure to create long-term relationships with Indian society and that systemic problems still impact India as it navigates the twenty-first century.

3. Ibid.
4. Ibid.
5. Ibid.

6. Ravindra Rathee, *True to Their Salt: The British Indian Army and an Alternative History of Decolonization* (HarperCollins India, 2020) tells the story of how India came to be colonized by a handful of Europeans in the eighteenth century, largely based on garnering the loyalty of Indian soldiers, and how the British held sway over the country for almost two centuries, including the use of Indian soldiers in global theatres for projecting imperial power. The book details how the Bengal army was deployed in the Anglo-Afghan wars with predominantly Purabia soldiers recruited from eastern UP, Awadh and what is now Bihar. It documents how, after the 1857 War of Independence, these very soldiers were taken off the list of martial races.

7. Jon Wilson, *India Conquered: Britain's Raj and the Chaos of Empire* (Simon & Schuster India, 2016).

8. Rodrick Matthew, *A New History of British India: Peace, Poverty and Betrayal* (C. Hurst & Co., 2021). The book tells a nuanced story of 'oblige and rule', the foundation of common purpose between colonizers and powerful Indians. *Peace, Poverty and Betrayal* argues that this was more a state of being than a system: British policy was never clear or consistent; the East India Company went from a manifestly incompetent ruler to, arguably, the world's first liberal government; and among British and Indians alike, there were both progressive and conservative attitudes to colonization.

9. Roderick Matthews, *A New History of India: Peace, Poverty and Betrayal*, p. 229.
10. Ibid., p. __.
11. Angus Maddison, *Class Structure and Economic Growth: India and Pakistan since the Moghuls (Economic History)* (Routledge, 2005) analyses the social and economic structure of India and Pakistan over the past 500 years and outlines the decline in the productive capacity of India.
12. Sayyid Ahmad Khan, *The Causes of the Indian Revolt* (Benaras Medical Hall Press, 1873), as quoted by Jon Wilson in *India Conquered* as outlined above in reference number 2 in this chapter.
13. Taluqdars refers to the people who were given charge of revenue collection at the taluka level and were most prominent in the provinces of Uttar Pradesh.
14. Jon Wilson, *India Conquered: Britain's Raj and the Chaos of Empire* (Simon & Schuster India, 2016).
15. Macaulayism: Wikipedia, https://en.wikipedia.org/wiki/Macaulayism, Thomas Babington Macaulay instigated a system of education that gave primacy to English education over education in local languages. His minutes on education led to a tendency to 'marginalize inherited learning' and uproot academics from traditional Indian modes of thought, inducing in them 'a spirit of self-denigration (ISO: hīnabhāvanā)'. Macaulayism has been criticized as it uprooted Indian traditions in sectors such as finance and replaced them with a foreign system that was unsuited to India. Macaulayism caused foreign systems of thought to become prioritized over Indian systems of thought.
16. Dharampal, *The Beautiful Tree: Indigenous Indian Education in the Eighteenth Century* (Rashtrotthana Sahitya, 2021), is a book that outlines the Indian education system before a colonial education system with English as the primary language was imposed on India. *The Beautiful Tree* documents local educational traditions that were destroyed through neglect and active imposition of an education system inspired by Macaulay's minutes on education that created the primacy of English as a language of education.
17. Jon Wilson, *India Conquered: Britain's Raj and the Passions of Empire* (Simon & Schuster India, 2016).
18. Ibid.
19. Ibid.
20. This phrase comes from the excerpts of the speech that David Hume is reputed to have given as a prelude to the formation of the Indian National Congress. Read the poem by the British founder of the Congress that exhorts Indians to make their own nation—https://scroll.in/article/778465/read-the-poem-by-the-british-founder-of-the-congress-that-exhorts-indians-to-make-their-own-nation.
21. Rodrick Matthew, *A New History of British India: Peace, Poverty and Betrayal* (C. Hurst & Co. 2021), p. 309.
22. Ibid., p. 309.
23. Diane L. Eck, *India – a Sacred Geography* (Harmony, 2013). The author shares a methodology that helps imagine India before the nation-state era. Eck explores the 'prehistory' of the concept of India, tracing it back to the location of Hindu pilgrimage and spiritual practice. The author demonstrates how the imagination of India was deeply rooted in the shared meanings created by the geographical landscape, each place anchored by a myth or story, and connected in turn to another place, myth and story through travels and pilgrimage, refuting the Orientalist idea that India was a creation of the British who benevolently provided political unity to warring communities.

24. Michel Danino, *Sri Aurobindo and India's Rebirth* (Rupa Publications India, 2018) presents, through chronological excerpts from Sri Aurobindo's political writings, speeches and essays as well as conversations with and letters to followers, his opinions on Jawaharlal Nehru, Subhash Chandra Bose, Gandhi's strategy for achieving freedom through ahimsa as well as his contribution to developing the nationalist movement. Sri Aurobindo's vision of a new India combines the spiritual with the political, foretelling the issues India would face post-Independence and his confidence that India would overcome these.

25. Ravindra Rathee, *True to Their Salt: The British Indian Army and an Alternative History of Decolonization*, (HarperCollins India, 2020), p. 155.

26. Priya Satia, *Time's Monster—History, Conscience and Britain's Empire* (Allen Lane, 2020). This book recounts the conquest of India and the consolidation of imperial rule in India, the Middle East, Africa and the Caribbean through a new perspective. The book outlines how a narrative of the development of imperial governance licensed the brutal suppression of colonial rebellion. Their reimagining of empire during the two world wars compromised the force of decolonization. The book shows how many historians not only interpreted the major political events of their time but also shaped the future that followed.

27. Isabel Wilkerson, *Caste: The Lies that Divide Us* (Penguin, 2020) explores the relation of caste and race both in North America and in India. It outlines the society-wide system of social stratification characterized by notions such as hierarchy, inclusion and exclusion, and purity. The author does so by comparing aspects of the experience of American people of colour to the caste systems of India. P. (6).

28. Vijay Joshi, *India's Long Road: The Search for Prosperity* (Allen Lane, 2016), p. 226. The book lays out a penetrating analysis of the country's recent faltering performance, set against the backdrop of its political economy, and charts the course it should follow to achieve widely shared prosperity. The author argues that for India to realize its huge potential, the relation among the state, the market and the private sector must be comprehensively realigned. Deeper liberalization is very necessary but far from sufficient. The state needs to perform much more effectively many core tasks that belong squarely in its domain: 'The decentralizing intentions of the constitutional amendments have been neutered by state governments.'

29. Pankaj Mishra, *From the Ruins of the Empire: The Revolt Against the West and the Remaking of Asia* (Penguin UK, 2013), p. 254. The book is organized as a collection of intellectual biographies of early Asian critics who discuss the best ways to counteract the violent invasion and disruption caused by the arrival of European nations into Asian politics and culture. It traces the first intellectual push-back to colonialism by thinkers in India, China, Japan and Afghanistan.

Chapter 6: Democracy: Two Nations at Seventy-Five

1. While the Declaration of Independence was written in 1776, it was only in 1781 that independence was gained, and the constitution was written over the subsequent three years, being adopted by all the thirteen states in 1787.

2. James Surowiecki, *The Wisdom of Crowds* (Anchor, 2005) explores the premise that large groups of people are smarter than an elite few. They are more adept at problem-solving, promoting creativity, making prudent judgements and even foreseeing the future. The book explores a wide range of topics, including psychology, ant biology, behavioural economics, artificial intelligence, military history and politics to demonstrate how this concept can teach us valuable

lessons about how to live our lives, choose our leaders, manage our businesses and view the world.

3. Eric Cowan and Lennis G. Echterling, *Nature's Sage: The Influence of Sacred Indian Literature in Henry David Thoreau's Walden* (Journal of East West Thought, 2017). The book examines the close connection between the individual and environment, the embeddedness of self-experience and a capacity for participation, with a profound influence on generations of Americans. Ancient Indian literature, such as the Bhagavad Gita and the Upanishads, had a significant impact on Thoreau's writing. The work examines how Eastern philosophy influenced Thoreau's thinking and his perception of nature, and draws conclusions about how to apply these Eastern viewpoints to experiencing nature.

4. Ross Baird, *The Innovation Blindspot: Why We Back the Wrong Ideas and What to Do about It* (BenBella Books, 2017). The book argues that while big companies in the American economy have never been more successful, entrepreneurial activity is at a nearly thirty-year low. More businesses are dying than starting every day. Investors continue to dump billions of dollars into photo-sharing apps and food delivery services, solving problems for only a wealthy sliver of the world's population, while challenges in health, food, security and education grow more serious. It says a handful of people in a handful of cities are deciding, behind closed doors, which entrepreneurs get a shot to succeed. The resulting system creates rising income inequality, stifled entrepreneurial ambition, social distrust and political uncertainty.

5. Ron Chernov, *Washington: A Life* (Penguin, 2011) describes Washington's troubled boyhood, his precocious feats in the French and Indian wars, his creation of Mount Vernon, his heroic exploits with the Continental Army, his presiding over the Constitutional Convention and his magnificent performance as America's first president.

6. John Meacham, *Thomas Jefferson: The Art of Power* (Random House, 2013) brings to life Thomas Jefferson, giving an account of Jefferson the politician and president, a great and complex human being forever engaged in the wars of his era. Philosophers think, politicians manoeuvre. Jefferson's genius was that he was both and could do both, often simultaneously.

7. Paul Johnson, *A History of the American People* (Weidenfeld & Nicholson, 1997), p. 7. The book presents an in-depth portrait of American history from the first colonial settlements to the Clinton administration. The book brings out the story of the men and women who shaped and led the nation and the ordinary people who collectively created its unique character. Filled with letters, diaries and recorded conversations, it details the origins of their struggles for independence and nationhood, and with the 'organic sin' of slavery and the preservation of the Union to its explosive economic growth and emergence as a world power.

8. Ibid.

9. Source: https://www.archives.gov/founding-docs/declaration-transcript

10. Source: https://www.archives.gov/founding-docs/declaration-transcript, Ibid.

11. Jon Wilson, *India Conquered: Britain's Raj and the Chaos of Empire* (Simon & Schuster India, 2016).

12. Deepak Gupta, *The Steel Frame: A History of the IAS* (Roli Books). The author examines developments from history, its present status and the future of the IAS in a well-researched and detailed work. Even though a lot has changed, the Indian Administrative Service still possesses some fundamental traits from the past. Additionally, he makes recommendations for how it may reinvent itself to fulfil the significant function that our Constitution's framers had in mind.

13. Tripurdaman Singh, *Sixteen Stormy Days: The Story of the First Amendment of the Constitution of India* (Vintage Books, 2020). One of the key moments in Indian political and constitutional history as well as the site of its first significant intellectual conflict, *Sixteen Stormy Days* tells the tale of the First Amendment to the Constitution of India. The First Amendment severely limited freedom of speech and describes a harried Nehru wanting to assert control through the government, limiting the rights of citizens that had recently been agreed to by the Constituent Assembly.

14. Andrew Jackson | *Facts, Biography and Accomplishments* | Britannica, outlines how, after a distinguished career on the frontier, Andrew Jackson, won the highest number of votes at 100, with John Quincy Adams at eighty-seven votes and Henry Clay at thirty-seven votes. Clay as the speaker of the house gave Adams his support, and in the bargain got appointed the secretary of state, confirming what most thought was a corrupt bargain.

15. John Meacham, *American Lions: Andrew Jackson in the White House* (Random House, 2009) describes a man who rose from nothing to create the modern presidency. Beloved and hated, venerated and reviled, Andrew Jackson was an orphan who fought his way to the pinnacle of power, bending the nation to his will in the cause of democracy. Jackson's election in 1828 ushered in a new and lasting era in which the people, not distant elites, were the guiding force in American politics.

16. Paul Johnson, *A History of the American People* (HarperCollins, first published in 1997).

17. Ibid., outlines how 'slave ownership betokens not only the possession of wealth, but indicates a gentleman of leisure', p. 441.

18. George Friedman, *The Storm Before the Calm: America's Discord, the Crisis of the 2020s and the Triumph Beyond* (Anchor Books, 2020) focuses on the United States, predicting how the 2020s will bring dramatic upheaval and reshaping of American government, foreign policy, economics and culture. In his riveting book, examining the clear cycles through which the United States has developed, heaved, matured and solidified, Friedman breaks down the coming years and decades in cycles—particularly a seventy-eight-year 'institutional cycle' that has defined it (there are three such examples—the Revolutionary War/founding, the Civil War and World War II).

Chapter 7: Culture: Inner Resource of National Strength

1. Paul Lienwand and Cesare Maindari, *Strategy that Works: How Winning Companies Close the Strategy to Execution Gap* (Harvard Business School Publishing, 2016) explains why companies lack the resources necessary to implement their strategies. They pinpoint established company procedures that unintentionally cause a disconnect between strategy and implementation. They also argue that changing culture is difficult and can only be done over time. Using culture to drive strategy is a key recommendation of the book. P. 120.

2. Tansen Sen, *India, China and the World: A Connected History* (Rowman and Littlefield, 2017), provides a comprehensive examination of India–China interactions in the broader contexts of Asian and world history. By focusing on material exchanges, transmissions of knowledge and technologies, networks of exchange during the colonial period, and interactions between the Republic of India and the People's Republic of China, the book argues that the analysis of India–China connections must extend beyond the traditional frameworks of nation-states or bilateralism.

3. T.N. Ninan, *Turn of the Tortoise: The Challenge and Promise of India's Future* (Oxford University Press, 2017). The paradox of a 'premature superpower' is explored by the author as Martin Wolf once described India in the *Financial Times*. Although fundamentally different from China and overshadowed by it in the struggle for influence in a region that extends from Asia to Africa, the author evaluates India's position as a natural counterweight to that of China and outlines the possibility of it overtaking the Chinese Hare.
4. Isaac Stone Fish, *America 2nd: How America's Elites Are Making China Stronger* (Scribe Publications, 2022). The book charts the emergence of the Chinese influence on America. It demonstrates how American policymakers first embraced China's involvement in the American economy in the hope that it would result in a more democratic China. It demonstrates that despite this not happening, America has become reliant on China to the extent of not questioning it. Beijing's influence has been through influential individuals such as Disney CEO Bob Iger, past Secretary of State Henry Kissinger, Madeleine Albright and Bush family members. The 3Ts are mentioned on page 138 as a hidden code of self-censorship in China.
5. 'China's Communist Party Hails President Xi as "Helmsman"', 12 November 2021, https://www.reuters.com/world/china/president-xi-is-helmsman-chinas-rejuvenation-says-party-official-2021-11-12/.
6. https://journals.sagepub.com/doi/pdf/10.1177/0956247813501139, cites that in September 2004, the Beijing municipal government decided to carry out 'environmental improvement' projects in 231 Village-in-City or VICs accommodating 33,935 households, aiming to complete these projects in 171 VICs before the 2008 Olympic Games. The projects were overseen by a municipal organization, the 2008 Environmental Construction Head Office, set up in December 2005, working with other district governments. It was estimated that the demolition of 171 VICs led to the eviction of about 74,100 permanent village residents.
7. Fritjof Capra, *Uncommon Wisdom: Conversations with Remarkable People* (Simon & Schuster, 1988), p. 35. The book outlines the connections between contemporary physics and Eastern mysticism and gives a systems perspective that encompasses ecology and spiritual awareness. The author's conversations with philosopher Jiddu Krishnamurthy, physicists Werner Heisenberg and Geoffrey Chew, psychologists Stanislav Grof and R.D. Laing, economists Hazel Henderson and E.F. Schumacher, as well as figures such as systems theorist Gregory Bateson, cancer therapist Carl Simonton and feminist Charlene Spretnak, are the basis of his insights.
8. Francis Fukuyama, *The Origins of Political Order* (Profile Books Ltd., 2012). The book investigates the routes used by various societies to arrive at their contemporary political order. It investigates economics, anthropology and geography, beginning with the origins of humanity and ending before the French and American Revolutions. The book is a classic study on how humanity became politically alive. P. 121.
9. Ibid.
10. Ibid., p. 161.
11. Ibid.
12. Will Durant, *The Story of Civilization: Our Oriental Heritage* (Simon and Schuster, 1935). A historical and philosophical classic, the book examines the history of civilization through a broad overview of the Orient: the Egyptians, who perfected monumental architecture, medicine and mummification; the Babylonians, who made advancements in astronomy and physics; the Judeans, whose culture was preserved in the timeless books of the Old

Testament; and the Persians, who ruled the largest empire in recorded history prior to Rome.

13. Parag Khanna, *The Future is Asian: Commerce, Conflict and Culture in the 21st Century* (Simon & Schuster, 2019). The book argues that Asia is maturing, spurred on by pride in the continent's history and its intrinsic diversity. It explores the long history of Asia's vibrant patterns of trade and culture, as well as the rediscovery of those linkages in the post-Cold War era, and presents intriguing theories on the possibility of an 'Asianization' of the international system. He claimed that Asia provides a perfect counterbalance to the West's waning predominance.

14. Jessica Chen Weiss, *A World Safe for Autocracy: China's Rise and Future of Global Politics* (Foreign Affairs, 2019). The book illustrates the domestic-international linkages in Beijing's approach to issues ranging from sovereignty and homeland disputes to climate change and COVID-19, in order to highlight this variation and prospects for conflict and cooperation. The author proposes that Beijing's foreign policy preferences and actions across issue areas are influenced by domestic politics and through this lens, one can understand the approach China takes to international issues.

15. Duane W. Roller, Eratosthenes' Geography Fragments collected and translated, with commentary and additional material, Princeton University Press, Princeton and Oxford, p. 82, 70 (IIIB8). Pliny, Natural History 6.56 . . . the Hemodi [Emodos] Mountains rise up, and the Indian peoples begin, who not only live near the Eastern Ocean but also the Southern, which we call the Indian. The part facing the east extends in a straight line to a bend, and at the beginning of the Indian Ocean it totals 1875 miles, and from there to where it bends to the south is 2475 miles up to the Indos River, which is the western border of India, as Eratosthenes records.

16. Fritjof Capra, *The Hidden Connections: A Science of Sustainable Living* (Flamingo, 2003).

17. Ibid., p. 30.

18. Ibid., p. 59

19. S.N. Balagangadhara, *What Does It Mean to Be 'Indian'?* (Notion Press, 2021). The book presents the findings of forty years of scholarly research in the field of comparative science of cultures. By examining ideas about people, society, culture, experience, the past, the effects of colonialism, etc., the book seeks to transcend the political division between 'the right' and 'the left'. It brings out the challenges of interpreting our world view, where a cultural perspective plays a key role, differentiating the interpretation of various fields of science and arts given the differing cultural positions of the West and India.

20. Will Durant, *The Story of Civilization: Our Oriental Heritage* (Simon and Schuster, 1935), p. 2.

21. Richard Lannoy, *The Speaking Tree: A Study of Indian Culture and Society* (Oxford University Press, 1971). The book seeks to uncover the underlying culture of India. It does this by providing an in-depth analysis of Indian culture and society. The non-technical and philosophical examination of Indian philosophy, values and aspirations is brought out in the book with the idea of identifying various issues prevalent and a deep examination of the Indian cultural milieu.

22. Alvin Toffler, *The Third Wave: A Classic Study of Tomorrow* (Bantam Books, 1980).

23. List of cities in India by population—Wikipedia. https://en.wikipedia.org/wiki/List_of_cities_in_India_by_population.

24. Ashutosh Varshney, *Battles Half Won: India's Improbable Democracy* (Penguin, 2014) analyses the deepening of Indian democracy since 1947 and the challenges this has created. It examines concerns ranging from federalism to caste conflict and civil society, the north-south economic divide and the politics of economic reforms. It portrays the successes and failures of our experience in a new comparative perspective, enriching our understanding of the idea of democracy. He relates the rise of enterprise in the south to an early start made in the south to lower caste differences and the surge of the backward castes.

25. Richard Lannoy, *The Speaking Tree: A Study of Indian Culture and Society* (Oxford University Press, 1971).

26. Pavan K. Varma, *The Great Hindu Civilization: Achievement, Neglect, Bias and Way Forward* (Westland Publication, 2021), p. 3. The book argues, 'The Bhakti movement was Hinduism's response to the violent and proselytizing Islamic invasion. If Hinduism had not shown the suppleness and energy to reinvent itself, and had remained brittle and fossilized, without the mass support enabled by the Bhakti movement, it may have suffered the same fate that befell it (and Buddhism) in Indonesia with the advent of Islam.'

27. Vanita Viswanath, '*Indian Culture and Traditions: "Circles of Trust" for Next Gen Aspirations*' (2019). The paper explores circles of trust that define how most of rural India interprets its societal relationships. These circles often encompass family as well as local communities. These trusted relationships are not ordained by law, but through family, community and often through faith.

28. National Geographic Society and GlobeScan, '*Greendex™ 2009: Consumer Choice and the Environment—A Worldwide Tracking Survey*', a comprehensive measure of consumer behaviour in sixty-five areas relating to housing, transportation, food and consumer goods. Greendex 2009 ranks average consumers in seventeen countries according to the environmental impact of their discretionary and non-discretionary consumption patterns, where India was the number one country.

29. Richard Evans, *Deng Xiaoping and the Making of Modern China* (Penguin, 1997). A major study of the life of Deng Xiaoping, a revolutionary and one of the most influential figures of the twentieth century, who shaped China and its place in the modern world. It gives details of how Deng was a key player in the long March with Mao, and how his fall from grace and then his rejuvenation created space for modern China to emerge as an economic superpower.

30. Jeremy Lent, *The Patterning Instinct: A Cultural History of Humanity's Search for Meaning*, p. 170.

31. John Dewey, *Democracy and Education* (first published 1917) addresses the challenge of providing quality public education in a democratic society. The approach calls for a renewal of public education, arguing for the fusion of vocational and contemplative studies in education and for the necessity of universal education for the advancement of self and society. First published in 1916, *Democracy and Education* is regarded as the seminal work on public education by one of the most important scholars of the century.

32. Diane L. Eck, *India: A Sacred Geography* (Harmony, 2013), p. 6. The book describes the sacred geography of India and the passage of pilgrims from one end to the other as a defining feature of Indian civilization.

Chapter 8: Udyamita: New Thinking, New Building

1. Amitav Ghosh, *The Nutmeg's Curse: Parables for a Planet in Crisis* (University of Chicago Press, 2021). The book examines the roots of our current planetary

predicament, tracing it back to the extractive and colonizing philosophy of the West. It suggests that the dynamics of today's climate change are a result of a long-standing geopolitical structures created by Western colonialism. The now-common spice nutmeg lies at the heart of Ghosh's story, where he seeks a new alternative through the philosophies that are non-extractive and those that respect nature.

2. Jon Wilson, *India Conquered: Britain's Raj and the Chaos of Empire* (Simon & Schuster India, 2016).

3. Ibid.

4. Ibid.

5. Angus Maddison, *Class Structure and Economic Growth: India and Pakistan Since the Moghuls* (Routledge, 2005).

6. Ibid.

7. Philip Mason, *Matter of Honour—An Account of the Indian Army, its Officers and Men* (Penguin, 1977) is about Indian soldiers and about certain virtues— loyalty to comrades, fidelity to an oath, courage under stress. Without virtues, an army is nothing. The book provides an understanding of the individual psychology of the soldier and how, despite weapons, equipment and training, it is personal honour and integrity that emerge as the most important assets of an army. Mason looks into history—the Indian Army's role during the two world wars, the birth of the Indian Army and studies it as it finds its identity. P. 242.

8. Angus Maddison, *Class Structure and Economic Growth: India and Pakistan Since the Moghuls* (Routledge, 2005).

9. Ibid.

10. Sumit Kumar Majumdar, *Lost Glory: India's Capitalism Story* (Oxford University Press, 2020, p. 65) deconstructs India's industrialization story based on careful and detailed empirical analyses of India's industrialization over a period of almost seven decades. The book provides a deeply nuanced account of the history of political economy that has affected India's industrialization, based on evidence-based surveys of India's industrial landscape. It includes a detailed historical description of the intellectual origins of India's modern industrialization, anchored in a privileged view of economic policymaking. Molecular economy is described as 'an alternate model of economic life, embodying ancient moral glory, could be found in India's thousands of villages'.

11. Ibid.

12. *Full Potential Revival and Growth: Charting India's Medium Term Journey'* (PwC, 2020) is a publication that sought to explore the possibilities of India's economic recovery after COVID-19. It investigated ten key sectors that comprise 75 per cent of the Indian GDP and highlighted a medium-term recovery strategy. One of the key findings was that COVID-19 revealed frictions in the Indian economy, which could be overcome by a whole-of-nation approach so that a bigger economic bounce-back can be achieved by deepening and widening the economy post-COVID.

13. *'Future of India—the Winning Leap: Breaking New Ground by Deploying Solutions for Rapid, Sustainable, and Resource Efficient Growth'*, PwC, 2014, is a report that seeks to create a strategic view of India's growth story by asking the question: What would it take to create growth and improve the Human Development Index significantly? The name comes from the findings that a linear approach to this growth will not succeed, it is only through creating new solutions that India will be able to achieve such targets in a resource efficient way.

14. Ibid.

15. https://en.wikipedia.org/wiki/Income_inequality_in_India. While it is difficult to measure inequality in India due to the sketchy data on income tax, IMF, in

a report in 2016, calculated that the Gini coefficient rose from 0.45 (1990) to 0.51 (2013). N.C. Saxena of the National Advisory Board attributed this to the lower economic possibilities of rural areas. Rural employment schemes were not reputed to be working while urban areas, well-connected to global markets, grew rapidly in that duration.

16. Adam Smith, *The Wealth of Nations*, (London, 1776). This classic book outlines the principle of free trade. It gives an insight into the creation of a nation's wealth while examining concepts such as division of labour, the origin and use of money, the division of stock, the rise and progress of cities and towns after the fall of the Roman Empire, the systems of political economy and the taxes on various private revenues.

17. Kevin Kelly, *The Inevitable: Understanding the 10 Technological Forces That Will Shape Our Future* (Penguin, 2017, p. 123) provides an optimistic road map for the future, showing how the coming changes in our lives from virtual reality in the home to an on-demand economy to artificial intelligence embedded in everything we manufacture can be understood as the result of a few long-term, accelerating forces. Kelly both describes these deep trends—flowing, screening, accessing, sharing, filtering, remixing, tracking and questioning—and demonstrates how they overlap and are co-dependent on one another.

18. World Bank paper, '*Entrepreneurship and Firm Foundation across Countries*' (2007), Policy Research Working Paper 4313, Klapper, Amit, Geullian, and Quesada, gives this definition. The paper is a study of entrepreneurship across nations and therefore seeks a common definition to measure this across countries and markets. P. 3.

19. Ibid. Klapper, Amit, Geullian, and Quesada cite Gough 1969 giving this definition. P. 3.

20. Josh Lerner and Antoinette Schoar, *International Differences in Entrepreneurship* (University of Chicago Press, 2010) explains how a country's institutional differences, cultural considerations and personal characteristics can affect the role an entrepreneur plays in its economy. It outlines the origins of entrepreneurs as well as the choices they make. In addition, the book outlines how environmental factors of individual economies, such as market regulation, government subsidies for banks and support for entrepreneurial culture, affect the industry and the impact such enterprise can have on growth in developing nations.

21. Alain De Botton, *The Architecture of Happiness* (Vintage Books, 2006). This delightful book explores the appreciation of architecture through a philosophical examination of houses. The book asks and tries to answer basic questions of aesthetics—what makes a house truly beautiful? Why are many new houses so ugly? Why do we argue so bitterly about sofas and pictures—and can differences of taste ever be satisfactorily resolved? He also details how western Europe started its industrial journey by designing and manufacturing elite goods (fripperies) that were for the pleasure of the few.

22. Ludwig Erhard, *Prosperity through Competition* (Fredrick A. Prager, 1958). The book lays down the economic thrust of the author's economic thinking, which refers to bridging the gap between unbridled liberalism and soulless state control. He also focused on supporting the medium-sized companies in Germany which strengthened what became the spine of the German economy, the Mittlestadt.

23. Silvia M. Lindtner, *Prototype Nation: China and the Contested Promise of Innovation* (Princeton University Press, 2020), is an examination of China's shifting place in the global political economy of technology production and its growth of mass manufacturing and 'copycat' production in the global tech imagination. The book offers a transnational analysis of how the promise

of democratized innovation and entrepreneurial life has shaped China's governance and global image.

24. Peter Thiel, *Zero to One: Notes on Startups and How to Build the Future* (Random House, 2014) focuses on building a valuable company that others are not building. He focuses on creating new ideas by developing a 'moat' that resembles a monopoly. He asserts that doing what we already know how to do takes the world from 1 to n, adding more of something familiar. Every new creation goes from 0 to 1, and he focuses on that. This book has become a must-read for those pursuing the unicorn dream.

25. Josh Lerner and Antoinette Schoar, *International Differences in Entrepreneurship* (University of Chicago Press, 2010), p. 2, see above.

26. Swavalambi Bharat Abhiyan is a national movement initiated by collaborators within the RSS fraternity to create district level enterprise and employment centres that can create a strong nation. www.swavalambi.in.

27. Township and Village Enterprises—Wikipedia, outlines how the complexity of this arrangement led to the labelling of collective (township and village) TVE property rights as 'fuzzy'. This lack of a true system of property rights collapsed in a short amount of time, as townships and villages expropriated the use rights using their ownership rights. TVEs thrived from 1978 to 1989, and were largely dismantled between 1989 and 1996. https://en.wikipedia.org/wiki/Township_and_Village_Enterprises.

28. Hernando De Soto, *The Mystery of Capital: Why Capitalism Triumphs in the West and Fails Everywhere Else* (Basic Books, 2003) takes up one of the most pressing questions the world faces today: why do some countries succeed at capitalism while others fail? It posits that success is determined by cultural and legal structure of property and property rights. These rights are ill-defined in developing nations, which lowers the deployment of such capital and diminishes development.

29. Clayton M. Christensen, *The Prosperity Paradox: How Innovation Can Lift Nations out of Poverty* (Harper Business, 2019). The book highlights the shortcomings of typical top-down approaches to economic development and proposes a new paradigm for economic growth based on entrepreneurialism and market-creating innovation. Ford, Eastman Kodak, Singer Sewing Machines and Toyota are just a few of the successful examples Christensen, Ojomo, and Dillon utilize to demonstrate how successful comparable models have performed in other regions, including Japan, South Korea, Nigeria, Rwanda, India, Argentina and Mexico.

30. Rama Bijapurkar, *A Never-Before World: Tracking the Evolution of Consumer India* (Portfolio, 2014) analyses India's consumer economy—demand structure, supply environment, income demographics, social and cultural changes and much more—and pinpoints the existing opportunities, the unserved needs, the incorrect assumptions and the strategic imperatives that can better serve these markets. P. 140.

31. '*Future of India—the Winning Leap: Breaking New Ground by Deploying Solutions for Rapid, Sustainable, and Resource Efficient Growth*', PwC, 2014.

32. Thomas L. Friedman, *Thank You for Being Late: An Optimist's Guide to Thriving in the Age of Accelerations* (Farrar, Straus and Giroux, 2016) documents the tectonic shifts that that are reshaping the world today and explains how to get the most out of them and cushion their worst impacts. It includes analyses of how to understand the news, the work you do, the education your kids need, the investments your employer has to make, and the moral and geopolitical choices that a country has to face in this new world.

33. James Manyika, Susan Lund, Jacques Bughin, Jonathan Woetzel, Kalin Stamenov and Dhruv Dhingra, *'Digital Globalization: The New Era of Global Flows'*, McKinsey, 24 February 2016, highlights how the digital economy and its flows, non-existent only twenty years ago, now exert a larger impact on GDP growth than the centuries-old trade in traditional goods. Through this shift, it is possible for international companies to reach markets faster and with less asset-intensive models than before.

34. Yuen Yuen Ang, *China's Gilded Age: The Paradox of Economic Boom and Vast Corruption* (Cambridge, 2020), argues that not all types of corruption hurt growth, nor do they cause the same kind of harm. The book unbundles corruption into four varieties: petty theft, grand theft, speed money and access money. While the first three types impede growth, access money—elite exchanges of power and profit—cuts both ways: it stimulates investment and growth but produces serious risks for the economy and political system.

35. Dan Senor and Paul Singer, *Startup Nation: The Story of Israel's Economic Miracle* (Twelve, 2011). The book outlines how it is that Israel—a country of 7.1 million, only sixty years old, surrounded by enemies, in a constant state of war since its founding, with no natural resources—produces more start-up companies than large, peaceful and stable nations such as Japan, China, India, Korea, Canada and the UK. It talks of a culture of enterprise that has been created by the country to stimulate enterprise. P. 37.

36. Ibid.

37. https://niti.gov.in/sites/default/files/2021-01/IndiaInnovationReport2020Book.pdf, which describes the innovation ranking, where globally India is now in the top fifty nations, as well as regional innovation assessment, although, as a percentage of GDP, the amount of spend on R&D remains small.

Chapter 9: Citizen: Our Protagonist for the Middle

1. Alex Tocqueville, *Democracy in America* (University of Chicago Press, first published 1835). The author (1805–59) came to America in 1831 to see what a great republic was like. What struck him most was the country's equality of conditions, its democracy. The book he wrote on his return to France, *Democracy in America*, is considered one of the best written books on democracy and describes American life then.

2. UK Population Estimates 1851 to 2014, Office for National Statistics (ons.gov.uk).

3. These numbers have been arrived at by dividing the number of citizens by the number of MPs and the number of citizens by the total number of districts.

4. Samuel P. Huntington, *Political Order in Changing Societies (The Henry L. Stimson Lectures)* (Yale University Press, 2006). The book is an examination of the development of viable political institutions in emerging nations and is considered a significant contribution to modern political analysis. It examines the relationship between development and stability and sheds light on the comparative politics of nations.

5. Ibid.

6. Niall Ferguson, *The Square and the Tower: Networks, Hierarchies and the Struggle for Global Power* (Penguin, 2018). The book argues that while the twenty-first century has been hailed as the Age of Networks, networks have always been with us, from the structure of the brain to the food chain, from the family tree to freemasonry. Throughout history, hierarchies housed in high towers have claimed to rule, but often, real power has resided in the networks

in the town square below, for it is networks that tend to innovate and it is through networks that revolutionary ideas can spread.

7. Thomas Piketty, *Capital in the Twenty-First Century* (Harvard University Press, 2017). His research team amassed a mountain of data, much of it going back centuries, suggesting that the concentration of wealth in ever fewer hands is not an anomaly or a recent development. Without a significant force to counterbalance rising wealth inequality, the research indicates, a capitalist economy will drift predictably toward oligarchy. The book argues this case with charts and graphs but does so with great ease and facility. P. 490.

8. Ibid., p. 98, where Margaret Thatcher in Britain and Ronald Regan in the US promised to 'roll back the welfare state' that had allegedly sapped the animal spirits of Anglo-Saxon entrepreneurs.

9. Ibid., p. 491.

10. Thomas Malvern, *Inside the Nudge Unit: How Small Changes Can Make a Big Difference* (WH Allen, 2016).

11. Jamie Susskind, *Future Politics: Living Together in a World Transformed by Tech* (Oxford University Press, 2018). The book examines the emerging dilemmas in politics driven by digital power. Previously, politics was animated by this question: How much of our collective life should be determined by the state, and what should be left to the market and civil society? The book argues that the debate today is different: To what extent should our lives be directed and controlled by powerful digital systems—and on what terms? Digital technologies—from artificial intelligence to blockchain, from robotics to virtual reality—are transforming the way we live together. Those who control the most powerful technologies are increasingly able to control the rest of us.

12. Thomas L. Friedman, *Thank You for Being Late: An Optimist's Guide to Thriving in the Age of Accelerations* (Farrar, Straus and Giroux, 2016).

13. Thomas W. Malone, *Superminds: The Surprising Power of People and Computers Thinking Together* (Little, Brown Spark, 2018). The author, the founding director of the MIT Center for Collective Intelligence, shows how groups of people working together in superminds—such as hierarchies, markets, democracies and communities—have been responsible for almost all human achievements in business, government, science and beyond. And these collectively intelligent human groups are about to get much smarter. Using examples and case studies, the book shows how computers can help create more intelligent superminds simply by connecting humans to one another in a variety of new ways.

14. Ibid., p. 15.

15. Jonathan Haidt, *The Righteous Mind: Why Good People are Divided by Politics and Religion* (Penguin UK, 2013, p. 113.

16. Ibid., p. 116.

17. Ibid., p. 117.

18. Ferdinand Tonnies, *Gemeinschaft to Gesellschaft, German Sociologies*, July 1855–April 1936. The book outlines a dichotomy where social ties can be categorized, on one hand, as belonging to personal social interactions, and the roles, values and beliefs based on such interactions, *Gemeinschaft*, are commonly translated as 'community', where social ties can belong to indirect interactions, impersonal roles, formal values, and beliefs based on such interactions, *Gesellschaft*, commonly translated as 'society' as in association, corporation, including company, modern state and academia.

19. Francis Fukuyama, *Political Order and Political Decay* (Hachette Book Group USA, 2016), takes up the question of how societies develop strong, impersonal and

accountable political institutions. The book starts from the French Revolution, comes eventually to the so-called Arab Spring and goes to contemporary American politics. The book examines the effects of corruption on governance and why some societies have been successful at rooting it out. It explores the different legacies of colonialism in Latin America, Africa and Asia and offers insights into why some regions have thrived and developed more quickly than others.

20. Ibid.
21. David Brooks, *The Second Mountain: The Quest for a Moral Life* (Random House Large Print, 2019), p. 287. The book details what happens when a person climbs the pinnacle of success and realizes that there are bigger challenges to conquer. They discover another, bigger mountain out there and embark on a new journey. On the second mountain, life moves from self-centred to other-centred. They want the things that are truly worth wanting, not the things other people tell them to want. They embrace a life of interdependence, not independence. They surrender to a life of commitment. P. 287, quoting Jonathan Sacks in 'The Home we Build Together'.
22. Samuel P. Huntington, *Political Order in Changing Societies (The Henry L. Stimson Lectures)* (Yale University Press, 2006).
23. Deendayal Upadhyaya, *Integral Humanism—An Analysis of Some Basic Elements* (Prabhat Prakashan, 2020), p. 48. In this book, the author outlines how Indian socio-political structures are informed by *Bharatiya sanskriti* and created the concept of *Chitti*, writing that 'Society is not just a conglomeration of individuals, it is a living entity by itself.'
24. Deoria in this book refers to the Deoria parliamentary constituency which has three Vidhan Sabhas in Deoria administrative district and two Vidhan Sabhas in Kushinagar administrative district. Deoria administrative district has seven Vidhan Sabha constituencies, some of which are in Salempur and Bansagaon.
25. The per capita income of Uttar Pradesh in 2019 was $909. Research in 2011 shows that the per capita income of Purvanchal was around three-fifths of the average GDP of Uttar Pradesh. https://timesofindia.indiatimes.com/india/What-will-happen-if-Uttar-Pradesh-is-split-into-four-parts/articleshow/10776028.cms.
26. Brief Industrial Profile of Deoria District, MSME Institute, 2016. The report analyses different economic activities in the district of Deoria and was authored in 2016 by the MSME Institute. The quote is from the export section 3.3.
27. Jon Wilson, *India Conquered: Britain's Raj and the Chaos of Empire* (Simon & Schuster India, 2016).
28. Ibid.
29. Ibid.
30. Ibid.
31. Shashi Tharoor, *An Era of Darkness: The British Empire in India* (Aleph Book Company, 2016). The book reveals how disastrous British rule was for India. Besides examining the many ways in which the colonizers exploited India, ranging from the drain of national resources to Britain, the destruction of the Indian textile, steel-making and shipping industries to the negative transformation of agriculture, he demolishes the arguments of Western and Indian apologists for the Empire on the supposed benefits of British rule, including democracy and political freedom, the rule of law and the railways.
32. Jon Wilson, *India Conquered: Britain's Raj and the Chaos of Empire* (Simon & Schuster India, 2016).
33. Ibid.
34. Ibid.
35. Ibid.

36. David Brooks, *The Second Mountain: The Quest for a Moral Life* (Random House Large Print, 2019), p. 267.
37. Armin Ishkanian and Simon Szreter, *The Big Society Debate: A New Agenda for Social Welfare?* (Edward Elgar Pub, July 2013). David Cameron placed the 'Big Society' at the heart of his efforts to rebuild Britain's 'broken society'. The essays in this volume probe the historical origins of the concept and seek to evaluate it in the light of both historical and contemporary evidence. The 'Big Society' is relevant as it neither believes in state-led development nor in the dominance of the private sector. Instead, it seeks to harness energies of local citizens and their efforts in development.
38. David Brooks, *The Second Mountain: The Quest for a Moral Life* (Random House Large Print, 2019), p. 273.
39. Ibid.
40. Jonathan Haidt, *The Righteous Mind: Why Good People are Divided by Politics and Religion* (Penguin UK, 2013), p. 80.
41. Panchayati raj in India – Wikipedia. https://en.wikipedia.org/wiki/Panchayati_raj_in_India.

Chapter 11: Digital: Human Networks in the Middle

1. CERN stands for the European Organization for Nuclear Research, known as CERN (French acronym) that operates the largest particle physics laboratory in the world. Tim Berners-Lee, a British scientist, invented the World Wide Web (WWW) in 1989 while working at CERN. The web was originally conceived and developed to meet the demand for automated information-sharing between scientists in universities and institutes around the world. The first website at CERN—and in the world—was dedicated to the World Wide Web project itself and was hosted on Berners-Lee's NeXT computer. On 30 April 1993, CERN put the World Wide Web software in the public domain. Later, CERN made a release available with an open licence that led to its dissemination and the web to flourish.
2. https://www.businesstoday.in/technology/story/india-to-have-1-bn-smartphone-users-by-2026-deloitte-study-323519-2022-02-22. The number of smartphones in 2022 is estimated to be 750 million.
3. Scott Hartley, *The Fuzzy and the Techie: Why the Liberal Arts Will Rule the Digital World* (Penguin Portfolio, 2018), reveals the counter-intuitive reality of business today: it's actually the fuzzies, the liberal arts—not the techies—who are playing the key roles in developing the most creative and successful new business ideas. The book challenges the view that only technically qualified people can lead startups.
4. Thomas L. Friedman, *Thank You for Being Late: An Optimist's Guide to Thriving in the Age of Accelerations* (Farrar, Straus and Giroux, 2016).
5. Albert-László Barabási, *Linked: How Everything is Connected to Everything Else and What it Means for Business, Science and Everyday Life* (Basic Books, 2014), tells the story of the true science of the future and of experiments in statistical mechanics on the Internet. It strives to prove that social networks, corporations and living organisms are more similar than previously thought.
6. Ibid.
7. Ravi Agrawal, *India Connected: How the Smartphone is Transforming the World's Largest Democracy* (Oxford University Press, 2018), reveals both the dimensions and the implications of how one tiny device, the smartphone, is effecting staggering changes across all facets of Indian life, and how widespread Internet use is poised to transform everyday life in India. The book, based on

the author's experiences as the CNN New Delhi bureau chief, focuses on how the identity of the common Indian will be linked with the smartphone.

8. U.S. Rural Population 1960–2023 | MacroTrends

9. Study: Federalism and Decentralization in Germany (reformgestaltung.de).

10. 'Meet the World's Most Connected Population and Future Home For Digital Commerce Growth'—Euromonitor.com, report author Michelle Evans, outlines the advances made by South Korea in creating a digital economy and a connected life linked by digital technology. South Korea ranks high in both the use of digital in purchasing as well as in other modes of life.

11. https://lmflux.com/french/protecting-american-investments-in-ai-war-on-the-rocks/ refers to this quote.

12. Thomas L. Friedman, *Thank You for Being Late: An Optimist's Guide to Thriving in the Age of Accelerations* (Penguin, 2016).

13. Ibid.

14. Ravi Agrawal, *India Connected: How the Smartphone is Transforming the World's Largest Democracy* (Oxford University Press, 2018), p. 117.

15. 'Global Flows in a Digital Age: How Trade, Finance, People, and Data Connect the World Economy', Global Flows in a Digital Age | McKinsey, 2014, argues that the global flows are getting increasingly digital and that the flow of value can benefit small and medium companies, https://www.mckinsey.com/capabilities/strategy-and-corporate-finance/our-insights/global-flows-in-a-digital-age

16. The Boston Consulting Group, '*The Mobile Revolution: How Mobile Technologies Drive a Trillion Dollar Impact*', BCG 2015, posits that globally, mobile technology has emerged as a primary engine of economic growth, stimulating enormous private-sector spending in both R&D and infrastructure, and profoundly changing daily lives—everywhere.

17. Omidyar Network India, '*Unlocking Digital for Bharat: $50 Billion Opportunity*', Omdiyar Network India, 2018. The report, prepared in collaboration with Bain & Co., argues that while 40 million new Internet users per year are added to online transactions, only 40 per cent of India's 390 million Internet users in 2018 transact online. There is potential to unlock over $50 billion in online commerce in India by driving awareness, usage and transactions among the current and next set of Internet users and shoppers. This will be driven by more than 500 million Indians, who will constitute the next wave of online consumers. The report also outlines significant problems that come in the way of this usage.

18. Survey conducted by Lok Foundation and Oxford University, administered by CMIE, in 2019, finds that just 6 per cent of respondents said they could speak English, less than what the 2011 census showed. Between mother tongue, second and third language, the 2011 census records that over 10 per cent of Indians reported being able to speak some English. English is far more an urban than a rural phenomenon; just 3 per cent of rural respondents said that they could speak English, as against 12 per cent of urban respondents, with a class element at work—41 per cent of the rich could speak English as against less than 2 per cent of the poor.

19. Ibid.

20. Jamie Susskind, *Future Politics: Living Together in a World Transformed by Tech* (Oxford University Press, 2018), challenges readers to rethink what it means to be free or equal, what it means to have power or property, what it means for a political system to be just or democratic, and proposes ways in which we can—and must—regain control given the influence of technology on all walks of life.

21. Ibid.
22. Accenture Consulting, 'Government as a Platform: Coming Soon to a Government Near You', Accenture, 2018.
23. https://www.e-resident.gov.ee/, Estonia offers e-residency through which residents can register online and work with some attendant benefits given by the state.
24. Benjamin H. Bratton, The Stack: On Software and Sovereignty (Software Studies) (The MIT Press, 2016), p. 6. The Stack, an unintentional megastructure, is suggested to be both a technological tool and a prototype for a new geopolitical architecture in a comprehensive political and design theory of planetary-scale computation. The book analyses the blurring of boundaries caused by digital to the physical boundaries of the nation.
25. Ibid.
26. Ibid.
27. Anirudh Suri, The Great Tech Game—Shaping Geopolitics and the Destinies of Nations (HarperCollins India, 2023). The book offers us a big-picture view by weaving a masterful story of the world we are living in and how we got here. Technology is the new wealth of nations, and the 'great tech game' is the global contest for technological, economic and geopolitical success. This contest is transforming the distribution of power in the world, intensifying economic rivalries, forging new geopolitical alignments and changing the nature of war.
28. Indian Unicorn Landscape: Startups, Growth, FDI, Investors (investindia.gov.in).
29. Hamish McRae, The World in 2050: How to Think About The Future (Bloomsbury, 2022), traces how the complex forces of change—demography, the environment, finance, technology and ideas about governance—affect our global society. And how, with so many unknowns, should we think about the future? Drawing on decades of research and combining economic judgement with historical perspective, the book weighs up the opportunities and dangers we face, analysing the economic tectonic plates of the past and present in order to help us chart a map of the future.
30. (15) Non-Kinetic Warfare : The New Game Changer in the Battle Space | Martti Lehto—Academia.edu, refers to warfare done through means that employ cyber, electronic warfare and other methods that do not use kinetic force.
31. Jamie Susskind, Future Politics: Living Together in a World Transformed by Tech (Oxford University Press, 2018), p. 8.

Chapter 12: Integration and Innovation: A Unified Rise

1. Dr Surat Narain Mani, A Commoner's Struggles in Life (1980).
2. Angus Maddison, Class Structure and Economic Growth: India and Pakistan since the Moghuls (Routledge, 2005).
3. Ibid.
4. Ibid.
5. Ibid.
6. India | Data (worldbank.org), the World Bank gives the total GDP of India as $3.14 trillion, which is 3.25 per cent of the global GDP at $96.4 trillion.
7. 'Future of India—the Winning Leap: Breaking New Ground by Deploying Solutions for Rapid, Sustainable, and Resource Efficient Growth', PwC, 2014.
8. Clayton M. Christensen, The Prosperity Paradox: How Innovation Can Lift Nations Out of Poverty (Harper Business, 2019).
9. Future of India – the Winning Leap: Breaking New Ground by Deploying Solutions for Rapid, Sustainable, and Resource Efficient Growth', PwC, 2014, p. 6.

10. Ibid.
11. Ibid.
12. 'Full Potential Revival and Growth: Charting India's Medium Term Journey' (PwC, 2020).
13. Ibid.
14. Edmund Phelps, Mass Flourishing: How Grassroots Innovation Created Jobs, Challenge, and Change (Princeton University Press, 2013). In this book, the author, a Nobel laureate, draws on a lifetime of thinking to make a new argument about what makes nations prosper. He analyses why prosperity exploded in some nations between the 1820s and 1960s, creating not just unprecedented material wealth but 'flourishing'—meaningful work, self-expression and personal growth—for more people than ever before. Phelps makes the case that the wellspring of this flourishing were modern values such as the desire to create, explore and meet challenges. These values fuelled grassroots dynamism that was necessary for widespread, indigenous innovation.
15. Ibid.
16. Corporatism—Wikipedia, https://en.wikipedia.org/wiki/Corporatism. Corporatism is different from capitalism as it involves some form of collusion between large companies and between companies and government.
17. Edmund Phelps, Mass Flourishing: How Grassroots Innovation Created Jobs, Challenge, and Change (Princeton University Press, 2013).
18. John Rawls, A Theory of Justice (Harvard Press, 2005 print), aims to express an essential part of the common core of the democratic tradition—justice as fairness—and to provide an alternative to utilitarianism, which had dominated the Anglo-Saxon tradition of political thought since the nineteenth century. Rawls substitutes the ideal of the social contract with a more satisfactory account of the basic rights and liberties of citizens as free and equal persons, based on advancing the ideas of Rousseau, Kant, Emerson and Lincoln.
19. UN estimates for population predicts it will be 9.8 billion by 2050, growing to be 11.2 billion by 2100.
20. India's population will peak by the middle of the century and then decline to 1.1 billion by 2100.
21. Thomas L. Friedman, Thank You for Being Late: An Optimist's Guide to Thriving in the Age of Accelerations (Farrar, Straus and Giroux, 2016).
22. CO2 emissions (metric tons per capita)—China, India, United States | Data (worldbank.org).
23. Bill Gates, How to Avoid a Climate Disaster: The Solutions We Have and the Breakthroughs We Need (Allen Lane, 2021), p. 58.
24. Yorker Magazine, 18 March 1923, as reported in an article titled 'Climbing Mount Everest Is the Work of Supermen' where this quote is taken from. https://graphics8.nytimes.com/packages/pdf/arts/mallory1923.pdf
25. Thomas L. Friedman, Thank You for Being Late: An Optimist's Guide to Thriving in the Age of Accelerations (Penguin, 2016).
26. 'India's Solar Power Capacity Increased More than 11 Fold in Last 5 Years', Energy News, ET EnergyWorld (indiatimes.com).
27. https://data.worldbank.org/indicator/EN.ATM.CO2E.KT?locations=IN-1W&name_desc=false.
28. Abhyankar, Nikit Mohanty, Priyanka Deorah, Shruti M., et al., 'Pathways to Atmanirbhar Bharat: Harnessing India's Renewable Edge for Cost Effective Energy Independence by 2047', https://escholarship.org/content/qt9211h0mf/qt9211h0mf.pdf?t=rrgtbx
29. Indian Forest Act, 1927—Wikipedia, https://en.wikipedia.org/wiki/Indian_Forest_Act,_1927. The Indian Forest Act of 1865 extended British colonialism

and its claim over forests in India. The 1865 act was a precursor to the Forest Act of 1878, which truncated the centuries-old traditional use by communities of their forests and secured the colonial governments' control of the forests. The act of 1865 empowered the British government to declare any land covered with trees as a government forest and make rules to manage it. The government mainly used the wood for railway sleepers' manufacture.

30. Partha Chatterjee, 'Agrarian Relations and Communalism in Bengal, 1926–35', in Ranajit Guha, *Subaltern Studies I: Writings on South Asian History and Society* (Oxford University Press, Delhi, 1982).

31. https://doughnuteconomics.org/about-doughnut-economics, Kate Rawthorn.

32. Clayton M. Christensen, *The Prosperity Paradox: How Innovation Can Lift Nations Out of Poverty* (Harper Business, 2019).

33. René Descartes, *Treatise on Man and its Reception* (Springer, 2017), p. 108, offers a critical discussion on the different versions of L'Homme. the book attempts to explain the workings of the human body by drawing an explicit comparison between a hypothetical 'machine' which operates, ostensibly, 'like we do'. Descartes spends the best part of the Treatise outlining the ways that this machine's senses are informed by the singly material operations of the cardiovascular and nervous systems. Working on a heat model, Descartes discusses how blood in the heart, and what he calls animal spirits in the brain, cause the human machine to function just 'as we do'—without the supposed necessity of the soul.

34. Amitav Ghosh, *The Nutmeg's Curse: Parables for a Planet in Crisis* (University of Chicago Press, 2021). The book argues that the nutmeg's violent trajectory from its native islands is revealing of a wider colonial mindset which justifies the exploitation of human life and the natural environment, and which dominates geopolitics to this day. Starting with a massacre by the Dutch Army in the island of Banda in present-day Indonesia, it traces events from climate change, the migrant crisis and the animist spirituality of indigenous communities around the world, offering a sharp critique of Western society, and reveals the profoundly remarkable ways in which human history is shaped by non-human forces.

35. While the quote has been attributed to Mahatma Gandhi, who died in 1948, the first reference to it can only be traced to 1967 when it was attributed to Gandhi in a documentary. However, it has been used in the context of Gandhi many times as an apocryphal quotation attributed to him, and is similar to the quick response he gave to a journalist when he said that the king was wearing enough clothes for both of them.

36. J. Robert Oppenheimer Explains How He Recited a Line from Bhagavad Gita: 'Now I Am Become Death, the Destroyer of Worlds'—Upon Witnessing the First Nuclear Explosion | Open Culture.

37. Edward Humes, 'Over Hear—How the GI Bill Transformed The American Dream' (Harcourt Inc, 2006), p. 55.

38. Albert Einstein: 'We Cannot Solve Our Problems with the Same Thinking We Used When We Created Them' | PEP UNLIMITED LLC, https://pepunlimited.com/business/albert-einstein-problem-solving/.

39. Pankaj Mishra , *From the Ruins of the Empire: The Revolt Against the West and the Remaking of Asia* (Penguin UK, 2013). The book is organized as a collection of intellectual biographies of early Asian critics who discuss the best ways to counteract the violent invasion and disruption caused by the arrival of European nations into Asian politics and culture. It traces the first intellectual push-back to colonialism by thinkers in India, China, Japan and Afghanistan.

40. P.P. Divakaran, *The Mathematics of India: Concepts, Methods, Connections* (Hindustan Book Agency, 2018). The book identifies three of the exceptionally fruitful periods of the millennia-long history of the mathematical tradition of India: the very beginning of that tradition in the construction of the now-universal system of decimal numeration and of a framework for planar geometry; a classical period inaugurated by Aryabhata's invention of trigonometry and his enunciation of the principles of discrete calculus as applied to trigonometric functions; and a final phase that produced, in the work of Madhava, a rigorous infinitesimal calculus of such functions. The main highlight of this book is a detailed examination of these critical phases and their interconnectedness, primarily in mathematical terms but also in relation to their intellectual, cultural and historical contexts.

41. Ibid.

42. Dharampal, *The Beautiful Tree: Indigenous Indian Education in the Eighteenth Century* (Rashtrotthana Sahitya, 2021). In this book, the author uses a political and historical perspective to trace the decline of indigenous education through detailed analysis of commissioned surveys of the East India Company, which sheds light on how the education system in India prior to the arrival of the British was doing well and how it was systematically ignored and destroyed.

43. James Plunkett, *End State: 9 Ways Society Is Broken and How We Fix It* (Trapeze, 2021).

44. Chaturvedi Badrinath, *Swami Vivekanand: The Living Vedanta* (Penguin, 2015). While Vivekananda's landmark address at the Parliament of Religions in Chicago in 1893 established him as modern India's great spiritual leader, his popularity and appeal is attributed to his ability to integrate his human side with his profound spiritual side. In this beautifully written biography, Chaturvedi Badrinath liberates Vivekananda from the confines of the worship room and offers an unforgettable insight into the life of a man who was the very embodiment of the vedanta that he preached.

45. Silvia M. Lindtner, *Prototype Nation, China and the Contested Promise of Innovation* (Princeton Press, 2020).

46. Karen Armstrong, *Sacred Nature: How We Can Recover Our Bond with the Natural World* (Penguin Random House, 2022), p. 11. The book argues that if we want to avert environmental catastrophe, it is not enough to change our behaviour; we need to learn to think and feel differently about the natural world, to rekindle our spiritual bond with nature. For most of human history, and in almost all the world's cultures, nature was believed to be sacred, and our God or gods to be present everywhere in the natural world. When people in the West began to separate God and nature in modern times, it was not just a profound breach with thousands of years of accumulated wisdom, it also set in motion the destruction of the natural world.

47. Deepak Chopra, *MetaHuman: Unleashing Your Infinite Potential* (Rider, Random Penguin House, 2021). The book claims that higher consciousness is accessible right now. The book presents the case that it is possible to go beyond ordinary life and enter into states of heightened awareness. The book also gives a concrete plan to achieve that state of heightened awareness through a methodical practice of meditation and yogic discipline.

48. A shloka from the Bhagavad Gita. *Urdhva-mūlam*—with roots above; *adhah*—downward; *śhākham*—branches; *aśhvattham*—the sacred fig tree; *prāhuh*—they speak; *avyayam*—eternal; *chhandānsi*—Vedic mantras; *yasya*—of which; *parṇāni*—leaves; *yah*—who; *tam*—that; *veda*—knows; *sah*—he; *veda-vit*—the knower of the Vedas. The world is like a huge Aśhvatth tree for the soul. Its roots are going upwards (ūrdhva-mūlam) originating from God, nourished and

supported by Him. The trunk and branches which are extending downwards (adhaḥ-śhākham) encompass all the life forms from different abodes of the material realm. Its leaves are the Vedic mantras (chhandānsi), which describe rituals, ceremonies and their reward.

49. Edmund Phelps, *Mass Flourishing: How Grassroots Innovation Created Jobs, Challenge, and Change* (Princeton University Press, 2013).

50. Alexander and the Gymnosophists | MANAS (ucla.edu). The name given by the Greeks to certain ancient Indian philosophers who pursued asceticism to the point of regarding food and clothing as detrimental to purity of thought. It translates to 'naked wise men' in Greek. On arriving in India and defeating Porus, Alexander is supposed to have quizzed ten such wise men, and as per Plutarch, 'These philosophers were reputed to be clever and concise in answering questions.'

51. Isaiah Berlin, *The Proper Study of Mankind: An Anthology of Essays* (Farrar, Straus and Giroux, 1949), p. 246.

52. Ibid.

53. Tim Brown, *Change by Design: How Design Thinking Transforms Organizations and Inspires Innovation* (Harper Business, 2013). Refutes the myth of innovation that brilliant ideas leap fully formed from the minds of geniuses. The reality is that most innovations come from a process of rigorous examination through which great ideas are identified and developed and are realized as new offerings and capabilities. The book introduces ideas of design thinking and the collaborative process by which the designer's sensibilities are employed to match people's needs. In short, design thinking converts need into demand. It's a human-centred approach to problem solving that helps people and organizations become more innovative.

54. Kabir said the following in relation to the musk deer roaming the forest: '*Kasturi kundali base, mrig dhundhe ban mahi, aise ghati ghati ram hain, duniya dekhai nahi.*'

55. Isaiah Berlin, *The Proper Study of Mankind: An Anthology of Essays* (Farrar, Straus and Giroux, 1949), p. 254, referring to Herder and his philosophy.

56. Siddarth Shrikanth, The Case for Nature: The Other Planetary Crisis (Penguin Random House, 2023), p. 155. The book presents a compelling vision for tackling the global collapse of ecosystems. This other crisis has to be resolved by rethinking our relationship with nature in economic, social and even personal terms. The book argues that we can create flourishing economies and societies by preserving and restoring our planet's 'natural capital'. The book also calls attention to reflect on the roots of this crisis, drawing upon indigenous world views to show that nature must be woven into our modern societies, not set apart.

57. Name of the tour guide disguised for confidentiality. I undertook this visit to the institute in 2022, where the guide took me and my family on a two-hour tour of the Norbulingka Institute in Dharamshala, Himachal Pradesh.

58. An Asian Development Bank report states that ten of Asia's major rivers flow from the Tibetan plateau and fill river basins that provide water to more than 1.35 billion people, a fifth of the world's population. Demand for this water is soaring while supply is under increasing pressure from accelerated melting of Himalayan glaciers and other factors. A water crisis looms. Overall, Asia has the world's lowest per capita water availability and arable land.

59. Edmund Phelps, *Mass Flourishing: How Grassroots Innovation Created Jobs, Challenge, and Change* (Princeton University Press, 2013).

60. Ibid.

61. Jagriti's work is based on a 3xI framework for India. It believes that Inspiration, Innovation and Incubation are intimately linked for udyamita. This theory has been tested in Purvanchal at the work in the Jagriti Enterprise Centre–Purvanchal and during the Jagriti Yatra.
62. Clayton M. Christensen, *The Prosperity Paradox: How Innovation Can Lift Nations Out of Poverty* (Harper Business, 2019).
63. Ibid.
64. Ibid.
65. Ibid.
66. Ross Baird, *The Innovation Blindspot: Why We Back the Wrong Ideas and What to Do about It* (BenBella Books, 2017).
67. India—Urban Population per cent of Total), 2023 Data 2024 Forecast 1960–2021 Historical (tradingeconomics.com).
68. The rate of migration has shown a consecutive decline in the last three censuses. In most other countries, this has happened only once the urban population grows to around 55 per cent of the total population. However, in India, the deceleration began as early as when the share of urban population hit 25 per cent.
69. Anna Tsing, *Friction: An Ethnography of Global Connections* (Princeton University Press, 2004). The book develops friction as a metaphor for the diverse and conflicting social interactions that make up our contemporary world. The book focuses on one particular 'zone of awkward engagement'—the rainforests of Indonesia—where in the 1980s and the 1990s capitalist interests increasingly reshaped the landscape not so much through corporate design as through chains of legal and illegal entrepreneurs that wrested the land from previous claimants.

Chapter 13: Future: A New Promise

1. Shashank Mani, *India: A Journey Through a Healing Civilization* (HarperCollins, 2007), which recounts the story of the first train journey, Azad Bharat Rail Yatra, undertaken in 1997, and which seeded Jagriti Yatra, p. 163.
2. Will Durant, *The Story of Civilization: Our Oriental Heritage* (Simon and Schuster, 1935), p. 633.
3. Rajiv Malhotra, *Artificial Intelligence and the Future of Power: 5 Battlegrounds* (Rupa and Co., 2021). The book argues that the ongoing AI-driven revolution will have an unequal impact on different segments of humanity. There will be new winners and losers, new haves and have-nots, resulting in an unprecedented concentration of wealth and power. After analysing society's vulnerabilities to the impending tsunami, the book raises troubling questions that provoke immediate debate: Is the world headed towards digital colonization by the US and China? Will depopulation eventually become unavoidable?
4. Fritjof Capra, *Uncommon Wisdom: Conversations with Remarkable People* (Simon & Schuster, 1988), p. 232.
5. Mariana Mazzucato, *The Entrepreneurial State: Debunking Public vs Private Sector Myths* (Penguin, 2018). The book challenges an old paradigm that innovation is best left to the dynamic entrepreneurs of the private sector, and government should get out of the way. The book highlights how many national endeavours are not possible without the energy and the resources of the government. It seeks to show that from Silicon Valley to medical breakthroughs, the public sector has been the boldest and most valuable risk-taker of all.
6. Mariana Mazzucato, *Mission Economy: A Moonshot Guide to Changing Capitalism* (Allen Lane, 2021). To solve the massive crises facing us, we must

be innovative—we must use collaborative, mission-oriented thinking while also bringing about a stakeholder view of public-private partnerships, which means not only taking risks together but also sharing the rewards. To fix these problems, the book looks at challenges in a radically new way, arguing that we need to think bigger and mobilize our resources in a way as inspirational as the moon landing—this time for the most 'wicked' social problems of our time.

7. Raghunath Mashelkar, Gautam Bambawale, Vijay Kelkar, Ganesh Natarajan, Ajit Ranade and Ajay Shah, *Rising to the China Challenge: Winning through Strategic Patience and Economic Growth* (Rupa Publications, 2021), promotes India's rethinking of how to manage a more dangerous China. With the events of Doklam and Ladakh, India now faces the prospect of a hostile relationship with China, with this problem playing out on a strategic scale. The book develops an intellectual framework for Indian strategy to impact a broad swathe of Indian policy planning and a strategic response.

8. Get My Parking and Atlan are two ventures started by alumni of Jagriti Yatra. Get My Parking co-founders Rasik Pansare and Chirag Jain met on the Jagriti Yatra and started the company, SocialCops, co-founded by Pakulpa Sanker and was thereafter acquired by Atlan.

9. James Plunkett, *End State: 9 Ways Society Is Broken and How We Fix It* (Trapeze, 2021).

10. Thomas L. Friedman, *Thank You for Being Late: An Optimist's Guide to Thriving in the Age of Accelerations* (Farrar, Straus and Giroux, 2016).

11. Edmund Phelps, *Mass Flourishing: How Grassroots Innovation Created Jobs, Challenge, and Change* (Princeton University Press, 2013).

12. Jamie Susskind, *Future Politics: Living Together in a World Transformed by Tech* (Oxford University Press, 2018).

13. Edmund Phelps, *Mass Flourishing: How Grassroots Innovation Created Jobs, Challenge, and Change* (Princeton University Press, 2013).

14. Ibid., p. 307.

15. Ibid.

16. Ibid., p. 175.

17. Ibid, p. 309.

18. John Rawls, *A Theory of Justice* (Harvard Press, 2005 print).

19. Mariana Mazzucato, *Mission Economy: A Moonshot Guide to Changing Capitalism* (Allen Lane, 2021).

20. Ibid.

21. James Plunkett, *End State: 9 Ways Society Is Broken and How We Fix It* (Trapeze, 2021).

22. See Appendix 2 on the Banyan Revolution, where I have attempted to define it and give an initial quantification as outlined by Jagriti.

23. More details on Middle of Diamond Institute at www.jecp.in or by writing in to the author at shashank@shashankmani.in.

24. William Easterly, *The White Man's Burden: Why the West's Efforts to Aid the Rest Have Done So Much Ill and So Little Good* (Penguin, 2007).

25. Edward Humes, *Over Here: How the GI Bill Transformed the American Dream* (Harcourt Inn, 2006).

26. Richard Evans, *Deng Xiaoping and the Making of Modern China* (Penguin, 1997).

27. Corporatism—Wikipedia, is different from capitalism.

28. Regional Disparities in China: Time For a Lift Up—CKGSB, https://english. ckgsb.edu.cn/knowledges/regional-disparities-in-china-time-for-a-lift-up/

29. '*Full Potential Revival and Growth: Charting India's Medium Term Journey*', PwC, 2020.

30. Kate Raworth, *Doughnut Economics: Seven Ways to Think like a 21st Century Economist*' (Penguin Random House, 2017), the book identifies the seven

critical ways in which mainstream economics has led us astray—from selling us the myth of 'rational economic man' to obsessing over growth at all costs—and offers instead an alternative roadmap for bringing humanity into a sweet spot that meets the needs of all within the means of the planet.

31. Sumit K. Majumdar, *Lost Glory: India's Capitalism Story* (Oxford University Press, 2018), deconstructs India's industrialization story, challenging contemporary ideas about her economy. Based on careful and detailed empirical analyses of India's industrialization, for a period of almost seven decades, the book provides deeply-nuanced depictions of the history of political economy that have affected India's industrialization over the course of a century. This quote is at the end of the book as the author links the book's content to the ideals of Netaji.

32. Quit India movement—Gandhi's 'Do or Die' speech inspired India, The Better India.

33. Jagdish Bhagwati, 'Democracy Vs Development: New Thinking on an Old Question' (1995).

34. Hannah Arendt, *The Human Condition* (University of Chicago Press, 1958). The book considers humankind from the perspective of the actions which it is capable of. The problems Arendt identified then—diminishing human agency and political freedom, the paradox that as human powers increase through technological and humanistic inquiry, we are less equipped to control the consequences of our actions—continue to confront us today

35. Sankar, *Vivekanand: The Monk as a Man* (Penguin, 2015), p. 60.

36. Will Durant, *The Story of Civilization: Our Oriental Heritage* (Simon and Schuster, 1935), p. 166.

37. Sankar, *Vivekanand: The Monk as a Man* (Penguin, 2015), p. 166.

38. Ibid.

39. Pavan Varma, *The Great Hindu Civilization: Achievement Neglect, Bias and the Way Forward* (Westland Publication, 2021).

40. Arnold J. Toynbee, *A Study of History* (Oxford University Press, 1988).

41. Bibek Debroy, Anirban Ganguly, Kishore Desai, *Making of New India: Transformation Under Modi Government* (Wisdom Tree, 2022) is a compendium of essays by different authors. This quote is from an essay titled 'Narendra Modi and India's Second Renaissance' by Makarand Paranjape, p. 28.

42. Will Durant, *The Story of Civilization: Our Oriental Heritage* (Simon and Schuster, 1935), p. 425.

43. Diane Eck, *India: A Sacred Geography* (New York: Three River Press, 2012).

44. John Rawls, *A Theory of Justice* (Harvard Press, 2005), p. 383.

45. Will Durant, *The Story of Civilization: Our Oriental Heritage* (Simon and Schuster, 1935), p. 166.

Appendix 2: New Modernity for Environmental Sustainability: An Investigation

1. Jeremy Lent, *The Patterning Instinct: A Cultural History of Humanity's Search for Meaning* (Prometheus Books, 2017). The book offers a glimpse into the minds of a vast range of different peoples: early hunter-gatherers and farmers, ancient Egyptians, traditional Chinese sages, Indian philosophers, the founders of Christianity, trailblazers of the Scientific Revolution, and those who constructed our modern consumer society. It shows how mediaeval Christian rationalism acted as an incubator for scientific thought, which in turn shaped our modern vision of the conquest of nature. The author probes our current crisis of unsustainability and argues that it is not an inevitable result of human

nature, but is culturally driven: a product of particular mental patterns that could conceivably be reshaped.

2. Amitav Ghosh, *The Nutmeg's Curse: Parables for a Planet in Crisis* (Penguin Allen Lane, 2021), Ibid.

3. Karen Armstrong, *Sacred Nature: How We Can Recover Our Bond with the Natural World* (Vintage, 2023), The book argues that if we want to avert environmental catastrophe, it is not enough to change our behaviour: we need to learn to think and feel differently about the natural world—to rekindle our spiritual bond with nature. For most of human history, and in almost all the world's cultures, nature was believed to be sacred, and our god or gods to be present everywhere in the natural world. When people in the West began to separate god and nature in modern times, it was not just a profound breach with thousands of years of accumulated wisdom; it also set in train the destruction of the natural world.

4. Siddarth Shrikanth, *The Case for Nature: The Other Planetary Crisis* (Penguin, 2023). The book presents a compelling vision for tackling this other crisis by rethinking our relationship with nature in economic, social and even personal terms using ecosystems as his framing. The book argues that we can create flourishing economies and societies by preserving and restoring our planet's 'natural capital' and introduces the pioneers of this nature-positive revolution with examples from across the world. The book also calls upon readers to reflect on the roots of this crisis, drawing upon indigenous world views to show that nature must be woven into our modern societies, not set apart.

Appendix 4: Translation of some Sanskrit words

1. Rajiv Malhotra, Satyanarayanan Dasa Babaji, *Sanskrit Non-Translatables: The Importance of Sanskritizing English* (Infinity Foundation, 2020). The book contends that certain Sanskrit words cannot be translated glibly into English, for it takes away the core meaning of that word in the original language. It suggests that English speakers should use these words in the original, so that the core idea of the word, that has interconnectedness to Indic culture, is not lost.